Neuropsychedelia

The Revival of Hallucinogen Research
since the Decade of the Brain

Nicolas Langlitz

UNIVERSITY OF CALIFORNIA PRESS

Berkeley · Los Angeles · London

University of California Press, one of the most
distinguished university presses in the United States,
enriches lives around the world by advancing
scholarship in the humanities, social sciences, and
natural sciences. Its activities are supported by the UC
Press Foundation and by philanthropic contributions
from individuals and institutions. For more
information, visit www.ucpress.edu.

University of California Press
Berkeley and Los Angeles, California

University of California Press, Ltd.
London, England

Library of Congress Cataloging-in-Publication Data

Langlitz, Nicolas, 1975–.
  Neuropsychedelia : the revival of hallucinogen
research since the decade of the brain / Nicolas
Langlitz.
      p.   cm.
  Includes bibliographical references and index.
  ISBN 978-0-520-27481-5 (cloth : alk. paper)   —
ISBN 978-0-520-27482-2 (pbk. : alk. paper)
    1. Hallucinogenic drugs—Research.
2. Neuropsychopharmacology.   3. Hallucinogenic
drugs and religious experience.   I. Title.
  BF209.H34L36   2013
  154.4—dc23
                              2012022916

Manufactured in the United States of America

21   20   19   18   17   16   15   14   13
10   9   8   7   6   5   4   3   2

In keeping with a commitment to support
environmentally responsible and sustainable printing
practices, UC Press has printed this book on 50-pound
Enterprise, a 30% post-consumer-waste, recycled,
deinked fiber that is processed chlorine-free.
It is acid-free and meets all ANSI/NISO (z 39.48)
requirements.

Cover image and design: Thomas Ng

Contents

Figure section follows p. 131.

Acknowledgments

Although I happen to be an anthropologist not primarily interested in cultural differences, let me point one out: in Germany, we keep acknowledgments short or omit them altogether (somewhat in the spirit of the proverb *Nix gesagt ist genug gelobt:* nothing said is praise enough). In American academic publishing, by contrast, this peculiar genre has come to blossom and sprawl exuberantly since the late twentieth century. A critical and reflexive ethnographic gaze has unmasked these public expressions of gratitude and confessions of intellectual debt as a form of gift giving that promotes the cohesion of a scientific community as well as the author's career by repaying elders for their guidance and protection through displays of reliance, esteem, and loyalty (Ben-Ari 1987). However, following the ethos of the ongoing revival of psychedelic research, which has given up the countercultural rebellion against social conventions and the power of science, this book aspires to be reflexive but not critical. Thus, its German author will do his best to be a good participant observer and join in the ritual of acknowledgments, if not as lavishly as might be expected in an American publication these days.

"'Gratitude is heaven itself,' says Blake—and I know now exactly what he was talking about," wrote Aldous Huxley after his experiences with mescaline and LSD. The drugs had helped him understand many of the more obscure utterances to be found in the writings of the mystics, he claimed, for example, the unspeakable sense of thankfulness for the privilege of being born into this universe. Being more Kantian than

Swedenborgian in temperament, I will not chime in with this lyric enthusiasm, but I believe I also have an inkling of what Blake and Huxley meant (and, to the extent that a person rather than a molecule could claim credit for this insight on my part, it would be Mügül Andrews whose Sufic spirituality strangely infused my persistent materialism). However, what seems to make the mere fact of existence a privilege rather than a curse is the company of family, friends, colleagues, and students whom I would like to thank.

Among these numerous people, I am particularly grateful to Franz Vollenweider and Mark Geyer, who were kind and trustful enough to host this anthropologist in their laboratories and endure his nagging questions; my dear friends Boris Quednow and Felix Hasler, who shared so much more with me than juicy stories (better to be published in a later edition) and their office; and all their most generous and forthcoming coworkers populating the pages of this book. I would also like to express my heartfelt gratitude to Paul Rabinow for his intellectually fostering and fondly caring mentorship in the trenches of the Anthropology Department at Berkeley. Lorraine Daston's Department II and especially Fernando Vidal's Cerebral Subject research group at the Max Planck Institute for the History of Science in Berlin provided an atmosphere of scholarly leisure, academic rigor, and intellectual stimulation that facilitated postdoctoral rumination of my ethnographic findings. In the course of this, the Volkswagen Foundation's European Platform for Life Sciences, Mind Sciences and the Humanities provided an experientially rich opportunity to rethink the relationship between ethnography, philosophy, and neuroscience in ways that I can only begin to articulate in this book. My colleagues and students at the New School for Social Research in New York must take credit for creating and sustaining a warm and vibrant milieu, in which I feel at home as in no other institution before. I could go on and on and there would at least be an anecdote to tell in appreciation of every single person. But since this will either happen in the chapters to come or is really between me and the wonderful people who have helped this book see the light of the day, I will not even try to clear my debts. Instead I sincerely apologize for the formalist brevity and list the remaining benefactors in alphabetical order: Daniel Allemann, David Andel, Peter Andrews, Matthew Baggott, Oliver Bosch, Philippe Bourgois, Rudolf Brenneisen, Scott Brown, Carlo Caduff, Rael Cahn, Suparna Choudhury, Adele Clarke, Lawrence Cohen, Philipp Csomor, Talia Dan-Cohen, Jörg Daumann, Rick Doblin, Richard Doyle, Paul Dietschy, Hubert Dreyfus, Alex Gamma, Gantt Galloway,

John Gilmore, Euphrosyne Gouzoulis-Mayfrank, Jeffrey Guss, Michael Hagner, Anne Hermann, Lawrence Hirschfeld, Dominique Holstein, Amelie Ulrika Magdalena Hoshor, Randi Irwin, Reed Malcolm, Emily Martin, Maja Maurer, Valdas Noreika, Thomas Metzinger, Hamilton Morris, Michael Kometer, Bia Labate, Dave Nichols, Francisco Ortega, Torsten Passie, Susan Powell, Margarete Pratschke, Vincent Quinn, Hugh Raffles, Vyjayanthi Rao, James Redfield, Tobias Rees, Victoria Risbrough, Janet Roitman, Nikolas Rose, Stephen Ross, Gary Bruno Schmid, Pete Sharp, Ann and Alexander Shulgin, Renée Stadler, Meg Stalcup, Jakob Tanner, Sharika Thiranagama, Miriam Ticktin, Ann Stoler, Erich Studerus, Julie Van Pelt, Gabriel Vignoli, Scott Vrecko, Anthony Wallace, Daniel Wetzel, Charles Whitcroft, Kelly Whitmer, Jennifer Windt, Allan Young, and Jared Young (no relation). Finally, I also want to thank my parents for, well, the privilege of being born (a fundamental precondition for the authoring of any book). Donya Ravasani not only challenged me as an intellectual interlocutor but also served as such an invaluable source of inspiration, care, and love that mentioning her in an acknowledgment must appear to be a preposterously scanty gesture. But what else can I do here?

To conclude this acknowledgments section (by now of American proportions), I also wish to thank the publishers of the following articles for allowing me to use these previously printed materials in revised and expanded form in this book: "Ceci n'est pas une psychose: Toward a historical epistemology of model psychosis," *BioSocieties* 1 (2) (2006):158–180; "The persistence of the subjective in neuropsychopharmacology: Observations of contemporary hallucinogen research," *History of the Human Sciences* 23 (1) (2010):37–57; "Political neurotheology: Emergence and revival of a psychedelic alternative to cosmetic psychopharmacology," in *Neurocultures: Glimpses into an Expanding Universe,* edited by Francisco Ortega and Fernando Vidal, 141–165 (Frankfurt/M.: Peter Lang, 2011); "Delirious brain chemistry and controlled culture: Exploring the contextual mediation of drug effects," in *Critical Neuroscience: A Handbook of the Social and Cultural Contexts of Neuroscience,* edited by Suparna Choudhury and Jan Slaby, 253–262 (London: Wiley, 2012).

Introduction

Neuropsychopharmacology as Spiritual Technology

Neuropsychedelia is about the revival of psychedelic research since the "Decade of the Brain." When US president George H. W. Bush (1990) dedicated the 1990s to neuroscience, he paid tribute to the unprecedented public valorization of this prospering branch of medicine and the life sciences. By contrast, the investigation of hallucinogenic drugs had enjoyed less government support in the preceding two decades. Most academic and corporate research projects had been closed down or run out of funding after the clash between the "counterculture" and the "Establishment" in the 1960s. Only in the underground had experimentation with this class of substances continued to flourish. But, as the twentieth century was coming to an end, some of those who had been young during the so-called psychedelic era and who had subsequently chosen not to "turn on, tune in, and drop out," but to pursue careers in medicine or science, were running their own research groups and sensed that the time was ripe for a second attempt to introduce hallucinogenic drugs into the academy and the Western pharmacopoeia. The growing public esteem of brain science helped them to relegitimate their research interest in psychedelics, not as symbols of social dissent or as magic drugs, but as tools to study different neurotransmitter systems, the neural correlates of consciousness, or the biological substrates of schizophrenia.

The two neuropsychopharmacological laboratories at the center of this anthropological inquiry have played key roles in the revival. Franz

X. Vollenweider's lab in Zurich has arguably been the most important research facility studying the effects of hallucinogens on human subjects, while Mark A. Geyer's animal lab in San Diego developed an important and widely used experimental paradigm taking hallucinogen-intoxicated rodents as a model of schizophrenia to screen for new antipsychotic drugs. Even though the current renaissance of psychedelic research has emerged from many countries simultaneously, this study's focus on Switzerland and the United States also sheds light on the central transnational axis of this process connecting American psychedelic culture with the home country of LSD. The ethnographic investigation of the two laboratories, mostly conducted during nine months of fieldwork in 2005 and 2006, followed by many visits, interviews, telephone conversations, and e-mails, sheds light on the scientific practices and the ethos informing the scientists' work. This close-up perspective reveals that the current resurgence of psychedelic science is not just another story of disenchantment (from magic mushrooms to 5-HT_{2A} receptor agonists) but has produced a form of laboratory life that continues to be suffused with the peculiar kind of mysticism that emerged from the psychedelic culture of the 1950s and 1960s. Rather than presenting one more case study of the biologistic reduction of the human to "bare life," *Neuropsychedelia* explores the assemblage of a precarious figure of *anthropos* as a being situated between animals and gods, between the bestial and the divine. From the thick of anthropological fieldwork, it generates a meditation on spiritual venues open to those living under conditions of late-modern materialism.

LISTENING TO MOKSHA IN THE AGE OF SOMA

As the Decade of the Brain and of the Human Genome Project, the 1990s saw countless media reports about just discovered genes for this and brain centers for that human trait or state. The sociologist Nikolas Rose (2007: 188–192) identified this period as the turning point when a neurochemical understanding of human mental life became hegemonic, flattening out the deep psychological space that had dominated Euro-American conceptions of the mind since the days of Freud. What distinguishes these rearticulations of naturalism and materialism from their nineteenth- and early twentieth-century predecessors is that biology is no longer accepted as fate but has been made into an object of biotechnological and psychopharmacological intervention. A prominent event in this transition was the introduction of the selective serotonin reuptake inhibitor Prozac, which was soon reported to not only restore the premorbid self of patients suffering from depression but to make healthy people feel even "better than well." Some claimed that the drug had allowed them to finally become their "true selves" (although they had never experienced anything comparable before). By "listening" to the drug, the American psychiatrist Peter Kramer (1993: xi, xv) and his patients came to rethink what was essential and what was contingent about people's personalities, "what in them was biologically determined and what merely . . . experiential." Kramer's account of so-called cosmetic psychopharmacology set the terms for the ensuing discussion of the use of drugs for nonmedical purposes such as the enhancement of mood and cognition.

Consequently, in contrast to the 1960s, not hallucinogens, but antidepressants and stimulants dominated the popular problematization of psychopharmacology at the time of the revival of psychedelic research. As Prozac prescriptions skyrocketed, the drug was first hyped and then demonized for increasing the risk of suicide and murder and for robbing its consumers of authenticity. The physician and philosopher Carl Elliott (2004) read the case histories surrounding Prozac as indicating a sense of spiritual emptiness and existential alienation, which psychiatrists treated as if they were purely internal neurochemical matters, whereas they actually pointed to a mismatch between the ways people were living their lives and the structures of meaning that told them how to do so. But not only were they disoriented, they also did not know what could possibly provide an ethical orientation. In the conventional accounts of modernity, such nihilism is associated with the grand narrative of the disenchantment of the world. The psychopharmacological response to this conundrum, Elliott (2004: 129) argued, made the situation even worse by overlooking the fact that "alienated people are alienated from something—their families, their cultures, their jobs, or their Gods."

During the presidency of George W. Bush Jr., this cultural critique was shared by the President's Council on Bioethics, which the physician and public intellectual Leon Kass chaired from 2002 to 2005. Kass (2002, 2008b) and another prominent member of the council, the political economist Francis Fukuyama (2002), emphasized the analogies between this historical diagnosis and the dystopian future envisaged in Huxley's *Brave New World* (1932).[1] The novel describes a totalitarian social order preventing political unrest, among other things, by controlling its subjects' brain chemistry. Citizens are urged to use the fictive drug soma, which makes them content and docile. It lulls them into a false sense of happiness and imprisons their minds in a gilded cage. "Religion, Karl Marx declared, is the opium of the people. In the Brave New World this situation was reversed," Huxley (1959: 100) commented. "Opium, or rather soma, was the people's religion. Like religion, the drug had power to console and compensate, it called visions of another, better world, it offered hope, strengthened faith and promoted charity."

In Kass's and Fukuyama's readings of Huxley, two peculiarities were striking. First of all, both ignored the fact that *Brave New World* describes a totalitarian system. They presented the novel as a mirror of bioethical developments in liberal democracies. Unlike Huxley, they did not warn against the emergence of a particularly perfidious regime of mind control by the state but against the temptations of new technologies (Fukuyama 2002: 5–6; Kass 2002: 9; Morgan et al. 2005). The citizens of Kass's and Fukuyama's Brave New World were present-day Americans seduced by the most recent advances of biotechnology—from genetic engineering to brain implants and from cloning to neuropsychopharmacology. In Kass's (2002: 13) view, secularization and pluralism had corrupted the liberal principles at the heart of America's political identity. In this world of mere appearances, cognitive performance was improved by Ritalin, but the results were not the subject's own achievements. Prozac made people feel "better than well," but their happiness was false and shallow, and so on.

Following the philosopher Michael Sandel (2002), yet another member of the President's Council on Bioethics, Kass (2003, 2008a), a practicing Jew, advocated the development of a "religious sensibility" resonating "beyond religion" and acknowledging the giftedness of life. "Respect for a being created in God's image means respecting everything about him, not just his freedom or his reason but also his blood," Kass (2002: 21) wrote. Any attempt to overcome the limits and burdens imposed on the individual by God or nature was supposed to entail a loss of humanity and human dignity. Human nature was to be protected against its biotechnological transgression and deformation. Consequently, nonmedical interventions into body and mind would lead us onto a slippery slope, to Huxley's Brave New World, as understood by these neoconservative thinkers. To forestall this development, Kass called for "a new bioethics and a new biology: a richer ethic of *bios* tied to a richer *logos* of *bios*, an ethical account of human flourishing based on a biological account of human life as lived, not just physically, but psychically, socially and spiritually. In the absence of such an account we shall not be able to meet the dehumanizing challenges of the brave new biology" (21).

The second peculiarity in Kass's and Fukuyama's frequent references to Huxley's work was their omission of the fact that Huxley had written not only a dystopian but also a utopian novel in which drug use figures equally large. In contrast to *Brave New World, Island* presents a spatialized, not a temporalized, utopia (Koselleck 2002). It conjures up a contemporary alternative rather than a foreshadowing of sociotechnical developments to come, located on a faraway island instead of a distant future. Thereby Huxley suggested that, in principle, the idyllic society of Pala was already possible without any science-fiction technologies. The islanders' use of the drug moksha (named after the Hindu term for liberation from the cycle of death and reincarnation) for spiritual purposes was modeled on Huxley's (2009/1954) own experiences with the hallucinogens mescaline and LSD, as described in his essays *The Doors of Perception* and *Heaven and Hell*. Unlike soma, moksha neither serves escapism nor does it rob its users' lives of authenticity, quite the contrary. In an initiation ceremony, the drug is administered to young people with the goal of "ceasing to be what you ignorantly think you are and becoming what you are in fact," as one inhabitant of Pala puts it (Huxley 1962: 173). The insights gained under the influence of the drug help them obtain true happiness. Whereas the superficial cheerfulness induced by soma is the outcome of a "holiday from the facts" (Huxley 1932: 280), a purely subjective sense of happiness ignoring the subject's actual situation of repression and alienation, the happiness and insight provided by moksha are presented as genuine. Their truthfulness consists in a correspondence with both the paradisiacal social life described in *Island* as well as with a spiritual reality transcending individual psychology. A Palanese explains to the European protagonist of the novel that his people do not dismiss their drug experiences as mere hallucinations because they presuppose a different neurology:

> You're assuming that the brain produces consciousness. I'm assuming that it transmits consciousness. . . . You say that the moksha-medicine does something to the silent areas of the brain which causes them to produce a set of subjective events to which people have given the name "mystical experience." I say that the moksha-medicine does something to the silent areas of the

brain which opens some kind of neurological sluice and so allows a larger volume of Mind with a large "M" to flow into your mind with a small "m." (Huxley 1962: 140–141)

Thus, moksha does not provide quick fixes. Instead the drug initiates a lasting spiritual transformation. It is a "drug for life," but not for everyday life (see Dumit 2002). To be effective it does not have to be taken continuously like soma. The Palanese use moksha once or twice a year. But the resulting mystical experiences of unity with the cosmic mind and of boundless compassion pervade their whole worldview and way of living.

Island responded to a diagnosis of the state of society similar to, but not identical with, that of Kass and Fukuyama. Since the discovery of a multitude of new mind drugs in the 1950s, the consumption of performance-enhancing and euphoriant amphetamines, as well as tranquilizers alleviating anxiety, had spread rapidly in the American population. The anxiolytic Miltown, for example, first helped businessmen cope with job-related stress and then soothed exhausted housewives (Pieters and Snelders 2007; Rasmussen 2008; Tone 2008; Herzberg 2009). The nontherapeutic employments of psychopharmaceuticals by the white middle class could be described as cognitive enhancement and cosmetic psychopharmacology *avant la lettre*. When Huxley (1959) saw the societal consequences of this so-called psychopharmacological revolution, he believed that *Brave New World* had become a reality much sooner than he had expected. Looking for a way out, he found inspiration in cultural anthropology. Analogous to Margaret Mead's (1928) ethnographic account of Samoa as a society of noble savages, Huxley dreamt up another halcyon island where psychedelic drugs were used in the service of an enlightened primitivism. "Pala," noted literary scholar Jerome Meckier (1978: 78), "is the utopia one might build if evils were merely the product of imperfect social conditions, as Mead maintained." By contrast, Fukuyama and Kass did not blame social conditions but the emergence of new biotechologies that required stricter regulations. Distrusting the utopian potential of primitivism, Meckier pointed out that *Island,* even though forward-looking, was "an exercise in nostalgia for an ideal whose day is already over before Huxley gets it right" (80).

In *Island,* Huxley gave literary form to a reconceptualization of hallucinogenic drugs, which he himself had helped to initiate. Since the 1920s, these substances had been used to model schizophrenia in healthy human subjects. In this context, the drugs were called psychotogens or psychotomimetics: drugs producing or mimicking psychoses. One of the key figures in this research was the psychiatrist Humphry Osmond. It was through him that Huxley got the chance to try mescaline in 1953. Since the publication of *Brave New World* two decades earlier, Huxley had undergone a conversion from cynical British intellectual to committed Californian mystic. In light of his new worldview, he described his first encounter with mescaline as a mystical experience and felt that pathologizing terms such as *hallucinogen* or *psychotomimetic* did not do justice to the effects of the drug (Huxley 2009/1954). In dialogue with Osmond (1957: 429), Huxley (1980: 107) invented a new name for this class of pharmaceuticals: *psychedelics,* that is, mind-manifesting drugs. As the passage from *Island* quoted above indicates, the mind that was supposed to manifest itself in these experiences was not that of the person taking the drugs (as in contemporaneous psychoanalytic or "psycholytic" applications) but a cosmic mind, which the more confined individual psyche was then able to commune with. Instead of deluding the subject, psychedelics were meant to open up the brain to dimensions of reality usually hidden from human perception for lack of immediate survival value but beneficial to spiritual life. Hence, the term implied a neurology and an anthropology very different from those underlying model psychosis research. Here, human beings did not appear as caught up in phantasmal representations of both world and beyond but as spiritual animals endowed with a brain that, under the influence of psychedelic drugs, could connect to a metaphysical truth concealed by everyday neurochemistry.[2]

In his reverent self-experimentation with hallucinogens, Huxley believed to have found what, in his *Perennial Philosophy* (2004/1944), he had previously described as the transhistorical and transcultural core of all religions, the ultimate reason for human existence: first-hand knowledge of the one divine Reality underlying the phenomenal multiplicity of the world, traditionally achieved by way of strenuous and at times physically harmful spiritual exercises (from prolonged fasting to violent self-flagellation). Now this knowledge was readily and safely available to everybody through modern pharmaceuticals. In Huxley's eyes, this religious interpretation of hallucinogen action was not at odds with scientific investigation. In fact, the claims to universality of the *philosophia perennis* matched the universalism of brain science. Mystics reported the same experiences across history because "we have fairly good reasons for supposing that there have been no considerable changes in the size and conformation of human brains for a good many thousands of years" (Huxley 2004/1944: 16–17). The fictive society described in *Island* even established a scientific discipline to study the relationship between physiology and spirituality, for which Huxley invented the word *neurotheology* (Huxley 1962: 94, 144; Horgan 2003: 74)—half a century after philosopher and psychologist William James used nitrous oxide to introspectively explore religious ecstasies and three decades before *neurotheology* came to designate the quest for the neural correlates of a universal spiritual experience by way of neuroimaging studies of meditating Buddhist monks and praying Carmelite nuns (Newberg et al. 2001; Beauregard and Paquette 2006).

As more and more people came to try out hallucinogens from the late 1950s onward, Huxley's writings provided a vocabulary and interpretive framework shaping the drug experiences of his numerous readers in the decades to come. Understood against the background of this worldview, further elaborated by Timothy Leary and his coworkers, the subjective effects of psychedelic drugs were conceptualized as "the psychedelic experience" and soon came to inform a whole subculture known as psychedelia. In the course of the 1960s, Huxley's *Island* became one of the most influential books in the so-called counterculture rebelling against the Protestant ethic and the spirit of capitalism (Weber 1992/1920): a utopian blueprint for a psychedelically enlightened society (Stevens 1987: 184). Among the hippies, *Island* inspired experiments in living set up in opposition to the lifestyle of the "plastic people" staffing the "Establishment," including their use of drugs to improve professional efficiency and to stabilize bourgeois family life (Miller 1991: 23–50).

Ironically, central elements of the hippies' social critique also entered into the discourse of conservative bioethicists such as Leon Kass. Both Kass and the hippies rejected an alleged dehumanization pervading technological society in general and expressed contempt for middle-class drug use for the purpose of self-optimization. Like the youthful rebels of the sixties, the self-identified "old-fashioned humanist" defended the notion of an authentic human existence (Miller 1991: 30; Kass 2002: 3–4, 15–17). In *The Making of a Counter Culture,* the historian Theodore Roszak described the movement named after his book primarily as an opposition to "technocratic society" that called into question the validity of the "conventional scientific world view."[3] As a sympathetic observer, Roszak (1968: xiii) adopted this antimodern concern and predicted, "If the resistance of the counter culture fails, I think there will be nothing in store for us but what anti-utopians like Huxley and Orwell have forecast." Likewise, Kass (2002: 29–53) identified technology as the greatest problem of modern society and warned against its dehumanizing powers, which, especially when used to intervene in the human body and mind, would make Huxley's dystopian vision come true.

But, despite their convergent diagnoses, Kass and the flower children could not have differed more profoundly on how to prevent their debauched American society from sliding down the slippery slope toward the realization of *Brave New World*. While Kass (2002: 277–297) saw the solution in a restrictive biopolitics guarding the natural limits of humanness against their biotechnological transgression, many hippies put their hopes on overcoming the confines of the human mind with the help of consciousness-expanding drugs. If the spiritual is the universal part of every human being, Kass sought to protect it against external intervention, whereas the hippies had hoped to advance it through neuropsychopharmacology as spiritual technology (see Rabinow 1999: 11, 179). Unlike Kass, they did not conceive of human nature as an unchanging moral landmark but as a vast realm of unexplored potential. Even though they were against pharmacological self-optimization for the sake of the "growling machinery" of capitalism, they did not object to facilitating human flourishing with the help of drugs, as a realization of novel and more fulfilling forms of life (Miller 1991: 34–50).[4]

Just like the "straight" majority of white middle-class Americans, the hippies were children of the psychopharmacological revolution, which had produced not only Miltown but also LSD. They, too, believed in the power of drugs. Like their prim and proper fellow citizens, they distinguished between good drugs and bad drugs—except that they largely reversed the psychopharmacological order of things. Alcohol, legally available stimulants, and sleeping pills were conceived of as detrimental. Propagating contemplative mind expansion, the so-called heads also disapproved of heroin and stimulants (the former being popular among veterans of the fiercely rejected Vietnam War; the latter among the so-called freaks, that is, hippies more interested in hedonistic kicks than in spiritual insights). Although illegal, these despised substances allegedly only enabled their consumers to bear "cheap, neon, plastic, ugly Amerika [*sic*—the German spelling emphasized the fascist character attributed to the United States]" (Miller 1991: 46). The good drugs collectively referred to as "dope" comprised marijuana and psychedelics. They were meant to give rise to authenticity, human warmth, and a spiritual life. This put them at the center of a counterculture modeled on *Island* rather than *Brave New World* (Davis and Munoz 1968; Miller 1991).

This social conflict, as well as growing concerns over drug safety in general, eventually led to the prohibition of hallucinogens in the late 1960s. Legal impediments in combination with more subtle mechanisms, such as restrictions of funding or the curtailment of career advancement, created major obstacles to the scientific investigation of psychedelic drugs. By the 1970s, all hopes that research in this area would allow scientists to push "human consciousness beyond its present limitations and on towards capacities not yet realized and perhaps undreamed of" (Masters and Houston 1966: 316) were shattered. At the same time, the use of hallucinogens for model psychosis research received a second, purely scientific blow as the newly introduced dopamine hypothesis of schizophrenia discredited the modeling of psychoses with a class of drugs primarily affecting the serotonergic and the glutamatergic neurotransmitter systems. Consequently, from 1970 to 1990, academic hallucinogen research broke down.

In the last decade of the twentieth century, however, a new generation of scientists reanimated the field in the United States, Switzerland, Germany, Great Britain, Spain, and Russia. They reinscribed their endeavors into the inherited conceptual matrix opening up between experimental psychosis and experimental mysticism. Both paradigms gained traction again as more complex neurochemical conceptions of schizophrenia emerged in the 1980s and novel neuroimaging technologies made the search for the cerebral "God spot" front-page news in popular magazines. Even though a closer historical and ethnographic look will reveal the conceptions of model psychosis research and neurotheology not to be mutually exclusive, the tension between them continued to polarize the field. It is striking, however, that all major players renounced the countercultural struggle against the Establishment. Instead they sought to integrate hallucinogenic drugs into mainstream science and society. Thereby, they constructed an intellectual and political framework for nonmedical drug use beyond both the gloomy vision of *Brave New World* and the conviction that a better world was only possible on a remote *Island*. Did these efforts help to fulfill the unrealized potential of the first episode of psychedelic science in the age of Prozac and Ritalin? Could contemporary neuropsychopharmacology refashion psychedelics into spiritual technologies fostering the good life?

PAST PROBLEMS, PAST ANTHROPOLOGIES

Uses of hallucinogens, not in the laboratory, but in religious settings, have been studied by anthropologists since the late nineteenth century (Mooney 1896; Lumholtz 1902; Slotkin 1955; Perrine 2001; Zieger 2008). Until the 1950s, the literature focused on the diffusion of peyotism among Native American tribes (LaBarre 1960). The social and political problem to which this body of scholarship responded was the role of the peyote cult in the formation of a so-called pan-Indian religion. Penned up with other tribes in reservations, groups that previously had not used any hallucinogens began to concoct a syncretic assemblage of their own time-honored ideas and ceremonies, peyote rituals as traditionally practiced by other indigenous groups, and Christian elements adopted from white missionaries. The emergence of these composite forms of religiosity, which would soon be institutionalized by the Native American Church, was either interpreted as an attempt at cultural adaptation and assimilation (e.g., Petrullo 1934; Barber 1941) or as resistance to acculturation and white domination (e.g., Jones 1953; Kluckhon and Leighton 1946; Thompson 1948). In the conflicts between Native Americans and the US government, prominent anthropologists publicly and successfully pleaded for the indigenous population's right to continue using the otherwise prohibited plant drug peyote for religious purposes: an exclusive right based on race and cultural identity (Boas et al. 1937; LaBarre et al. 1951; Boller 2005: 71).

In the late 1960s and early 1970s, hallucinogens continued to attract scholarly attention against a new sociopolitical background. This time anthropologists responded to the spreading use of hallucinogenic drugs among white and educated members of the middle class who felt alienated from their own Euro-American societies. As this group had previously not been associated with deviant drug consumption—and deviant the consumption of psychedelics had become after their prohibition in the late 1960s—this social problem raised public concern and, thus, funding opportunities for social scientists. As the population most affected by the problematic happened to be the group from which the majority of academics were recruited, some of those entranced by their own drug experiences found a way to give their preoccupation with these substances a socially acceptable form by making them the subject matter of scientific inquiry. Before "going native" and becoming a shaman himself, anthropologist Michael Harner claimed that his discipline had long underestimated the importance of hallucinogens in shamanism and religious experience, because few of his older colleagues had experienced the mind-altering effects of these substances themselves (Harner 1973: vii). However, considering that James Mooney (1896) and Carl Lumholtz (1902) had already taken part in peyote rituals in the late nineteenth century, it rather seems that Harner's generation of anthropologists just immersed themselves in exotic drug rituals for different reasons: sharing a widespread discontent with their own culture, they not only wanted to understand other ethnic groups but were looking to them for better ways of life.[5] The most famous example of this kind of anthropology as cultural critique is Carlos Castaneda's (1968) supposedly ethnographic, but largely fictive, master's thesis on his apprenticeship with the Yaqui shaman Don Juan, which became a major source of inspiration for the counterculture.

Other anthropologists studying the use of hallucinogens in so-called traditional societies reported that the drugs' embedment in ritual settings and cosmological worldviews prevented the disruptive effects they had on American and European youth. Elsewhere, it seemed, psychedelics even served to stabilize the social order. In a Huichol initiation ceremony, for example, the ingestion of peyote turned the adolescent into a full member of his tribe. The drug experience allowed the young person to get to know for himself the supernatural spirit realm that provided the group with a normative structure and ethical orientation. In these settings, "doing drugs" validated the moral and religious order according to which the tribe lived (Furst 1972; Myerhoff 1975, 1976; Dobkin de Rios and Smith 1977). Against this background, anthropological studies of drug use in other cultures appeared to be a promising and timely way of counteracting the aggravating drug problem Western governments were facing. In nonmodern societies, ritual rather than legal means sufficed to control the consumption of mind-altering substances (Dobkin de Rios 1984: 205–214). Instead of prohibiting their use altogether, such ritual guided it toward specific cultural goals. Thus, somewhere far from home, anthropologists might learn from other peoples how to integrate hallucinogens into their own societies, rendering the recently declared and ultimately futile "War on Drugs" superfluous.

Furthermore, broadly based cross-cultural comparisons were meant to reveal an almost universal use of intoxicants by different ethnic groups all over the world and in all periods of human history. By demonstrating that, from a global perspective, Western opposition to ecstatic states was the exception rather than the rule, anthropology helped to legitimate the pharmacological quest for altered states of consciousness and corroborated the assumption of a perennial philosophy (Weil 1972; Bourguignon 1973; Furst 1976; Dobkin de Rios 1984). The cultural historian Andy Letcher (2006: 25–48) argues that these claims to the universality of hallucinogen use might tell us more about the utopian sentiments accompanying the psychedelic revolution of the 1960s than about other cultures or the human condition.

HALLUCINOGENS TODAY: FROM WONDER AND SHAME TO INQUIRY

Irrespective of these scholarly endeavors, both hallucinogen hype and scare eventually took care of themselves. The drugs did not bring about the cultural revolution announced by Timothy Leary and other pros- elytizers. Alongside the high hopes of the countercultural sixties, the widespread enthusiasm for these odd substances simply waned. By now, despite the revival of psychedelic research, hallucinogens are no cause for major public concern anymore. Their consumption has been reported to have stagnated or declined since the mid-1970s. Even in the neopsychedelic techno and rave scene emerging in the 1980s, the drugs of choice were amphetamines and especially MDMA (ecstasy), while psychedelics proper remained marginal (Reynolds 1999). The German authorities noticed a decline of LSD seizures (Amendt 2008: 103–104). Although concerned about their marketing on the Internet and by so- called smartshops, an EU report from 2006 stated: "The proportion of current users among those who have ever used is lower for the use of hallucinogenic mushrooms than it is for cannabis and ecstasy. It has been reported that the effects of hallucinogenic mushrooms limit the appeal of regular use" (Hillebrand et al. 2006: 9).[6] In the same year, the US Drug Enforcement Administration (2006) announced that "LSD trafficking and abuse have decreased sharply since 2000, and a resur- gence does not appear likely in the near term." The resumption of a moral panic would sound different.[7]

Today, hallucinogens are located in a problem space very different from those of the early ethnographies of peyotism or the anthropologi- cal cultural critiques of the 1960s and 1970s. This inquiry departs from a less timely problematic and follows a very different anthropological trajectory. It grew out of an existential rather than political concern. When I took LSD for the first time in 1993, shortly after my eighteenth birthday, I temporarily suffered from a loss of self. But I did not become one with the universe. It is a sociological commonplace that peer leaders are members of a group that others identify with. Under the influence of LSD, however, I *literally* mistook myself for the classmate whom I was emulating by taking the drug. As I resurfaced from the depths of this deeply delusional experience, I was filled with joy about being me rather than the other person. I felt reconciled with myself and the world. Everything is as it should be, I thought. "This sense of happiness," I wrote into my adolescent diary, even though I was taking pride in my materialism and abhorred all things ecclesiastical, "must have something to do with God." As a fervent rationalist, I was dumbstruck by this experience of cosmic comfort. In its wake, I prayed for the first time since my childhood (for my mother and her partner who were about to separate). In the diary entry, I was quick to counteract this awkward piety with a set of slightly precocious and naïve scientific questions: "How about the activity of the *locus coeruleus* in children? Is it stronger than in adults? Do children experience the world like adults under LSD?" These questions merged Huxley's (2009/1954: 25) claim that a drug-induced breakdown of what he called the "cerebral reducing valve" enabled the eye to recover some of the perceptual innocence of childhood with what Solomon Snyder's popular science book *Drugs and the Brain* (1986) had taught me about the neuroanatomical substrates of the LSD experience. After all, it was the Decade of the Brain. The neurosciences were on the rise and I wanted to become a brain researcher myself. When talking to my friends about my drug experiment, which I took to be one of the most important experiences in my young life, I felt perfectly confident speaking about the neurochemistry underlying its breathtaking aesthetic dimension. But I felt too ashamed to mention either my self-loss or that, even long after the drug effects had worn off, I continued to think of my first trip as a profound, if ill-defined, spiritual experience.

Shame is an affect marking the return of social consciousness after having lost oneself in one way or another (Fisher 2002: 65–70). My secular orientation made it difficult for me to acknowledge any kind of religious sentiment. Max Weber (1958/1919: 155) articulated the contempt of the moderns—and modern I deemed myself in every respect—for those unable to endure the disenchantment of the world: "To the person who cannot bear the fate of the times like a man, one must say: may he rather return silently, without the usual publicity build-up of renegades, but simply and plainly. The arms of the old churches are opened widely and compassionately for him. After all, they do not make it hard for him. One way or another, he has to bring his 'intellectual sacrifice'—that is inevitable. If he can really do it, we shall not rebuke him." These condescending sentences were spoken in 1917 to university students who, in Weber's eyes, were all too prone to give up science for the sake of religious enthusiasm. Today, Weber's pathos sounds antiquated. I never felt that my chemically mediated glimpses into a spiritually transfigured world compromised my philosophical or scientific work. Even though I had also got to know the psychotic dimension of hallucinogenic experiences, I did not feel the need to reduce them in their entirety to the delusions of an intoxicated brain, either. Nevertheless, nothing could have been more alien to me than seeking refuge in the arms of a church. The space of possibilities generated by the nineteenth-century *Kulturkampf* between pious conservatives and scientifically minded progressives could no longer provide the orientation I sought.

And yet Weber's challenge cannot be casually brushed aside: How can a spiritual experience be meaningful if it is caused by a drug? What kind of referent should it have other than the psychoactive compound by which it was induced? Was the supernatural not really a fancy of us human beings? During my fieldwork, one of the psychopharmacologists I worked with spoke of "double-entry bookkeeping" to designate the intellectually dishonorable practice—which he knew firsthand—of holding a belief in a spiritual reality while being unable to justify it in naturalist or materialist terms. Thus, both the shame and the wonder I felt in response to my psychedelic experience was as much about feeling as about knowing. They were not just psychological quirks but reflected a distinctly modern order of nature, shared by my contemporaries, that had no more space for the super- and preternatural but restricted its ontology to nature and culture. The deep sense of wonder I felt over the drug-induced violation of my materialist sensibilities, over the incursion of the sacred into a world that I had previously experienced as completely profane, had no place in the modern rationality I was committed to. Since the Enlightenment, wonder had become a disreputable "cognitive passion" in science (Daston and Park 1998). Consequently, I kept this embarrassing experience to myself for many years. In retrospect, however, it marked the beginning of the following empirical philosophical inquiry. The starting point of reflection, the anthropological problem, *tout court*, lies indeed in the unavoidable fact that *anthropos* is that being who suffers from—and, I may add, feels ashamed about—too many *logoi* (Rabinow 2003: 6).

Before anthropologists began to include Western societies in their investigations, anthropology was exercised as the study of premodern by modern people. Religious and other supernatural interpretations of hallucinogenic experiences prevalent in these "traditional societies" have been at the heart of the classical ethnological literature. Already the seventeenth-century Christian missionaries (preceding anthropological researchers in the zone of culture contact) thought of the Native Americans' peyote-induced visions as "fantasies and hallucinations" lacking any truth value. In contrast to latter-day anthropologists, however, the Spanish Inquisition attributed these misbeliefs neither to the nature of the ingested drugs nor to indigenous culture but to "the suggestion and intervention of the Devil, the real author of this vice" (quoted in Leonard 1942: 326). When, in the late nineteenth century, the first Euro-Americans tried peyote in the laboratory (Prentiss and Morgan 1895) or during anthropological fieldwork (Mooney 1896), it became clear to them that the plant itself was psychoactive. But anthropologists like James Mooney also noted that white subjects reported very different experiences than Native Americans who ingested peyote in the context of religious rituals rather than scientific experiments. From the start, these differences were attributed to culture. Western test persons experienced "horrible visions and gloomy depression" because they were afraid of the drug in the first place, whereas "the Indian" had acquired a sense of "pleasant anticipation" from earliest childhood (11). Mooney also pointed to the "difference between the Indian life, with its comparatively regular routine and freedom from worries, and the civilized life with all its stress of thought and irregularities of habit" (11). Subsequently, the assumption that hallucinogen-induced experiences were fundamentally shaped by historically and culturally contingent expectations and situations came to dominate the anthropological discourse on hallucinogen use throughout the twentieth century (e.g., Shonle 1925; Petrullo 1934; Wallace 1959; Dobkin de Rios 1984).

This perspective stands in stark contrast to the perennial philosophy informing psychedelia. Contingency as "modern society's defining attribute" (Luhmann 1998: 44–62) appears to be at odds with a reduction of the multitude to mystical oneness. Although marked by a pervasive countermodern longing and ressentiment, this body of anthropological scholarship remained decidedly modern in attributing religious interpretations of drug experiences to culture. They were taken to be the product of suggestion facilitated by drugs that function as active placebos. Hence, all claims that psychedelics could establish a connection to the supernatural had to be relegated to the realm of meaning making. From a modern point of view, giving religious value to drug experiences is no longer condemned as inspired by the Devil, but it continues to appear as a form of idolatry: a worshipping of culturally constructed divinities.

At the time of my fieldwork, anthropology had long since given up confining itself to studying premodern ethnic groups. The moderns had themselves become an object of anthropological inquiry. According to one prominent if dated definition, modernity is constituted by a unidirectional transition from religion to science. At first glance, such a process of secularization seems to inform the current psychedelic revival as well. After the failure of Leary and other psychedelic evangelists to defend the consumption of hallucinogens in the name of religious freedom, it is no coincidence that the attempts to relegitimate their uses in the West discussed in this book have taken the route of science, not religion. Hence, it would make sense for an anthropology of modernity to study the disenchantment of hallucinogenic drugs in the psychopharmacological laboratory. By shedding light on cases of secular scientific uses in Europe and the United States, this book could then be taken to complement the kind of cross-cultural comparison of hallucinogen use that Richard Blum (1969) and Marlene Dobkin de Rios (1984) initiated but limited to supposedly traditional societies.

However, as the following ethnographic account will show, the neuroscientific revitalization of psychedelia has not purged the investigated drugs from their mystical connotations. Theological questions and spiritual experiences continue to serve as a moral motor of the ongoing revival of scientific studies of hallucinogenic compounds. Thus *Neuropsychedelia* is about a formation that is not modern. Provisionally, I will call it *contemporary* in Paul Rabinow's (2003, 2008) sense (a bit like we have come to distinguish between contemporary and modern art). At the end of this book, however, I will argue that *perennial* might be a more suitable term for what I have in mind. But I am getting ahead of myself. For the time being, what matters is that this book does not proclaim an epochal break with the past (the hallmark of all grand narratives of modernity) but describes the emergence of a not yet stabilized and possibly ephemeral assemblage of heterogeneous temporalities. Past, present, and future intermingle, for example, when more or less time-honored religious conceptions meet cutting-edge neuropsychopharmacology to generate a moral economy of hope. This configuration is examined as a response to the long-standing problematization of the relationship between science and spirituality. Where the classical anthropological literature studied non-Western religious and shamanistic perspectives on hallucinogens, this book explores how naturalist and supernaturalist *logoi* of *anthropos* are disaggregated and reaggregated in contemporary Western science, eventually giving rise to a new form that I will call *mystic materialism.*

In this respect, *Neuropsychedelia* can indeed be read as a contribution to the ethnographic archive documenting human unity and diversity. The French anthropologist Philippe Descola (2005, 2006) has mapped and analyzed the distribution of four ontological predispositions—animism, totemism, analogism, and naturalism—across cultures, or what naturalist anthropologists take to be "cultures." For the ordering of the world in terms of nature and culture is no more ontologically neutral than an animistic worldview that regards plants as persons to be communicated with through hallucinogenic drugs or, as in totemism, groups particular human beings with particular nonhuman animals instead of other humans belonging to a different ethnic group. Just like the other three ontologies, naturalism, as Descola defines it and as I will continue to use the term throughout this book, is a dualist scheme of metaphysics. It is characterized by the assumption of continuity in the exterior realm (a biological nature shared not just by all humans but by humans and animals alike) and discontinuity in the interior realm (each *ethnos* is distinguished by its own *Volksgeist* or culture; animal minds are fundamentally different from the human mind because they lack an immortal soul, consciousness, reason, language, etc.).[8] Descola demonstrates that this cosmology has become and continues to be hegemonic among modern Euro-Americans while being ethnologically and historically contingent. For example, Margaret Lock's (2002) cross-cultural study of the reconceptualization of death as brain death shows how the idea of a living body, in which the person is no longer present, was adopted quite willingly in Europe and North America while meeting fierce resistance in Japan. Descola, however, also argues that, more recently, the bipartite ontology of naturalism thus understood has become unstable and is about to give rise to and will possibly be replaced by a different scheme. This emergent ontology not only promises to leave behind the timeworn modern dichotomies of nature and culture or mind and body but will break with the more fundamental underlying dualism, which, according to Descola, has structured all previous ontologies: a genuine anthropological revolution, it would seem. As an ethnographic case study, this book examines this ongoing transformation of dualist naturalism into monist materialism. It focuses on a mystical variety of the latter, eventually looked at in a perennialist framework that emphasizes recurrence over radical novelty (thereby diverging from Descola's ontological trajectory and analytic approach).

Since the 1980s, many Anglo-American sociocultural anthropologists (most prominently Asad 1986) have come to question the value of such ethnographic archives in light of doubts about cross-cultural translatability of supposedly universal anthropological categories. Yet this study, although contrasting the United States and Switzerland (and sometimes Germany), does not presuppose or reveal any kind of incommensurable cultural difference. It would be put to good use if readers decided to compare it with other, especially non-Western ethnographic cases—and I will briefly gesture at animistic hallucinogen use in Amazonia when examining an animal experiment with a synthetic ayahuasca concoction in chapter 5.

However, the overall project of *Neuropsychedelia* does not in itself aim at such ethnology. Instead it aspires to a peculiar kind of philosophical anthropology. It refunctions ethnography as a form of "fieldwork in philosophy" (Austin 1970; Rabinow 1989, 2003; Bourdieu 1990) that has not grown out of an encounter with cultural otherness (the point of departure of so many ethnographic narratives) but with a different sort of alterity: a pharmacologically altered state of human consciousness. It presents a working through of this experience not in psychological but in cultural and biological terms. Historical epistemology and ontology add temporal depth to the project's ethnographic breadth (Daston 1994; Hacking 2002; Rheinberger 2010b). Ultimately, however, the goal is not to show how a new scientific fact has made us into a different kind of human being (which has been the rationale of numerous anthropological studies of medicine and science in the past two decades) but to find a way out of the stale standoff between science and spirituality.

For this purpose, the inquiry will not look to supposedly premodern cultures for solutions to a modern conundrum. Even though the author is neither Swiss nor American, but German, *Neuropsychedelia* falls into the genre of "anthropology at home" (see Peirano 1998), in that the ethnographer has not only been shaped by philosophy seminars but also graduated from medical school shortly before setting out for fieldwork in two psychopharmacology laboratories investigating hallucinogenic drugs in Zurich and San Diego. Considering that my disciplinary identity is multiple, my approach to this field is not confined to ethnographic observations and historical narration but will occasionally extend into the realms of philosophy and psychopharmacology itself. This shunning of the intellectual asceticism marking strictly disciplinary perspectives is the methodological correlate of my personal engagement with the problem at the heart of this inquiry. The book will show that fresh ways of responding to a problematic situation do not necessarily have to be sought in far-flung idylls but can often be found by attending to marginalized and therefore only partially realized possibilities in one's own domains (Dreyfus and Rabinow 1982: 262–263; Dreyfus 1991: 329–331).

When I set out on this research project, the use of hallucinogens promised to have the liberating potential of such marginal practices. Where Prozac had come to be seen as a quick fix for a profound spiritual vacuity, psychedelics were taken as "entheogens," as drugs revealing the "God within" (Wasson et al. 1978). Prozac was criticized for making subjects temperamentally more alike, a psychopharmacological makeup robbing people of their individuality. The ease it gave seemed to lure consumers into social conformity. Hallucinogens, on the other hand, continued to be identified with authenticity and nonconformism. Prozac was said to adjust people to the competitive spirit of capitalism while hallucinogen-inspired drug mysticism appeared to undermine the underlying Protestant ethic. And while mescaline had been described as a vessel taking us on a journey into the terra incognita of the "mind's antipodes" (Huxley 2009/1954: 86), Prozac was accused of producing complacent subjects who had given up looking for anything other than their medically prescribed happiness (Kass 2008b).[9]

Despite this stark contrast between the discursive constructions of Prozac and the psychedelics, hallucinogenic drugs have been part and parcel of the emergence of late-modern materialism and its identification of mind and brain as a space of psychopharmacological intervention. In fact, the recent popularization of neurochemical self-conceptions had been anticipated by Timothy Leary's writings from the 1960s that teemed with brain metaphors and *neuro-* prefixes. The immediate and mind-blowing effects of hallucinogenic drugs were even better suited than Prozac to convince their consumers of Leary's (1965: 123) message that consciousness was a biochemical process—and that consequently chemicals were the keys to its expansion. As the following ethnographic account will show, early twenty-first-century hallucinogen researchers continue to "listen" to all sorts of psychopharmaceuticals, which have taught them, just like Peter Kramer's patients, to conceive of the human mind in neurochemical terms. But, mediated by Huxley's perennial philosophy, this materialism has taken a mystical form.

IN A NUTSHELL

The book is organized in six chapters and a conclusion. As it is about the revival of academic hallucinogen research since the Decade of the Brain, the first two chapters provide a historical explanation of what happened to make such a revival necessary in the first place. Jointly framed by an ethnographic account of the 2006 LSD Symposium in Basel, Switzerland, chapter 1 lays out the rise, fall, and resurgence of psychedelic science in the United States, while chapter 2 examines the prominent role of Switzerland in the transnational dynamics of this process. The American part of the narrative reveals that, due to broader developments in drug regulation, hallucinogen research was already on the wane before this class of substances came to be associated with the counterculture's resistance to the Protestant work ethic. It outlines the "political neurotheology" underlying the subsequent clash between psychedelia and the Establishment, which eventually led to the prohibition of hallucinogens and the breakdown of most research. Based on interviews with several key actors of the current revival, the first chapter also shows how this new generation of scientists and activists employed both disenchantment and spiritualization of psychedelic drugs as political strategies to overcome the ruinous antagonisms surrounding this class of drugs.

Chapter 2 turns to Switzerland, where the historical continuities were as important as the caesura of "1968." Oral-history accounts of the government administrator in charge of research with controlled substances and his closest scientific ally track the emergence of the regulatory framework of contemporary psychedelic science at the time of Swiss drug policy reform in the 1990s. Largely untroubled by the aggressive ideological rifts that had divided American society, the Swiss government not only permitted but actively supported hallucinogen research. Exploiting such transnational differences between regulatory regimes, psychedelic entrepreneurs and philanthropists from the United States funded human experiments in Switzerland: an engagement producing both synergies and tensions. Thus, the investigation of hallucinogen action, which chapters 3 and 5 will reveal as molded by local context, is simultaneously a global phenomenon.

The remaining chapters zoom in for ethnographic close-ups of laboratory life in Zurich and San Diego. Based on observations of Franz Vollenweider's group and this anthropologist's own participation in one of their experiments, chapter 3 examines the relationship between subjectivity and objectivity in psychopharmacological research, including the correlation of psychometric and neurophysiological measurements and pilot studies in which the scientists provisionally served as test subjects themselves. Gradually, the chapter moves from second-order observations of these activities to an ontological argument: shaped by "set" (the subject's personality, mood, and expectations) and "setting" (her social, cultural, and physical environment), hallucinogenic drug action is maintained to be a hybrid phenomenon of nature and culture and both a natural and a human kind. This account calls into question randomized placebo-controlled trials as the methodological gold standard of neuropsychopharmacology. A positivist proposal from the days when anthropology was still a holistic discipline is unearthed and reconsidered in the context of current attempts to move beyond the nature/culture divide: should placebo controls be supplemented by culture controls? Eventually, however, it turns out that the wild and overly complex neurochemistry of psychedelic drugs escapes both cultural and pharmacological attempts at controlling their effects and thereby threatens the global assemblage of contemporary hallucinogen research.

While the experiments at the center of chapter 3 mostly fall into the category of experimental mysticism, chapter 4 contrasts this rationale with experimental psychosis research. As the downfall and reanimation of the hallucinogen model of psychosis had reasons internal to psychopharmacology not covered by the preceding social and political analysis of the 1960s, the chapter adds this historical strand to the narrative. Ethnographically, it looks at model psychosis research through the eyes of a test subject, a theater director, drawing an analogy between the performative character of the experiment in which he participated and the break with representation in modernist aesthetics. In response to the exceeding complexity of the mind-brain, the revived psychotomimetic rationale constitutes an "enactive model" of psychosis that does not aim at a naturalistic depiction of schizophrenia but at a comparative investigation of drug intoxication and mental disorder as two distinct states situated on the same ontological level. They are used to shed light onto each other without one serving as a transparent representation of the other. Thereby, the question of whether supposedly mystical hallucinogen experiences are really psychotic (or the other way round) receives an unexpected answer: in a pragmatist frame of noncontradiction, the hallucinogenic experience appears multifaceted but not plural. It is not simply psychotic or mystical but takes different, practically mediated forms that are partially connected and coordinated through a shared historical matrix.

A discrepancy between experimental psychosis research in humans and animals then takes the reader from Switzerland to California. Chapter 5 relates how one enactive model of schizophrenia, based on the hallucinogen-induced modulation of the startle reflex, grew out of Huxleyan drug mysticism and a fairy tale by Hermann Hesse that was popular in the sixties. The chapter examines the ethics and epistemology of neuropsychopharmacological animal research, especially how scientists deal with the problems of set and setting and nonhuman forms of subjectivity. Difficulties in the translation between human and animal studies uncover a crisis of animal models in psychiatry. At the same time, they point to a molecularization of the *differentia specifica* of philosophical anthropology and the emergence of a recombinant anthropological form that joins the natural and the divine.

How this mystic materialism was lived and reflected upon by contemporary psychedelic researchers is described in the last chapter. The scientists' incessant joking in the face of a supposedly unprecedented neuroscientific revolution of our image of humankind reveals the persistence of a dualist anthropology. At the same time, however, some of the actors transvalued monism into biomysticism. In contrast to the neurotheological interest in the biology of mystical experiences discussed in chapter 3, this mysticism of the biological reveres life itself. It is associated with different practices, such as a philosophical quest for "experiential invariants" pursued through systematic self-experimentation, artistic work employing photography to reflect the unity of materiality and spirituality, and the conduct of science not as a vocation but as cosmic play. Through the lives of many of the characters populating this book, the last chapter takes stock of the revival of psychedelic science so far.

The conclusion disambiguates this anthropologist's cognitive dissonance regarding my materialist persuasions and the spiritual drug experience I had as a young man. Revisiting many insights from the substantive chapters, it moves from ethnography to anthropology and reflects on how the fieldwork in perennial philosophy previously laid out from a third-person perspective responds to first-person philosophical concerns. For this purpose, this last part of the book reconfigures the chronotope of the contemporary into the perennial. It advocates an anthropological reorientation toward a new or, rather, contemporary form of universality.

1

Psychedelic Revival

HOFMANN'S HUNDREDTH BIRTHDAY

13 January 2006. Guided by security personnel, Albert Hofmann, the father of LSD, bent by a century to a height of barely five feet, took the stage on crutches. Almost two thousand people rose from their chairs in the Basel Convention Center. Thunderous applause. Dozens of photographers and cameramen—professional and hippie—were jostling in front of the centenarian birthday boy (see figure 1). The LSD Symposium took place in honor of Hofmann's one-hundredth birthday. But it also served as a fair of the contemporary world of psychedelia, presenting itself in front of two hundred journalists who had come to cover the event. Fragile, but quite sprightly for his age, probably the only person in the hall wearing a tie, Hofmann briefly raised his hand to greet the crowd before sitting down with one of the organizers, a lively and stout middle-aged man with a full voice, president of the Psi Society Basel, a specialist for spiritual healing and otherwise involved in organizing trade fairs for esoterics. He asked Hofmann to tell one more time how he discovered his "problem child" and "wonder drug," LSD. Hardly a newspaper article or TV program preceding or following this spectacular celebration did not begin its report with this almost mythological origin story.

In the 1930s, the research chemist Hofmann developed new ergot alkaloids for the Swiss pharmaceutical company Sandoz. They were meant to stop bleeding after childbirth. Hofmann created a number of derivatives from lysergic acid, the molecular core of ergot. In 1938, he synthesized the twenty-fifth substance in this series of compounds: lysergic acid diethylamide, abbreviated LSD-25 (after the German *Lysergsäurediäthylamid*). The substance was tested on animals. They became restless and a strong effect on the uterus was established, but as neither the physicians nor the pharmacologists of Sandoz were particularly interested in the substance, these preclinical trials were discontinued. However, five years later—by now the rest of Europe was engulfed in war—Hofmann (1983: 14) followed what he called "a peculiar presentiment," a hunch, "that this substance could possess properties other than those established in the first investigations." He noted that "this was quite unusual; experimental substances, as a rule, were definitely stricken from the research program if once found to be lacking in pharmacological interest" (14). To make a long story short, Hofmann must have contaminated himself with a small amount of this highly potent substance, and he experienced an uninterrupted stream of fantastic pictures, extraordinary shapes with an intense, kaleidoscopic play of colors. Three days later, he conducted a self-experiment, ingesting what he (falsely) believed to be a small dose, and he experienced the first full-blown LSD trip in human history. The reason why this story is recounted over and over again is not the heroism of Hofmann's self-experiment—self-administration was not uncommon in pharmacology at the time—but his claim to have followed a "peculiar presentiment" when taking the seemingly insignificant compound from the shelf again (see, e.g., Nichols 2006). He discovered its mind-blowing effects accidentally because of a little sloppiness in his usually meticulous chemical bench work.[1] This led Hofmann to conclude that he did not find LSD but that it was LSD that found him. It must have been divine providence, not scientific method, admitting us to the enchanted world behind the "doors of perception."

However, Hofmann, who had had his first mystical experience as a boy walking in the forest, was quick to add that one did not need LSD anymore once the gateway had been opened in one way or another. His greatest hope was that one day state-controlled meditation centers would provide LSD to facilitate the spiritual development of those seeking access to this experiential plane. But, he said, he did not want to be a guru telling others what to do. The organizer closed the opening ceremony by saying, "Dear Albert, you're certainly the very best example to show that what you discovered is no infernal stuff!" Hofmann was presented with an enormous bunch of red roses. He expressed his thanks by saying that he was particularly grateful for the flowers, as our connectedness with other life forms, including plants, had become more and more important to him in recent years: "The feeling of co-creatureliness with all things alive should enter our consciousness more fully and counterbalance the materialistic and nonsensical technological development in order to enable us to return to the roses, to the flowers, to nature, where we belong." Tumultuous applause again.

Many of the media reports on Hofmann, his pharmacological problem child, and the three-day conference, with its abundance of lectures, discussion panels, workshops, and stalls, proclaimed a comeback of hallucinogen research. After its discovery in 1943, the story went, LSD soon escaped the walls of the laboratory. Its propagation by irresponsible scientists like Timothy Leary and its widespread abuse by the hippies was said to have eventually led to the criminalization of LSD and other hallucinogens in the 1960s. After scientific research on this class of drugs had subsequently been repressed for more than two decades, a more pragmatic attitude had finally gained the upper hand. Since the 1990s, it had given rise to a revival of hallucinogen research. Thus the framing of the event.

The proponents of this resurgence gathered at the LSD Symposium. A minority among the crowds of old hippies, New Age disciples, and psychedelic geeks, these brain researchers, pharmacologists, and psychiatrists used the occasion of Hofmann's hundredth birthday to demonstrate the restored vitality of their scientific field. Many of the preclinical and clinical studies conducted in recent years were, for the first time, presented to a broad audience and received a significant amount of media attention. Even though many of the so-called psychedelic elders were still present, a new generation of American and European hallucinogen researchers had taken over, introducing these "magic drugs" into the age of cognitive neuroscience.

THE HEYDAY OF HALLUCINOGEN RESEARCH

But what exactly was being revived? And how was the revival different from the historic era, which it sought to resume? In the mid-twentieth century, hallucinogenic drugs came to play a key role in psychiatric and psychopharmacological research. Much has been written about this important chapter in the history of science and medicine. Let me briefly recapitulate to lay the ground for my account of the current revival of psychedelic science.

Hallucinogens became an object of scientific investigation in the course of the nineteenth century as Europeans and Americans observed their uses in other cultures. The French psychiatrist Jacques-Joseph Moreau de Tours brought hashish from a trip to the Orient, which, in the 1840s, he used to both model and treat mental illness. The spreading use of peyote among Native Americans in the second half of the century led US and English researchers like Silas Weir Mitchell or Henry Havelock Ellis to study the effects of the cactus. Through a series of self-experiments, the German chemist Arthur Heffter identified and isolated mescaline as its pharmacologically active principle in 1897. And two decades later, his colleague Ernst Späth managed to synthesize the substance (Perrine 2001).

From the 1920s onward, German and French psychiatrists such as Kurt Beringer, Ernst Joëll, Fritz Fränkel, and Alexandre Rouhier returned to Moreau's psychopharmacological modeling of mental disorders, administering mescaline instead of hashish to healthy subjects. After LSD was discovered in 1943, it was first used in this tradition of experimental psychiatry. But Hofmann's chance find also marked the beginning of a profound transformation of the field. In the course of the 1950s, more than 750 scholarly articles were published on LSD alone.[2] During this period, the first antipsychotic chlorpromazine and the first tricyclic antidepressant imipramine were discovered as well. This second wave of biological psychiatry differed from its predecessor in that the "psychopharmacological revolution" of the 1950s left behind the therapeutic pessimism prevalent in the late nineteenth century (Shorter 1997). The cerebral substrate of mental illness no longer seemed to be a matter of fate but rather a target of biomedical intervention (Rose 2007). When it was found that chlorpromazine could antagonize some of the effects of LSD, an experimental system emerged that seemed to allow exploration of causes as well as potential treatments of schizophrenia in the laboratory. Model psychosis research was no longer confined to mimicking the experience of mental illness but turned into a quest for its biochemical cause: a psychotogenic molecule resembling LSD or mescaline. Psychiatry finally seemed to get a chance to meet the scientific standards and therapeutic expectations set by other medical specialties (Caldwell 1970; Ulrich and Patten 1991; Novak 1997; Thuillier 1999; Vannini and Venturini 1999; Healy 2002: 107; Langlitz 2006a; Dyck 2008: 32–52).

In brain research, this sudden upswing of psychopharmacology supplemented anatomical and electrophysiological conceptions of the brain with a neurochemical one. In contrast to mescaline, which was only psychoactive in doses of several hundred milligrams, LSD was active in the microgram range. The fact that extremely low doses could have such profound pharmacological effects strongly supported the emergent theory of neurotransmission and spawned the "dream of molecular specificity": if the number of molecules were not enough to swamp the entire brain, there had to be specific sites of action; neurotransmitters and drugs had to fit into receptors like keys into locks (Healy 2002: 180; Rose 2007: 199–200). The finding that LSD, with a core structure closely resembling that of serotonin, turned out to antagonize the effects of serotonin was soon used to explain its psychotomimetic qualities and helped to establish a tight connection between brain chemistry and behavior (Green 2008). The sociologists Joëlle Abi-Rached and Nikolas Rose (2010) have shown how this new "neuromolecular gaze," breaking up the holism of psychic life into a multiplicity of receptors, neurotransmitters, ion channels, second messengers, and membrane potentials, eventually led to the birth of the neurosciences in the 1960s.

One of the proponents of this molecularization of psychiatry was Humphry Osmond. Together with his colleagues at Saskatchewan Mental Hospital in Weyburn, Canada, the British physician investigated mescaline-like substances that cause a biochemical imbalance underlying schizophrenia. In her book *Psychedelic Psychiatry,* medical historian Erika Dyck (2008: 13–31) points out that this research on hallucinogens was supported by the leftist government of the province as part of its commitment to health-care reforms. Demonstrating the biochemical nature of mental illness entailed its destigmatization: psychiatric patients were meant to be treated just like any other patient population.

But in the course of his exchange with Aldous Huxley, Osmond turned away from such reductionist accounts, reconceptualizing "hallucinogens" and "psychotomimetics" as "psychedelics" and paving the way for a spiritual explanation of their effects. Historian of psychopharmacology David Healy (2002: 202) emphasizes the Janus-faced character of this class of drugs: "It is probably no coincidence that biological thinking crept into psychiatry on the back of a group of drugs like the psychedelics, which gave rise to 'spiritual' thinking." Religious interpretations of the hallucinogenic experience also inspired the use of these drugs in the treatment of alcoholism, where LSD was administered to address addiction as a spiritual rather than biomedical condition. Considering that the scientific interest in psychedelics had been triggered by observations of their religious uses in other cultures, psychedelic therapists had come full circle (Dyck 2008: 53–78).

This association of hallucinogenic drugs with spirituality was primarily a North American phenomenon. The more secular Europeans mostly used them to facilitate psychoanalytically oriented psychotherapies, hoping that they would assist the unconscious to reveal its secrets (Passie 1997; Sandison 1997; Vannini and Venturini 1999; Snelders and Kaplan 2002; Roberts 2008). But the rationale of such narcoanalysis or psycholytic therapy was also of interest to the CIA and the US Army, who were looking for a "truth serum" to make interrogations more efficient. The brain was imagined as a locus in which truthfulness could be instilled and from where truth could be extracted. Eventually, the hallucinogen research program of the CIA was closed down in the late 1960s because the effects of these drugs on interrogations turned out to be unpredictable (CIA Historical Review Program 1977; Lee and Shlain 1992; Langlitz 2007; Tanner 2009).

By that time, most hallucinogen research had already been or was about to be terminated. Much of this was due to the politicotheological battles fought over psychedelic drugs in the 1960s, which will be discussed in the next section. But we should also note—and to many readers this might come as more of a surprise—that the field was already in decline before Timothy Leary entered the scene, at a time when the term *hippie* had not even been coined.

In the late 1950s, physicians' nonchalant dealings with pharmaceuticals, especially with not (yet) approved "investigational drugs," began to be problematized within the medical profession. In 1961, the thalidomide disaster came to the fore: 8,000 children with gross anatomical malformations, an unknown number of abortions, and many patients suffering from peripheral neuropathy. The US Congress passed the Kefauver-Harris amendments in the following year, giving the Food and Drug Administration (FDA) control over all investigational drugs (Daemmrich 2004: 60–69). LSD happened to be such an investigational drug just like thalidomide. A drug safety study on Hofmann's problem child, also published in 1962, warned against the risks of suicide and prolonged psychotic reactions (Cohen and Ditman 1962). Regulations were tightened. Consequently, researchers could no longer mail a form to Sandoz, receive LSD in return, and administer it to patients without even informing them about the experimental nature of their treatment. Now they had to undergo the newly created Investigational Exemption to the New Drug Application process. Henceforth, the FDA had to give prior approval for all testing of experimental drugs. Additionally, Sandoz had grown concerned about its reputation and restricted the provision of LSD in the United States to researchers associated with the National Institute of Mental Health, Veterans Affairs hospitals, and to state commissioners of mental health. As a result, the number of researchers who had access to psychedelics was reduced from several hundred to approximately 70 (or, according to another source, even 13). They were all scientists working within federal and state agencies or they had obtained grants or permissions from such agencies (Masters and Houston 1966: 66; Stevens 1987: 182–182; Novak 1997; Doblin 2000).

Up to this point the history of the medical uses of hallucinogens had been part of a much broader history of controlling pharmaceuticals in the United States. What was at issue when scientific applications of hallucinogens were subjected to a strict regulatory regime in the early 1960s was not spiritual liberation through consciousness-expanding drugs and their association with the politics of the counterculture, but medical paternalism and pharmaceutical marketing practices. After all, the distribution of thalidomide and LSD as investigational drugs primarily served to acquaint doctors with new products and to establish a lucrative therapeutic application from which industry could profit. The expansion of the FDA's duties and power was meant to protect American citizens from ruthless or adventurous physicians, scientists, and businessmen. It belonged to a profound transformation of medical decision making, challenging and curbing physicians' professional dominance with a commitment to individual rights. In the 1960s, trust in medical authority was shaken and thereafter doctors and researchers had to make their decisions about patients and test subjects, treatments and study designs alongside lawyers, judges, legislators, members of ethics committees, and FDA officers (Rothman 1991). These developments in the medical sector were part of an even more far-reaching restructuring of the governance of technological change in industrialized countries that was responding to public concern about the risks accompanying scientific and technological innovation (Brickman et al. 1985: 19). But this was only the beginning of the end of hallucinogen research.

POLITICAL NEUROTHEOLOGY

In 1960, an established middle-aged personality psychologist went on a vacation to Mexico before taking up a new position at Harvard's

Center of Personality Research. In the area where Timothy Leary was staying, the New York banker and amateur mycologist Gordon Wasson had rediscovered and widely publicized the ritual use of hallucinogenic mushrooms only five years earlier. Interested in experiencing their effects for himself, Leary bought such *Psilocybe* mushrooms at the market, tried them—and had what he would later describe as a religious epiphany (Leary 1970: 13–14). By the time he arrived in Cambridge, he had decided to make the effects of psilocybin, the pharmacologically active compound of the toadstool (just isolated and synthesized by Hofmann), the center of his new research program (Greenfield 2006: 110–114).

The last experiment, which Leary supervised during his short tenure at Harvard in 1962, instantiated a science, which Huxley (1962: 94, 144) simultaneously envisaged in *Island* under the newly coined rubric of *neurotheology*. It is in this work of fiction that the term was coined to designate a discipline studying the relationship between physiology and spiritual experience (Horgan 2003: 74). Considering that the academic discipline of theology traditionally studies and elaborates a rational system of religious beliefs, it is debatable whether the biological investigation of spiritual experiences is aptly characterized as neuro*theology*. But, since this is how the term has been used ever since, I will adopt the concept of neurotheology to describe this emergent discourse instead of replacing it by the possibly more appropriate designation *neurospirituality*. Following William James's (1958/1902: 298–299) association of drug-induced mind states and divine illumination, Leary and his doctoral student Walter Pahnke administered psilocybin to twenty theology students who attended the Good Friday sermon at Boston University's Marsh Chapel. Subsequently, they compared the participants' experience reports with experiences described in the mystical literature and concluded that hallucinogens could facilitate genuine mystical experiences (Pahnke 1963; Pahnke and Richards 1966; Lattin 2010: 73–84).

But the situation was becoming more and more difficult for Leary and his allies. As in any university department, there were power struggles between them and other factions in the psychology faculty. At a time when behaviorism reigned, there was much opposition to their introspective approach to psychopharmacology. Ethically, Leary was also criticized for ignoring the medical risks associated with the administration of psilocybin and for his use of graduate students as experimental subjects. Legend has it that he was eventually dismissed from Harvard in 1963 when undergraduates became involved in his experimentation as well. But, in fact, it was Leary who declared himself fired on a TV talk show, fashioning himself as a repressed but rebellious countercultural hero. It was not just Harvard that drove him out but also he himself who turned his back on Harvard (Greenfield 2006: 195–199; Das and Metzner 2010: 81–91; Lattin 2010: 85–106).

Even after Leary had decided that he was "through playing the science game" (quoted in Jonnes 1996: 229), he remained intellectually rooted and continued to influence the field of psychology (Devonis 2012). But he also metamorphosed into the prophet of a pharmacologically revitalized religious movement (Leary 1968). "Drugs are the religion of the twenty-first century," Leary (1970: 44) announced. He propagated hallucinogens as a psychopharmacological cure for all social ills: "It seemed to us that wars, class conflicts, racial tensions, economic exploitation, religious strife, ignorance, and prejudice were all caused by narrow social conditioning. Political problems were manifestations of psychological problems, which at bottom seemed to be neurological-hormonal-chemical. If we could help people plug into the empathy circuits of the brain, then positive social change could occur" (Leary 1983: 49–50).

This optimism resonated with the high hopes inspired by the psychopharmacological revolution. A decade or two earlier, drugs had hardly been accepted as remedies of mental disorders. But since the mid-1950s, Americans had grown convinced that no illness was beyond the capacities of pharmaceutical science. Leary took this new confidence in biological psychiatry one step further, from the clinic to society at large, which he declared a suitable target of pharmacotherapeutic intervention. Moving from scientific detachment to social activism, Leary (1983: 50) plotted a "neurological revolution": "Bolshevik bomb throwing was out. The new bombs were neurological. You don't blow up the Czar's palace. You blow minds" (quoted in Greenfield 2006: 333).

The rhetorics of Leary's "politics of ecstasy" were radical and new. New because of the abundance of brain metaphors and *neuro-* prefixes. They might appear less striking against the background of the current hype around the neurosciences. But when Leary invented this vocabulary, he was among the first to introduce such loose brain talk into popular discourse. His biologizing manifestos and sermons were also radical in that they advocated the liberation of people's "divine bodies" from a repressive "robot society." Consciousness-expanding drugs were meant to facilitate the "opening" of the cortex and its "liberation from the cultural self" (Leary 1965: 69, 93, 141). In contrast to much critical scholarship in contemporary anthropology, Leary's impatience for liberty did not turn to historical and cultural contingencies but to biospiritual universals, framed by Huxley's perennial philosophy, as a way out of a societal situation experienced as overly restraining. In this respect, the counterculture was not just a subculture opposing the Establishment but a culture against culture per se. But however novel and extreme these calls for a consciousness revolution were, Leary did not simply see himself in the tradition of political avant-gardism. He cast himself as involved in a recurrent transhistorical battle that every new generation had to fight all over again to recover the wisdom already possessed by Gautama Buddha two and a half millennia ago: a reminder that *revolution* described a circular motion before it came to designate the singular historical breaks that have come to serve as the hallmark of modernity (Leary 1965: 84–89; Koselleck 2004: 46).

Despite this neurotheological agitation, Leary's agenda was ostensibly apolitical. He followed the worldview underlying Huxley's *Island* that all evils were the product of imperfect social relations and not of human nature. Leary's anthropological optimism was—like Huxley's—religious, not political, assuming that even within a bad society happiness was possible by turning inward and seeking mystical revelations (Meckier 1978). "The choice is between being rebellious and being religious," Leary declared (quoted in Greenfield 2006: 303). "Don't vote. Don't politic. Don't petition. You can't do anything about America politically" (Leary 1965: 6). He was convinced that militant opposition as practiced by student activists (whom he mocked as "young men with menopausal minds") (quoted in Greenfield 2006: 303) only led to further subjection to the alienating and oppressive "games" of society. He told an audience in San Francisco, "My advice to people in America today is as follows: If you take the game of life seriously, if you take your nervous system seriously, if you take the energy process seriously, you must turn on, tune in, and drop out" (Leary 1965: 133). And taking LSD—short for "Let the State Disintegrate!" (quoted in Greenfield 2006: 303)—appeared to be the fastest way of reaching this goal. Like early Christians, Leary invoked spiritual transcendence to distance himself from and passively resist the political powers that be (Adam 2006).

Of course, this kind of theology represented a political stance of its own right. At least in Bruno Latour's (1993) somewhat idiosyncratic reading, the historians of science Steven Shapin and Simon Schaffer (1985) have shown how Thomas Hobbes and Robert Boyle, in response to decades of religious civil war in seventeenth-century Britain, established the political ontology of modernity, dividing the world into nature and society while removing God from both realms. To preserve peace, the "crossed-out God" was deprived of all agency by simultaneously locking Him out into infinite transcendence and locking Him into men's heart of hearts. Leary and the psychedelic counterculture challenged this modern cosmological order by invoking a direct drug-mediated experience of the divine, bringing the kind of religious enthusiasm, which had politically destabilized early modern Europe, to twentieth-century America.

In the United States, the political turbulence of the 1960s went hand in hand with a far-reaching reconfiguration of the religious landscape. This decade marked the beginning of the so-called Fourth Great Awakening in American history. In contrast to the previous three revitalizations of religious life, which were dominated by asceticism and subordination to biblical authority, this latest revival has been described as a turn toward unusual experiences taken as instances of direct and personal contact with the divine. It affected mainline churches and gave rise to contemporary evangelical movements. But it also led to the emergence of alternative forms of spirituality, syncretically combining the appreciation of Eastern religious thought, a rediscovery of natural rather than revealed religion, and the mystical illuminations induced by psychedelic drugs (McLoughlin 1978: 179–216; Fuller 2000: 84–89; Luhrmann 2005). These developments challenged the established political system from different directions.

The emergence of psychedelic enthusiasm did not fail to provoke resistance. The mixture of "psychotropic hedonism" and "instant mysticism" associated with the use of hallucinogens conflicted with the widespread attitude of "pharmacological Calvinism," which rejected the use of drugs to achieve pleasure or enlightenment. The term *pharmacological Calvinism* was coined in 1972 by the psychiatrist Gerald Klerman. Since the nineteenth century, Calvinism had come to be associated with "un-American" tendencies such as the oppression of freedom of thought, religious intolerance, fatalism, and so on (Davis 1996). Thus Klerman's use of the term was not purely analytic but also served a polemical purpose. He criticized the underprescription of psychiatric drugs by physicians and psychotherapists who relied instead solely on the therapeutic effects of verbal insight (Klerman 1972; Healy 1997: 226–231, 1998: 535). Even though biological psychiatry was already on the rise and pharmacotherapy was quickly gaining support, Klerman identified the youth culture of the early 1970s as the most serious challenge to Puritan reservations about drugs. It seems questionable whether the moral rejection of medical and nonmedical drug applications can be accurately described as Calvinist. But this label is suitable for conceptualizing the opposition to drug mysticism insofar as Calvin was convinced that spiritual experiences were illusionary: faith was not to be proven by mere feelings but through "good works." The this-worldly orientation of Calvinism entailed a spiritual dignification of mundane activities, including the pursuit of economic gain, which, according to Max Weber's (1992/1920) famous if contested thesis, eventually inspired the development of capitalism. Pharmacological Calvinism is part of the Protestant work ethic in that it rejects drug use as a means to experiencing pleasure or religious ecstasy and advocates more industrious routes to salvation.

The opposition of pharmacological Calvinism and psychedelic pharmacospirituality mirrors Weber's distinction between two ideal types of religious ethic: asceticism and mysticism. According to Weber, the asceticism characteristic of the Protestant ethic played a particularly important role in the formation of American capitalism. Through work, this ethic seeks to master the original depravity of man, transforming the quest for salvation into a worldly business. Mysticism, on the other hand, aims at contemplation and ecstasy. Progress in the inner life requires detachment from narrow materialistic pursuits. Following Weber, it cultivates a "world-denying love" at odds with the unbrotherly spirit of capitalism. Mysticism conceives of the hustle and bustle of working life not as the way to heaven, but as a soteriological obstacle. The contrast to the asceticism of the Protestant work ethic could not be any starker (Weber 1958/1919; Bellah 1999).

Already in the 1960s, sociologically informed observers and self-reflexive members of the American counterculture described that culture's drug mysticism against the background of Weber's work. For example, the Stanford psychologist Richard Blum (1964: 283) noted, "For the user [of LSD] who does move in the direction of contemplative mysticism, there is a fleeing from the world and the re-establishment of the ethic of brotherhood, symbolized in becoming more loving." And the countercultural activist Jerry Rubin explained: "Drug use signifies the total end of the Protestant ethic: screw work, we want to know ourselves. But of course the goal is to free oneself from American society's sick notion of work, success, reward, and status and to find oneself through one's own discipline, hard work, and introspection" (quoted in Jonnes 1996: 239). This blend of drug mysticism and the desire for self-knowledge was articulated in opposition to what was imagined as the Protestant spirit of capitalism (Davis and Munoz 1968).

Representatives of the psychedelic movement presented their conflict with the so-called Establishment as a fight over religious values. This framing enabled them to defend the use of "sacramental biochemicals like LSD" (Leary 1970: 18) by claiming their constitutional right of religious liberty. In a Senate hearing, one of them even warned against a "religious civil war" that would break out if Leary was arrested for drug possession (Greenfield 2006: 274). In the course of the 1960s, the struggle over hallucinogens became a political struggle over the spiritual foundations of America's social and economic order. Soon, Leary's political neurotheology became so influential that the Nixon administration came to see him as public enemy number one in its "War on Drugs"— even though the opponents of the counterculture preferred to present the situation as a moral threat and a public health crisis rather than a religious conflict (Davenport-Hines 2002: 265; Greenfield 2006: 343).

The attribution of a political neurotheology to Leary and the psychedelic movement evokes not only the late Huxley's sense of biospirituality but also Carl Schmitt's *Political Theology* (2005), originally published in 1922. Of course, politically and theologically, the far-right Catholic jurist from Germany and the libertarian high priest of the American psychedelic movement could not have been further apart. Schmitt's famous dictum that "all significant concepts of the modern theory of the state are secularized theological concepts" (36) led him to embrace authoritarianism. In his eyes, Hitler restored a dimension of political transcendence by reoccupying a position of sovereignty above the law— analogous to the omnipotent God of theist theology.

Leary, on the other hand, drew from an antistatist tradition equally inherent in Christianity. Here, God did not appear as celestial king upon a throne in heaven. Instead of identifying Him with a position in a symbolic system that ordered the social and political world, Leary (2001) proclaimed: "Your brain is God!" The divine was to be found as inner experience, and psychedelics served as chemical keys to this God within: "Religion is consciousness expansion, centered in the body and defined exactly the way it sounds best to you" (Leary 1965: 9). Antithetical to Schmitt's authoritarian politicotheological order, Leary called for an anarchist drug mysticism: "You must start your own religion. You're God—but only you can discover and nurture your divinity.

No one can start your religion for you" (7). This was both spiritual and legal advice followed by numerous "dope churches" that quoted the freedom of religion to defend their use of illicit drugs (Leary 1965: 12–15; Miller 1991: 31–34). But only members of the Native American Church and, since 2006, of the syncretist churches União do Vegetal and Santo Daime were granted the right to use peyote and ayahuasca for religious purposes (Stewart 1987: 213–238; Fuller 2000: 177–190; Dobkin de Rios and Rumrrill 2008).[3]

The attempt to introduce psychedelic drugs as mediators of the divine into the modern world threw 1960s America into a crisis. Eventually, however, this moment of conflict and indetermination was resolved by legislators. The spreading consumption of hallucinogens among white middle-class youth (probably promoted more effectively by Ken Kesey's hedonistically oriented electric Kool-Aid acid tests than by Leary's tongue-in-cheek proselytizing [Wolfe 1968]), along with a growing number of drug-related accidents and their scandalization in the media, resulted in the gradual prohibition of this class of drugs between 1966 and 1970. Consequently, the utopian visions of an alternative drug culture, which Huxley's novel *Island* had inspired at the beginning of the decade, were shattered.

THE DARK ERA

Even though hallucinogen research was drastically curbed in the late 1960s, it never came to a total standstill. Despite the numerous hurdles and restrictions limiting the freedom of science it was, in principle, still possible to pursue research on psychedelic drugs and, in fact, some scientists did obtain licenses that allowed them to go ahead. Two of them, the chemist David Nichols and the neuropsychopharmacologist Mark Geyer, would later play a crucial role in the resurgence of hallucinogen research. For those holding a special permit, chemical analysis and synthesis as well as pharmacological studies in animals were legally possible throughout the 1970s and 1980s. There were even a very few human studies during the period that Geyer ironically referred to as "the Dark Era" (e.g., Francom et al. 1988; Lim et al. 1988). In Germany and the Netherlands, the psychiatrist Hanscarl Leuner and the psychoanalyst Jan Bastiaans were also allowed to continue using hallucinogens in therapeutic settings until they retired in the mid-1980s (Passie 1996/97; Snelders and Kaplan 2002). Of course, the scale of this medical research was infinitesimal in comparison to the vibrant scientific experimentation in the 1950s, but it was enough to demonstrate that such research was not categorically prohibited. The mechanisms that led to its deterioration were subtler. Scientists were not officially denied their academic freedom and yet they were discouraged, worn down, and guided away from further work on these compounds. A subtle microphysics of power (allocation of funding, having to guard one's reputation, approval of research projects, recruitment of test subjects, etc.) led to an almost total breakdown of academic hallucinogen research.

At the same time, however, psychedelic science flourished in the underground. The central figure of this nonacademic hallucinogen research was Alexander Shulgin. Invited to a symposium at the University of California, San Diego, in 2006, Shulgin indicated that in the nineteenth century the Western world had only known two psychedelic drugs: marijuana and peyote. By the 1950s, it already knew dozens. And at the beginning of the twenty-first century, the number was about two hundred—many of which Shulgin had invented himself (see Shulgin and Shulgin 1991, 1997). If this logarithmic growth continued, Shulgin calculated, there would be about 2,000 compounds by 2050. Since the birth of the Internet, largely contemporaneous with the revival of hallucinogen research in the 1990s, clandestine psychedelic science has found a highly efficient venue for publication and collaboration (Langlitz 2009). It blossomed in the shadow of prohibition. But this is for another book.[4]

AFTER THE COUNTERCULTURE: THE REVIVAL OF PSYCHEDELIC RESEARCH

In 2010—by now the revival had been simmering for two decades—I went to visit Rick Doblin, one of its most important initiators, to talk about how this comparatively quiet return of psychedelics into academic science had begun. Together with his wife, three children, and a dog, Doblin was living in Belmont, an affluent suburb of Boston, just a short bus ride away from where Timothy Leary had brought hallucinogen research into disrepute. Some neighbors demonstrated their patriotism by planting little Star Spangled Banners in their well-trimmed front gardens, while Doblin was advocating scientific and recreational drug use. Yet the exuberant outgrowths of the War on Drugs, which President Obama's newly appointed drug czar had only rhetorically ended, seemed worlds apart (Kerlikowske 2009). And so we spent a peaceful afternoon talking next to a Jacuzzi on the rooftop. The only noise interfering with my interview recording was the soft rustling of leaves.

Asked about the sixties, Doblin stated: "Most people explain the breakdown with psychedelic experiences going wrong in a recreational context. But I would say that it had more to do with psychedelic experiences going right: people having unitive mystical experiences that changed their political perspectives and which got them involved in social justice movements challenging the status quo." However, he not only held an uptight and anxious American society responsible but also blamed Leary. Doblin (1991, 1998) had conducted follow-up studies on two of Leary's experiments and had found that Leary had committed scientific fraud. Together with his doctoral student Walter Pahnke, Leary had furthermore concealed the fact that one subject from the Good Friday experiment had become so severely psychotic that he had to be tranquilized with an antipsychotic drug. "Tim justified this in his mind as, 'The society is demonizing these drugs, so if I fudge things a bit, it's excusable because I'm fighting a bigger evil,'" Doblin explained. On the opposite side, Doblin saw a society not prepared for those "incredible dynamic energies." In response to the drugs' gradual association with cultural rebellion, this society equally distorted the facts, exaggerated risks, and suppressed research "to keep the stories going about how terrible these things were."

But Doblin saw the ostracism of hallucinogens in a much broader temporal framework. Following historical speculations about the use of hallucinogenic drugs in initiation ceremonies at Eleusis in ancient Greece (Wasson et al. 1978), Doblin said: "The Eleusinian Mysteries were wiped out by the Church in 396. That was the last time in Western culture that psychedelics had been integrated in a central way. So our mission is a 1600-year mission to try to bring psychedelics back into the core of our culture."

For Doblin, however, the escapism of the counterculture—the fantasy of self-actualization on a remote island as envisioned by Huxley's novel—had turned out to be a dead end. "The self-definition of the counterculture was inherently destructive. If you're separated from the core of society, you will eventually be overwhelmed. That's why I have a picket fence, a station wagon, and a boring middle-class life. That's the route, though. It's to mainstream these things and take them away from cultural rebellion and use them for cultural renewal. I long for a conventional life that has psychedelics and spirituality as part of it." Doblin is Jewish, but his this-worldly mysticism is inspired by the Mahayana Buddhist figure of the Bodhisattva who puts off nirvana to help others: "Even the idea that you could be done on Earth and then you're off the wheel of reincarnation is distasteful to me. It implies that you have no sense of social responsibility and that there is something more spiritual than what we have here on Earth, which I don't think there is. I think this is it. This is the playground, the proving ground. I don't believe in heaven."

Doblin started working toward the mainstreaming of psychedelics in 1984, when MDMA was about to be prohibited as well. A friend of his had founded a nonprofit organization, Earth Metabolic Design Laboratories, dedicated to the development of alternative energy. Since the friend did not use the organization, Doblin took over, reinterpreted its mission as being about "mental energies," and began working against the US Drug Enforcement Administration (DEA): "This was about moving from 'I'm a criminal, I'm a draft resister, I'm a drug user, I'm a countercultural person' to—wow!—this system has also created a mechanism for change within it that will give us the ability to take money from people who get tax reductions to fight the system." With the money it raised, Earth Metabolic Design Laboratories sponsored a toxicity study testing MDMA on dogs and rodents as well as a first preclinical trial on humans (Downing 1986; Frith et al. 1987).

Doblin quickly turned into a psychedelic entrepreneur and lobbyist, speaking out in favor of ecstasy and other psychedelics in TV talk shows and at the World Health Organization in Geneva. When, in 1985, all efforts to prevent the illegalization of MDMA had failed, he abandoned Earth Metabolic Design Laboratories and planned to build a "psychedelic orphan drug pharmaceutical company." The following year, Doblin established it as another nonprofit organization called Multidisciplinary Association for Psychedelic Studies (MAPS). It assembled a network of drug researchers and raised funds from private donors to support its work. MAPS also made a sustained effort to develop a respectful relationship with the FDA to improve communication between the psychedelic community and regulators. For this purpose, Doblin enrolled in the PhD program of Harvard's prestigious Kennedy School of Government, where he wrote a dissertation on the regulation of medical uses of psychedelics (Doblin 2000). Through an internship program for graduates interested in careers in the federal government, Doblin managed to develop strong ties to the FDA officers in charge of hallucinogen studies, and he learned from them how to create admissible research protocols before returning to MAPS. The ultimate goal of his organization was to get MDMA and other psychedelic drugs tested in clinical trials in order to register them as prescription medicines.

But MAPS did not remain the only organization promoting the revival of hallucinogen research. On both sides of the Atlantic, further associations emerged for MAPS to collaborate and compete with. In the United States, the Heffter Research Institute, named after the German chemist who had first isolated mescaline, arrived on the scene in 1993. At the LSD Symposium in 2006, the institute's president and cofounder, David Nichols, a professor of medicinal chemistry, related how this virtual institution, connecting laboratories and research groups at various universities in America and Switzerland, was conceived:

> I began my career in 1969, concentrating on research on psychedelics, and it has been a major focus of my life ever since. *[Turning to Hofmann who was sitting in the audience:]* Albert, thank you! My life would be very different had LSD not been discovered. And certainly less interesting and colorful. After I got my PhD in 1973, I started thinking about the fact that clinical research had stopped. I thought this was really too bad. I would go to scientific meetings and share beers with colleagues, saying, "You know, there should be clinical research." And they would say, "No, no, you can't do it." And I would say, "Well, you can do it. You can't get the government to pay for it, but you need private money." Around 1990, I would be telling the same story to someone, and I thought, "Dave, you gonna be ninety years old sitting in a rocking chair telling the same story." So I decided to start the Heffter Research Institute.

Holding a so-called Schedule I permit, which allowed him to handle even the most tightly controlled psychoactive compounds, Nichols had been one of the very few people able to pursue their scientific interest in hallucinogens continuously since the late 1960s. In his laboratory at Purdue University, he synthesized a range of new substances and tried them out on animals. As a well-respected chemistry professor, he never experienced any difficulties with government agencies—even after the prohibition of hallucinogens. The red line not to be crossed, however, was human research.

In 1990, Nichols's colleague Rick Strassman, a psychiatrist at the University of New Mexico, was the first to test the regulatory limits. He was particularly interested in the short-acting but extremely powerful hallucinogen N,N-dimethyltryptamine (DMT) because it was the only psychedelic endogenously produced by the human body and was possibly involved in naturally occurring psychedelic states such as birth, death and near-death, psychosis, and mystical experiences. Strassman believed it was excreted by the "mysterious pineal gland," which Descartes had taken to be the seat of the soul and where both Eastern and Western mystical traditions had located "our highest spiritual center" (Strassman 2001: xv). In Strassman's eyes, DMT was the key to our humanity. As a Buddhist, he believed that human life began forty-nine days after conception when the spirit ensouled the fetus. The neurobiological correlate of anthropogenesis, Strassman speculated, was a pineal gland release of the "spirit molecule" DMT (xvii).

Strassman proposed to start off with a randomized double-blind dose-response study. He stuck to the unwritten rules, asking to study DMT as a "drug of abuse" and focusing on its pharmacology instead of psychotherapeutic applications (which would have suggested that there was a benefit to taking an illegal drug). He was backed by Daniel Freedman, one of the most powerful figures in American psychiatry at the time (a former president of the American Psychiatric Association and editor of the highly prestigious journal *Archives of General Psychiatry*), who had conducted LSD research himself in the 1950s and 1960s. Despite the damaged reputation of hallucinogens, Strassman's colleagues at the medical school also turned out to be supportive of his project. In 1988, he submitted a research protocol to the Human Research Ethics Committee of his university. In the first phase of hallucinogen research, such institutional review boards had not yet played a major role. Their emergence was part of the institutionalization of medical ethics as well as the establishment of a new regulatory regime in the course of the 1960s (Rothman 1991). Being situated within the research institutions themselves, these bodies were—at least in part—composed of fellow researchers. The underlying idea was to enable scientists to check up on themselves by assigning each other the roles of auditors and auditees (Strathern 2000). Such an autonomous self-regulating apparatus was meant to guarantee, but also to shape and delimit, the freedom of science. In his book *DMT: The Spirit Molecule* (2001), Strassman provided a detailed account of how the precautionary measures demanded by the ethics committee came to affect the experience of his test subjects. Thus the regulatory apparatus not only constituted the external conditions of research but also entered into the outcome of the experiments by transforming the subjects' experiences.

Strassman also had to gain approval from the FDA to use an investigational drug and from the DEA because DMT was a controlled substance. This process was greatly complicated by the fact that DMT was not readily available. He contacted various pharmaceutical companies. But they were either unwilling to provide all the information about the manufacturing process required by the FDA, arguing that it was a trade secret, or refused the liability for human use of their product, fearing lawsuits. Others demanded outrageous sums (up to $50,000) to cover their insurance as well as the uneconomical production of small quantities of an obscure drug. Finally, Dave Nichols offered to synthesize the necessary amount of DMT for $300 and the FDA agreed. In November 1990, two years after the application process had begun, Strassman received the go-ahead for what he presented as the first hallucinogen study in more than two decades (Strassman 2001: xv, 108–118).

When Strassman got approval to giving a psychedelic as powerful as DMT to humans, it seemed as if there could be no fundamental obstacles to administering other hallucinogens as well. Thus, Nichols, Strassman, Geyer, Charles Grob, Dennis McKenna, and George Greer founded the Heffter Research Institute in 1993. In contrast to MAPS' focus on clinical applications of MDMA, Heffter concentrated on psilocybin and, at least initially, emphasized basic research rather than medical applications. Like MAPS, the institute tried to spread a spirit of optimism to attract private funding: "We are at a historic moment. Old social orders are rapidly changing. Economic powers are restructuring for the future. There is widespread popular interest in the brain and the mind as never before. Interest in research with psychedelics seems to be growing, and yet organized financial support for this work is on the wane. The Heffter Research Institute is uniquely poised to be THE key player in the revival of psychedelic research" (Heffter Research Institute n.d.: 1).

It is no coincidence that the reinvigoration of hallucinogen research coincided with US president George H.W. Bush's (1990) announcement of the Decade of the Brain. As in the sixties, the biology of the mind was presented as the last great frontier (Crick 1990: 17; Farber 2002: 29). Psychonautic self-exploration had been replaced (or, as we will see, supplemented) by brain scanners and other new technologies, but drugs continued to serve as probes of the neurochemistry of consciousness. The Heffter members used this opportunity to promote their pet molecules. "Research with psychedelic substances offers an unparalleled opportunity for understanding the relationship of mind to brain in ways not possible using other methods," they claimed (Heffter Research Institute n.d.: 1). Heffter used the neuroscience hype of the 1990s strategically to relegitimize human research with hallucinogenic drugs (Grob 2002: 280).

Even though MAPS and Heffter were pursuing different scientific and political agendas, one of the things both organizations agreed on was that hallucinogen research should not lapse back into the antagonism between "culture" and "counterculture." As the consequences of sixties radicalism continued to unfold and resurge in civil society (O'Donnell and Jones 2010), their common objective was to return this class of drugs to mainstream science and society. In this respect, the psychedelic revivalists managed to break out of the Huxleyan framework, which has shaped so much public debate around psychopharmacology. For them, the choice was not between societal repression and lulling *(Brave New World)* on the one hand and a freedom that could only be found faraway from modern society *(Island)* on the other. They wanted to transform Western culture with its own means, bringing psychedelic perennialism into the twenty-first century.[5]

THE POLITICS OF DISENCHANTMENT AND SPIRITUALIZATION

The Heffter Research Institute was working toward this goal by pursuing what Mark Geyer, in a conversation with me, called "the dispassionate approach of mainstream science." The Heffter researchers presented themselves as free of religious and political fervor. Founder Dave Nichols (2004: 168) emphasized the disenchantment of hallucinogenic drugs through neuropsychopharmacological research: "The tools of today's neuroscience, including in vivo brain imaging technologies, have put a modern face on the hallucinogens. Scientists can no longer see them as 'magic' drugs but rather as 5-HT_{2A} receptor-specific molecules that affect membrane potentials, neuronal firing frequencies, and neurotransmitter release in particular areas of the brain." The message was that psychedelics were ready to inconspicuously join the modern psychotropic pharmacopoeia.

In its mission statement, the Heffter Research Institute (2001: iv) declared that it would "neither condemn psychedelic drugs nor advocate their uncontrolled use. The sole position of the Institute in this regard will be that psychedelic agents, utilized in thoughtfully designed and carefully conducted scientific experiments, can be used to further the understanding of the mind" (Heffter Research Institute 2001). Dare to know! This sense of value neutrality was incompatible with the religious zeal that had dominated the public perception of psychedelia in the 1960s. A pharmacologist from the Heffter lab in Zurich told me that his generation differed from Leary's in that they had lost a sense of mission. They had given up the hope that mind-altering drugs would revolutionize society. The psychedelic experience was no longer presented as a catalyst of nonconformism and rebelliousness. If, as anthropologists have shown, the ritual use of hallucinogens in tribal societies could also serve to "validate and reify the culture" (Furst 1976: 16), then, another Heffter member argued, Westerners should also be able to use them to reinforce "cultural cohesion and commitment" (Grob 2002: 283). Following these cues, it was the neuroscientific disenchantment and depoliticization of hallucinogen research that rendered its revival possible. Such a narrative of the psychedelic revival—from the idealistic and revolutionary 1960s to the pragmatic and civil 1990s— would affirm historian of science Michael Hagner's (2009) diagnosis of a "neuroscientific Biedermeier."[6]

But the moral terrain of contemporary hallucinogen research is too rugged to fit into any epochal zeitgeist diagnosis. First of all, like Leary's withdrawal from politics into the spiritual realm, the alleged depoliticization qua scientification was itself a political maneuver. In an ideologically charged field like hallucinogen research, professions of soberness and the display of dispassionate objectivity were used rhetorically to reinstate the legitimacy of scientific and therapeutic uses of psychedelics. The intended rapprochement between these ostracized drugs, biomedicine, and the authorities was supposed to change the legal status and the social acceptability of hallucinogen use. Thus, instead of abandoning the psychedelic revolution for good, it was rather transformed into a reform movement, in which Heffter was playing a cautious role as well.

MAPS, on the other hand, presented itself as avowedly political but aimed at translating its enthusiasm not into another cultural civil war but into civic engagement. In a special issue of the *MAPS Bulletin* dedicated to the organization's vision, Rick Doblin (2002a) first laid out a five-year, five-million-dollar plan for developing MDMA into a prescription medicine to assist the psychotherapeutic treatment of post-traumatic stress disorder. MAPS was particularly interested in the treatment of soldiers and police officers: "We want to show that MDMA can be helpful for people in the heart of the power structure, in the mainstream," Doblin (2007) explained their strategy in an interview. A second article of the special issue represented MAPS' politicospiritual vision. Significantly, the latter was not written by Doblin or any other member of the psychedelic community. To emphasize the reconciliation of psychedelia with "the Establishment," MAPS reprinted a speech delivered by a member of the US House of Representatives. "Though definitely not written as a psychedelic manifesto," MAPS introduced Dennis Kucinich's piece as "one of the clearest examples of the political implications of mystical experience," also reflecting MAPS' own utopian hopes: "There is an idealism at the core of the psychedelic community that is difficult to explain. It's based in part on the conviction that even partial unitive mystical experiences, whether or not catalyzed by psychedelics, can have a transformative effect. The hope is that the lasting effects of these experiences include more tolerance and appreciation of diversity of all kinds, enhanced environmental awareness, solidarity with the poor and oppressed, and a willingness to work through difficult emotions rather than project them onto an external enemy or scapegoat" (MAPS' lead-in in Kucinich 2002: 19). Thereby, MAPS took up Leary's psychobiologization of political problems and his advocacy of the psychedelic experience as contributing to their solution. Pharmacospirituality was meant to promote peace: "Societies more open to psychedelic experiences are likely to be less blind to their own demons and prejudices, and perhaps less likely to wage wars of all types" (Doblin 2003).

However, Doblin refrained from reducing the political spirituality associated with psychedelics to a potentiality lying within the drugs themselves (an essentialist perspective that Richard DeGrandpre [2006] termed "pharmacologicalism"). Even though Doblin told me that "of all psychedelics, MDMA is the most inherently therapeutic, the most inherently warm and loving," he also knew that "Charlie Manson used LSD for brainwashing and to get people to kill"; and he referred to an article in the Israeli press that reported on Hamas fighters using ecstasy from Tel Aviv as "go pills" for their night missions (the anthropological literature is full of examples of hallucinogen use for bellicose purposes [Dobkin de Rios 1984: 213]). "It's not about the drug," Doblin concluded. "It's how you use it. The context is more powerful than the drug."

Despite this more cautious attitude, it is certainly questionable whether MAPS' politicized drug mysticism harmonized with either mainstream science or society. But the casting of psychedelia's countercultural identity engendered a new ethos less antagonistic toward the Protestant ethic of capitalism. It was a this-worldly mysticism that no longer required "dropping out" of society. Instead it tried to translate the experience of unity and transcendence into forms of "active citizenship" (Kucinich 2002: 19). Rather than rejecting the entrepreneurial spirit and wealth generated in the American economy, this new stance sought to enlist the resources of capitalism in the service of advancing the psychedelic agenda. MAPS presented itself as a "membership-based non-profit pharmaceutical company" (Doblin 2002b: 3) and raised money for its projects from successful business people. In this respect, the culture vs. counterculture conflict had indeed been overcome.

When the revival began, drug mysticism could also connect more easily with elements of the Protestant ethic because, in the wake of the 1960s, American Protestantism had changed as well. The discrepancy between the Protestant focus on the scriptures and the drug mystics' emphasis on intense spiritual experience was less pronounced than thirty years earlier. Not just the counterculture, but also the baby boomer generation more broadly had turned toward experience-centered forms of spirituality shared, for example, by evangelical Christianity and the New Age movement (Luhrmann 2003). In his book on the impact of the counterculture on mainline denominations, Mark Oppenheimer (2003: 6) goes so far as to argue that "by the mid 1970s, the counterculture had become the culture."

This new appreciation of religion as experience (rather than normative order) inspired a growing number of attempts to bridge the gap between science and spirituality. Under the rubric of neurotheology, brain researchers began to study the neural correlates of altered states of consciousness induced by meditation, prayer, or transcranial magnetic stimulation (Joseph 2002). When we spoke, Doblin contended "that we have science and religion coming together in a way that they had not since Galileo." The growing attention paid to this encounter had two roots. On the one hand, meditation was considered to be work on the self that led to increased concentration, heightened cognition and awareness, and emotional control. As such it was part of a broader interest in enhancement technologies. The culture of self-improvement provided a common matrix for both neurotheology and cosmetic psychopharmacology. On the other hand, the burgeoning neuroscientific interest in spiritual practices also reflected the changing role of religion in certain corners of the life sciences in the last two decades. Cognitive anthropologists came to acknowledge religious thought as part of human nature, contending that it could be explained in evolutionary terms (Boyer 2001; Atran 2002). After the limited success of two centuries of secularization, they had come to realize that religiosity was unlikely to succumb to the kind of materialist proselytizing practiced by many of their late nineteenth-century predecessors (Hecht 2003; Shapin 2008a). At about the same time, some of the brain researchers who had come of age during the Fourth Great Awakening and had followed the turn toward unchurched forms of spirituality had become powerful figures in their fields, setting their own research agendas. In the last ten or twenty years, the traditionally materialistic field of brain research has become significantly more accommodating toward scientists who break with this ontology and publicly express their belief in a "spiritual reality" (Monastersky 2006).

In fact, such avowals have even helped to obtain funding from private organizations. The Mind and Life Institute, for example, financed experiments, conferences, and retreats exploring the mental activities of Buddhist meditators (Tresch 2011). The Fetzer Institute, founded by a radio and television magnate, funded scientific projects fostering "the awareness of the power of love and forgiveness."[7] And the John Templeton Foundation, run by an evangelical philanthropist, promoted the employment of scientific methods to discover "spiritual realities" (Schüle 2006).

In an academic milieu that provided hospitable niches to those interested in the scientific investigation of religious experiences, a number of researchers came to apply the tools of cognitive neuroscience, especially neuroimaging technologies and electroencephalography, to spiritual practices. Hallucinogen research also profited from this assemblage of science, religion, and philanthropy. The Fetzer Institute, for instance, cofunded a number of psychedelic research projects together with MAPS and the Heffter Research Institute (e.g., Walsh and Grob 2005; Cahn 2006). Partially financed by the Council on Spiritual Practices, Roland Griffiths and colleagues' (2006) study on psilocybin-induced mystical-type experiences mostly replicated the findings of Walter Pahnke's famous Good Friday experiment in a more controlled setting, but it received such a significant amount of media coverage that it brought the return of psychedelic science at major research universities such as Johns Hopkins to the attention of a wider American public. Such neurotheological studies of the physiological correlates of the *unio mystica* rescued spiritual experiences from the realm of the subjective (or even imaginary), endowing them with some kind of reality. This "reality" was interpreted in two contradictory ways: either as reducing spirituality to an epiphenomenon of neural processes or as proof that the brain could be turned into a sense organ capable of perceiving the immaterial but nonetheless real dimensions revealed in such altered states (d'Aquili and Newberg 2002).

In contemporary neurotheology, an experience-centered spirituality and the heuristic individualism of cognitive neuroscience meet in the abstraction of experience from its social and cultural context. Mysticism is narrowed down to peak experiences and isolated neural events. Thereby it is also stripped of cultural difference and antagonism. This is certainly no big loss if one continues to pursue a "liberation from the cultural self," as Leary (1965: 93) called it in a homage to Huxley. The neurotheological assumption of the universality of mystical experience has been inherited from Huxley's *Perennial Philosophy* (2004/1944). The notion of *philosophia perennis,* which Huxley popularized in the twentieth century, is rooted in a tradition even predating Gottfried Wilhelm Leibniz's early modern quest for religious unity (Ch. Schmitt 1966). The supposed transcultural nature of drug-induced mystical revelations lends itself to a politics of confessional reconciliation, which had already been the goal of the perennial philosophy in seventeenth-century Prussia (Jordan 1927; Wake et al. 1934; Whitmer 2010). Whereas Leibniz and his contemporaries responded to interconfessional tensions between different Protestant sects, Catholics, and Jews, MAPS promoted psychedelics in America in the face of the political antagonism between liberals and the religious right, which had brought US president George H.W. Bush to power. Doblin (2008) advocated a "global spirituality" that was meant to bridge the divide between organized religion and a scientifically enlightened liberal lifestyle open to drugs: "There is a rise in religious fundamentalism at a time when that world view is more and more difficult to sustain. . . . The fundamentalists are scared that psychedelics might delegitimize their particular religion, but I think psychedelics can reinvigorate religion and make people appreciate their traditions. Global spirituality is not inherently anti-religion." The political neurotheology of the psychedelic revival oscillated between disenchanted but politically defensive atheism and mystically inspired libertarian activism. In accordance with MAPS' mainstreaming strategy, Doblin deemphasized the marked ideological differences between the reanimated psychedelic movement and the powerful advocates of American conservatism who had also dominated Leon Kass's President's Council on Bioethics (Briggle 2009).

THE GLOBAL ASSEMBLAGE OF HALLUCINOGEN RESEARCH

And yet, even at our meeting in 2010, Rick Doblin was still worried that the political climate would change and that everything MAPS had built up over the past two decades could be torn down again. From the very beginning, such concerns had led the psychedelic revivalists to develop an international strategy. As Doblin told me: "We need multiple places where this stuff is happening. If there is a backlash in any one of them, hopefully there is a refuge elsewhere."

Thus, the revival of psychedelic science was not restricted to the United States. In the late 1980s and early 1990s, new research projects were simultaneously budding in Russia, Britain, Spain, Germany, and Switzerland. Many of the protagonists of this development had known each other for many years through the conferences of the International Transpersonal Association established by the Czech psychedelic researcher Stan Grof in 1978. Grof and his allies promoted a form of psychology that studied self-transcendent aspects of human experience, including those induced by drugs. "They were going all over the world trying to unify scientists over spirituality and looking for a place to start this," Doblin remembered. But not everybody involved in the global reanimation of hallucinogen research was an adherent of transpersonal psychology. In Germany, for example, the group around the biological psychiatrists Manfred Spitzer, Leo Hermle, and Euphrosyne Gouzoulis-Mayfrank was more interested in experimental psychosis than in experimental mysticism. The symposia of the European College for the Study of Consciousness, a virtual institution founded in 1985 by the German psychiatrist Hanscarl Leuner, provided a meeting place for the small but burgeoning scene of European hallucinogen researchers, mostly from Germany and Switzerland. Here, members of different ideological camps came together. Advocates of psycholytic therapy exchanged ideas with basic science researchers, while stern biological psychiatrists spoke to anthropologists practicing neoshamanism.

It did not take long until Europeans and Americans met. In a 1989 newsletter that MAPS sent out to its supporters, Doblin (1989a) mentioned the possibility of conducting MDMA research in the Soviet Union before FDA permission was granted for US studies. A small group of scientists was already active in Moscow and Leningrad. Since 1985, for example, the Russian psychiatrist Evgeny Krupitsky had treated alcoholics and heroin addicts with the hallucinogen ketamine. As the Iron Curtain fell and the USSR began to disintegrate, an opportunity seemed to open up for MAPS: "Soviet state-funded science is in a crisis. It is now possible to assemble a world-class psychedelic research group for a fraction of the cost here in the US" (Doblin 1992).

At about the same time, in 1988, the Swiss Federal Office of Public Health gave permission to a group of physicians, the Swiss Medical Association for Psycholytic Therapy (SAPT; Schweizer Ärztegesellschaft für Psycholytische Therapie), to treat patients with LSD, psilocybin, and MDMA. Doblin was thrilled: "Finally, somewhere in the world, psychotherapeutic research with MDMA is taking place," he wrote in a MAPS newsletter article titled "Switzerland Leads the Way" (Doblin 1989b). He was hopeful that the Swiss experience would help MAPS convince American regulatory agencies of the value of psychedelic research: "The fact that hundreds of patients have been successfully treated with MDMA in Switzerland strengthens the circumstantial case for research into the therapeutic use of MDMA" (1).

When the Heffter Research Institute was founded in 1993, the axis between American and Swiss psychedelic scientists was further consolidated. It was the fiftieth anniversary of Hofmann's discovery of LSD. To mark the occasion, the academic conference "50 Years of LSD" was organized by the Swiss Academy of Medical Sciences and sponsored by Sandoz and the Swiss Federal Office of Public Health. On this occasion, Dave Nichols, Mark Geyer, and Rick Strassman traveled to Switzerland, where they met Spitzer, Hermle, and Gouzoulis from Germany. Soon Geyer's lab began to cooperate with Gouzoulis. Yet a second encounter would turn out to have even greater bearing on the future of Heffter. Franz Vollenweider was a young Swiss researcher building up a laboratory at the Psychiatric University Hospital in Zurich, where he was conducting the first neuroimaging studies on the effects of psilocybin. Nichols remembered that they immediately realized that Vollenweider was very bright and promising—if "a bit scrambled." But in Vollenweider they saw not only a highly talented young brain researcher with a passionate interest in psychedelics but also a potential collaborator who had access to neuroimaging technologies none of their allies in the United States had at their disposal. Even more importantly, Vollenweider was based in Switzerland, a country with a significantly more permissive drug policy and regulatory regime. Despite the optimism Nichols, Geyer, and Strassman were spreading when addressing potential donors, they still felt distressed about the resistance that psychedelic research met in America. After all, Strassman's study had only been approved after struggling for two years with various regulatory bodies, and it was not clear whether other universities would be equally accommodating. Geyer recalled: "After meeting Franz and setting up the collaboration, I first told the Heffter people about this: There is actual research going on in Europe! What we had been frustrated about getting going in the US was happening in Germany and Switzerland."

The fact that Vollenweider could conduct clinical research in Zurich became even more important when Strassman left Heffter. Strassman had been the only person at Heffter with access to a clinical research facility. But he became increasingly dissatisfied with his work. He resented the restrictions imposed by the ethics committee and the pressure to stick to the biomedical model, in which mechanisms were more important than the psychedelic experience (Strassman 2001: 278–293). After pushing through the clinical study, which lent so much credibility to Heffter's enterprise, Strassman also refused to acknowledge Nichols as president of the organization. Claiming a leadership role for himself, he expected his colleagues to join him in New Mexico, where he wanted to build up a center for psychedelic studies. But they refused. Strassman complained: "It was easier to talk about the transformative value of the psychedelic experience than it was to put into practice some of its contents. My colleagues may have had inspiring experiences, but they were not committed to goals that required work and sacrifice" (282). Or, as Geyer told me: "Despite experiences with these compounds, people still had egos to contend with." Eventually, Strassman resigned from his academic position and withdrew from Heffter. He also turned his back on his Buddhist community after they spoke out against his association of psychedelics with spirituality. Instead, he returned to his Jewish roots and began to study the Hebrew scriptures in an attempt to further understand the role of endogenous DMT. In 1996, the Heffter Research Institute integrated Vollenweider's lab as a new site to conduct clinical studies in Switzerland. But how had this small, politically introverted country become so central to the global assemblage of hallucinogen research?

Swiss Psilocybin and US Dollars

"LSD—killer drug! LSD—killer drug!" around 150 protesters chanted on the second day of the LSD Symposium in front of the Basel Convention Center. They belonged to the Citizens Commission on Human Rights, Switzerland, an organization cofounded by the Church of Scientology, which was well-known for its antipsychiatric activism. They handed out flyers titled *LSD: The Cruel Time Bomb,* accusing psychiatrists—many of whom were said to have gathered in the conference building—of giving LSD to their patients to worsen their mental problems so they could maintain power over them.

And, indeed, while the scientological human rights activists were protesting, one of those psychiatrists administering hallucinogenic drugs (even though not LSD) to healthy volunteers (not patients) was giving a workshop inside. Franz Vollenweider and his collaborator, Felix Hasler, were hosting a panel titled "Preconditions for Work with Hallucinogens in Switzerland." They mostly explained the regulatory framework of their research to an international lay audience. During the question and answer period one listener asked: "The research you're doing is relatively controversial and I could imagine that you encounter some rough resistance. Where does this resistance come from? Colleagues? Pseudoreligious groups? Politicians? And how do you deal with it?" Considering the intense politicization of psychedelic drugs and the regulatory hurdles Rick Strassman had had to overcome in the United States, Vollenweider's answer came as a surprise:

> We have done about fifty studies and examined 600 to 700 people, but I haven't experienced any resistance so far. Once, there was criticism from

the USA because of an MDMA study we did. They claimed that our doses came close to those given to animals and that this might be dangerous. We checked this meticulously, but our doses were significantly lower than those used in animal models where MDMA is suspected to be toxic. That was the only discussion I had with American colleagues and such disagreements are argued out at conferences.[1] But, interestingly, we have never had any problems here in Switzerland. If there is resistance, it comes from psychiatry insofar as we are seen to be doing too much biology. People always want psychological models. But, of course, doing psychology without biology is nonsense. Psychology is a brain function and the brain is a function of the psyche. It's a vicious circle. This kind of prattle can be ignored. If someone is still a dualist today, he is behind the times.

Obviously, Vollenweider did not consider the scientologists spreading antipsychiatric conspiracy theories in front of the Convention Center a serious threat to his research. Whereas the Church of Scientology was suspiciously watched by the Swiss authorities (it had repeatedly been accused of exploiting its members and harassing its critics), Vollenweider could count on government support for his scientific work with hallucinogenic drugs. The fierce antagonism between authorities and psychedelic culture that had marked the American field after the prohibition of hallucinogens in the late 1960s had no direct match in Switzerland. It was because of this historical and cultural difference that Rick Doblin had reason to hope that Switzerland would lead the way to a revival of hallucinogen research.

HELVETIC COUNTERCULTURE

However, Switzerland had not been spared the sociopolitical conflicts sparked by the appearance of the so-called counterculture. In fact, the Alp republic had already been home to such experimentation with alternative lifestyles many decades before Theodore Roszak coined the term to designate the heterogeneous ensemble of protest movements mushrooming not only in the United States but in almost all industrial countries in the course of the 1960s. Between 1900 and 1920, the small Swiss-lake village of Ascona attracted many disgruntled members of the European *Bildungsbürgertum,* such as the novelist Hermann Hesse and the psychoanalyst Otto Gross, who were looking for alternative ways of life. They experienced what one of these visitors, the German professor of economics Max Weber (1992/1920: 123–124), described as a sense of living in an "iron cage": a world increasingly rationalized, bureaucratized, and populated by a modern vocational humanity *(Berufsmen-*

schentum) that had grown out of, but had become unmoored from, the spiritual foundations of the Protestant moral asceticism so profoundly shaping the country of Calvin and Zwingli (Whimster 2001). To counter this stifling side of modernity, the intellectuals frequenting Ascona defied "society": they advocated anarchy and pacifism, practiced free love, attempted to square individual self-liberation and the renewal of deeply rooted group bonds, rebelled against science and medicine, and sought to experiment with the potential of their own and each others' bodies. They longed for a return to nature while devising this-worldy forms of religiosity that reconciled monism and mysticism. Like their successors half a century later, some of these spiritual dissidents experimented with drugs. Especially after a young woman died of an overdose of cocaine, the Swiss authorities considered the Asconan milieu to be highly undesirable and dangerous and began to take legal action against its most exposed members. But eventually this early counterculture did not disappear due to police action. When the First World War broke out, many members of this scene were drafted for military service, persecuted for refusing to fight for their country, or were simply no longer able to cross borders to travel from their home countries to the Swiss resort. The spirit of Ascona, however, lived on and manifested itself in very different forms as the twentieth century began to take its course (Green 1986).

One of these recurrences involves the events called to mind by the year 1968. Like their counterparts in other Western countries, the Swiss protest movements of the late 1960s revived many of the Asconan ideas by associating them with the political order of the day: protests against the Vietnam war and imperialism, challenges to technocracy, and advocacy of Maoism, feminism, environmentalism, and libertarianism (Linke and Scharloth 2008; Studer and Schaufelbuehl 2009). These ideological currents connected countercultural rebels from San Francisco to Zurich and from Berne to Berlin. While American hippies dropped out to live in small communes in rural California, Swiss youth, most prominently the so-called *Bärglütli,* sought harmonious relations to nature, fellow human beings, and themselves in the Alps, where they practiced herbal medicine, organized workshops in Sufi dancing, and took LSD together (Bittner 2009). As elsewhere, these protests against the established social order resulted in violent clashes between rebellious youth and police forces (Zweifel 1998).

But there was also a distinctly Swiss flavor to the revolts in this part of the world. On the one hand, in Switzerland 1968 was a less apparent historical break than in other countries. In contrast to France, a political takeover did not even seem a faint possibility. Unlike Italy, no sustainable alliance emerged between students and workers. The Swiss government and bureaucracy were not laced with former Nazis and no leftist radicalization gave rise to terrorism as happened in Germany. Having grown up in a notoriously neutral country, Swiss youth were not at risk of having to serve in Vietnam, nor did their society experience the kind of racial tensions that brought together black civil rights activists and the student movement in the United States. Thus, in the case of Switzerland, the historical continuities were as significant as the caesura of '68 (Schär 2008).

On the other hand, the Swiss suffered from what, in 1964, was first diagnosed as the "Helvetic malaise." The term was coined by a member of the Free Democratic Party, classically liberal in its political orientation, who was soon seconded by intellectuals such as the writers Max Frisch and Friedrich Dürrenmatt who sympathized with the nonconformist youth. They all expressed a growing discontent with the "spiritual defense" of Switzerland: a political and cultural movement that had emerged in the early 1930s to protect values and customs perceived as genuinely Swiss against the totalitarian ideologies of national socialism, fascism, and later on communism. In the 1960s, however, both liberals and leftists came to experience this political culture as intellectually suffocating and as an impediment to an open democratic society flourishing by way of permanent self-reflection and self-critique (Färber and Schär 2008).

This convergence of liberal reform and radical protest movements led the Swiss historian Bernhard Schär (2008) to interpret 1968 in Switzerland—despite the Marxist self-conceptions of many of its leftist actors—as a revival of the values of the failed liberal bourgeois revolutions of 1848. Like their nineteenth-century predecessors, Schär argues, this generation of activists fought for more inclusive democratic participation and emphasized individual freedom. The quest for consciousness expansion was not so much about a return to the ecstatic communion of a premodern collective as it was about mental self-determination and the fulfillment of one's own potential. This reading seems further justified—and maybe even applies beyond the borders of Switzerland—when considering the unintended economic effects of 1968: the experimentation with alternative lifestyles facilitated the transition from industrial to consumer capitalism, new markets came to cater to the demand for self-realization, and, certainly in the United States, the counterculture gradually merged into a lucrative cyberculture. Hence, it was also the tranquil history of Switzerland, especially the relative tameness of its sixties, that predisposed the country to helping alleviate the conflict between culture and counterculture.

COMPETITIVE ADVANTAGE

The fact that, in the 1990s, Switzerland came to be at the forefront of the revival of hallucinogen research was not only because it was the homeland of LSD but also because this small country, at the heart and yet outside of Europe, had a history of resisting the internationalization of drug policy. At the beginning of the twentieth century, the problems and conflicts caused by the global opium trade led to the emergence of drug control as an issue of international concern. In 1912, the Hague Convention was passed as the first international drug policy treaty, even though it did not become operational until after World War I (McAllister 2000). The cause was subsequently adopted by the League of Nations (which would be replaced by the United Nations in 1945). However, Switzerland refused to enter into the convention. In part, this might be explained by the nation's long-standing reservations toward international involvements (Suter 1998). Additionally, the Swiss pharmaceutical industry served as one of the world's biggest suppliers of heroin. Its successful lobbying prevented Switzerland from ratifying the Hague Convention until 1925, when the Swiss government finally gave in to massive international pressure from the United States and the League of Nations (Tanner 1990; Boller 2005: 145–146).

Although Switzerland did not become a member of the United Nations until 2002, it signed the UN Single Convention on Narcotic Drugs in 1961 and the Convention on Psychotropic Substances in 1971. The latter was presented as ushering in a new age of drug control and included the international prohibition of hallucinogens. But this gradual surrender of Swiss neutrality to the US-driven War on Drugs only occurred reluctantly. The Swiss historian Jakob Tanner remarked: "Generally, one can say that the power of the United States to define what is and what is not a drug has been crucial. Particularly the Single Convention of 1961, which replaced or abolished almost all previous agreements had a very characteristic trademark. I think that it wouldn't have occurred to Switzerland to prohibit opiates. Probably, one would have continued to manage this by way of laws regulating the manufacture and distribution of medicines *[Arzneimittelverordnungen]* as had been the case before the Narcotics Law" (quoted in Vannini and Venturini 1999: 266).

Regarding the prohibited substances listed by this law, Tanner told me that "in general, one wanted to keep the list short or at least one wanted a list that did not restrain the innovation potential of the chemical and pharmaceutical industry." While in the United States a problematization of drug use had already set in around the turn of the century, the isolationist mountain state deemed itself immune from the world's drug problems. Even in 1967, the writer Frank Arnau still claimed that intoxicants of any kind were foreign to the Swiss national character (Boller 2005: 151). But, however grudgingly, Switzerland eventually decided to join the international community in adopting a more repressive drug policy. By the late 1960s, Swiss policy makers had to acknowledge that their citizens were not as impervious to the temptations of inebriants as once thought. In a major revision of the Narcotics Law of 1951, LSD was prohibited in 1975 (in comparison with 1966 in the United States and 1967 in neighboring Germany), and for about fifteen years Switzerland adopted a primarily repressive course. As in the American case, the illegalization of hallucinogenic drugs seriously hampered their scientific investigation even though half a dozen researchers continued to work in the field (Vannini and Venturini 1999: 285–305).

A second and more momentous parallel to the development in America was the exacerbation of the "drug problem" despite—or maybe because of—these repressive measures. Paradoxically, the availability and consumption of cocaine increased as the American drug war grew fiercer during the 1980s (Davenport-Hines 2002: 338–383). Simultaneously, more and more Swiss became addicted to heroin. The artificial scarcity of heroin produced by police operations made the drug significantly more expensive and, consequently, the crime rate skyrocketed. Soon political pressure began to mount as an increasing number of citizens were affected by thefts, robbery, and the public display of abject misery in the neat streets of Zurich and Berne.

The United States responded to the failure of its counternarcotics policy by stepping up its interdiction efforts. The country imprisoned ever more drug users at home and reinforced its police and military operations in drug-producing countries abroad. The Swiss, however, decided on an almost antithetical response to the problem. In 1994, the Swiss Federal Office of Public Health (SFOPH) began to distribute heroin to addicts under medical supervision—a decision not without controversy, especially in the French- and Italian-speaking cantons, but overall it was supported by the Swiss citizenry (Fahrenkurg 1995).

In the late 1980 and early 1990s, the civil servants of the SFOPH were also grappling with a very different drug-related problem. The Swiss Medical Association for Psycholytic Therapy (SAPT) had asked for permission to use LSD, psilocybin, and MDMA for psychotherapeutic purposes. In 1988, the group received a special permit to administer these controlled substances to patients (Styk 1992/93; Saunders 1993). But this exemption remained problematic. In 1989, a new government official took over the Department of Pharmacy at SFOPH, where he would be in charge of both the logistics of the heroin program and the scientific and medical applications of hallucinogenic drugs. After initial skepticism, Paul J. Dietschy approved both uses. Neither America, trying to form a united front in its War on Drugs, nor the United Nations that was advocating a similarly repressive stance were pleased about the Swiss pullout from the internationally established hard line on the use of controlled substances. Representing Switzerland on the International Narcotics Control Board, the Commission of Narcotic Drugs, and the Commission Pompidou of the Council of Europe, Dietschy had to bear the brunt of international criticism. However, when Claudio Vannini and Maurizio Venturini interviewed him for their history of Swiss psychedelic science, Dietschy stressed the importance of drug research for Switzerland:

> In the international research community, our experiments with heroin or hallucinogens have aroused much interest. In the past, the Americans were at the forefront of this area. But then their government did not approve of such research anymore for political reasons. (This attitude has recently begun to change again.) Switzerland is one of the few countries in which such experiments are possible at all. Politically, our experiments provoke much skepticism [on the international level]. This is not voiced publicly but has been articulated repeatedly in discussions with us. . . . Apart from that, the international treaties leave a lot of freedom to the member states as to the conduct in one's own country as long as the interests of other countries are not affected. This freedom must be used for the benefit of Switzerland. (Quoted in Vannini and Venturini 1999: 269)

Here, the very technocracy that the counterculture had rebelled against by using psychedelic drugs endorsed their scientific investigation. This government support contributed significantly to the competitive advantage of Swiss hallucinogen research and helped to make

Franz Vollenweider such an interesting collaborator in the eyes of his American colleagues.

When, during my fieldwork in 2005, I first came across Dietschy's advocacy of the Swiss drug and drug policy experiments, I began to wonder about the relationship between the Swiss government's backing of psychedelic science and its heroin program. Was there an underlying policy, a comprehensive plan, a broader cultural matrix constituting the regulatory conditions of the work I was about to observe in the lab? To find out, I arranged a meeting with Dietschy who, it turned out, was no longer working for the Swiss Federal Office of Public Health but had moved to Swissmedic, a new federal agency comparable to the American FDA that had just taken over the regulation of medicines (but not of controlled substances) from the Swiss cantons to establish a nationally uniform regulatory regime.

Paul Dietschy was an authoritative man in his fifties with a long moustache. He wore a dark gray suit, white shirt, and a paisley silk tie. We met in one of the conference halls of the new Swissmedic building. Glass walls separating the room from the foyer gave the institution an appearance of transparency. Dietschy had invited a second person to our conversation: a tall bearded man of about the same age, but more casually dressed in a gray shirt and a sweater. Rudolf Brenneisen was a professor of pharmaceutical science at the University of Berne. The careers of Dietschy and Brenneisen had been closely entwined. During the turbulent years of Swiss drug policy reform, Brenneisen had become Dietschy's closest scientific ally. He conducted most of the basic science research, which Dietschy needed to back up his often difficult administrative decisions. Together they had shaped one of the most adventurous episodes in the history of twentieth-century drug policy. Reminiscing about the 1990s, they looked back on a time when the current regulatory regime governing the scientific and medical uses of controlled substances in Switzerland was still in the making. Dietschy began:

> When I started my job in 1989, there was a medical association for psycholytic therapy, which wanted to do research on patients with LSD, ecstasy, and psilocybin. As these substances are prohibited, the Swiss Medical Association for Psycholytic Therapy had to get a federal license according to Article 8, paragraph 5 of the Narcotics Law. Hence, they asked the SFOPH for permission. My predecessor Dr. Jean-Pierre Bertschinger and the then director kept putting this off. It wasn't quite clear how to deal with it. Nobody had any experience in Europe. What did one have to take into account? Thus there was a vacuum and the response was continuously postponed.

But then this medical association complained to the minister in charge. He gave brief directions to the federal office: No matter what, but come to a decision! In 1987 or 1988, the SAPT was given authorization without further requirements. When a renewal was due in '89, my then chief of staff came up to me and told me where to sign. I glanced over the document and asked, "Where is the approval of the ethics commission?" And he said, "The ethics what?" At this point in time, ethics commissions were only just being introduced into human trials in Switzerland. This was pushed by the Swiss Academy of Medical Sciences. The state didn't care yet. Shortly after I began my job, I had a meeting with this group of physicians and I told them, "Hey, the ethics commission is missing and I can't see a neat study design. I want to see more."

Considering that, in the United States, institutional review boards had been introduced in 1966 (Rothman 1991), it is striking that, on the federal level, Switzerland only came to police pharmaceutical research activities in the 1990s. In 1989, Dietschy was among the first to make the approval of an ethics commission a requirement. At the time, drug regulation was organized by the cantons, that is, the states of the Swiss confederation—some strict, some more permissive. To homogenize the Swiss regulatory landscape, an intercantonal control agency coordinating cantonal regulations issued guidelines for clinical trials in the mid-1990s. Only in 2002, when Swissmedic was established, did the Swiss state put an end to the cantonization of its regulatory regime. "We were in a field that was just emerging," Dietschy remembered. In the late 1980s, the Narcotics Law only stated that the SFOPH could grant special permits for scientific research and limit medical applications of prohibited substances. "A completely open wording," Dietschy said. "This provided us with latitude, which we don't have anymore today."

But this regulatory freedom was accompanied by much uncertainty, especially when internationally prohibited drugs like heroin or hallucinogens were involved. "We had zero experience with this," Dietschy recalled. "Apart from England, there was no research on illicit drugs in Europe, which could have served as a foundation. I was a civil servant who actually had nothing to do with research. My task was a different one. But I always got applications for research projects. I was in the situation that I constantly had to face problems for which I couldn't find an answer anywhere."

This was how Rudolf Brenneisen became involved. The administrative decisions Dietschy had to make were politically and medically risky. As the prohibition had also choked off pharmacological research on heroin and the hallucinogens, a lot of information he would have needed was missing in the medical literature. Consequently, the SFOPH invited Brenneisen to conduct the studies necessary to fill in the blanks. Brenneisen scientifically supported Dietschy, who was in charge of the logistics of the Swiss heroin program. But he also helped him assess applications from the renascent field of hallucinogen research. For this purpose, Brenneisen's doctoral student Felix Hasler generated drug-safety data for psilocybin, which the SFOPH needed in order to assess applications like the one submitted by the Swiss Medical Association for Psycholytic Therapy.

It did not take long for Dietschy to realize how vital questions of drug safety were in this area. In 1990, one of the patients treated by SAPT president Peter Baumann died during a therapy session. After a number of prior irregularities, Baumann had taken the woman to a remote, ill-equipped lodge in France (not Switzerland), far away from an emergency room, where he gave her ibogaine, a powerful plant hal-lucinogen used for ritual purposes in the West African spiritual tradi-tion of Bwiti. Ibogaine was not among the substances approved of by the SFOPH. Dietschy also claimed that, after this fatal incident, other patients came forward reporting that, while in the clinical trial, they had come to suffer from severe depression. "Probably their serotonin supplies had been depleted," Dietschy said. "Exactly the opposite of what one had aimed for had happened. They were not, as they told us, taken care of. The doctor just pushed them aside because it didn't fit into his preconceptions." Soon charges of medical misconduct were filed against a second member of the SAPT.

By this time, Dietschy had grown deeply mistrustful of the orga-nization: "We became very reserved. We felt that there was a lack of scientific seriousness. They were freaks who thought, 'Here we get a chance to make our mark.' My impression was, they don't want to stick to the rules." Because of the experiences and data provided by Bren-neisen, however, Dietschy continued to believe that psychedelic drugs might have a great potential to treat severe mental disorders. Therefore, he told the SAPT that he was not opposed to hallucinogen research in principle but that, in the future, he would only support applications that had a clear study design and were approved by an ethics commission.

At this point, Franz Vollenweider entered the scene proposing to test psilocybin on humans. Dietschy was impressed:

> The application was scientifically perfectly neat and correct. I have rarely seen such a solid documentation. The SFOPH waved it through relatively quickly and, to a certain extent, we also supported his research because it was

an important part of the puzzle for us to be able to decide later on whether to test these drugs in humans again. This is how Vollenweider got involved and I have to say that I have always only seen top-quality work from him. Few researchers—Brenneisen and Vollenweider among them—never had any problems with us regarding approvals. The SFOPH also supported them financially. Today, Swissmedic doesn't have research funds anymore. Back then we had budgets for international projects and for research. When you saw a new problem, you could decide relatively spontaneously. Those were the days.

And Brenneisen seconded: "It was an enormous privilege to have authorities that massively supported research. I admit, for me this was *the* chance of my academic career. Without the politics and the research support of the SFOPH, financially and ideationally, this would not have been possible."

Paul Dietschy (PJD) and Rudolf Brenneisen (RB) brought their account of hallucinogen research to a close by relating two more reminiscences explaining how Vollenweider's lab managed to leave behind its local rivals and move to the forefront of the global resurgence of psychedelic science.

PJD: Reminiscence 1: I left SFOPH in 2001 and gave up these responsibilities. Until then, the SAPT did not get another approval. Within ten years they did not manage to turn in a dossier complying with the usual standards of good clinical practice. The second point is a funny reminiscence: At the beginning of the 1990s, we got some psilocybin back for disposal, as we were the authorities in charge of this. It was really ancient material.

NL: *Who gave it to you?*

PJD: We got it from someone who had used it for experiments, syntheses, for various things. The laboratory assistant called and said, "Mr. Dietschy, I got some psilocybin. How shall I dispose of it?" I took a look, called Brenneisen, and said, "I would like to know whether the substance still meets any quality standards." The answer came a few days later: "It meets all standards!" Suddenly we had 100 g of pure psilocybin. Nobody else in the world had such an amount. And the production was very expensive. To give you an example: When I went to an international conference of the US Drug Enforcement Administration, I mentioned this in an aside to people from DEA labs.

They said, "What? You really got that? We need this for our kits." I asked, "How much do you need? I'll bring it to you to the next conference in Washington." Today, this would be inconceivable. These were really easygoing times.

RB: That's the cue: the link to the US. Of course, they were following what was going on here, also on the level of psychiatric research. "What can Switzerland do? Why can't we do this as well? Aren't we allowed to do that too?" There was Rick Strassman in Albuquerque. They got DMT and other materials with FDA approval. But unfortunately his project failed and Strassman left the US for personal reasons. Then David Nichols took over that role.

PJD: I don't know whether Vollenweider would ever have been able to start his work if we had not had that psilocybin. If he had had to synthesize it, he would probably not have been able to pay for it. Hence, a number of lucky coincidences came together and made this possible. (Figure 2 pictures some of this Swiss psilocybin freshly encapsulated.)

THE MANIFOLD MATRIX OF SWISS DRUG POLICY

After a short coffee break, Dietschy and Brenneisen recounted in equal detail the no less venturesome development of the heroin program and Swiss cannabis research and policy in the 1990s. Their accounts were captivating and comprehensive. But when, three hours later, we went for lunch, I still could not see how these different plots added up to a distinctive policy approach. Dietschy had already told me in his first response to my query that, "from the end of the '80s to the mid-'90s of the last century, there was no continuously planned and stringently designed research policy concerning hallucinogens at SFOPH" and that, "in the first half of the 1990s, important decisions were rather made on an ad hoc basis."

Swiss drug policy was an assemblage of heterogeneous governmental strategies. In the language of policy makers, this was called the Fourfold Approach (Vier-Säulen-Modell), comprising four strategic trajectories or "pillars": repression (law enforcement), prevention (keeping citizens from using drugs in the first place), therapy (treatment and reintegration of former drug users), and harm reduction (survival support). In an alternative jargon, borrowed from Michel Foucault (2007), one could also speak of an assortment of elements from three different apparatuses: law, discipline, and security. The law constitutes a purely negative form of normativity, which prohibits particular acts within a confined territory, for example, the manufacture, sale, and consumption of drugs like heroin and LSD in Switzerland. Discipline ideally aims at a continuous panoptic observation of individuals responding even to minute deviations from a norm by disciplinary measures. Close monitoring of all people having to do with illicit substances can serve as an example. Drug scenes were infiltrated by undercover narcotics officers; dealers and consumers were prosecuted; scientists studying controlled substances needed special permits and their laboratories could be subject to inspections. At the same time, addicts willing to undergo therapy were registered ("Nobody could enter into a heroin trial without the permission of the SFOPH," Dietschy told me); they were tested for the additional use of street drugs (based on a method developed by Brenneisen) and had to inject the heroin provided by the Swiss state under supervision in special outpatient clinics. The heroin-assisted treatment programs served to enmesh addicts in the safety net of the otherwise not overly developed Swiss welfare state. These measures were highly effective. In the course of the 1990s, many patients enrolled in these programs managed to return to a well-ordered life, and the number of addicts declined significantly—in part because the heroin programs destroyed the image of the junkie as countercultural hero defying society by making him into a welfare case dependent on the state (Aarburg and Stauffacher 2004).

However, total control of society has remained a totalitarian utopia. As neither proscriptions nor treatment or continuous monitoring of individuals could guarantee the desired outcomes, a third strategy was developed: security. The emergence of security as a form of government can be interpreted as a response to the limits of legal and disciplinary instruments. Here, the aim of total control is replaced by the modulation of a preexisting milieu in order to regulate a population at large. While discipline is based on sustained interventions, security adopts, at least to a certain extent, a laissez-faire attitude, only intervening as a last resort and after observation and evaluation of the specific tendencies of a given situation (Foucault 2007: 1–86). As a key element of biopolitical government (which aims at the promotion rather than the repression of life), Foucault's notion of security differs from the traditional sense of the term. It is not based on the restriction of civil liberties for the sake of protecting the population through preventive exclusion of malign agents. The biopoliticized security apparatus of the advanced liberal state monitors and manages the chances and risks associated with the largely unhindered activities of its citizens (Dillon and Lobo-Guerrero 2008).

This strategy was integrated into Swiss drug policy in the late 1980s as the problematization of drug use shifted from the repression of ine-briation and addiction to fostering the health and safety of consumers and other citizens (Boller 2005: 10). It was briefly pursued when the municipality of Zurich temporarily tolerated drug trade in a confined area known as Needle Park before the heroin program was initiated. At the time of my fieldwork, the Foucauldian security *dispositif* was actualized in the form of a drug-checking program.[2] On the weekends, a mobile lab with cutting-edge analytic machinery, including a high-performance liquid chromatograph, run by the Cantonal Pharmacist's Office, Berne, was moving from party to party allowing ravers to test the quality and dosage of their black-market drugs. This enabled rec-reational users to make informed and responsible decisions about the drugs they consumed. As products of poor quality were quickly identi-fied and abandoned, this measure improved the quality of the drugs traded (for better or worse).

In this circumscribed context, the Swiss state accepted that illicit drugs were taken and tried to reduce the harm they caused by making the black market more transparent. At the same time, the drug-checking lab allowed the authorities to carry out spot checks, which in turn let them monitor the black market and track consumption patterns. The collected information was mostly used to develop more effective preven-tion strategies and to warn users, through flyers and postings on party scene–related websites, against adulterated and mislabeled drugs. The mobile lab also provided associated social workers an opportunity to approach users of illegal drugs in an informal but direct manner. Even though it would be misleading to reduce the development of Swiss drug policy in the 1990s to the formation of this security apparatus, the integration of such elements appears to be its most distinctive feature in comparison with the hard-line policies of the United States or neigh-boring European countries such as France or Germany.

At a panel discussion titled "Modern Drug Policy" at the LSD Sym-posium, Thomas Kessler, the former delegate for drug issues from the municipality of Basel, argued that progress in drug policy equaled differentiation regarding substances and patterns of consumption: heroin-assisted treatment programs for opiate addicts, drug checking for so-called recreational users of party drugs, strictly regulated sales of strong alcoholic beverages and absinthe, approval of psychotherapeutic applications of psychedelics despite their prohibition in nonmedical settings, and so on. Measured against this metric of differentiation, Switzerland had already gone further than most other countries. If there was a shared matrix in which the different aspects of Swiss drug policy developed in the 1990s, it was this attentiveness to pharmacological differences paired with a businesslike approach to the corresponding perils and possibilities. Pharmacologist Felix Hasler (2007: 42), a native of Liechtenstein, described his Swiss neighbors as "reasonable pragmatics who weigh benefits and risks and value individual responsibility."

The Swiss government's liberal technocratic attitude toward drugs required both more and a different kind of knowledge than mere repression did. If a drug was simply prohibited, all the state needed to know was how to detect it for forensic purposes. But if a state decided, for example, to prescribe heroin medically, it also had to learn about its pharmacokinetics to determine an appropriate form of application (tablets, cigarettes, injections, etc.). It also needed to understand the drug's pharmacodynamics, adverse effects, interactions with other medications, and so on. The SFOPH funded some of Brenneisen's and Vollenweider's research on the basic pharmacology of psilocybin to establish a firm foundation for the assessment of future applications for clinical trials. The rationalization of government according to the value of truth that has taken place in the West requires that regulators protect themselves by drawing on scientific authority (Rose 1999: 24–28). At least in Switzerland, this will to and need for knowledge facilitated the revival of hallucinogen research.

In the United States, a legal culture in which government agencies could easily be sued led to a particularly pronounced tendency of administrators to seek refuge in bureaucratic formalism alongside massive government funding of research (Brickman et al. 1985: 304, 309). In Switzerland, on the other hand, state bureaucracy remained relatively restricted. Much social regulation took place on the community level, mediated through more informal relations. The historian Manfred Hettling (1998) speaks of sociability *(Geselligkeit)* as the predominant form of societal self-organization in Switzerland. Sociability even seemed to be at work within Swiss bureaucracy (and, to some extent at least, this might apply to modern bureaucracy more generally). In principle, a bureaucracy is meant to make decisions in a strictly formalistic manner according to rational rules and "without regard for persons" (Weber

1946: 215). However, when asked whether Vollenweider's reputation as a sober scientist had anything to do with the approval of his clinical research, Dietschy admitted point-blank that it did play a significant role in the decisions of the SFOPH. In a contentious field like hallucinogen research, seriousness and respectability were of great importance. Had there been any incidents, it would have been Dietschy as chief administrator who would have been called to account. For this reason, he only wanted to work with people he could trust as responsible scientists.[3]

The fact that Switzerland's drug policy was generally liberal and the regulatory conditions for hallucinogen research beneficial did not mean that there was no social control. On the contrary, the regulatory regime was close-meshed—at the time of my fieldwork even more so than in the early 1990s. Special permits were required for research purposes and, by then, institutional review boards had also been established in Switzerland. The densely woven social fabric of this small country lent even more weight to a person's standing in the community. People carefully observed the behavior of their neighbors—to the extent that the East German theater director Michael Schindhelm polemically called Switzerland "the better GDR," alluding to the widespread spying of East Germany's citizens on each other. In fact, Switzerland had a major scandal in 1989, the so-called Fiches Affair, when it became publicly known that the Swiss authorities kept files on 900,000 of 6,500,000 Swiss citizens, including many countercultural activists, supposedly to protect the country from communist subversion (Studer and Schaufelbuehl 2009). Thus, Switzerland provided a tightly controlled and regulated, but permissive, research environment that was created and supported by government agencies. The freedom of science they granted was not a "negative liberty," leaving people alone to do what they wished without interference (Rose 1999: 67). Instead it was carefully framed by legislators, administrators, ethics committees, and funding agencies to hold scientists and therapists accountable.

This was the regulatory apparatus that gave Vollenweider and other Swiss drug researchers a certain competitive advantage, which liberal Swiss politicians vigorously defended against international pressure. As the former Basel drug delegate Thomas Kessler put it: "One has to be incredibly careful not to destroy the great possibilities, which this research presents. . . . Switzerland, as a research site, must take care that its scientific experiments do not disappear in the machinery of a crude and undifferentiated drug policy" (quoted in Vannini and Venturini 1999: 274).

REGULATORY DIFFERENCES AND CAPITAL FLOWS

Thomas Kessler's former political superior, Luc Saner, also took part in the drug policy discussion at the LSD Symposium. Saner was a politician. As a member of the Free Democratic Party, he promoted economic liberalism in conjunction with libertarianism. In the 1990s, when Kessler was working at Basel's Department of Justice, Saner championed a liberalization of Swiss drug policy. He advocated making all generally prohibited substances legally available in a differentiated manner by subjecting them to a variety of legal regulations (Saner 1998). On the panel, Saner said:

> I think that, in the case of LSD, one must try to get research projects through in order to create the possibility of registering this substance, so that it can be prescribed by physicians. But I have to tell you that this process is highly complex. Registering a drug is not an easy job. Usually, it costs enormous sums, hundreds of millions. And there is only an interest if there is a prospect of profit. The substance must be patentable and there must be an economic incentive. That's often not easy with such designer drugs. Maybe the patent has already been issued and cannot be renewed. In this context, we have proposed that the state steps in. Here, the liberal calls for the state. Thomas is laughing at me, but that's how it is. The state needs to take a leadership role making sure that the legal preconditions are created to provide some sort of access to these substances. The state would have to take over the registration.

After the discussion, some people from the audience approached Saner to ask further questions. A remarkable encounter ensued. Among those wanting to speak to Saner was an American man in his late forties. From their outward appearances, John Gilmore and Luc Saner could not have differed more. Saner was a slick Swiss politician wearing shirt and tie. Gilmore, on the other hand, had come from California with long hair and a goatee, dressed in a purple batik shirt and sandals. He told Saner that he had miscalculated the costs of registering substances like LSD or MDMA. The hundreds of millions of dollars for the successful development of one drug, which Saner had mentioned, actually included a pharmaceutical company's costs of amortizing all the drugs that failed somewhere along the pipeline. In the case of LSD and MDMA, however, we already knew about their safety and therapeutic efficacy and only had to demonstrate them scientifically. Hence, Gilmore reckoned, the costs for registering these substances would be closer to five to ten million dollars. Saner readily accepted the objection, but asked in reply: "Okay, but who would pay those five to ten million dollars? The pharmaceutical industry would only be interested if there was the prospect of profit, but the patents for these substances have long run out." Gilmore said: "I could do it. I'm a businessman and a philanthropist. If someone presented a reasonable plan, I would be willing to pay for it." Looking slightly stupefied, Saner offered Gilmore one of his business cards.

John Gilmore was raised in a middle-class family and started to work in information technology at a time when this did not yet require a college degree. He was not only a world-famous hacker but had also been the fifth employee of Sun Microsystems. As such, he quickly made "too much money," as he said, by which he meant "more than I could usefully spend on myself in my lifetime and more than I wanted to leave to someone else as an inheritance, because it tends to corrupt people to receive large amounts of money for nothing." Hence, he decided to become a philanthropist, sponsoring projects that ranged from legal aid for detainees at Guantanamo Bay to the development of free software and psychedelic research. What tied these projects together for Gilmore was a certain libertarian agenda supporting civil liberties, from drug use to firearms possession: "The focus is on individual rights, individual responsibility, and freedom to do what you choose to do."

I first met Gilmore at the LSD Symposium after I had given a talk about hallucinogen research in Switzerland. Based on my fieldwork in the Vollenweider lab, I had addressed the fact that the Swiss branch of the Heffter Research Institute received money not only from the Swiss Federal Office of Public Health but also from private, mostly American donors. After my presentation, Gilmore introduced himself as one of the people I had spoken about. As one of its donors, he asked me for an evaluation of Heffter, as he was unsure whether the institute served his cause. He had decided to spend ten million dollars in ten years on ending the War on Drugs, which in his eyes caused a large amount of human suffering. The most promising strategy to achieve this goal, he thought, was to get illegal drugs registered for medical applications. Hence his interest in Luc Saner's suggestion. Gilmore had grown concerned that Heffter might be spending too much money on basic research instead of focusing on making psilocybin into a medicine. Formally, a registration with the FDA only required the demonstration of a drug's safety and efficacy. The mechanism of action, Gilmore argued, could still be explored at a later point in time when a preceding registration would have made it easier for researchers to study the controlled substance in question. To reach this goal, John Gilmore (JG) had a plan.

JG: People have struggled to improve drug policies forever, but mere advocacy seldom works because the governments are so resistant to change. What you actually have to do and what I have been trying to fund are projects that require the governments to change, that don't merely suggest that they change. If we actually completed a full drug development program, it would require the government to change its scheduling, to move the drug out of Schedule I, which has no medical use, into another schedule that allows physicians to prescribe it. Then it would not be optional on the government's part to make that change.

NL: *You said that your goal was to end the War on Drugs. On your website, you write about the huge number of people who get incarcerated for drug-related crimes. This might apply to cannabis. But the share of people who go to jail for crimes related to psychedelics in particular is fairly low. So why focus on this class of substances?*

JG: Partly because most other donors in drug policy focus on marijuana. If I depend on them to largely handle marijuana, I can expand the efforts to also include psychedelics rather than psychedelics being left behind when marijuana becomes legal.

NL: *And the substances responsible for the majority of imprisonments, like heroin and cocaine, are off-limits anyway. You won't get them legalized.*

JG: Right. And opiates are already widely used in medicine. OxyContin, for example, is a prescription drug that is widely abused, but doctors are free to prescribe it. There is nothing to fix there in the legal situation unless you're aiming at full legalization, which I think is a harder problem than the ones I'm trying to solve.

NL: *Is there no medical use for cocaine in the United States?*

JG: No, there is. It's in Schedule II. It's used as an anesthetic for people who have corrective surgery on their noses, for example.

NL: *Yeah, or in eye surgery. But if there was a medical use for psychedelics, they would probably be put into Schedule II as well.
However, that would still be restrictive enough to continue to
fuel the War on Drugs, just as heroin and cocaine do. The question is whether the approval of a medical use would really end
the War on Drugs.*

JG: It wouldn't end the War on Drugs. Indeed, I don't think I will end
the War on Drugs by 2010, which was my goal. But, like with the
Berlin Wall, I'm hoping to take a few big stones out and then it
will probably fall on its own accord, but through normal social
processes. The medical use of marijuana has clearly improved
the public's opinion of its recreational use. In each state where
medical use has been allowed, you can see over the succeeding
years more and more support for recreational use among the
public in polls and in voting. That's because the fear factor goes
away. When everyone knows somebody who uses marijuana
medically, and they don't turn into a demon and they don't lose
their job and they don't go out raping small children, then they
wonder, what is all this trouble with marijuana about anyway?
If they want to use it, let them use it.

Gilmore's strategy of ending the War on Drugs by funding clinical research was a response to regimes of government built on the
production of knowledge that provided authority to their authority.
The rationalization of government brought about a situation in which
knowledge was heavily invested with power relations and vice versa.
This was especially true in the United States, where the legal system
made regulatory agencies vulnerable to attacks from various private
interest groups—from transnational corporations to litigious libertarian
activists like Gilmore. As a result, there was a high degree of polarization in American science. As Brickman and colleagues (1985: 309–310)
point out:

> The expansion of the government's scientific research capacity in response
> to political pressure is one aspect of a more general phenomenon in the
> United States. American regulators, being more politically exposed than their
> European counterparts, have a greater need to support their actions through
> formal analytical arguments. . . . The structure of the American rule-making
> process subjects the analytical case for regulation to intense political scrutiny.
> Any weaknesses are exploited, and the uncertainties and shortcomings of the
> relevant scientific base are readily exposed. . . . In this adversarial setting,
> participating scientists often appear as advocates of particular regulatory

outcomes rather than disinterested experts. . . . The polarization induced by the U.S. regulatory process has tainted even the federal government's own research institutions, undermining their credibility as a source of unbiased expertise.

The greatest loss of credibility in US government-funded drug research in the recent past occurred in 2003 when psychopharmacologist George Ricaurte—the colleague who had previously accused Vollenweider of giving dangerously high doses of MDMA to human subjects—had to withdraw his sensational study on the neurotoxicity of the substance published in *Science* one year earlier (Ricaurte et al. 2002, 2003). Based on primate research funded by the National Institute of Drug Abuse, Ricaurte had postulated such a high degree of neurotoxicity for MDMA in doses regularly consumed at raves that ecstasy users should have died very frequently. Many of those who had seen the drug being used in their own social environment regarded Ricaurte's claims with suspicion. Eventually, he had to concede that he had actually administered the significantly more toxic methamphetamine (speed) to the monkeys. This mistake had been based on a mislabeling of containers, he claimed.

Such crises of confidence in government-funded research were exactly what Heffter's competitor MAPS was trying to take advantage of to relegitimize various medical and nonmedical applications of psychedelic drugs. MAPS founder Rick Doblin explained at the LSD Symposium: "The key point here is to build credibility. The government has lost credibility about the risks because they completely exaggerate them. The government has also lost credibility about benefits because they completely deny them. So we need to be at the forefront of looking at risks and at benefits." The goal was to acquire greater scientific authority than either countercultural propagandists or experts supported by the US government. As an activist organization, MAPS funded both research and lawsuits against the US Drug Enforcement Administration, employing the scientific knowledge it helped to generate to pursue its political goals.

Even though the Heffter Research Institute also had as a goal the registration of psilocybin as a medicine, the organization tried to stay out of the trenches of the drug war. It was key to Heffter's strategy of depoliticization to support and conduct clinical research and basic science alike—an approach Gilmore criticized as not sufficiently goal-oriented. The tensions manifesting in this situation arose from a regulatory regime in which the supposed value neutrality of science was simultaneously claimed and undermined by the warring parties. The

War on Drugs was also a war of knowledge, in which victories were occasionally based on new scientific findings. But the sharpest weapons blunt rapidly when wielded with too much fervor.

In *Society Must Be Defended* (2003), Foucault argues that the eighteenth century was characterized by "an immense and multiple battle, but not one between knowledge and ignorance, but an immense and multiple battle between knowledges in the plural—knowledges that are in conflict because of their very morphology, because they are in the possession of enemies, and because they have intrinsic power-effects" (179). Technological know-how, trade secrets, and much tacit knowledge were guarded jealously and used to one's own advantage in economic and political conflicts. The establishment of the modern university around 1800 forced a temporary (and certainly not complete) end to these epistemic struggles by selecting and domesticating, policing and disciplining the polymorphous and heterogeneous forms of knowledge. In the context of psychedelia, many deviant epistemic forms inspired by the aberrant states of mind these drugs induce had been disqualified and eliminated from academic institutions since the 1960s. Timothy Leary (1965: 113–114) had been proven wrong when he predicted that, within a generation, universities would open departments of psychedelic studies, no longer expanding their students' consciousness with books but with drugs. However, the epistemic confrontations reignited by the revival of hallucinogen research in the 1990s were not primarily a clash of respectable science and obscure esoteric lore, of knowledge and counterknowledge. The core conflict took place *within* an academic framework. Many of the key players held positions in universities, usually even in one of the most established and normalized faculties: the medical school. Here, neurotoxicity studies and the investigation of drug-induced neuropsychological deficits were countered with therapeutic trials and quality of life rating scales. But the front lines were not always clear: a neurotoxicity study could also demonstrate lack of toxicity, while a therapeutic trial might reveal new side effects. In this homoepistemic conflict, all sides were committed—or at least subjected themselves—to the metric of scientific methods and a naturalist or materialist ontology.

John Gilmore was certainly not the only donor to organizations like Heffter and MAPS and, without systematic research on this culture of patronage, it is difficult to determine in what ways he was and was not representative. What did seem typical though was that he made his money in information technology. Many of the American philanthropists sponsoring psychedelic research got into the computer, software, and Internet business at the right time and made a fortune. Their affinity for hallucinogenic drugs was not surprising. After all, Silicon Valley was not only located in geographical proximity to the San Francisco hippie community; many people at the forefront of the personal computing revolution had been part of this culture of psychedelic drugs, social experimentation, and political protest (Roszak 1986; Markoff 2005). When, by the 1990s, they had entered the entrepreneurial world of the New Economy, their ideals and practices had not simply been crushed or co-opted by the forces of consumer capitalism and high technology, which they had opposed in the 1960s. Instead the counterculture had been associated with these forces all along. It had never managed to completely break away from the society it abhorred and, eventually, reformed. In the 1990s, this made it easy to leave the countercultural ideology behind while continuing to pursue the transformation of individual consciousness and society at large through "personal" technology such as desktop computers and psychedelic drugs (Turner 2006). The Decade of the Brain was also the era of the dot-com bubble.

Throughout this period, Heffter's most important donor had been the late Bob Wallace, one of the founding members of Microsoft. Until his death in 2002, he had single-handedly sponsored most of Heffter's research, but with very different intentions than Gilmore. When I asked about key events in the history of Heffter, Mark Geyer, one of the virtual institute's founding members, answered:

> The two important events, the two biggest ones that shaped the course of Heffter, were finding and having Bob Wallace join us and having Bob Wallace die. Bob was certainly a recreational pharmacologist, a self-experimenter, avowedly and openly. He was wealthy. He was one of the first five or six in Microsoft. And he was perfect for Heffter because he—more than any other donor that we have had—appreciated the need for basic research. I don't just mean animal research. I mean doing the basic work to assess dose-response characteristics, assess and understand the neurobiology, physiology, and pharmacology of these compounds at a more fundamental level. The classic donor for Heffter is someone who wants us to skip past all of that and go right into treating some patient population. But it's a field that doesn't have the basics yet. Franz [Vollenweider] and I really feel that we need to start with the more mundane. But the more mundane work isn't very sexy and the donor doesn't see a lot of bang for his buck. So Bob was unusual if not unique in being willing to support both the infrastructure of Heffter and the kind of basic pharmacological studies, with the faith that this would eventually evolve into more clinically relevant work. He was intellectually fascinated by the chemistry, the phenomenology, and the underlying neuro-

biology, even if it didn't have the promise of some health-related or world-saving consequence or benefit. For him it was the same as it is for me and for Franz, I would say, a matter of great intellectual fascination. That's not the common donor. Bob was committed to $200,000 per year on a regular basis. When he died, we have never recovered from that loss.

A significant part of the money Heffter received from its American sponsors was channeled into its Zurich branch to fund human studies in Switzerland. Such transnational flows from a more restrictive to a more permissive regulatory regime are well-known from different contexts. Adriana Petryna (2009) has analyzed the ethical variability at work in the globalization of drug trials. Over 40 percent of clinical trials were shifted from the United States and western Europe to eastern Europe, South America, or India, where an abundance of preferably treatment-naïve test subjects were available and regulatory conditions more lenient. In the absence or after the collapse of basic health care, different ethical standards seemed to apply to these research sites, where any kind of medical attention, even in the context of a drug experiment, was better than what patients could otherwise expect. Of course, the outsourcing of hallucinogen research from the United States to wealthy Switzerland was not motivated by any such grave socioeconomic gaps, but it also exploited differences in nationally organized regulatory regimes. Like stem-cell research—another field marked by significant ethical variability between well-developed nation states—psychedelic science was part of what Sarah Franklin (2005) calls "the global biological": a transnational scientific research apparatus stretching across distant sites and linked to the flow of global capital.

Today, hallucinogen research also has a global quality insofar as the results of neuropsychopharmacological experiments are supposed to apply to every human being on the planet. In the next chapter, however, we will see that, in a very peculiar sense, it is also a "local biological," to use another term coined by Franklin. Not only can the interpretations of experimental findings differ according to the observers' perspectives and background assumptions. Despite all efforts to universalize the validity of the facts established in the laboratory, they remain more closely associated with the conditions under which they were found than many other phenomena of biological life. The fact that hallucinogens make an organism more susceptible to its surroundings and the increased impressionability they induce bring about a situation in which locality and social context are strongly implicated in the findings of hallucinogen experiments. What is true in the lab is not necessarily true in a different setting, and what is true about one test subject is not inevitably true about every other user of psychedelic drugs. This curious quality also contributed to making psychedelics into pharmacological "problem children." Not just because of the widespread abuse implied by the title of Albert Hofmann's (1980) famous book, but because of the difficulties in integrating hallucinogens into an increasingly normalized pharmaceutics. The historian of psychopharmacology David Healy (2002: 383–384) wrote:

> From the pharmaceutical industry's point of view, the problem drugs are not the opiates or cocaine but the hallucinogens, the drugs so indelibly associated with the 1960s. The problem is not that these drugs could tell us a lot about ourselves and this knowledge might foment revolution, although these do seem to be possibilities. The problem is that with each dose every individual is likely to have a different experience. This is the very antithesis of quality as corporations currently define it. It seems difficult to see how hallucinogens can be brought into the arena of standardization.

Research in Heffter's Zurich branch also had a local character inasmuch as Vollenweider's laboratory could not be reduced to an outpost of American psychedelic science. Ever since Hofmann's discovery of LSD and psilocybin, hallucinogen research had been prospering in Switzerland. The Vollenweider lab had emerged from this local tradition at the intersection of Swiss drug policy reform and the worldwide neuroscience hype in the 1990s. It received funds from the Swiss Federal Office of Public Health, American philanthropists like Wallace and Gilmore, the Fetzer Institute promoting a reconciliation of science and spirituality, and national and international science foundations funding basic and clinical neuroscience projects. Just like its US-based counterparts, it was a conglomerate of both local and global trajectories. Contemporary hallucinogen research is a global assemblage territorializing highly mobile and abstractable elements of technoscience and transnational flows of global capital at specific sites subject to national regulatory regimes (Ong and Collier 2005).

WHAT REVIVAL?

15 January 2006. After three days of talks, discussions, and celebration, the LSD Symposium in honor of Albert Hofmann's hundredth birthday came to a close. All speakers were asked to come onto the stage of the main conference hall. I felt uncomfortable, somewhat like a square peg in a round hole. Originally, I had only planned to attend the event as an ethnographic observer. But at the time I was doing fieldwork at Vollenweider's laboratory and the pharmacologist Felix Hasler, struggling to keep up with the usual workload, had asked me to take over one of the three presentations he had agreed to give at the conference. When I was told to come on stage, it occurred to me that, in an uneasy way, I was about to become part of the field that was the object of my study. There were chairs for us to sit in during the closing ceremony. As the stage was filling up with the notables of psychedelia, the speaker next to me bent over and whispered reverentially, "Isn't it incredible who is up here with us?"

After short speeches by the organizers, we, the speakers, were given the opportunity to address the symposium's guest of honor and the gathered psychedelic community. With his sonorous voice, the German cultural anthropologist and drug guru Christian Rätsch called in Nepalese, "Here, we have come together to pay tribute to the true father of our tribe: Albert Hofmann!!!" Several minutes of tumultuous applause and hooting cheers followed. Then numerous people expressed their gratitude to Hofmann for having discovered LSD. MAPS founder Rick Doblin announced a Chinese translation of Hofmann's book *LSD: My Problem Child* and promised him translations into several other languages as well, so that "the whole world can hear the voice that you heard first." Poems were read out. The Swiss shaman Carlo Zumstein asked us and the entire audience of more than 2,000 people to hum together (a very impressive sound!), guiding us through a quick visionary voyage to connect with the spirit of LSD. Ralph Metzner made the crowd sing and dance the Bardo Blues with him, a song based on the psychedelic adaptation of the *Tibetan Book of the Dead,* which he had coauthored with Richard Alpert and Timothy Leary (Leary et al. 1964). In the middle of these lively performances, one of the organizers presented a petition signed by Hofmann and the conference speakers advocating scientific research on psychedelic drugs, which would be sent to the press, the authorities in Berne and Brussels, "and perhaps also to Washington, even if it won't be heard there." After all, the hope that had inspired the conference, the organizers said, was "that LSD will take up the place among us humans and in history, which it deserves."

The many press reports covering the conference could not have been more divided about the significance of the event. For some, the symposium indicated "a scientific coming-out party for the drug Hofmann fathered" (Harrison 2006) and a "quiet comeback of LSD & Co." (Olff 2006). For others, it was a gathering of diehard hippies vainly trying to rehabilitate LSD (Büttner 2006; Halter 2006; Rühle 2006). Was there a revival after all?

One of the voices in this cacophony of newspaper comments was Felix Hasler's. In addition to his research in the lab, the pharmacologist regularly worked as a science journalist for Swiss newspapers and the weekly *Die Weltwoche*. Hasler's judgment about the alleged LSD revival was suitably acidic (no pun intended):

> The LSD revival caused by Hofmann's birthday is not going to last for long anyway. Simply because there is no LSD revival. Neither in research nor in psychotherapy or society. This is confirmed not only by the conference presentations but also by the latest statistics of the German Federal Bureau of Criminal Investigation. In 2005, the share of LSD in drug-related crime was rounded up to mere 0.1%. When the current spring tide of newspaper articles, which the birthday sparked off, will have petered out, LSD will presumably return to where it peacefully resided in the three decades preceding Dr. Hofmann's great jubilee day: in great proximity to insignificance. (Hasler 2006: 13–14)

However, as a neuropsychopharmacologist who had himself played a role in the latest episode of hallucinogen research, Hasler immediately qualified his critique: "Still, it could be possible that psilocybin, the little and less infamous brother of LSD, will have a career in research and psychotherapy. This cosmic spice acts shorter, has a more clear-cut pharmacology, and in its mind-altering effects it is much more user-friendly that the notoriously bitchy and moody LSD. Credit where credit is due: After all, this agent has also been isolated and synthesized (and, of course, tried) by Albert Hofmann" (14).

Of all reporters writing about the symposium, Hasler was by far the best-informed—at least as far as scientific research was concerned. In fact, most of his fellow journalists had called him during their own investigations, interviewing him as an expert in the field of hallucinogen research. Hasler's observation concerning the nonexistence of an LSD revival was certainly justified in the light of the ongoing research activities. At the time of the symposium, not a single human study employing LSD was taking place anywhere in the world. DMT, psilocybin, and ketamine had played important roles since the 1990s, but LSD had not been part of the story. Because of its notoriety, the administration of lysergic acid diethylamide to humans would have attracted much public attention and political opposition. Additionally, LSD was said to cause "bad trips" more often than other hallucinogens, and the duration of its effects—eight to twelve hours!—would have been a burden on the scientists having to look after their test subjects during the whole time. And, last but not least, LSD was seen as a "dirty drug" affecting many neurotransmitter systems simultaneously. Unlike psilocybin, it did not appear to be a suitable tool for precise neurochemical interventions that allowed correlating the manipulation of a specific neurotransmitter receptor with certain psychological or neurophysiological effects.[4]

As a hallucinogen researcher, Hasler was not only a particularly well-informed observer of the field but also a strongly positioned actor whose career had been closely associated with psilocybin, not LSD. In his doctoral research in Brenneisen's laboratory at the University of Berne, Hasler had laid out its basic pharmacology. The resulting publications served as the foundation for subsequent preclinical and clinical research with the drug, in which he also got involved when joining Franz Vollenweider's team in Zurich. In his representation of the field, Hasler omitted that other conferees at Basel were forcefully trying to initiate the LSD revival he negated.

At the time, the most prominent figure in these attempts was John Halpern, a psychiatrist at Harvard. In collaboration with MAPS, Halpern had been struggling to gain approval for a first therapeutic application of LSD. He wanted to restart LSD research at this symbolically charged place in Cambridge, Massachusetts, where psychedelic science had allegedly come to an end after Leary had declared himself fired. Having established a track record in hallucinogen research, Halpern and his colleague Andrew Sewell had forged a link to Clusterbusters, a cluster headache patient organization. This controversial self-help group claimed that small doses of LSD and psilocybin efficiently reduced cluster headache pain and prevented and interrupted cluster headache cycles even in patients resistant to treatment with legally available medications. This appeared to be a promising venue to reestablish a therapeutic application of psychedelic drugs. The fact that they would be used to treat a seemingly tangible neurological condition instead of a hazy psychiatric disorder could help overcome the resistance of those highly skeptical of psychotherapeutic uses of hallucinogens. After all, LSD treatment of cluster headaches was not about consciousness expansion, spiritual healing, or facilitating access to the contested realm of the unconscious but about fixing a neurochemical disorder. Moreover, based on anecdotal reports from patients recruited through the support group and an Internet-based survey, Halpern and Sewell argued that even subhallucinogenic doses might be effective. Thus cluster headache patients could possibly be spared the suspect and potentially dangerous "psychedelic experience." Treatment would be compatible with everyday life. Neither panic attacks, psychotic reactions, and suicides nor mystical revelations and ethical reorientations would have to be feared. The rationale of the project made it seem a viable strategy for the reintroduction of hallucinogens into mainstream medicine. By supporting Halpern, Doblin was hoping to win the race for the first human LSD study since the 1960s crackdown. He wanted to use the highly visible LSD Symposium to present formal approval of the study to the press, nicely wrapped up as a birthday present to Hofmann. But this plan did not work out.

History seemed to repeat itself. Again, LSD research at Harvard got caught up in a scandal. In 2000, the chemist William Leonard Pickard was arrested by agents of the Drug Enforcement Administration for manufacturing what was reported to be the largest amount of LSD ever seized in the DEA's history, in a decommissioned nuclear missile silo turned into an extravagant subterranean palace in rural Kansas (US Drug Enforcement Agency 2003).[5] Soon it was reported that Pickard had given Halpern $300,000, possibly from drug sales, for his research. The Heffter Research Institute was also accused of having received money from Pickard, but could disprove these allegations, while Halpern was drawn into the criminal investigation (Rosenfeld 2001). In a field as sensitive as hallucinogen research, mere suspicion was enough to seriously threaten a scientist's reputation. Instead of being able to announce the first LSD study, Halpern's presentation at the conference was interrupted by someone in the audience accusing him of having turned informant to the US authorities—just as Timothy Leary had reduced his prison sentence for illegal drug use from ten to three years by giving away some of his former friends (Jonnes 1996: 237).

Among the members of Heffter, there was grave concern that the rumors burgeoning around this case could bring the whole field into disrepute. Even without the uproar caused by the Pickard connection, the use of LSD in a human study seemed questionable to them. The infamous three-letter word could all too easily summon up the heated sentiments of the 1960s. However, it was precisely the symbolic and affective charge of LSD that also attracted the attention of certain donors to whom the acronym brought fond memories. But apart from the political risk of falling back into the trench warfare of the psychedelic era, there were also the scientific reasons, outlined above, that militated against a scientific application of LSD. Instead of Hofmann's problem child, the Heffterites placed their hopes in the less infamous psilocybin. At the symposium, Heffter president Dave Nichols announced its registration as a medicine as the organization's main objective.

Two years after the LSD Symposium, Albert Hofmann died. That same year, in 2008, MAPS and the reinvigorated Swiss Medical Association for Psycholytic Therapy got permission from the Swiss authorities to initiate the first clinical trial in over thirty-five years to evaluate a therapeutic application of LSD: the treatment of end-of-life anxiety in cancer patients (Langlitz and Hermann 2012).[6] Nevertheless, for research purposes, psilocybin continued to be the most widely used hallucinogen. Slowly but surely, the field was picking up steam. Journalistic accounts claiming that the psychedelic resurgence was essentially the nostalgic pipe dream of a few aging flower children were clearly misguided. Of course, many ideas and practices of the sixties lived on, not only in the psychedelic revival, but in Euro-American culture at large. However, despite their internal differences, both MAPS and the Heffter Research Institute had distanced themselves from the field's countercultural past. They did not rebel against technocracy and Western rationality. On the contrary, they embraced modern science as the best way of relegitimizing psychedelic drugs and managed to build friendly relations with government administrators. As Vollenweider said, the problem was not political repression—even though everybody continued to be nervous about a possible backlash. The real problems were scientific— and maybe spiritual. How could one stabilize and pin down the neuropsychopharmacological effects of such unruly substances? How could their seemingly evanescent benefits be demonstrated? And how could these drugs be used to help people flourish as human beings?

3

The Varieties of Psychedelic Lab Experience

Before all sixty-four electrodes had been fixed to my head to measure my brain waves, my circulation broke down and I fell through a dark tunnel into a void. The walls of the tunnel were covered with colorful spots and shapes. I felt terrified and absolutely helpless. At first I struggled, then I surrendered. Only when my seat was folded back did I come around again. A glass of water brought me back to the cramped, soundproof room in which the EEG measurement was to take place. Twenty minutes before, I had ingested eighteen capsules of psilocybin, which were now kicking in. I still felt giddy and asked for a break before the two researchers continued to prepare my EEG cap. But their schedule was tight. Another scientist had booked the room for the afternoon. They could not afford to lose more time. If further difficulties ensued, they said, the experiment would have to be broken off. I realized that I needed to pull myself together. If I didn't stick it out, I would give away my only chance of building rapport with the group I was hoping to study.

This was how my ethnographic fieldwork among Swiss hallucinogen researchers began in the summer of 2005. I gained access to Franz Vollenweider's Neuropsychopharmacology and Brain Imaging Laboratory in Zurich as an experimental test subject. So far, my affiliation as a doctoral student with the University of California, Berkeley, had turned out to be an obstacle rather than an entry ticket to the world of academic hallucinogen research. "When they see LSD and California, they think fun and games," as a psychedelic scientist from the West Coast would explain to me later on. Initially, Vollenweider had not responded to my requests to come to his lab as an ethnographic observer. But, eventually, one of his postdoctoral researchers referred me to an American PhD candidate from Vollenweider's group who was looking for volunteers to participate in his psilocybin study. Seizing the opportunity, I traveled to Switzerland to make contact.

I arrived on a warm summer day. Zurich's time-honored Psychiatric University Hospital, the Burghölzli, was located on the outskirts of the city. From the trolley stop, I walked down a lane and cut across a small field to get to the fortress-like nineteenth-century clinic. Here, about a century earlier, Eugen Bleuler had invented the concept of schizophrenia, while Carl Gustav Jung had reconciled depth psychology and spirituality by helping his patients relate their individual lives to the "collective unconscious" manifest in art, myth, and religion. The Burghölzli's extensive grounds comprised a pasture with apple trees and sheep as well as a forested hill with a scenic view of Lake Zurich (see figure 3). The Vollenweider lab was situated in two buildings somewhat apart from the main complex: a more imposing one housing Vollenweider and his secretary's offices and the EEG laboratory; and the clinic's former washhouse, home to about ten doctoral and postdoctoral researchers.

I was welcomed by Boris Quednow (figure 4), the German postdoc with whom I had established initial contact. Quednow and I had probably met before, presumably more than ten years ago when I used to go to techno parties in my hometown of Cologne, Germany. At the time, I was a high school student and went to raves and electronic music clubs almost every weekend. But I was too much of a nerd and did not take enough drugs to become more than a perpetual bystander and observer of the rave scene. The sense of not belonging had never left me since the first time I had been turned away at the door of a club. Back then, in the early 1990s, Quednow worked as a doorman at some of the places I frequented. A massive long-haired bodybuilder, he decided who was hip enough and who was not. When we sat in the Burghölzli's sunlit cafeteria, it briefly occurred to me that life repeated itself. Again I was trying to gain access to a group of people, and again Quednow seemed to serve as the gatekeeper. However, this time I came as an anthropologist interested in a group of neuropsychopharmacologists who were studying psychedelic drugs. Since our last unnoticed encounter, Quednow had become one of them.

When he was still working as a bouncer, Quednow must have been a bit of an oddball himself. He had a laboratory in the basement of his father's private clinic in the spa Bad Neuenahr, where he isolated a broad range of alkaloids from plants—not for consumption (many drugs of abuse belong to this class of compounds), but out of curiosity. In 1991, he even won a prize for his chemical analysis of the poisonous alkaloid cytisine contained in leaves and seeds of the tree *Laburnum anagroides*. Too much of a misanthrope to follow in his father's footsteps and become a physician, and too interested in the mind to become a chemist, he eventually studied psychology and underwent five years of psychoanalysis. He did his PhD at the university hospital in Bonn, studying the neurotoxicity of ecstasy, the most popular drug in the clubs he used to work for (Quednow 2005). A few months before my arrival, he had moved from Germany to Switzerland. He joined the Vollenweider lab to examine whether the brains of long-term MDMA users suffered from a lack of the neurotransmitter serotonin, a pathology that might come to affect many members of "Generation Ecstasy" (Reynolds 1999) in the future. I would soon come to realize that such links between the scientists' lifeworlds and their research interests were not uncommon in the field of psychedelic research. Considering that this still sturdy but by now shaven-headed contemporary and I had spent formative years in the same scene, sharing a scientific curiosity with respect to drugs, brains, psyches, and people, it was not surprising that we immediately took to each other.

FRACTAL CAVES, ILLUSIONARY TRIANGLES, AND OBJECTIVE MEASUREMENTS

But there were more hurdles to make. In the early afternoon, I met with Rael Cahn, the American doctoral researcher running the study I had come to take part in, and his Swiss coworker, the psychology student Michael Kometer. Formally, Cahn did his PhD in Mark Geyer's laboratory at the University of California, San Diego, which investigated the effects of hallucinogenic drugs on rodents. But Cahn was primarily interested in altered states of consciousness induced by psychedelics and meditation, which were impossible to investigate in animals. In the United States, the prospect of getting approval for a human study with hallucinogenic drugs seemed too uncertain, even for a reputable lab such as Geyer's. Therefore, Cahn went to Switzerland, where the regulatory conditions were more favorable and Vollenweider, a close friend and ally of Geyer's, provided the facilities and expertise necessary to compare the neural correlates of the psychedelic experience in normal subjects with the neurobiological substrate of meditation as practiced by experienced meditators. Cahn told me that his motivation for examining these altered states of consciousness was personal:

> I came here because I was interested in looking at the effects of psychedelics and to do this kind of comparative study. In particular, I came here because more than in anything else I was interested in using the tools of science, some brain-imaging method—it didn't matter to me too much which one, but it ended up being EEG—to look at what's happening in the brain when someone experiences a really clear sense of being one with everything. This experience, which I have had in my own life and which was very much catalytic to my going into this direction, was so striking and real to me that I felt it was important to consider it, not just as an internal experience, but as reflecting something that's real about our collective reality and the greater sense of my own life and experience. I had the hope that more people could have that kind of experience and it would positively change the way in which they interacted with the world.

Cahn wanted to study what was happening in the brain when a human subject experienced a sense of oneness with the world—theologically speaking, a *unio mystica*. His research question was thus situated in the budding field of neurotheology. In contrast to other neurotheological accounts that reduced religious experiences to brain chemistry, Cahn's project was true to the Huxleyan origins of the term *neurotheology* in that he believed that these altered states revealed a reality usually concealed by everyday consciousness. Experiencing them was supposed to have a profoundly positive impact on the conduct of one's life by facilitating "transformative mystical and loving ways of relating," as Cahn put it. He also followed Huxley's perennial philosophy, as expressed in *Island* (1962: 188–189), in assuming that hallucinogens and meditation took subjects "to the same place." And, finally, he considered Huxley's dualism—the assumption of a consciousness transcending its neurobiological manifestations—a real possibility:

> It also does seem likely that good-quality neuroscientific work addressing these domains will shed significant light on the neural "bases" (or lack thereof) of consciousness. The ways in which this may occur are hard to predict specifically, given that there is still such a huge explanatory gap and mystery surrounding the definition of consciousness. But certainly if, in the extreme case, consciousness is truly not dependent on the brain for its existence, it is only work in such domains as altered states of consciousness

and parapsychological studies that are likely to provide the key evidence to support such a major shift of worldview within science.

Cahn's faith in the healing power of psychedelics and meditation had inspired him to enter medical school in California. As a physician he was hoping to contribute to the development of "integrative medicine," a medical philosophy originating in the nineteenth century that merged biological and spiritual conceptions of the human (Harrington 2008). Cahn wanted to bring together "the power and perspectives that are available through the biological materialist view on the human body with perspectives that are based on the power of thought to interact with the body, to stimulate healing, and to see how such methods can be helpful to people who aren't being helped very much by standard Western biomedicine."

But, in the laboratory, Cahn had come to experience tensions between this vocation and the norms, expectations, and requirements structuring the field of cognitive neuroscience. Vollenweider was supportive of the proposal to compare meditating brains with brains under the influence of hallucinogenic drugs, but he also demanded a solid foundation in what Thomas Kuhn (1962) would have called "normal science." As the outcome of research on a phenomenon as elusive as conscious-ness (not to speak of its supposed expansion) seemed too uncertain, Vollenweider had decided to play it safe and integrate some classical neuropsychological paradigms into the study. If fishing for altered states should turn out to be a failure, the trial would still produce valuable data leading to publications in established neuroscience journals. Cahn, on the other hand, was concerned that subjecting test subjects to the disciplinary regime that structured neuropsychological measurements might create an experimental setting inimical to the experience of feeling one with the universe. Eventually, the experimental design turned out to be a compromise between the quest for the neural correlates of mysti-cal experience, which Cahn wanted to pursue, and a number of more focused neuropsychological tests that subjects had to undergo in the second part of the trial.

Before I could take part in this study, I needed to pass a psychi-atric interview. Cahn asked me about crises in my biography as well as mental disorders in my family. Questionnaires and psychological rating scales helped to generate a psychopathological profile of myself, allowing him to judge whether I was eligible for being administered a hallucinogen as powerful as psilocybin. Test subjects who appeared to be vulnerable were excluded from the trial. A single case of prolonged hallucinogen-induced psychosis or suicide could bring down the whole laboratory. However, some of the questionnaires also aimed at uncovering a different predisposition, quantifying my bent for the mystical and supernatural. Fortunately, this-worldliness did not serve as an exclusion criterion for the drug study. Thus my journey into the world of neuro-psychedelia took its course.

Trip to Outer Space: Day 1 of the Psilocybin Experiment

When I emerged from the dark tunnel, still nervous and sweating, I was certain that I had not received a placebo on this first day of the experiment. The trial was supposed to be double-blind. Neither the scientists nor I knew in advance whether the capsules I had washed down with a glass of water contained an inactive control substance, a low dose of psilocybin (125 µg/kg body weight), or a high dose (250 µg/kg). For a 70 kg person like myself, the latter amounted to 8.75 mg. These different doses were to be administered randomly on three days separated by at least one week from each other to give my organism enough time to completely metabolize the drugs and return to its normal state before the next experiment. The sudden breakdown of my circulation left little doubt that I had ingested a hefty dose on that first day. But, after drinking a sip of water and settling back into the massive leather armchair, everything seemed fine again. A calm, sunny day was peeking through the window. And, as if to remind me of the entanglement of 1960s counterculture and contemporary cyberculture, the computer screen in front of me generated a flow of colorful psychedelic visualizations of the soft electronic music trickling from its speakers. Soon, Cahn and Kometer continued to prepare the EEG cap on my head (see figure 5).

The procedure seemed to take forever, but finally they were done. The sunlight was shut out and the chamber darkened. The researchers retreated to the adjoining room that contained monitors and computer equipment, from where they could observe me through a window. The door closed. Total silence. I was on my own now. The desired correlation of first-person perspective (on this side of the observation window) and third-person perspective (my brain waves on the monitor next-door) should not be perturbed by the presence of other people in the room. Social relations counted as confounders. When the measurement began, I was supposed to keep my eyes closed for fifteen minutes, while continuing to concentrate on my breathing, to produce an EEG recording that could be compared to the experienced meditators' meditations. Every time I felt that something peculiar was happening to me, I was supposed to press a button to describe my experience through an intercom system. Cahn and Kometer were hoping to identify the neural correlates of these introspective reports in the EEG recordings later on.[1] Thereby, my subjective experiences would be given an objective corporeality and, I began to worry, traces of my most private inner life, however unrecognizable, would become accessible to public view.

The second my eyelids went down, an enormous cave opened up in front of me. All surfaces were covered with geometric patterns, spinning fractals in shades of dark red. There was something uncanny, almost demonic about the scenery. I looked around anxiously; and then, as I realized that no imminent danger was looming, more curiously. Curiously, but without the particular kind of pleasure marking the joy of discovery—an oddly affectless state of mind. Despite the warm tones, the impression was cool. I did not like the aesthetics of the vision. It reminded me of gaudy psychedelic paintings. For a moment, I felt irritated by the fact that my brain could not do better than imitate the geometric forms prevailing in psychedelic art. Or did these patterns result from the neurochemical effects of psilocybin, like the "form constants" (lattices, spirals, tunnels, cobwebs) that the psychologist Heinrich Klüver (1966) had postulated in his laboratory study of peyote-induced visions in 1928? Did they mirror certain architectural features of the visual cortex, as the mathematician and computational neurobiologist Paul Bressloff (Bressloff et al. 2001) had claimed more recently?

I also heard whirring sounds in stereo, moving from the right to the left. They were pseudohallucinations: I could tell that they were not out there in the laboratory, even though they traversed some sort of space. I wondered whether it was the phenomenal space of my mind or the surface of my cerebral cortex. I also experienced real auditory hallucinations, hearing a radio from afar sending inaudible messages. They frightened me. As a former medical student, I knew that "hearing voices" was one of the hallmarks of schizophrenia. I told Cahn and Kometer about this. Speaking to them was a way of surfacing from the trip and reestablishing contact with the familiar world out there. It gave me a moment to get my breath back before returning to the strange fractal cave behind my eyelids.

Overall, the visionary world I experienced appeared bizarre and alien, more outer space than my inner life. I did not feel at home there. Only toward the end of those fifteen minutes did I begin to relax. Finally,

I felt a touch of joy and serenity reminiscent of what I had experienced as a teenager on LSD. This must have changed my facial expression: Cahn turned on the intercom and told me that they had detected an increase of muscle tension in my face, and it was interfering with the EEG recording. He asked me to relax again. While I was still wondering how they could expect me to reach a state of ecstasy if I needed to control the minutiae of my facial play, the lights turned on and I had to rate three dimensions of my experience—self-transcendence, anxiety, and intensity of hallucinations (a simplified version of the APZ questionnaire to be discussed below). The first item received the lowest score. I had missed my chance of rapture.

The neuropsychological testing that followed provided no more opportunity for bliss. A fast and incessant sequence of flashing images was raining down on me from the computer screen. In response, I had to press different buttons. One time, I needed to distinguish little blue circles from big blue circles and checkerboards, but I always failed to remember how big the big circles were and how small the small circles unless I saw them right after each other. Another time, I had to distinguish concrete black triangles from their illusionary counterparts (so-called Kanizsa triangles; see below). Then a circle was brightly flickering on the screen. I was meant to count the number of flashes I perceived while the loudspeakers fired volleys of a distracting rat-a-tat-tat. And, finally, I had to detect faces in a rapid succession of black and white images popping up in front of me. During this phantasmagoria of neuropsychological tasks, I experienced extreme difficulties in keeping to the point. Just focusing my attention on the screen turned out to be demanding. Again and again my mind began to wander. I realized that my performance was very poor. Often I became aware of mistakes I had just made, but I could not keep abreast of the onslaught of flashing images. On top of that, Cahn repeatedly asked me to control my nictitation to avoid disturbing the EEG measurement (for example, I was not meant to blink after seeing a big blue circle or when recognizing a face). Time and again, they told me to relax certain facial muscles, while random thoughts and existential questions continued to crop up. It was impossible to juggle all these things simultaneously. I felt harassed, overstrained, and self-alienated by the fact that my nervous system could not cope with this rush of visual exigencies and sensory stimuli.

When the whole measurement was finally over at 1:30 PM, I was exhausted and ill-tempered. As the effects of the drug began to fade away, Cahn, Kometer, and I passed by the hospital cafeteria to grab some food before climbing up the wooded hill on the clinic premises. They took their experimental subjects here to chill out. I was glad to have escaped the laboratory, and the hilltop offered a scenic view over Lake Zurich, but I was too worn out to enjoy the panorama. We sat down on a bench and talked about the experiment. The researchers interviewed me in a casual manner, asking questions about how I experienced different parts of the trial. At the same time, I was trying to find out from them what the purpose of all this had been. Often they refused to reveal their aims, fearing that such knowledge could influence my behavior during the two measurements to come. I was still scatterbrained, jumping from one subject to the next. But, overall, I was coming to understand that, in the neuropsychological tasks, Cahn and Kometer were less interested in my performance (whether I had pressed the right button at the right time) than in the electroencephalographic inscriptions of my neuronal responses, the so-called event-related potentials, to the stimuli presented on the computer screen. With the help of the EEG tomography technique LORETA, they would later on compute from the scalp-recorded voltages the three-dimensional neuroanatomical trajectories of these electrical signals.

In contrast to the first part of the study, where my lived experience had been decisive—after all, it had prevented me from experiencing the sense of oneness with the world that Cahn was after—the subsequent neuropsychological measurements had only recorded my brain's immediate responses to the presented stimuli. This was meant to sidestep the intricacies of subjectivity. Whether I felt overwhelmed or grumpy supposedly did not affect how my visual cortex processed blue circles and illusionary triangles—as long as the researchers managed to keep me disciplined enough to pay attention to the tests instead of tripping off. Investigating the relationship between stimulus and response presupposed a complicated communicative action, an implicit agreement between experimenter and experimental subject. Ethnographic observation reveals that, beyond the relationship of first-person and third-person perspective (much discussed in the philosophy of mind), neuroscientific experiments on human subjects also involve a second-person dimension (Roepstorff 2001; Lindemann 2005; Cohn 2008). Researchers guide and instruct test persons to make sure that they participate as intended. Even though historically the epistemic norm of objectivity had emerged in response to the growing concern that the scientist's willful self might endanger scientific knowledge (Daston and

Galison 2007), an objective measurement of the effects psilocybin had on my brain was not possible without the researchers imposing their will on me. However, their goal was not to turn me into a passive object of investigation but to redirect my own will, sustaining my readiness to cooperate with them. By making me press different buttons in response to different stimuli, without being interested in whether or not I got it right, they tried to ensure that I focused on the set tasks and resisted the temptation of losing myself in what anthropologist Marlene Dobkin de Rios (1984: 8) called "one of the most subjective experiences available to psychological, sociological, or anthropological inquiry." Considering this persistence of the subjective and the volitional, the question arises: can the research described above count as objective science?

In his essay "What Happened in the Sixties?," a historical account of science studies, Jon Agar (2008) argues that the critiques of science articulated by the sociology of scientific knowledge in the 1970s and 1980s grew out of the counterculture, which, according to Roszak (1968: 205) also "called into question the validity of the conventional scientific world view." The primary target of these critiques was the myth of objectivity as the ideological foundation of technocratic rule that provided authority to the expert as the one "who *really* knows what is what" (208). In the wake of the sixties, a new generation of critical science studies scholars—many of whom were either part of or at least influenced by different strands of the counterculture (e.g., Clarke 2012)—dethroned these experts by showing that scientists were "'merely workers,' not highly trained instruments revealing the truth resident in nature," and yet their theories had powerful political implications (Star 1989: 2, 197). In her consciousness-raising "Cyborg Manifesto" (1991), Donna Haraway blended a wide array of counter-cultural currents, such as radical feminism, socialism, anticolonialism, and animal rights advocacy, calling for an acknowledgment of identi-ties and life-forms marginalized by patriarchal capitalism and Western science. Externalist sociological, ethnographic, and historical studies served to unmask the purported detachment of science by demonstrat-ing how it concealed class interests, masculine bias, racism, and corpo-rate greed. Just like the self-critical anthropologists of the 1980s who challenged the epistemic and moral authority of the anthropologist as author by arguing that ethnography could only produce partial, that is, incomplete and politically situated truths (Clifford and Marcus 1986), these science studies scholars maintained that there really was no such thing as genuine objectivity.

In parallel, however, alternative orientations emerged. Steven Shapin (1992: 357, 2010: 24–25)—who in the 1960s was an FDA laboratory technician involved in drug-safety research on LSD—described both his own historicist quarter of post-1960s history and sociology of science and the contemporaneous actor-network theory as "more interested in performing rites of disciplinary purification than in changing the world." In parallel to psychedelic researchers who disclaim their countercultural heritage, students of science such as Bruno Latour (1993, 2004c), Paul Rabinow (1996b, 2003), Nikolas Rose (2007), or Lorraine Daston (1992, 2009) have come to abandon a mode of radical critique that set up humanities and social science scholarship in opposition to the ills and evils of modern science. Even though some of this work attends to and even focuses on the entanglements of science and politics, it is not based on an externalist subject position enabling a critique of university and corporate science in social and political terms. This is also reflected by the objects of investigation. For instance, studies of patient activism, social movements, and emergent forms of "biosociality" have shown that contemporary forms of resistance do not necessarily come from outside but from inside "science" and "society," which have turned out to be less homogeneous domains than countercultural talk about "the Establishment" might have suggested (Epstein 1996, 2007; Rabinow 1999; Hess et al. 2007; Gibbon and Novas 2008). MAPS and the Heffter Research Institute are excellent examples of organizations that use scientific expertise as a means of challenging and reforming rather than exercising technocratic rule, in a way that is meant to benefit, not defy, both researchers and ordinary people. Of course, neither these forms of active scientific citizenship nor the postcritical scholarship informing this book would have been possible without the counterculture and its academic correlates.

Following those advances, as well as Matei Candea's (2010) initiative exploring the ways in which detachment and engagement are interwoven, I do not wish to call into question the objectivity of Cahn and Kometer's neuropsychological approach. Apart from telling me to relax my facial muscles to avoid artifacts, they did not interfere with the EEG's mechanical recording. Nor could I help but see the gestalts of the Kanizsa triangles and produce the corresponding brain waves when attending to the screen. The experimental paradigm was shaped by an ascetic will to will-lessness. For objectivity neither equals plain disinterestedness and value neutrality nor is it a mere myth. Objectivity is itself a genuine, consequential, and passionately defended value that profoundly transforms the scientific practices that it informs. It does not eliminate subjectivity and intersubjectivity but reconfigures them in ways that are meant to prevent the privacy of subjective experience from impeding the communicability of scientific findings (Daston and Galison 2007). Even though it is only one of many epistemic virtues that occasionally conflict with each other, objectivity was aspired to in most of the neuropsychopharmacological practices described in this book and also in parts of the ethnographic writing in the pages to come.

Illusions of a Decentralized Brain

Anthropologically, the most interesting thread running through different parts of the study conducted by Rael Cahn and Michael Kometer was the so-called binding problem. Since the outset of modernity, consciousness and the self have been conceived of as punctual or lacking extension—a point of convergence where sensory perceptions of the surrounding world were integrated (C. Taylor 1992). When, in the eighteenth century, the subject began to materialize in the brain, the idea of a center of consciousness was initially preserved. Hierarchically structured, the brain was thought to accommodate a higher-order observer overseeing everything else that was going on in this organ. Since the shift from such an "organ of the soul" to the modern brain as a decentralized biological structure at the beginning of the nineteenth century, this view has been replaced by various conceptions of the brain as a complex of discretely located but interacting mental properties and functions (Hagner 2000). One of the most recent and widely received alternatives assumed a network architecture, in which separate parts of the brain represented different aspects of an object (form, color, etc.) without running together in a superordinate center. Accordingly, there was no observer in the brain. Instead, consciousness emerged from interactions of different brain areas. But this raised the question of how neuronal processes taking place in different locations were coordinated to form a coherent whole. If there was no single nerve cell representing a specific object (like the famous "grandmother neuron" firing whenever someone sees his grandmother), how could an ensemble of cells representing different aspects of sensory perception code for common content?

In 1989, the German neuroscientist Wolf Singer and his American colleague Charles Gray offered an answer to this binding problem. The binding of features recognized as belonging to the same object took place in time, they claimed. By synchronizing their firing rates at about

40 Hz, that is, in the gamma range, neurons were able to generate a temporarily integrated system representing a certain object. However, for this content to also become an object of conscious awareness, yet another brain area needed to join in representing this representation. All these different parts of the brain had to be activated simultaneously, firing in time with each other (Singer 2002: 65–72).

Gamma range EEG activity was regarded as the electrophysiological substrate of binding phenomena closely associated with conscious awareness of objects. It was produced through circular interaction between thalamus and cortex, that is, within the cortico-striato-thalamo-cortical (CSTC) loop, which Vollenweider conceived of as the key structure in the generation of consciousness and its altered states. In their study, Cahn and Kometer examined the effects of psilocybin on this neural network and the resultant modulation of gamma activity. In the grant proposal, Cahn (2005) cited studies indicating that there was increased gamma activity in the frontal cortex of experienced meditators who were striving for self-dissolution as well as in the occipital-temporal-parietal cortex of members of the Brazilian Santo Daime church after they ingested ayahuasca as a religious sacrament. Following Singer and Gray, Cahn interpreted this localized gamma activity as underlying the conscious binding of experiential contents, in this case mostly the strong visual activity typically induced by ayahuasca use. Following these cues Cahn and Kometer were especially interested in their test subjects' gamma activity during the first introspective part of the study. But the neural correlate of binding gamma activity also took center stage in the neuropsychological tests in the second part of the experiment. The Kanizsa triangle task can illustrate how the neurobiological quest for consciousness was pursued experimentally.

The Kanizsa triangle is an optical illusion invented by the Italian psychologist Gaetano Kanizsa in 1955. It consists of three Pac-Man-like figures. If their "mouths" are turned toward each other (as shown in figure 6), we perceive the "subjective" or "illusory" contours of a nonexistent white triangle. Assembling the lines and corners in such a way that they are seen as parts of a coherent figure was said to require a binding process. To examine the neural activity underlying this illusory perception, Cahn and Kometer compared the event-related potential evoked by the presentation of a Kanizsa triangle with a control condition, the presentation of the three Pac-Men now looking into different directions. In the control condition, the test subject perceived the same three elements but did not recognize them as parts of a gestalt.

Hence, the gamma activity was significantly more pronounced when a Kanizsa triangle was shown. From Vollenweider's CSTC model, Cahn and Kometer derived the hypothesis that altered states of consciousness induced by psilocybin went along with a reduction of cerebral binding of perceptual information. At the same time, 5-HT_{2A} agonists such as psilocybin had been reported to induce cortical activity in the gamma range independent of sensory input, which could possibly explain how hallucinogenic drugs provoked hallucinations. This mechanism was hoped to shed light on the pathogenesis of schizophrenia also characterized by alterations in gamma synchronicity. When Cahn and Kometer made me look at the Kanizsa triangles, they wanted to test the assumed decrease of perceptual binding by comparing the gamma oscillations elicited by the stimulus under the influence of psilocybin with the placebo response (Kometer 2006: 19–21, 39–43).

The laboratory-type tasks of this last part of their experiment operationalized the concept of binding, which the first part of the study revolving around meditative introspection explored in a manner less clear-cut but closer to the lifeworld. The concept of binding implicated a new self-image of *Homo cerebralis*. Consciousness continued to be inseparably associated with the brain, but it did not appear as a control center anymore. Instead it emerged from the interactions within a decentralized and dynamic neural network constituted by cell assemblies temporarily synchronizing their activities. Cahn's interest in altered states of consciousness induced by meditative practices and psychedelic drugs was based on the assumption "that the ordinarily-experienced limited sense of self associated with an individual's body and personality is actually a very superficial aspect of the human self and that the true self as revealed through these domains of activity is actually universal and boundariless, timeless and at one with all else" (Cahn 2005: 1). Even though the "experimental mysticism" inspiring their project was at odds with the view of hallucinogen action as an "experimental psychosis," Cahn and Kometer studied the effects of hallucinogenic drugs with technologies and test paradigms that were also used in model psychosis research. It seemed as if these interpretive frameworks incorporating values and worldviews remained inconsequential to scientific practice.

Return to a Conflicted Self: Day 3 of the Psilocybin Experiment

After a tiresome but unspectacular placebo measurement on the second day of the experiment, on the third day I received the low dose of psilocybin, two weeks after my arrival in Zurich. In the case of placebo administration, I could clearly tell after half an hour that there was no drug action, despite the double-blind design of the trial. But low dose and high dose turned out to be more difficult to distinguish. This time, the drop of my blood pressure was less pronounced and did not frighten me, but emotionally the trip seemed even more intense. Instead of marveling at the exotic landscapes of a foreign wonderland, I was confronted with my own life. Visions triggered highly emotive and con-flicted trains of thought that mostly revolved around my partner, the question of having children with her, and my anxieties with respect to leading a bourgeois family life. Under the influence of the drug, I felt more accepting toward myself and less afraid of long-term commit-ments. Worries concerning daily life, my academic career, and my self-image took a back seat. What really mattered were the bonds of love. For the time of the trip and for a few days after, I experienced a resolve with respect to my most profound value judgments that vanished all too soon in the dissonances of everyday life. Twelve months later, my relationship of that time was broken and, thinking back to that drug-induced voyage to my innermost self, it appeared as if hallucinogens were worthy of their name.

Before leaving Zurich on the day after the experiment, I had an appointment with Franz Vollenweider. His office was smoky. On the shelf I discovered a portrait of Freud next to a picture of the Dalai Lama. The walls were covered with research awards, children's drawings, PET scans, a poster of Watson and Crick in front of the DNA double helix, and a photo of Vollenweider and his friend Albert Hofmann. I asked whether I could come back to do fieldwork in his laboratory. Vollen-weider agreed by explaining his own interest in our collaboration. One day, he wanted to write a book about the philosophical implications of hallucinogen research. But, at this point of his career, he could not afford to spend much time on elaborating such thoughts. The scientific rat race did not grant much leisure to reflect on the broader context of one's empirical work. Vollenweider regarded me as an intellectual interlocutor who might help him articulate and develop some of his ideas informally before he spelled them out in a more systematic fashion in the future. We agreed that I was going to come back in October to observe his group's research activities for half a year.

This first field experience in the lab left me with many questions that I was hoping to answer upon my return: How did these researchers handle the precarious relationship between the objectivity demanded by science and the exuberant subjectivity of the psychedelic experience? How did they bring together the paradigms of psychedelic mysticism and model psychosis research? How, if at all, did they reconcile spirituality and materialism? And how did their scientific work affect their lives—and vice versa?

LOOKING BEYOND BUT FROM A SOLID STANDPOINT

Vollenweider's research on altered states of consciousness originated in the early 1990s. In our first formal interview, he provided an autobiographical sketch of his background and development leading up to this enterprise. Franz Xaver Vollenweider (pictured in figure 7) was born in 1954, growing up in the hinterland of Zurich and in Lucerne, where his mother's family owned a bakery. His father was a businessman who worked for an American company but who was also interested in philosophy, the humanities, and the natural sciences. The Vollenweider family had a chemistry laboratory at home, where the father experimented in his spare time. Vollenweider remembered: "There was a strong tension between the maternal side, baking and selling bread, and the paternal side of the family, which was rather artistic, a lot of libertines. I always felt this tension enticing me from early on to look beyond bourgeois life. I can still hear my father say to my mother: 'For you the cash needs to be correct, for us the orchestra must play right.'"

As an adolescent, Vollenweider began to rebel against his mother's rigid Christian religiosity. Playing in a successful jazz-rock band devoured much of his time and, one year before finishing high school, he dropped out, broke with both his parents, left home, and moved to Zurich. He was torn between art and science. While doing an apprenticeship as a laboratory technician, he graduated from high school by correspondence course with excellent grades. He began to study chemistry, but he switched to medical school after two years because he was too interested in things human. An arduous reader of Freud since age seventeen, he went into psychoanalysis with a neo-Freudian analyst. In response to my question of why he had picked a Freudian, he answered:

> Even though Jung appealed to me with his archetypes and transpersonal ideas, Freud was like the natural sciences to me: something tangible. His theory of drives, the ego, the superego, and the id, these things seemed true to life. What there is besides my personal existence—ancestors, transpersonal realms, and what have you—can still be explored later on. This is still with me today: I always want to have a firmly established basis and then I want to

look beyond it, but from a solid standpoint. I think I got that from my father. Somehow he was crazy with his ideas, but he exemplified to me, through his own life, that one needs a stable basis and from there one can go on excursions: mentally, economically, or professionally. I never studied medicine because of the money, but I thought—this was another of those childish ideas—if all else fails, then I can still practice as a physician. *[Laughs.]* Maybe that's the mother with the bakery, baking little buns, security.

Vollenweider's analysis was not only a way of working through his family relations but also a quest for what Max Weber (1958/1919: 156) had called "the demon who holds the fibers of his very life." Eventually Vollenweider did find his vocation in a rigorous neuroscientific investigation of hallucinogen-induced states of mind. Here, his need for a firm ground was reconciled with the desire to venture out into the realm of ecstasy and psychosis on the far side of bourgeois waking life.

After a few years in neuroscience labs, Vollenweider began to work as a psychiatrist at the Psychiatric University Hospital in Zurich in 1990. The Burghölzli had always had a strong psychodynamic tradition that attracted those preferring the unconscious to neurotransmitters, philosophy and theology to biology, and social psychiatry to drug treatment. But Vollenweider came to work in the department of Jules Angst, who had conducted a significant amount of psychopharmacological research throughout his illustrious career. Angst had published scientific articles titled "Dangers of LSD" (1967) and "Hallucinogen Abuse" (1970), and he had been associated with some of the research projects on psychedelic drugs that had been conducted at the Burghölzli after Albert Hofmann's discovery of LSD in the 1940s.

PSYCHOMETRY OF ECSTASY

In Angst's department, the German psychologist Adolf Dittrich had studied altered states of consciousness, including those induced by psychedelic drugs, until about three years before Vollenweider's arrival. When Vollenweider and Dittrich met, the two researchers spent many a night together on the balcony of Dittrich's apartment; they shared a passionate interest in altered states of consciousness and a desire for a scientifically sound perspective on these extraordinary mental phenomena. Dittrich's work provided one of the building blocks from which Vollenweider would come to assemble his own approach.

Dittrich was first and foremost a psychological methodologist whose forte was statistics (Angst called him "my mathematician"), which he applied to data from mind states induced by a broad range of technologies: from meditation and hypnosis to sensory deprivation and drugs such as DMT, cannabis, and laughing gas. In part, Dittrich's methodological rigor was a response to the tensions evoked by research on illicit substances and altered states. His former partner Maja Maurer explained to me that "as a psychologist, if you didn't do mainstream work, methodology became a weapon." The animosities against which Dittrich had to defend his research were provoked by its political context and implications. In the introduction to his habilitation, he quoted an anthropological study according to which 90 percent of almost five hundred examined cultures had institutionalized altered states of consciousness, whereas the West differed strikingly in its disdain, pathologization, and criminalization of "non-ordinary waking states" (Bourguignon 1973). In Dittrich's eyes, the countercultural embrace of such forms of consciousness since the 1960s was no aberration but an "adjustment to the vast majority of other cultures" (Dittrich 1985: 5). But he did not approve of altered states under all conditions. Incurring the displeasure of the district attorney, he supported a study on the negative psychiatric consequences of sensory deprivation in solitary confinement. The frictions generated by the politics of consciousness contributed to Dittrich's departure from Angst's department in 1987.

Although Dittrich did not keep quiet about his political convictions, he was not an activist; he was a basic researcher whose most important work was the development of the self-rating scale APZ (*Abnorme Psychische Zustände,* or "abnormal mental states") that serves to quantitatively describe altered states of consciousness. To provide standardized and comparable data, one had to replace or complement free-experience reports with an itemized questionnaire. Based on a review of already existing rating scales from schizophrenia research and work in the psychology of religion, his own clinical experience, and self-experiments with hallucinogenic drugs and sensory deprivation, Dittrich (1985) collected about 800 potential items, 158 of which eventually proved their worth in empirical studies. He wanted to test both his rating scale and the hypothesis that all altered states of consciousness had a common denominator independent of how they had been induced. For this purpose, he tried out the APZ scale in studies that provoked such states pharmacologically (e.g., with DMT or laughing gas) and by way of sensory deprivation in an isolation tank (i.e., a container in which subjects float on a body-temperature magnesium sulfate solution in total darkness and silence, cutting them off from all perception of the outside world). Dittrich's statistical analysis of the results demonstrated that altered states could be clearly demarcated from normal waking consciousness as well as from the effects of psychoactive drugs that did not produce such states (e.g., antipsychotics or alcohol).

Despite their common core, factor analysis, cluster analysis, and multidimensional scaling allowed Dittrich to differentiate these states internally into three interdependent dimensions or subscales. Each of these subscales was constituted by a cluster of items, which experimental subjects had assessed in a highly correlated manner. Dittrich called the three dimensions oceanic boundlessness, dread of ego dissolution, and visionary restructuralization. Oceanic boundlessness, a term Freud (1961: 12) had taken over from the French writer Romain Rolland's work on Hinduism, designated a positively experienced state of ego dissolution, in its most pronounced form the ecstasy of mystical experience. But the disintegration of the self could also, at times simultaneously, be experienced as utterly terrifying—as in hallucinogen-induced "horror trips" but also in the sense of Rudolph Otto's (1958) notion of *mysterium tremendum*. Supposedly, this experience of dread, wonder, and reverential respect in the face of the divine was at the heart of all religions. The angst elicited by the breaking up of ego boundaries was quantified by the dread of ego-dissolution subscale. Finally, visionary restructuralization assessed the degree of perceptual alterations and distortions occurring in an altered state of consciousness (Dittrich 1985: 199–211, 1994). These three dimensions were meant to define operationally what Aldous Huxley (2009/1954) had called heaven, hell, and visions.[2]

The hypothesis, which Dittrich tested with this newly developed tool, was also derived from Huxley's perennial philosophy: the assumption of an experience of divine reality underlying all religions and especially the mystical currents within them. Dittrich (1989: 94) wanted to identify this "archetypal core" or "basic pattern of human experience" by means of quantitative psychology. He presented the fact that psychometric self-ratings of altered states of different etiologies overlapped as indicating (or "not falsifying," as Dittrich [1989: 91–92, 96–101] wrote, in the jargon of Karl Popper's critical rationalism) the postulated common denominator that characterized altered states of consciousness in general. This was the universal core experience identifying humankind as a spiritual species.

NEUROIMAGING AND THE PERSISTENCE OF THE SUBJECTIVE

Vollenweider had first read about Dittrich's research in a newspaper article in the late 1980s and was intrigued by Dittrich's claim that different psychological and pharmacological interventions led to similar outcomes. "I then had the idea," Vollenweider told me, "if Dittrich is right about different modes of induction leading to the same dimensions, then it must be possible to capture this neurobiologically. That is to say, if I provoke a certain degree of oceanic boundlessness with psilocybin and I do the same thing with ketamine, which has a completely different chemistry, and I reach the same result, then the effects converge in a common pathway and the overlap should be biologically detectable." What Dittrich had investigated psychologically, Vollenweider wanted to approach with the tools of contemporary brain research (see figures 8 and 9).

Jules Angst supported Vollenweider's project to provoke altered states in healthy test subjects with the help of hallucinogenic drugs. Vollenweider managed to obtain a grant from the Swiss National Science Foundation (which, at the time, was highly unusual for a young researcher like him), and he set up a collaboration with a research institute for nuclear physics about one hour from Zurich where he could use one of the first positron-emission tomography (PET) scanners in Switzerland. Thanks to his initiative, he was able to introduce functional neuroimaging to the Burghölzli while resuming the clinic's long-standing tradition of hallucinogen research in the age of cognitive neuroscience.

Of course, Vollenweider was not alone with his interest in psychedelics. Before Dittrich and himself, hallucinogen research had been conducted at the Burghölzli by Eugen Bleuler, Werner Arthur Stoll, Brigitte Woggon, and Martha Koukkou-Lehmann (Vollenweider 1992/93; Vannini and Venturini 1999). Vollenweider also knew members of the Swiss Association for Psycholytic Therapy. But he was not interested in psychotherapeutic applications and maintained a certain distance from their activities. He met mostly German colleagues at the conferences of the European College for the Study of Consciousness. At one of these events, around 1990, Vollenweider made the acquaintance of a group of psychiatrists associated with Leo Hermle who were about to reanimate model psychosis research with hallucinogenic drugs in Germany. However, despite this loose network of like-minded people and Switzerland's history of hallucinogen research, Vollenweider did not have a mentor, stayed apart from other groups, and slowly built up the necessary infrastructure for his project by himself. He belonged to a generation of scientists that had absorbed the entrepreneurialism of the 1960s counterculture and its individualist credo of everybody "doing their own thing" (Turner 2006; Agar 2008: 591).

The research that established Vollenweider's reputation in the early 1990s was a PET study of the effects of psilocybin and ketamine on the brains of healthy volunteers. He demonstrated that both hallucinogens—despite their very different pharmacological mechanisms of action—increased metabolic activity in the frontal cortex. The degree of this hyperfrontality correlated with the intensity of the experience of ego dissolution as measured by Dittrich's APZ questionnaire and two additional psychometric scales. Similar metabolic patterns had been found in schizophrenic patients suffering from acute psychotic episodes. Therefore, Vollenweider's findings provided further support for the revival of the hallucinogen model of psychosis. Both psilocybin and ketamine administration not only provoked "a psychosis-like syndrome that resembled in many ways acute schizophrenic experiences"; the two substances also led to similar neurophysiological changes in brain activity (Vollenweider et al. 1997a, 1997b).

In the media, but also in critical academic discourse, functional neuroimaging is often misconceived as being primarily about the colorful images it produces, which the press has made the hallmark of the neuroscience hype since the Decade of the Brain. However, the alleged "iconophilia of cognitive neuroscience" (Hagner 2006: 219) was first and foremost the iconophilia of clinical radiologists (Joyce 2008: 24–46), science journalists, and popular-science writers, not of neuroscientists. In an article on the iconoclasm of imagers titled "Images Are Not the (Only) Truth" (2002), Anne Beaulieu points out "that for researchers, if these pictures are pictures of anything, they are pictures of numbers. . . . The abundance of representations in neuroscientific contexts that overwhelms the neophyte clashes with the conceptions of researchers that they are involved in making measurements of the brain, not obtaining images of it" (59–60; cf. Dumit 2004: 90–95).

Methodologically, the point of Vollenweider's PET study on the effects of psilocybin (and ketamine) as a model of psychosis was to establish a correlation between numbers: "To explore the relationship between psilocybin-induced [psychological] reactions and metabolic alterations, the APZ . . . scores for hallucinatory disturbances, ego, and thought disorders were correlated with the changes of absolute metabolic rates of glucose or metabolic ratios [in different brain areas]"

(Vollenweider et al. 1997b: 365). He calculated the strength of the relationship between the quantified alteration of consciousness and the drugs' effects on spatially differentiated brain activity, using the Spearman correlation coefficient. This statistical method was developed in 1904 from the practice of correlation. Correlations had been invented a few years earlier to examine associations between two variables in domains of natural variation in which it proved difficult to establish clear lines of causation (Porter 1986: 270–314). The neurobiology of the human mind was such an area. Not only did it appear unlikely that a particular quality of experience was brought about by metabolic changes in one brain region alone, but the very idea of a causal relationship between mind and brain was a subject of heated debate. In a field deeply divided by ongoing philosophical trench warfare, statistics served as a common language facilitating exchange between ideologically opposed parties (Porter 1992). For correlations can indicate, but they do not require, a causal relationship between neural activity and human consciousness. It is this mathematical practice that constituted what the brain researchers Francis Crick and Christof Koch (1990) had christened the "neural correlates of consciousness."

Vollenweider's correlation of PET measurements and psychometric self-rating scales shows that neuroimaging does not necessarily lead to a marginalization of introspection (pace Hagner 1996: 193). In the late nineteenth century, self-observation was a key element of the emergent science of experimental psychology. But it was soon sidelined by the triumph of behaviorism (Ziche 1999; Baars 2003). The black box of mental processes was opened again in the second half of the twentieth century when cybernetics was introduced to brain research, examining the processes occurring between sensory input and motor output. When the resultant cognitive neurosciences came to widely employ functional neuroimaging, this led to a renaissance of introspection. The investigation of neural correlates of consciousness and subjectively experienced mental events (mystical experiences, anxiety, etc.) required that test subjects provide first-person accounts of their experiences (Jack and Roepstorff 2003). Otherwise, it would have been impossible to tell what the measured neural correlates were correlates of. After the "scientific taboo against consciousness" (Baars 2003) in the wake of behaviorism (that had inspired some of the fierce opposition to Leary at Harvard), neuroimaging led to a rehabilitation of introspection as the royal road to conscious experience. Hence, the test subjects' subjectivity was heavily implicated in the functional images. The reconceptualization of the relationship between mind and brain brought about by the cognitive neurosciences amounted to no mere biologization of mental life but rather to a "mentalization" of the brain. In the face of a supposedly materialist neuroscience, the subjective persisted and entered into a new arrangement with the objectivity of neurophysiological measurements.

As a consequence, neuroscience was also confronted with some of the key problems of first-person knowledge. One of them is that, like all subjective experience, psychedelic experiences are said to be ineffable— and yet they are shaped by the very language used in a vain attempt to describe them (Doyle 2011: 43–99). In the case of Vollenweider's experiments, this language consisted of not only the different vocabularies that individual test persons brought to the lab but also the prefabricated and standardized wording provided by the psychometric self-rating scales, which test subjects had to fill in. Moreover, their experiences were also affected by the clinical setting and the experimental procedures. Vollenweider explained the resulting methodological dilemma as follows: "It's extremely difficult to capture this inner truth or subjective reality. It can be mapped with rating scales and neuropsychological experiments, but these experimental interventions make these states collapse. There is something like Heisenberg's uncertainty principle in hallucinogen research: when you're observing the neurophysiology, the experience escapes you, and vice versa."[3]

One of Vollenweider's philosophical interlocutors, the philosopher of mind Thomas Metzinger, regarded the problem as even more foundational. The APZ questionnaire was meant to measure the affects accompanying drug-induced disintegrations of the self. But how could there be a first-person perspective on a situation characterized by the very fact that the first-person perspective had been dissolved? Even if one accepted that introspection was essentially retrospection, its application to experiences of complete depersonalization and "oceanic boundlessness" seemed questionable: "The major epistemological obstacle in turning such states—be they pathological or spiritual—into explananda for neuroscientific research lies in the logical contradiction inherent in all reports from a purportedly *auto*biographical type of memory" (Metzinger 2000b: 296).

PERSONAL KNOWLEDGE IN NEUROPSYCHOPHARMACOLOGY

In the preceding account of research in the Vollenweider lab, both subjectivity and objectivity have primarily been located on the side of the objects of investigation: mechanical measurements of brain waves and involuntary stimulus-response arcs were presented as objective while drug experiences and introspective self-rating scales counted as subjective. This distinction would not make sense in physics or chemistry, but in research on the mind-brain the object of research is a human subject, and this human subject is treated as an object. However, objectivity and subjectivity also play a role on the side of the scientists conducting such inquiries. Here, their relationship is both an epistemological and an ethical question. In hallucinogen research, this relationship was intensely problematized in the context of researchers' personal familiarity with the substances they studied. This problematization was most clearly articulated during my interview with Paul J. Dietschy (PJD), the administrator from the Swiss Federal Office of Public Health responsible for research with controlled substances, and the pharmaceutics professor Rudolf Brenneisen (RB).

RB: When my doctoral student Felix Hasler elucidated the metabolism of psilocybin in humans in the mid-'90s, we served as test subjects ourselves. I was one of them. At the time, I was an official consultant of the Swiss Federal Office of Public Health. That provoked a nice little conflict: a consultant of the SFOPH volunteers for a psychotropic experiment! The ethics committee required that neither medical students nor people from the street take part in this trial. It had to be people who knew what to expect and who had been screened extremely well by Vollenweider and his colleagues. If someone's grandmother had a psychiatric problem they were out.

PJD: I can add that, when I heard about this, I thought that it wasn't a good idea at all.

RB: That was the conflict we had.

PJD: We sat down together and I realized that this was a requirement of the ethics committee. Then we agreed that it made sense to conduct this study at a relatively high security level instead of taking anyone, maybe even paid test subjects or medical students who might end up enjoying it. We wanted test subjects who were knowledgeable and who also knew the risk they were taking. So I waved this through. But you are right, we fought with each other quite passionately.

NL: *Where did your original reservations come from?*

PJD: Brenneisen was in charge of the study. I said: In my eyes, the study director has to be independent. But that's hardly possible if he takes the substance himself.

Dietschy's concern about Brenneisen serving as a test subject in a study that he supervised cannot simply be attributed to his role as a regulator defining the external conditions of scientific activities without being involved in the actual research himself. What he evoked was an ideal that had emerged from within science, namely, objectivity.

Lorraine Daston and Peter Galison (2007) have shown how objectivity arose as an epistemic virtue in the mid-nineteenth century. It was preceded by the prevalence of "truth-to-nature," an attitude toward the objects of science that aimed at extraction of the typical. Truth-to-nature required scientists sufficiently experienced to tell the essential from the accidental. At about the same time, in the eighteenth and early nineteenth century, the scientist's self was also asserted confidently in the practice of self-experimentation. Experimenting on oneself was not only regarded as respectable but also distinguished a scientist as a superior source of knowledge. In a competitive field, both the self-experimenter's heroism and the fact that he had experienced certain phenomena first-hand with which his colleagues were personally unfamiliar served as sources of social distinction (Oreskes 1996; Strickland 1998).

With the emergence of objectivity, this view changed radically. Objectivity called for the effacement of the scientific self. This new scientific norm favored mechanical recordings to capture nature with as little human intervention as possible. Self-experimentation became suspect, as its results were now regarded as prone to distortion by the scientist's will. Objectivity was born out of a deep-seated distrust, even fear, of the subjective and its inclination to defile an impartial perspective on the world (Daston and Galison 2007: 49, 191–251). In the case of psychedelic science, the ardor with which a few vocal individuals from the previous generation of researchers had come to advocate drug use had raised grave concerns about whether drug experiences corrupted the dispassionate outlook expected from scientists.

But the question was not only whether drug experiences distorted the researchers' scientificity but also whether this scientificity distorted the researchers' experiences. When investigating psychedelics, the bias inherent in studies examining a select population of pharmacologists and psychiatrists might be particularly pronounced. Such a selection of subjects had not only been the case in the trial Brenneisen had supervised but was common practice in Germany, where, for ethical reasons, only medical professionals could serve as test subjects in hallucinogen experiments. Among such a group of people who dealt with these substances professionally, the subjects' mind-sets were likely to be more uniform or at least more developed. Furthermore, a self-experimenting scientist's expectations concerning the outcome of her self-experiment might affect its results, especially if the test subject's experience was the focus of attention. If the researcher's initial hypothesis and professional desires inflected her findings, her subjectivity undermined the scientific pursuit of objective knowledge.

Dietschy's defense of objectivity against Brenneisen's participation in the experiments of his doctoral student Felix Hasler (Hasler et al. 1997) was first and foremost a matter of principle. Dietschy might also have been worried about possible future studies focusing on the psychological effects of psilocybin. But the study Dietschy and Brenneisen fought over investigated the drug's pharmacokinetics, that is, its metabolization by the liver and kidneys. A distortion of the results by a subjective bias was not to be expected. However, the positive reasons both Brenneisen and Dietschy provided for why Brenneisen eventually took part in the experiment were ethical, invoking the heroic ethos of self-experimentation. Instead of "people from the street" or medical students who might get turned on to drugs, the mature, strong-minded, and self-sacrificing man of science was to go first (Altman 1987; Oreskes 1996). This outcome was presented as an acceptable compromise between ethics and epistemology as two antagonistic modes of reasoning.

In the experimental practice of the Vollenweider lab, the relationship between ethics and epistemology was more complex. In fact, these two domains were inextricably entwined. At the time of my fieldwork, Patrick Kossuth, an advanced doctoral researcher, and Anna Wagner, a biology student, were developing a study on psilocybin to produce data for Wagner's graduation thesis.[4] Although the consumption of hallucinogenic fungi containing psilocybin was no uncommon pastime among Swiss youth, it turned out that she had never taken any "magic mushrooms." In a discussion of her research project over lunch, another PhD student suggested that she try psilocybin herself before administering the drug to test subjects. The underlying rationale was spelled out by his more senior colleague Felix Hasler (2007: 40): "In the debate [over self-experimentation], there are two classical positions. Some people say that one shouldn't do self-experiments because this jeopardizes scientific objectivity. I don't agree with that. If I do hallucinogen research, I should know the effects of these substances firsthand. Besides, there is an ethical responsibility. If I expect my test subjects to put up with certain states, I should at least know from personal experience what they're going through." For LSD, the recommendation that psychiatrists first test the substance on themselves had already been issued in the late 1940s by the Swiss manufacturer Sandoz (Grob 2002: 17). Most hallucinogen researchers continued to subscribe to this view and, in the process of her socialization, Wagner soon came to adopt it.

Before long, Wagner and Kossuth set up a pilot study. They took turns serving as subjects in a trial version of their experiment. Her test run was smooth: some nausea at the beginning, colorful geometric patterns with eyes closed, mild hallucinations with eyes open, inhibited and perseverating thought processes, but neither emotional turmoil nor any quasi-psychotic episodes. The unpleasant surprise came when her more experienced coworker took the drug. Serving as a test subject in one of his colleague's experiments, Kossuth had already ingested psilocybin twice without encountering any difficulties. But this time it was different. The experiment involved an EEG measurement during which the subject was shown a series of images presented on a computer screen. Even though these pictures were supposed to be affectively neutral, they made Kossuth feel anxious. Eventually, he asked for the measurement to take place without the images. But deprived of this focal point of attention, things got even worse. All of a sudden, the small EEG chamber became bigger and bigger while Kossuth felt like a midget. A sense of profound solitude crept up—as if he were the only human being in the whole universe. He began to worry that his negative affects might interfere with the measurement. Eventually, he wanted to break off the experiment, but this made him all the more terrified: didn't it prove that he was in big trouble? Subscribing to the model psychosis paradigm, Kossuth conceived of his condition as gradually lapsing into a schizophrenia-like state. The situation was further complicated by the role reversal between Kossuth as the one leading the study and Wagner who now had to take care of him with nobody else directing her anymore. He later on remembered: "I tried to stay in charge, supervising how Wagner was looking after me, checking how I was affected by the stimuli, whether the room would be bearable for the subjects, etc. I tried to evaluate all of this. The problem was that I wanted to keep everything under control, which is simply impossible on psilocybin. That made me fully aware of the fact that I was losing control. So I got all worked up about this. You need to let go."

When Kossuth also started to feel dizzy and nauseous, Wagner decided to call Vollenweider for help. With an authority and sensibility based on personal familiarity with the drug, as well as with the whole spectrum of responses of a large number of experimental subjects, Vollenweider quickly managed to calm Kossuth down, enabling him to finish the trial. In the wake of this incident, Kossuth and Wagner redecorated the EEG chamber to make it look friendlier. They also replaced the computer images that Kossuth had perceived as frightening with pictures of a more positive emotional tone, hoping to spare their test subjects such "bad trips." Thereby, the researchers acknowledged that the drug effects could not be reduced to pharmacological properties of the ingested substance but were molded by the experimental setting.

At first glance, again the scientists' personal experiences seemed primarily implicated in the ethical dimension of their work—although in a different way than in Brenneisen's case. The Vollenweider lab did recruit "people from the street," mostly students eager to experience a hallucinogen trip in a supposedly safe setting or interested in earning some extra money by serving as test subjects in a clinical trial (a common procedure in pharmaceutical studies, which Brenneisen and Dietschy only regarded as problematic because psilocybin was classified as a drug of abuse). Whereas the measurement of Brenneisen's pharmacokinetics contributed to Hasler's findings, a pilot study like the one run by Kossuth and Wagner did not serve to generate publishable data. The scientists did not experiment on themselves to replace other test persons but to try out the methods, instruments, and drugs before a study with externally recruited subjects was launched. In such test runs, they familiarized themselves with the equipment and procedures and gained a better understanding of how their future subjects might experience the situation. For test persons were no mere objects of investigation that could be observed from a distance. For ethical reasons, it would not have been permissible to passively watch a subject sliding deeper and deeper into a state of horror. The scientists familiarized themselves with the effects of the applied substances to become more empathic and to be better equipped to take countermeasures if subjects were about to get emotionally unstable.

But bad trips were also detrimental to the scientific study as such. As participation in experiments was voluntary, test subjects had the right to break off measurements at any time if they felt too uncomfortable. In that case, the scientists would have lost their data. In both their own interests and their subjects', they could not sit back while their perfectly impartial measuring devices registered the neural correlates of exacerbating "dread of ego dissolution." Thus, the lab setting not only impeded full-blown mystical experiences but also saved subjects from the worst. Needless to say that both were reflected by the rating-scale scores and neurophysiological measurements. But, at this point, the hands-off attitude of objectivity had simply reached the limits of what was ethical and practicable.

Often, pilot studies also served as soundings to formulate a hypothesis or to check whether an envisaged experiment had sufficient potential. The results of these measurements were usually not published. At the beginning of the twenty-first century, no respectable scientific journal would accept a study based on systematic self-experimentation. Instead, one tried to reproduce and consolidate the findings from the pilot study with test subjects recruited from outside of the laboratory.

After completion of the actual study, personal drug experiences acquired in pilot studies receded into the background because the collected data was meant to speak for itself. However, even if the published interpretations of this data were purged of the scientists' first-person knowledge, their experiential background still occasionally helped them to weigh the significance of their data. For example, what might appear to be a hallucinogen-induced attention deficit could also reflect a lack of interest, which a tripping test subject experienced when having to perform test after test on a computer screen while confronted with the most elementary questions of life or a magical world of sublime beauty. As a British colleague of Vollenweider's put it graphically:

> It is well accepted that when under the acute influence of psychedelic drugs, performance on standard tests of intelligence, learning, memory and other cognitive functions, as well as certain psychomotor tasks, generally show impairment and sometimes show lack of change and only rarely show improvement (Carter et al. 2005). However, it is often difficult to get meaningful data from such measurements because subjects frequently become engrossed in the subjective aspects of the drug experience and lose interest in the tasks presented by the investigators. Psychological tests are often seen as absurd or irrelevant by the subjects, illustrated well by this quote from the psychologist Arthur Kleps, "If I were to give you an IQ test and during the administration one of the walls of the room opened up, giving you a vision of the blazing glories of the central galactic suns, and at the

same time your childhood began to unreel before your inner eye like a three-dimension colour movie, you too would not do well on an intelligence test." (Sessa 2008: 826)

As test subjects of pilot studies, most hallucinogen researchers had experienced such situations firsthand and were careful not to rush to drug-naïve conclusions. Such implications of the subjective produced a scientific practice that was not entirely objective. Of course, personal familiarity with the administered substances did not affect the mechanical recordings of the EEG or PET in any way, but such objective measurements were associated with practices informed by different epistemic norms. Daston and Galison (2007) have shown that there are more—and sometimes conflicting—epistemic virtues at work in science than the historically rather recent norm of objectivity. Researchers' participation in pilot studies was not regarded as compromising the scientificity of their work but rather as a way of acquiring a kind of practical wisdom. From their fleeting drug experiences, the scientists emerged as experienced subjects. Through subsequent reflection, temporary alterations of consciousness gave rise to and were integrated into more sophisticated forms of scientific subjectivity. Firsthand knowledge of what it felt like to be under the influence of a particular drug enabled researchers to develop the kind of empathy necessary to attend to their test subjects. Apart from such social skills, it also provided an experiential orientation that helped in designing experiments and interpreting results. Different forms of such skillful knowing and doing had always played a pivotal role in scientific practice but were hardly acknowledged and, if possible, practically marginalized under the absolutist reign of objectivity.

However, by the time Michael Polanyi (1958) put his finger on the importance of "personal knowledge" in the sciences, objectivity had already been structurally relocated (not replaced) by a new epistemic virtue, which Daston and Galison (2007) call "trained judgment," reinstating the scientist as subject. Trained judgment calls for the development of personal knowledge based on familiarity and experience that allows one to intuitively make sense of variation in empirical findings without returning to the ideal-typical representations of truth-to-nature. Despite this revaluation of the subject and the plurality of norms guiding scientific practice, objectivity has continued to maintain such a powerful position that, in public, it is almost equated with scientificity per se. Of course, the researchers I encountered were well aware of the value of experience. In the lab, they frequently talked about it. Despite the fact that not everyone in the lab knew psychedelics firsthand, and although acquiring such familiarity was rather taken as a psychopharmacological virtue than a categorical imperative, novices were subtly and gently encouraged to acquaint themselves with the drugs they were studying before administering them to test subjects.

Nevertheless, the role of personal knowledge was systematically excluded from the laboratory's publications. Here, the mechanical measurements and the procedural logic of method characterizing objectivity continued to prevail. The subjective was still highly vulnerable to criticism in a field that was divided by particularist interests while striving for universal knowledge. At the time of my fieldwork, I did not realize that I was documenting an epistemic culture on the wane: a few years later, as pharmacological experimentation was subjected to further regulations, the participation of researchers in pilot studies was officially terminated in Switzerland. In Germany, however, medical self-experimentation would continue to be not just a possibility but a requirement for any human research with hallucinogenic drugs.

THE HALLUCINOGENIC EXPERIENCE AS BOTH HUMAN AND NATURAL KIND

The interplay between personal drug experiences and psychopharmacological knowledge is bound to affect the self-conceptions of the scientists involved. In an interview, pharmacologist Felix Hasler (2007: 39) explained: "From experiments with hallucinogens I learned how manipulable the psyche is, how fundamentally our whole being and experience depend on our brain chemistry. The smallest amounts of a chemical substance lead to a restructuring of the whole of consciousness—seeing, feeling, thinking, space, time, ego, environment—everything gets mixed up." When such powerful neuropharmacological interventions shatter everyday consciousness, the identity of mind and brain presupposed by many neuroscientists seems to be transformed from an abstract philosophical postulate to an immediate experience. Hallucinogens taught Hasler and many of his colleagues to conceive of themselves as "neurochemical selves" (Rose 2003a). (Figure 10 pictures Hasler as a test subject in his own study.)

However, it was not hallucinogenic neurochemistry alone that brought about this identification of brain and person. When Peruvian or Siberian shamans ingested a plant hallucinogen or an inebriating toadstool, they were not struck by the fundamental dependency of their whole being on brain chemistry but rather communicated with the spirits of their ancestors (Furst 1976). Their visions were informed by different self-images and worldviews. In this respect, anthropologist Marlene Dobkin de Rios (1975: 402–407) speaks of the "cultural patterning of hallucinatory experience," which also takes place in the laboratory. Thus the researchers' own hallucinogenic experiences were mediated by their psychopharmacological knowledge and fed back into the generation of this knowledge.

If we followed Ian Hacking's (1995) historical ontology, this looping effect would make the hallucinogenic experience a human kind. In contrast to natural kinds, human kinds are transformed by their descriptions. New ways of talking about drug experiences certainly leave the drugs unchanged, but not the experiences, which they elicit in self-conscious human beings. There is little doubt that Hasler's neurologized hallucinogenic experience was strikingly different from the spirit quest of an Amazonian medicine man. It was the experience of a "cerebral subject" as it had emerged in Euro-American science and philosophy since the eighteenth century (Vidal 2009).

Hacking attributed the investigation of human kinds to the human sciences. According to Foucault (1973), these "sciences of man" emerged at the turn from the eighteenth to the nineteenth century alongside modern linguistics, economics, and biology as empirical bodies of knowledge constituting "man" as a speaking, working, and living being. In this new discursive formation, language, labor, and life appeared not only as objects of empirical inquiry but also as the quasi-transcendental conditions of any such inquiry. "Quasi-transcendental" because what makes up our humanness is also transformed and thereby historicized by human activity. For example, it is as living beings that biologists study life. Whatever they find out about their objects of study is bound to affect their self-conceptions as subjects of inquiry. The historically and culturally contingent epistemic figure of man, Foucault (1973: 318) argues, is simultaneously subject and object of its own understanding: "Man . . . is a strange empirico-transcendental doublet, since he is a being such that knowledge will be attained in him of what renders all knowledge possible." But these conditions of possibility simultaneously constitute the limits of this specific form of knowledge: it can never be complete. Consequently, this epistemological configuration has been haunted by a structural instability from the start: "Man became that upon the basis of which all knowledge could be constituted as immediate and non-problematized evidence; he became, a fortiori, that which justified the calling into question of all knowledge of man. Hence that double and inevitable contestation: that which lies at the root of the perpetual controversy between the sciences of man and the sciences proper" (344).

Where the neurosciences reflexively examine and naturalize their own epistemological preconditions, they enter into the precarious space of this "anthropological thought." In a public lecture titled "Ego Death and Ecstasy," which he gave in Zurich in 2005, Hasler articulated the concern about the epistemic finitude, defining the empiricotranscendental double as follows: "Can we investigate the neural basis of different states of consciousness? For this purpose, hallucinogens suggest themselves. However, here the observer and the observed are situated on the same ontological level. This raises the big question: Can a brain study the brain, can consciousness understand consciousness? Can man know himself?"

This reflexivity does not keep the neurosciences from treating the brain, consciousness, and humans as natural kinds. When reflecting on the cognitive limits posed by the scientist's own mind–brain to understanding the mind–brain as such, the resulting insights are not taken to feed back into the research process. In fact, it is an essential part of the construction of the mind–brain as scientific object to prevent or conceal such looping effects on the level of experimental knowledge production. What distinguishes the neurosciences from the human sciences is that reflexive concerns about the empiricotranscendental structure of the epistemological figure of man are not translated into scientific practices of reflexivity (R. Smith 2005).

Nevertheless, psychopharmacology—or "pharmacopsychology," as Emil Kraepelin still called it in the late nineteenth century (Müller et al. 2006)—is no pure natural science. Significant parts of the discipline are located at the intersection of the natural and the human sciences. Investigations of hallucinogen-induced alterations of consciousness are a striking example. If the psychedelic experience is affected by the subject's self-conception and understanding of the experiment, it must be considered a composite entity that is both human and natural kind— even though neither Hacking's dual ontology (which he himself has given up [Hacking 2007a]) nor the methodological armamentarium of psychopharmacology provide the tools necessary to study it as such. Does this failure reflect a fundamental epistemological limit of psychopharmacology and the human sciences or a contingent fact about the history of the disciplines?

WILD NEUROCHEMISTRY AND CONTROLLED CULTURE

When I returned to Zurich two months after my participation in Rael Cahn and Michael Kometer's experiment, they had already begun to work on the second part of their study. I had been the last of eighteen test subjects included in the first arm. The other seventeen had mostly been students recruited from an online job exchange for approximately $320 each. Suitable subjects for the second part of the trial were less readily available as they needed to have many years of meditation experience. Nevertheless, Cahn managed to recruit a number of long-term meditators from Swiss meditation centers and from among the readers of popular magazines such as *Buddhismus Aktuell,* as well as a famous monk from the entourage of the Dalai Lama, who had come to Zurich on the occasion of the "Buddhism and Neuroscience" conference in 2005 (but preferred to remain anonymous in the context of a drug study). The plan was to compare the brain waves of these supposedly "supranormal" individuals during meditation with those of "normal" test subjects under the influence of psilocybin. Cahn also wanted to examine whether meditators responded differently to the drug than the normal control group. The underlying assumption was that the psychophysiological traits, which had been shaped over the years by regular spiritual exercises, would be actualized in the specific mind-brain states examined during the experiment.

One day in December, Cahn invited me to observe one of his measurements because he had a particularly interesting test subject that day. When I arrived in the EEG lab, the experiment had already started. The room was only lit by the computer screen showing the subject's brain waves. Looking through the observation window, I could not see anything at first glance. But as my eyes got used to the darkness, I began to make out the shaven-headed meditator dimly illuminated by the monitor in front of him and sitting bolt upright in the leather armchair. A tangled mass of wires seemed to be coming out of the back of his head, disappearing in the dark. Jan Riedhammer, a Swiss meditation teacher in his fifties, had been administered psilocybin.[5] Cahn was excited: While Riedhammer was meditating and on psilocybin, his brain waves were particularly "calm," Cahn explained to me, showing comparatively strong activity in the alpha range. After the measurement, Riedhammer looked serene and happy.

Cahn interviewed him to learn more about the experience that had gone along with those unusual EEG patterns. Riedhammer recounted that, at the beginning of the test period, he had seen hideous faces and carnivalesque processions of ghosts. But then he remembered the *Tibetan Book of the Dead* and reminded himself that these were only projections of his ego. Eventually, he resorted to a simple mantra that he had learned as a novice, a meditation on two words, coupled with special attention to the physiological processes of inhalation and exhalation. Doing this, he managed to repel the spooky spectacle and was elevated to a "higher state of consciousness," culminating in an experience of oneness with the universe. Much to his surprise and even disappointment, this experience of cosmic unity was associated with the name of Jesus. It must have had to do with his upbringing in a Christian family, he mused. He was relieved and delighted when he subsequently thought of Buddha and this further deepened this state of ego dissolution. Compared to his everyday consciousness, he said, he gained a much more profound insight into the fact that the ground of all existence was love. "Divine love," he specified, "or even better: being." This occurred to him as an eternal truth: "It has always been that way and it will always be that way. When reaching that state," he told us, "I thought: This is it! This is it!" The state he had been striving for during three decades of meditation exercises.

Finally, Cahn had found a test subject who had had a unitive experience in the lab. But how was it possible that this meditation teacher had such a different response to the drug than Kossuth the brain researcher or me? How could one and the same substance send some people to heaven and others to hell? Cahn's and Kossuth's colleague Felix Hasler (2007: 39) explained the variability of the hallucinogenic experience as follows: "Hallucinogens enable you to have limit-experiences. Whether one regards such liminal states as mystical experiences or as psychotic delusions is mostly a matter of interpretation." Implicit in this statement is the cosmology of mononaturalism and multiculturalism: the perspectivist assumption that there is one world and many worldviews based on the ontological distinction between nature and a multitude of cultures (Viveiros de Castro 1998; Latour 2004b). The former is the object of the natural sciences; the latter are the objects of cultural anthropology. And indeed one of the first things this anthropologist noticed in the laboratory was that the scientists were starkly divided over the question of what sense to make of their own drug experiences. But does it follow that the meditator's religious ecstasy, the neuroscientist's "horror trip," and my own experience of overstrain and irritation were essentially the same mind-brain state, just differently interpreted?

The fact that hallucinogenic experiences can differ widely, dependent on the subject's cultural background and the context of drug ingestion, had already been observed in the late nineteenth century, when these substances were constituted as "boundary objects" (Star and Griesemer 1999) at the intersection of pharmacology and anthropology. The anthropologist James Mooney (1896) noted that Western test persons who had been administered peyote in scientific experiments tended to respond with anxiety and depression, whereas Native Americans eating the hallucinogenic cactus in religious rituals experienced a sense of spiritual elation. This conditionality on cultural context became one of the key topoi of twentieth-century anthropological research on hallucinogens (Shonle 1925; Petrullo 1934; Wallace 1959). Timothy Leary and colleagues (1963) coined the still current terms *set* and *setting* to describe the impact that a subject's personality, mood, and expectations, as well as her social, cultural, and physical environment, had on the psychedelic experience.

In the late 1950s, during the heyday of hallucinogen research, Anthony Wallace, an anthropologist well-known for his work on religious revitalization movements among American Indians, served as director of clinical research at the Eastern Pennsylvania Psychiatric Institute, where hallucinogen experiments were conducted. Like Mooney, he noticed how different the drug responses of the clinic's white test subjects were from those of Native American participants in peyote ceremonies. From this observation Wallace (1959) concluded that placebo-controlled studies— which, at the time, were only beginning to get established—had to be supplemented by "cultural controls." He proposed not only varying the pharmacological activity of the administered substance but also testing the same drug under different cultural and situational circumstances to systematically investigate (and subsequently control) the impact of these conditions on psychotropic effects. He speculated that these "cultural determinants" would affect not only the effects of hallucinogens but those of all psychopharmaceuticals. When, shortly after, LSD & Co. escaped the walls of the laboratory and the clinic, this discourse fueled the hope of developing a predictive social scientific theory of hallucinogenic drug action that, in combination with anthropological knowledge of the drugs' ritual uses in other cultures, would allow for social control over the effects of this unruly class of substances (Dobkin de Rios 1984: 214).

When Wallace spoke of culture-controlled trials, he used the term *culture* in a rather broad way. The suggested controls comprised the sociocultural background of test subjects, their personality and expectations vis-à-vis the experiment, their social treatment by laboratory staff, and the experimental setting as a whole. Against the background of the current debate about the "ontological turn" in anthropology (which is, as I understand it, the move from second-order observations of other cultures to first-order claims about the nature of the world as constituted by both human and nonhuman actors), Wallace's work might serve as a reminder that culture has not always been reduced to Geertzean "webs of significance" (see Candea's contribution to Carrithers et al. 2010: 172–179; Geertz 1973: 5). Before the progressive alienation of cultural from physical anthropology, as well as the advent of a symbolic and interpretive anthropology that cast an ethnographic quest for meaning against experimental science, human biology and material objects and practices had been key elements of anthropological accounts. Wallace's proposal of culture-controlled trials belonged to an era untouched by the epistemological critiques and postcolonial scruples of the *Writing Culture* generation (Clifford and Marcus 1986), when anthropology did not yet need science studies to reconnect the ontological domains of nature and culture.

But Wallace's proposition was stillborn. While placebo-controlled studies soon became the gold standard of pharmacological research (Marks 1997), culture-controlled trials never really caught on. Considering that the hallucinogen researchers I worked with were well aware of the impact that set and setting had on psychedelic drug action, it was striking that the predominant study design in the Vollenweider lab, just as in pharmacological research at large, continued to be the randomized double-blind placebo-controlled trial. In such experiments, all conditions are supposed to be kept identical while subjects randomly receive a pharmacologically active drug or an inactive placebo. Neither the researcher nor the test person is supposed to know whether the former or the latter is administered. The underlying assumption is that all psychosocial and cultural factors are also operative when the placebo is given. Hence, when subtracting the placebo's effects from the effects of the pharmacological agent, the drug's own activity is revealed in its purest form. If the psychotropic effect of the drug is affected by the organism's environment or mood, this influence is thereby rendered invisible.

For political, economic, and disciplinary reasons, biological psychiatry and psychopharmacology had an interest in attributing the effects of drugs to drugs alone. A contextualist conception of pharmacological activity did not fit the politics of antidrug campaigns based on the demonization of certain substances. Illicit drugs had to be portrayed as inherently bad. In the War on Drugs, there was no place for ambiguity and context dependence. Furthermore, for economic reasons, drug research was strongly shaped by the interests of industry. Since the 1962 revisions of US drug regulation in the wake of the thalidomide disaster and the uncontrolled clinical experimentation with LSD in the late 1950s, pharmaceutical companies needed to demonstrate specific and standardizable effects to register their products with the Food and Drug Administration. Additionally, they were marketing drugs as working in all circumstances, not only under particular conditions. And, finally, psychopharmacology was an important vehicle in psychiatry's aspirations to become a medical discipline like any other, based on firm natural scientific foundations. This project would have been jeopardized if the effects of psychotropic drugs had been shown to depend on patients' individual quirks, (auto)suggestion, and changing settings. In response to these constraints there emerged a view of drugs as having a pharmacological essence that determined human experience and behavior upon drug ingestion. As a shorthand for this mind-set, Richard DeGrandpre (2006), a behavioral pharmacologist turned historian, coined the term *pharmacologicalism*.

Pharmacologicalism prevailed because it helped psychiatry to be acknowledged as part of scientific medicine, enabled pharmaceutical companies to fulfill the FDA's regulatory requirements, and legitimized the War on Drugs. At the same time, culturalist approaches gained the upper hand in cultural anthropology. In the last quarter of the twentieth century, the disciplinary unity of anthropology broke apart as anthropologists came to reject the association of non-European peoples with early hominids and nonhuman primates that had been constitutive of US anthropology's holistic agenda but was enmeshed in the distinction between the West and the rest. The culturalist response to this complicity of anthropological holism and colonial racism was not to apply a biocultural perspective to humankind overall instead of non-European others alone but to exclude biological approaches and to focus on the study of cultures—both Western and non-Western (Clifford 2005; Segal and Yanagisako 2005). Rather than identifying the "cultural determinants" of psychopharmacological effects as Wallace (1959) had sought to do, culturally oriented studies of drugs focused on the drug as symbol (e.g., Myerhoff 1974) or on historically and culturally variable interpretations of supposedly identical neurochemical effects (e.g., Becker 1963; Dobkin de Rios 1984; Zinberg 1984). Having slipped through the cracks between cultural anthropology and psychopharmacology, Wallace's (1959) "method of cultural and situational controls" led a shadowy existence.

The revival of hallucinogen research in the age of science studies and an anthropology that has come to question the ethnocentrism of the modern cosmology of mononaturalism and multiculturalism provide an opportunity to critically reassess this development. What speaks against the assumption that drug-induced mystical experiences and anxiety-laden psychotic derailments are just different interpretations of the same neurochemical event are the results of Vollenweider's (1997b) early PET study. It endowed these antipodal experiences with objectivity by identifying their partly overlapping, partly distinct neural correlates.[6]

The fact that these mind-brain states were shaped by what Wallace had called the "cultural determinants" of hallucinogenic experiences was subsequently demonstrated by Vollenweider's doctoral student Erich Studerus (Studerus et al. 2012). Even though Studerus did not conduct any culture-controlled trials to directly test the causal impact of such nonpharmacological factors, he analyzed the pooled data from twenty-three placebo-controlled psilocybin studies. By statistically evaluating the psychological (self-)assessments of more than 250 participants, Studerus showed that, although dosage had the strongest impact on the subjects' experiences, nonpharmacological factors also played a significant role. High scores in oceanic boundlessness were correlated with the personality trait of absorption (i.e., the predisposition to get deeply immersed in sensory or mystical experiences). Surprisingly, neuroticism did not turn out to be a good predictor of "bad trips." A subject's mood in the weeks preceding the experiment proved to be more predictive. More sociable test persons tended to have less spiritual experiences. And the PET center in the basement of the nearby university hospital was found to be associated with anxious reactions to the drug; that setting, Studerus and his colleagues explained, was a "clinical and antiseptic environment" containing "lots of technical equipment, white walls, personnel in white lab coats," and so on (9).

This neuropsychopharmacological study and the ethnographic observations presented in this chapter suggest that the realm of the mental cannot be reduced to the brain but instead encompasses the organism's surroundings—a point that has also been made by philosophers supporting the "extended mind" hypothesis (Clark and Chalmers 1998; Noë 2004). Thus, to study the psychopharmacological activity of a drug, it is not sufficient to look only at its effects on the mind-brain while turning a blind eye to the environment in randomized placebo-controlled trials. The physical, atmospheric, social, and cultural qualities of the setting in which a drug is taken also determine how an organism responds to it. In allusion to Margaret Lock's discovery of "local biologies" (Lock 1995; Lock et al. 2010: 83–109) (in the sense of biological differences molding and containing subjective experience and cultural interpretations), the decisive role of the circumstances of drug ingestion can be taken to indicate the existence of "local neuropsychopharmacologies."

If a future psychopharmacology reinvented itself as a hybrid of natural and cultural science, one of the key questions would be whether any more general lessons could be drawn from the case of hallucinogens. Do set and setting play a similar role in other substances, as Wallace suggested? The effects of psychedelic drugs have been presented as particularly plastic. In the 1970s, the psychiatrist Lester Grinspoon and his colleague James Bakalar (1979: 90) wrote, "In experiments, most drugs make all the subjects feel more alike; LSD actually tends to accentuate any differences in mood that exist among subjects at the start." In a debate about an earlier version of the argument presented in this section, the Berlin psychiatrist Malek Bajbouj (2010) also argued that hallucinogens were a special case that did not allow any generalizations. Some clinical and more social scientific work suggests otherwise (Lindesmith 1938; MacAndrew and Edgerton 1969; Janke 1983; Gomart 2002; DeGrandpre 2006). At first glance, the study by Studerus and colleagues (2012: 1) seemed a compromise that largely reaffirmed psychedelic orthodoxy by emphasizing a significant impact of set and setting on hallucinogenic drug action: "Although set and setting influence the psychological effects of any psychotropic substance, including alcohol and nicotine, the effects of hallucinogens seem to be particularly strongly determined by these conditions." At closer inspection, however, their findings turned out to challenge the traditional psychedelic account. In an e-mail to me, Studerus stated his position boldly:

> Even though I wrote in the conclusion that set and setting played an important role, I also emphasized that drug dosage was the most impactful factor. We found a few significant non-pharmacological predictors, but overall the explained variance was only moderate. Therefore, one shouldn't overestimate the importance of set and setting the way Leary & Co. did. Leary has been quoted as claiming that 99% of the effects of hallucinogens could be attributed to set and setting. Of course, in the psychedelic movement such exaggerations fell on fertile ground because they implied that the effects of these substances were completely controllable if they were taken in the right

set and setting. Additionally, this overstatement allowed Leary to valorize his discipline. It made psychology look more important than pharmacology and biology. In other words, the mind is ranked above the body (a popular prejudice, which you can find in almost all esoteric-spiritual groups).

By questioning the weight that countercultural psychology and anthropology had placed on set and setting, Studerus also challenged the constructivist account of hallucinogen action, which I had defended in the scholarly debate with natural and cultural scientists mentioned above (Langlitz 2010b, partly translated as Langlitz 2012b). In this exchange, Studerus's colleague Boris Quednow acknowledged the role of set and setting as well-known from placebo effects, but he declared both factors to be mere "confounding variables." This went hand in hand with an ontology regarding the world as divided into competing shares of nature and culture:

> We know from placebo-controlled studies, with antidepressants, for example, how much expectations affect the efficacy of psychopharmaceuticals. In 13 to 52 percent of patients with major depression, the symptoms get better even though they have received a physiologically ineffective substance (Walsh et al. 2002). From the perspective of a psychopharmacologist, such subjective expectations are part of the basic noise, the effects of which need to be surpassed—for if the cultural influence on a drug effect is too big, this also means that its supposed neurobiological mechanism has to be called into question.
>
> For the pharmacologist, all forms of internal and external cultural modulation of pharmacological effects are confounding variables, which need to be minimized or—if that is not possible—controlled. When developing a medicine, its effects should preferably be the same in all cultures and a psychopharmacological experiment determining the neurobiological basis of our behavior should produce the same results all over the globe. Strong substances generate their effects independent of (or despite) culture. The other way round, one may assume that the influence of culture gets bigger as the intensity of a pharmacological stimulus decreases. (Quednow 2010b: 82)

Quednow's account was committed to an anthropology rooted in the nineteenth century that sought to determine the ratio of nature and culture in all things human. If a phenomenon is more natural, it has to be less cultural—and vice versa. In recent years, this dichotomy has lapsed into crisis, partly because Euro-Americans have come to conceive of their nature less as a fate and more as a space of cultural, for example, biotechnological or psychopharmacological, intervention (Rabinow 1996a; Rose 2007: 26; Malabou 2008). The case of hallucinogens shows that not only the effects of weak drugs are molded contextually. It will not occur to anyone who has ever experienced the mind-blowing effects of LSD or psilocybin that he might have taken sugar pills. And yet, as Studerus's study and the ethnographic vignettes presented in this chapter have shown, the activity of these substances is pharmacologically underdetermined. This is not about the fact that a weak pharmaceutical stimulus can receive different cultural interpretations, but about the observation that one and the same strong stimulus can produce very different, if partially connected biological—or rather, biocultural—effects.

By asserting this ontological stance, I have left the level of second-order observations—that is, (ethnographic) observations of other people's observations (the "native's point of view") that do not attend to the objects of the latter. The reader might have realized that I have treated in a realist manner not only my own carefully crafted ethnographic descriptions but also the psychological and neuroscientific studies discussed—with various caveats and qualifications based on my knowledge of how their truth claims were produced. But realism and constructivism are not mutually exclusive (Latour 1999). Without reverting to a mode of critique that would presuppose an external subject position countering the examined epistemic culture, I have positioned myself anthropologically and psychopharmacologically vis-à-vis the relationship between humans and drugs in opposition to two of my key informants. Not a comfortable situation for an anthropologist, even if I was not the first to encounter it. During his research on the Trobriand Islands in the 1910s, Bronislaw Malinowski developed a paradigm of anthropological fieldwork that would shape the discipline like no other, referring to his own aggressive interrogation of beliefs, which his informants took for granted, as pushing them "to the metaphysical wall"; and, in the process, he occasionally found himself up against this wall as well (Stocking 1992: 45–46). Such confrontations can be highly instructive, even though it took me a while to make sense of the disagreement I had provoked.

For only after this debate did I come to realize the value of Quednow's and Studerus's responses to what they had perceived as my overemphasis on set and setting. What they taught me was that, yes, set and setting did matter, but, more importantly, these theoretically controllable cultural determinants were much weaker than countercultural psychologists and social constructivist anthropologists had thought. Studerus and colleagues (2012: 9) wrote: "There were still relatively large proportions of unexplained variances in the outcome variables. For instance, more than 80% of the variance of the outcome variable *Anxiety* was left unexplained, suggesting that there is considerable unpredictability in anxious reactions to psilocybin—even under highly standardized conditions." The problem of being unable to stabilize the effects of psychotropic drugs under experimental conditions had haunted pharmacopsychology since its inception in late nineteenth-century Germany (Snelders et al. 2006; Balz 2010: 67–73), but it culminated a century later in psychedelic research. On the theoretical level, this wildness of hallucinogens and the complexity of cultural contexts pose a real challenge to both pharmacologicalism (assuming that strong drugs always have the same predictable effects) and social constructivism (presupposing that human culture has the power to shape the natural world in its own image). But it also poses a very practical challenge to the revival of clinical applications of hallucinogens.

When I interviewed Rick Doblin in 2010, he told me that the contingency and uncontrollable complexity of the effects of psychedelic drugs was turning out to be a real problem for MAPS' attempts to globalize its clinical trials with ecstasy, psilocybin, and LSD. At the time, MAPS-sponsored research groups were testing the MDMA treatment of post-traumatic stress disorder in the United States, Canada, and Switzerland. But they had also been trying to set up studies in Israel and Jordan, hoping that healing the wounds of war and terrorism would contribute to peacemaking in the Middle East. However, preliminary analyses of the ongoing trials revealed that treatment efficacy in Switzerland was less than half as good as in the United States—and the Israeli arm of the study had been so unsuccessful that it had to be closed down (partly because the psychiatrists had refused to acquire firsthand experience with the administered drug). In response, Doblin initiated an elaborate investigation of what was causing these profound differences. Video recordings of therapy sessions were subtitled and then analyzed cross-culturally by independent raters. "What we are finding," Doblin told me, "is that the therapist variable is very important. But there is also culture. Are Swiss people normally more emotionally reserved and more proper? That's their reputation: everything in order. The point about the Swiss results is that MDMA has been better than Zoloft and Paxil [so far the only drugs registered for the treatment of post-traumatic stress disorder]. So it has worked—it's just not phenomenal—whereas, in the US, it's like a cure. The Jordanian study is furthest away from our own culture. Can we make MDMA work even there?" In light of the lack of success in Israel and Switzerland, and considering how difficult it was to find out what exactly was going wrong, Doblin was seriously contemplating a painful step: "We are at the point where we may decide that all of the foreign studies are not working for us and we may abandon the foreign strategy and do all the research in the US."

Twenty years into the revival of psychedelic science, what Sarah Franklin (2005) has called the global biological was on the verge of tripping over all too local biologies and cultural psychologies. The practical problems that hallucinogens pose to twenty-first-century neuropsychopharmacology might serve as an incentive to revisit Wallace's proposal of complementing placebo-controlled trials with culture controls. But the complexity of the networks across which psychedelic drug action is distributed might be too high to be controlled successfully. This makes it difficult for laboratory scientists to extract statistically significant signals from the biocultural noise. Thus, Wallace's culture-controlled trials do not appear to provide a satisfying answer to the question of how to factor in complex environments. If experience is overdetermined by intricate contexts, then field studies, which by definition include rather than conceal the variegated features of place, appear to be a more suitable approach than controlled experiments. But they only play a very marginal role in psychopharmacology and cannot establish statistical correlations, not to mention causal links. Moreover, drug experimentation outside of controlled settings tends to put subjects at greater risk, as became apparent in early naturalistic studies with LSD and other experimental drugs (like the one conducted by Leary with New York artists and intellectuals, one of whom attempted suicide after ingesting mescaline—this was shortly before such research in the wild was curtailed by the Kefauver-Harris amendments in 1962 [Greenfield 2006: 138–142]).[7] Yet, one of the great challenges facing the life sciences today is to devise methods that do not—not even for heuristic purposes—aim at reduction but instead measure up to the complexity of life itself (Mitchell 2009). In the next chapter, we will see how contemporary model psychosis research can be seen as a response to this problem.

THE CEREBRAL REDUCING VALVE: BETWEEN THE ANIMAL AND THE DIVINE

In their book *The Varieties of Psychedelic Experience* (1966), the hallucinogen researchers Robert Masters and Jean Houston argued that, whether a subject lapsed into transient psychosis or had a genuine religious experience was determined by set and setting. Psychotic episodes were most likely, they claimed, in a clinical environment where scientific personnel mishandled the session by leading test persons to expect the experience of a "model psychosis" (51, 136). By contrast, in a supportive setting, 6 out of 206 subjects had what Masters and Houston counted as an authentic religious experience. Considering that these 6 were more mature people who had previously engaged in spiritual exercises such as meditation, or at least had demonstrated a sustained interest in unitive experiences, the researchers were not as exuberant about the possibility of a democratization of mysticism as Leary and other colleagues at the time (257, 307). A cultural relativist might take these findings to indicate that mystical and psychotic experiences are socially constructed (even though not just discursively: Masters and Houston emphasized the role of the physical environment as an "objective climate" [136]). Both types of experience are contingent on set and setting—and a good dose of chance.

However, in Huxley's rearticulation of the perennial philosophy, which had been so enormously influential in the psychedelic movement, a very different view prevailed. Truth value was equally attributed to mystical and psychotic experiences. This belief was based on a peculiar but momentous conception of neuronal humanity as situated between the animal and the divine, a belief that originated from late nineteenth- and early twentieth-century psychological and philosophical discourse. Following Henri Bergson, William James, and Charlie Dunbar Broad, Huxley (2009/1954: 22ff.) thought of the brain as an organ of filtration for spiritual life. From Bergson (1932: 272–273) and Broad (1949: 306), Huxley (2009/1954: 26) took over the assumption that "each person is at each moment potentially capable of remembering all that has ever happened to him and of perceiving everything that is happening everywhere in the universe. The function of the brain and the nervous system is to protect us from being overwhelmed and confused by this mass of largely useless and irrelevant knowledge, by shutting out most of what we should otherwise perceive or remember at any moment, and leaving only that very small and special selection which is likely to be practically useful." This filter mechanism barred access to the "beyond" while aiding biological survival. In his lecture titled "Human Immortality" (1999/1898), William James imagined that the brain's permeability for the constant flood of spiritual energy could rise and fall depending on whether one was asleep or awake. But, when the brain died, "the sphere of being that supplied the consciousness would still be intact; and in that more real world with which, even whilst here, it was continuous, the consciousness might, in ways unknown to us, continue still" (1111).[8] Against the background of his own mescaline experience, Huxley assumed that a hallucinogen intoxication would impair the efficiency of a "cerebral reducing valve." As a result, not only would the physical and sociocultural setting impress itself more than usual, but the normally filtered out cosmic stream of consciousness would inundate the individual mind:

> As Mind at Large seeps past the no longer watertight valve, all kinds of biologically useless things start to happen. In some cases there may be extra-sensory perceptions. Other persons discover a world of visionary beauty. To others again is revealed the glory, the infinite value and meaningfulness of naked existence, of the given, unconceptualized event. In the final stage of egolessness there is an "obscure knowledge" that All is in all—that All is actually each. This is as near, I take it, as a finite mind can ever come to "perceiving everything that is happening everywhere in the universe." (Huxley 2009/1954: 26)

Huxley's explanation contains a number of interesting elements that continued to play important roles in contemporary scientific and nonscientific discourses on psychedelic drugs. The fact that twenty-first-century hallucinogen researchers still employ the filter paradigm seems remarkable, for neuroscience has come to emphasize that the brain constructs its image of the world instead of being merely receptive—especially so in altered states of consciousness (Roth 1997: 23; Hobson 2001). Huxley (2009/1954: 22), however, followed Bergson and Broad in presenting the central nervous system as "*eliminative and not productive.*" Presenting the brain as a reducing valve rather than a system actively generating a mental picture of the world has both epistemological and ontological implications with respect to the psychedelic experience. If the brain does not autopoietically make up or add anything, then the inner experience needs to have an external referent. Accordingly, so-called hallucinogenic drugs do not actually produce hallucinations, illusions, and delusions; they provide access to a dimension of reality that remains inaccessible to human beings in normal waking states, a divine or supernatural sphere not conducive to biological survival but edifying to spiritual animals striving for more ethereal goals than self-preservation and procreation.

In the state of psychosis, Huxley (2009/1954) argued, the problem was therefore not that delusions and hallucinations made the subject lose contact with external reality. On the contrary. Schizophrenia, he claimed, "consisted in the inability to take refuge from inner and outer reality (as the sane person habitually does) in the homemade universe of common sense—the strictly human world of useful notions, shared symbols and socially acceptable conventions" (56). In Huxley's cosmology, culture protected the human brain against an otherwise overwhelming spiritual reality. Both hallucinogens and psychosis provided access to this realm, which could be experienced as heaven—but also as hell: "The schizophrenic is like a man permanently under the influence of mescaline, and therefore unable to shut off the experience of a reality which he is not holy enough to live with, which he cannot explain away because it never permits him to look at the world with merely human eyes, scares him into interpreting its unremitting strangeness, its burning intensity of significance, as the manifestations of human or even cosmic malevolence" (56).

Contemporary model psychosis research has adopted, but secularized, this filter paradigm. To explain altered states of consciousness, Vollenweider developed a neurocybernetic model of sensory information processing. In his cortico-striato-thalamo-cortical model, the thalamus appears as a filter reducing the flow of information from the sense organs to the cerebral cortex, protecting it against sensory overload, which would result in the formation of psychotic symptoms. As a cybernetic model it implies a theory that provides a set of testable hypotheses. Based on a circuit diagram of CSTC feedback loops showing the activating and inhibiting connections between different brain areas and neurotransmitters that enable these areas to regulate each other, Vollenweider postulated that a reduction of glutamatergic neurotransmission by the glutamate receptor antagonist ketamine, as well as a stimulation of the serotonergic system by the serotonin receptor agonist psilocybin, would equally result in an opening of the thalamic filter and, consequently, in sensory overload and metabolic activation of the frontal cortex. Moving from cybernetic representation to pharmacological intervention, Vollenweider corroborated this hypothesis experimentally by measuring the outcome with positron-emission tomography and psychometric questionnaires such as the APZ (Vollenweider et al. 1997b; Vollenweider 1998).[9]

Ironically, it was Rael Cahn and Michael Kometer's study, with all its Huxleyan undertones, that eventually came to call into question this filter, or "gating," paradigm. When analyzing the data of the Kanizsa triangle experiment, they found a dose-dependent decrease in a particular component of the electroencephalographic response that functionally correlated to a decreased binding of the illusionary triangles that had been found after administration of psilocybin and in schizophrenic patients. The weaker a brain responded to the gestalt between the three Pac-Men, the stronger were the visual hallucinations reported by the subject (Kometer et al. 2010). Was it possible that, after all, psychedelics did not provoke a sensory overload? Did people perceive even less—while imagining more?

Although they refrained from such speculations in their published article, Kometer and Vollenweider conjectured that their finding challenged the psychedelic filter paradigm. In light of a pilot study suggesting that psilocybin might possibly increase empathy, Kometer told me: "Psilocybin makes you emotionally more sensitive. That is why the setting has such a strong impact. And not because it enhances perception." For Vollenweider, this was puzzling. He explained to me:

> Michael Kometer's data show that external stimuli are processed differently while the internal production of stimuli is increased. This internal activation of frontal cortex and anterior cyngulate gyrus makes people turn inward. This is difficult to understand because, subjectively, you feel that you see the world more differentiated, more detailed, more intensive, almost microscopically. Sometimes everything becomes so big and you can see every grain of dust. But, when you look at the pathway where visual processing takes place, you see a deterioration throughout. That's paradoxical.

In the history of hallucinogen research, this paradox of subjectively enhanced and objectively impaired capacities had previously been encountered in studies on color perception (Hartman and Hollister 1963), musical tone discrimination (Vannini and Venturini 1999: 375–380), and artistic creativity (Berge 1999).[10] Did it point to a shortcoming of contemporary neuroscience in bridging the "explanatory gap" between subjective experience and brain mechanism (Levine 1983)? Or did these experiments indicate that subjects' drug experiences were completely illusory (as could be expected from a class of substances referred to as "hallucinogens")? And, if so, would such a determination prove these experiences spiritually worthless, maybe even harmful?

The question of the referent of drug-induced spiritual experiences echoed Cahn's hope that neuroscientific work would help corroborate unitive states as "reflecting something that's real about our collective reality." Here, the problem of the ontological status of the spiritual in relation to nature and culture was raised again in the form that late nineteenth-century psychic research had given to it (Monroe 2008). This form, adopted by Bergson, Broad, Huxley, and, in part, James, conceived of spiritual experience in analogy to perception. If the cerebral filter became more permeable, Bergson (1932: 274) reasoned, then "a gleam from this unknown world reaches us, visible to our bodily eyes," fortifying "belief in the life beyond." This belief, he hoped, could be "attained through the furtherance of scientific experiment" (274).

Kometer, by contrast, espoused a model closer to the pragmatist James of *The Varieties of Religious Experience* (1958/1902) than to the metaphysically speculative James of the lecture "Human Immortality" (1999/1898): "Of course, as a scientist, I would like to know what is true and what is not true," Kometer told me. "But, since our brain happens to be built the way it is, we cannot but perceive our environment in any other way. Therefore, I have come to accept the fact that we cannot determine the truth value of these experiences. We have to be pragmatic. What matters to me is that they really benefit me—no matter whether they are true or not." What can be gained from psychedelic experiences, Kometer said, was a sense of being part of a bigger context and of thinking in more collective than individualistic terms. Independent of whether they referred to an external reality or not, all states of mind were neurally conditioned, James had argued. Therefore, their significance had to be tested not for their origin but for their ethical and spiritual consequences.

Following in the footsteps of James, Bruno Latour (2002, 2005) has recently called for a reorientation of religion from transcendence to immanence by discarding the belief in a beyond. This stance conceives of religion as not about establishing or taking for granted the existence of supernatural facts but about bringing people closer together, here and now. Against this background, Latour argues against modeling religion on science (as in creationist readings of the Book of Genesis) or science on religion (as in psychical research). Of course, Latour's account of religion is prescriptive, not descriptive: philosophical, not ethnographic. But, considering the prominent role of the Jamesian tradition in the fields of psychedelic science and consciousness research, it helps to understand and conceptualize the relationship between science and religion in the pragmatist matrix of contemporary neuropsychedelia. In the following two chapters, we will see that this matrix accommodated not only hallucinogen researchers' reflections on experimental mysticism but also their research on experimental psychoses.

FIGURE 1. Celebration of Albert Hofmann's hundredth birthday at the LSD Symposium in 2006 (see chapter 1). Photo by author.
FIGURE 2. Swiss psilocybin, freshly encapsulated (see chapter 2). Photo by author.

FIGURE 3. Sheep looking down on the Burghölzli cafeteria (see chapter 3).
Photo by author.
FIGURE 4. Pharmacopsychologist Boris Quednow visiting the drug-checking
laboratory of the Cantonal Pharmacist's Office, Berne, at the Hive Club in Zurich
(see chapter 2 for the lab, chapter 3 for Quednow). Photo by author.

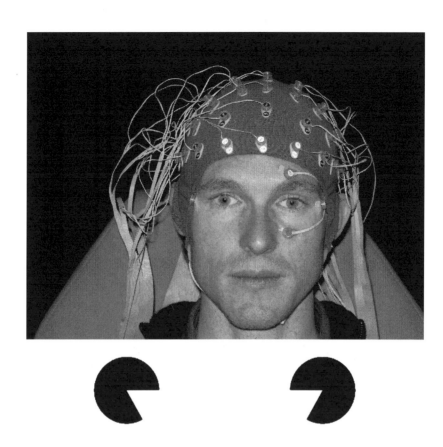

FIGURE 5. The anthropologist as experimental subject (see chapter 3). Photo by Felix Hasler.
FIGURE 6. Kanizsa triangle (see chapter 3). Drawn by author.

FIGURE 7. Franz Vollenweider in his laboratory (see chapter 3). Photo by author.
FIGURE 8. Neuroimaging facility at the University Hospital in Zurich (see chapter 3). Photo by author.

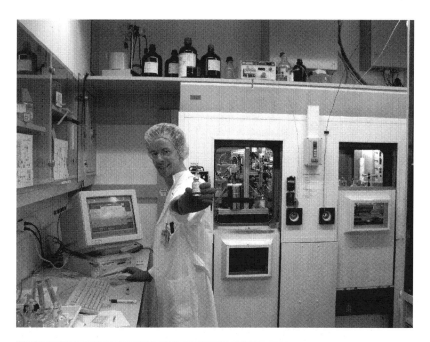

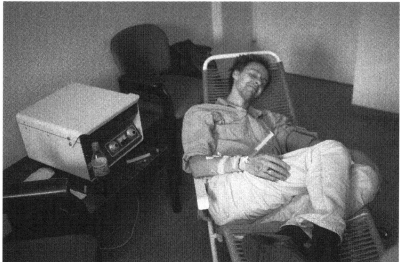

FIGURE 9. Pharmacologist Felix Hasler synthesizing a radio tracer for a PET scan (see chapter 3). Photo by author.

FIGURE 10. Felix Hasler serving as test subject in his own 1997 psilocybin study (see chapter 3)—the one that government official Paul Dietschy and pharmacology professor Rudolf Brenneisen had so passionately fought over. Courtesy of Felix Hasler.

FIGURE 11. Theater director Daniel Wetzel trying out computer goggles for the ketamine study, in which he participated as an experimental subject (see chapter 4). Photo by author.
FIGURE 12. Crammed experimental space in Mark Geyer's laboratory at the University of California, San Diego (see chapter 5). Photo by author.

FIGURE 13. Rat in the Plexiglas tube of a startle chamber (see chapter 5). Photo by author.
FIGURE 14. Psychopharmacologist and his mice before injecting them with angel dust (PCP) (see chapter 5). Photo by author.

FIGURE 15. Laboratory technicians hunting a rat, which escaped under the influence of pharmahuasca (see chapter 5). Photo by author.

4

Enacting Experimental Psychoses

CECI N'EST PAS UNE PSYCHOSE—OR IS IT?

Anthropological fieldwork is an erratic process. It has often been described as a form of participant observation. But participation presupposes that the people one intends to study welcome it. And there needs to be enough interesting activity to merit such sustained observation. Thus, before a stroke of luck brought me to Switzerland, I had spent a few months fishing for an appropriate field site. I briefly explored the psychonaut scene in California, visiting psychedelic chemist Alexander Shulgin and his wife, Ann, on their farm in Lafayette, and I talked to the founders of the drug website www.erowid.org at a Fungus Fair in Oakland (Langlitz 2009). In Germany, I had dinner with the photographer Andreas Gursky, whose aesthetic, even though far removed from the psychedelic art of the sixties, was inspired by his early LSD experiences (Gursky and Jocks 1999). When I eventually settled on academic hallucinogen research instead of underground science and art, I met the psychiatrist Torsten Passie, who was running an out-patient heroin clinic (based on the Swiss model) and, with his doctoral student Oliver Bosch, had conducted a psilocybin study at Hannover Medical School, in which I participated as a test subject. I also visited Euphrosyne Gouzoulis-Mayfrank, a Greek German professor of psychiatry at the University of Cologne who had previously been part of the group around Leo Hermle that had revived German model psychosis research in the mid-1980s. Even though both Passie and Gouzoulis were conducting hallucinogen research, they were doing it alongside their clinical duties and, because of Germany's peculiar ethics tradition, they had to find licensed physicians or other medical personnel as test subjects. For these reasons, there would have been little day-to-day research activity for me to observe. However, I used these encounters to conduct interviews.

Based on my conversations with Gouzoulis, as well as archival research on the history of the hallucinogen model of psychosis, I wrote an English article titled "Ceci n'est pas une psychose" (2006a). Alluding to the modernist problematization of representation in René Magritte's famous painting *Ceci n'est pas une pipe*, I argued that contemporary model psychosis researchers knew full well that hallucinogen intoxication was not a schizophrenic psychosis. Instead of making ontological claims about the nature of the psychedelic experience, they used the model in a pragmatic spirit to generate working hypotheses about schizophrenia. When I arrived at Franz Vollenweider's lab—thanks to Gouzoulis's assistant who had put me in touch with Boris Quednow—the researchers there invited me to present in their colloquium the paper I had written in light of my interviews with the Cologne group. During the discussion that followed, Vollenweider snarled at me: "There is absolutely no doubt that hallucinogens cause psychosis. That's already the case by definition. There is nothing to compare [between inebriation and psychosis]. In psychiatry, all ego dissolutions, including religious experiences, are pathological."

I was dumbstruck. Vollenweider's exclamation sounded like a reductionist inversion of what the philosopher of religion Walter Stace had said about the psychedelic experience in the sixties: "It's not a matter of being *similar* to mystical experience, it *is* a mystical experience" (quoted in H. Smith 1964: 524). But Vollenweider (1992/93: 20) himself had written in an early MAPS newsletter that "psychedelic experiences are not simply psychotic processes." Had he changed his mind? Was the statement in the newsletter nothing but lip service to MAPS, which disliked the pathologization of hallucinogen experiences? Did his response to my presentation serve as a reminder that these serious medical researchers did not want to be lumped together with esoteric drug mystics? It took me a long time to understand that none of this was the case. But to stay true to the logic of discovery in ethnographic work, we should start with another vignette.

A THEATRICAL PET SCAN

The experiment took place in the PET center located in the basement of the University Hospital in Zurich. At 8:30 AM, I met with Honza

Samotar,[1] the neuroscientist from the Vollenweider group running the study, and his test subject Daniel Wetzel.

Wetzel was a German theater director in his late thirties who usually lived in Berlin and Athens. He was in town for a production at Zurich's main playhouse. *Blaiberg und sweetheart19* was a theatrical performance without actors. The people on stage were laymen who did not play roles but were just themselves: presentation instead of representation. And yet this was no amateur theater. Wetzel and his two partners from Rimini Protokoll looked at the participants of their plays as "experts" of their particular spheres of life. The players were, on the one hand, a heart transplant patient and an assistant medical technician who worked with organ transplantations and, on the other hand, the manager of a dating agency that introduced Russian women to Swiss men as well as an organizer of so-called speed-flirting events. *Blaiberg und sweetheart19* (named for one of the first cardiac transplant patients and a typical screen name of a user of matchmaking websites) explored associations between these two contemporary economies of hearts. Rimini Protokoll had been a driving force in the recent renaissance of documentary theater in Germany. Each of the group's projects required a significant amount of "para-ethnographic" (Holmes and Marcus 2004) research to identify potential performers and to develop and entwine their stories in collaboration with them. In the course of such research, Wetzel had interviewed Samotar about the neurobiology of love. He had become interested in the suffusion of people's self-conceptions with medical knowledge after meeting the heart transplant patient from his play, who had largely come to conceive of herself in medical terms. Wetzel hoped to gain a better understanding of such forms of subjectivity by serving as a test subject in a medical experiment himself. That was how he got here, to the University Hospital in Zurich. He looked around the PET center and curiously followed what was happening to him. In his eyes, the neuroimaging facility was an alternative stage—in accordance with Rimini Protokoll's basic idea of looking for theatricality not in the playhouse but in real life (Dreysse and Malzacher 2007).[2]

The experiment was based on the hallucinogen model of psychosis and was designed as a blocker study. In his doctoral research, Samotar was examining to what extent the antipsychotic drugs ketanserin and haloperidol could block the psychosis-like deficits induced by the hallucinogen ketamine, in a manner that was neuropsychologically quantifiable and that changed brain perfusion as measured by positron-emission tomography. Wetzel was first injected with haloperidol, and only in the second half of the experiment, when he had already been lying in the PET scanner for forty-five minutes, was ketamine administered through an intravenous drip. Eventually, the results would be compared with those of a ketamine-only session, which Wetzel had already undergone. The whole measurement took one and a half hours, during which he had to lie still in the tube. During this time, he took neuropsychological tests on a computer screen built into a bulky pair of goggles fixed to his forehead (see figure 11). One ability that was assessed repeatedly was rapid visual processing, a measure of sustained attention. For this purpose, Wetzel had to follow a stream of fast-changing digits, pressing a button whenever certain three-figure sequences appeared—a task that required a significant degree of concentration. Ketamine, however, induced an attention deficit comparable to that suffered by schizophrenic patients (possibly on a neurochemical level, which is much more basic than experiential content of such existential importance that subjects would lose interest in the experimental situation altogether). The study examined whether this hallucinogenic effect could be counteracted by antipsychotic drugs. Furthermore, these findings were correlated with PET measurements of metabolic activity in different brain areas known to be involved in the pathogenesis of schizophrenia.

In the short intervals between scans and neuropsychological tasks, I took photos of Wetzel in the brain scanner. I walked around this massive machine trying out different angles. Shortly after the ketamine began running into his veins, this motion became part of Wetzel's trip. He was firmly fixed in the tube and had to stare at the ring of detector units enclosing the upper part of his body. But, in his peripheral vision, he could see me whirling around the room. Then he was out there with me and we were dancing together through a green space. In his synthetic phantasmagoria, my movements were transfigured into an elaborate choreography involving the two of us.

Wetzel's subjective experience was evaluated with an itemized questionnaire, a modified version of Adolf Dittrich's APZ, before the administration of haloperidol as well as before and after the additional infusion of ketamine. This was a lengthy and excruciating procedure, as the test subject needed to rate ninety-four items. With a loud, solemn, and monotonous voice, Samotar read out the whole questionnaire, point by point, while Wetzel had to use a trackball to assess each statement on a scale on the computer screen in front of him: "I felt like I was in a wonderful other world." "I felt like a doll on a string or a marionette." "A voice commented on everything I thought although no one was there." "I saw strange things, which I now know were not real." "I observed myself as though I were a stranger." "Worries and fears of everyday life felt irrelevant." "I felt connected to higher powers." "My experience had a religious character." All of a sudden, after the last of this extensive list of items, we heard Wetzel crying out in the PET scanner: "Heiner Müller! . . . This language! A great performance!"[3]

At long last, Wetzel was released from the interior of the machine. He seemed shaky. The ketamine would continue to affect his motor coordination for a few more minutes and his speech was still slurred. But soon he began to answer our questions concerning his drug experience. I asked him about his curious exit from the scanner. Samotar's voice, he said, had reminded him of the way the East German playwright and stage director Heiner Müller used to read texts, especially his own or those of Bertolt Brecht. Later on, Wetzel provided a more detailed explanation:

> I believe I exclaimed "Heiner Müller!" because the researcher had a very peculiar manner of reading out the questions from the questionnaire. It reminded me of how you could always hear the line breaks in Müller's readings. Thus, the spoken language was broken by the written text. His speech did not follow interpersonal discourse but vehemently called attention to the fact that it was reading. Probably, the researcher did not make these short, weird pauses at every line break like Müller, but tried to sound neutral.
>
> I think I called out "Heiner Müller!" to make a desperate joke, to produce a comic relief (unsuccessfully so) because being exposed to the vehemence of such a text-like speech in the experimental setting also had an unpleasant military feel to it. In contrast to Müller, who always read softly and calmly, the researcher spoke as if he had been implanted with a megaphone. That was my impression during the trial. There was something comical about that, since it sounded stilted, unnatural, forcedly neutral.
>
> And if you described the researcher's speech as a performative in Austin's sense, then it would be a speech emphasizing its textuality. With every word, even with every syllable, it stressed the elaborateness, the official character marking the sentences from the questionnaire. Far off from any spontaneous communication. A certain gesture of abstraction, a depersonalized speech, which you could often hear in Müller's productions in direct continuation of Brecht's aesthetics and theory of theater. There, the text was supposed to become audible as a completely independent parameter, cut off from techniques of empathy and the actor's desire for identification. For this purpose, it had to be depsychologized, formalized, and spoken on the basis of a structure contrary to psychological (bourgeois) semantics. In the experiment, the researcher sounded similar to that, making an exaggerated effort

to provide expressions for my state of mind ("I had a religious feeling") far beyond any empathy.

By looking at the performative dimension of the experiment, Wetzel read one of the leitmotifs of modernist art, the break with representation, into the scientific setting. It was one of Heiner Müller's credos that on stage the text had to be worked with, not as a mere representation of reality, but as a reality of its own. Any understanding had to be preceded by a sensual perception of the text's materiality (Birkenhauer 2004). In the attempt to objectify his subjective experience with the help of an itemized self-rating scale, Wetzel found a distant echo of the Brechtian alienation effects in twentieth-century theater that prevented the audience from losing itself in the character created by the actor. By calling attention to the theatrical practice of representation, Brecht had wanted to break its illusionism.

But the problem of representation also manifested on a second level. Samotar asked Wetzel how he had experienced the simultaneous ingestion of both psychotomimetic and antipsychotic drugs in comparison with the previous session, in which he had received the hallucinogen alone. Wetzel answered that, qualitatively, the experiences had not been very different from each other. In fact, under the influence of haloperidol the visions might have been even more pronounced. To my own astonishment, Samotar was not surprised. Most test subjects, he said, reported that, subjectively, haloperidol made hardly any difference. Vollenweider (1998) had actually previously written about the fact that such classical antipsychotics intensified rather than ameliorated LSD- and psilocybin-induced psychoses (see Colpaert 2003: 319). Furthermore, Wetzel not only felt that questionnaire items such as "I had a religious feeling" did not apply to his experience but also could not imagine that it resembled a state of schizophrenia. For him, the experience seemed to have been primarily a matter of aesthetics. Nevertheless, hallucinogen intoxication was supposed to serve as a model of psychosis. How, then, was this pharmacologically induced deviation from everyday consciousness used to represent schizophrenia, and what did neuropsychopharmacologists gain from this application of hallucinogenic drugs?

WHAT IS IT LIKE TO BE MAD?

At the end of the eighteenth century, medical researchers' attempts to mimic mental disorders by administering different kinds of drugs (wolfsbane, camphor, opium) had already been discussed in Kant's *Anthro-pology from a Pragmatic Point of View* (2006/1798: 322). Then, in the late 1830s, while accompanying a patient traveling in the Middle East, the French psychiatrist Jacques-Joseph Moreau de Tours heard an Egyptian talking about his encounter with a djinn, according to Arab and Muslim mythology a spirit ranking between angels and humans. Moreau attributed the man's experience to his consumption of hashish and decided to try the drug for himself. He believed that the resulting experience resembled that of his mentally ill patients. Back home, he began to experiment with hashish at the Hôpital de Bicêtre and in a Paris salon, the Club de Haschischins. In his study *Du haschisch et d'aliénation mentale: Études psychologiques* (1845), Moreau described the effects of hashish on healthy subjects—among them poets such as Charles Baudelaire, Honoré de Balzac, Théophile Gautier, and Gérard de Nerval. He wrote, "In the way in which it affects the mental faculties, hashish gives to whoever submits to its influence the power to study in himself the mental disorders that characterize insanity, or at least the intellectual modifications that are the beginning of all forms of mental illness" (quoted in Jay 1999: 20).

The goal of this psychiatric appropriation of the effects of the drug was to allow physicians and artists to acquire personal insights into the supposed nucleus from which all psychopathological phenomena spread. Having experienced such states firsthand, and being well suited to articulate these *états mixtes,* self-experimenting physicians and artists were meant to serve as mediators between the worlds of madness and reason (Solhdju 2011: 89–144). As a student of Jean Etienne Dominique Esquirol, Moreau was committed to the reform of French asylums and hoped that psychiatric self-experimentation with hashish would enable his colleagues to better understand their patients. The epistemic move from external observation of visible symptoms to grasping mental illness from within was meant to help overcome the social exclusion of the mad based on the fact that, experientially, psychiatric patients had remained alien to their doctors (Foucault 2006: 277–284). However, as a medical practice, Moreau's approach did not gain currency. The historian of psychopharmacology David Healy (1997: 113) writes: "Despite the widespread use of a variety of consciousness-altering agents during the nineteenth century, Moreau's idea was too radical. It was a century before it was picked up again."

When, in 1921, the German psychiatrist Kurt Beringer adopted Moreau's approach at the University of Heidelberg, he used mescaline (a synthetic version had become available two years prior) instead of hashish and considered the intoxication a model of psychosis, not of delirium.[4] In *Der Meskalinrausch* (1927), Beringer described how he had tried to use mescaline diagnostically as a probe to explore a patient's personality. Anticipating psycholytic therapy, he expected the contents of the psychotic experiences provoked by the drug to reveal something about the subject's individual constitution and unconscious processes. Although he did find that the momentary psychological condition influenced the effects of the drug, he could not identify any stable relationship between character and drug experience. No inner truth came to the fore. Instead Beringer reported a variety of misperceptions of reality. Mescaline induced disturbances of perception, illusions, and visual, but sometimes also acoustic, hallucinations and synesthesias; profound alterations in time perception; psychomotor inhibition; and varying alterations in affect and thought. In his eyes, this symptomatology was sufficiently similar to that of acute schizophrenia to justify the employment of mescaline-induced states as an artificial "model of psychosis," a term first used by Emil Kraepelin (1882; cf. Müller et al. 2006). Such a model would allow studying psychoses under controlled experimental conditions on the level of phenomenology as well as objective psychopathology.

In Heidelberg, Beringer established Moreau's approach as a pedagogical practice. The majority of the participants in his mescaline trial were medical students and doctors. Often his own residents were given the drug, not only in a laboratory, but also while working on the psychiatric ward. By serving as test subjects they not only contributed to the methodical production of psychiatric knowledge; the induction of an artificial psychosis also allowed them to learn, by way of personal experience, about one of the conditions they were treating. Being trained in the heyday of phenomenological psychiatry, Beringer's residents were expected to know what it was like to be schizophrenic.

In his textbook *General Psychopathology* (1963; first published in 1913), Beringer's Heidelberg colleague Karl Jaspers addressed the problem of subjectivity in the way it had emerged in the nineteenth century, as the radical privacy of mental states: "Since we can never perceive the psychic experiences of others in any direct fashion, as with physical phenomena, we can only make some kind of representation of them" (55). In Beringer's model of psychosis, the medium of representation was the self-experimenting subject's own mind. The mescaline experience served as a model of the experience of the acute stages of schizophrenia. This,

Beringer (1927: 31–32) hoped, would allow the (future) physicians participating in his trial to improve their clinical skills by sharing and understanding the experience of their schizophrenic patients.

Although the training model proposed by Moreau and Beringer was occasionally discussed throughout the twentieth century, it was never systematically implemented. In the spirit of optimism preceding the prohibition of psychedelics, hallucinogen researcher Humphry Osmond (1957: 424) was hopeful that one day such a self-experimental pedagogy would take hold:

> I know of no study dealing specifically with the application of these substances to the training of the workers engaged in many different disciplines who work together in psychiatry. Such training has resulted from experimental work, but only incidentally. Hyde and others have used these substances to enlarge the sympathy of members of a psychiatric staff for patients in their care. Such a journey of self-discovery may one day be obligatory for those working in psychiatry. Although it might not always be pleasant, with care and understanding this experience would be very useful to the trainee.

But from the 1950s onward, the similarity of hallucinogenic experience and schizophrenia was called into question. It might speak to the ambiguity, which the encounter with the writer and mystic Aldous Huxley had induced in this model psychosis researcher, that Osmond played a prominent role in this process as well. Alongside the tightening of legal restrictions, growing doubts about the likeness of psychedelic and schizophrenic experience would undermine both the pedagogic model Osmond was advocating and his biochemical quest for an LSD- or mescaline-like psychosis-inducing molecule in the human metabolism. He wrote: "It is curious that in the lengthy and sometimes heated discussions about the relationship of model psychoses to schizophrenia that smoldered for nearly 50 years, not until 1951 was the difference between a transient, artificially induced, experimental state in a volunteer under laboratory conditions and the prolonged, insidious, creeping illness in an unsuspecting victim whose social life progressively atrophied, clearly recognized" (Osmond 1957: 424).[5] Thus, Osmond began to challenge the hallucinogen model of psychosis, which had framed his own work, by emphasizing that both drug experience and schizophrenia were determined not only by their respective biologies but also by the given circumstances.

The experiential model of psychosis can be analyzed as what Michel Foucault (1997: 199) called a "historically singular form of experience." Foucault proposed to study the historical conditions and consequently also the limits of possibility of particular experiences by attending to three axes: types of understanding, forms of normativity, and modes of relation to oneself and to others—or knowledge, power, and ethics (see Jay 2005: 390–400). Such an analysis allows demarcating the experiences of Beringer's test subjects from that of his schizophrenic patients. His colleagues' self-reports collected in an appendix to *Der Meskalinrausch* indicate that these psychopathologically and pharmacologically literate self-experimenting physicians and medical students had a significantly different understanding of their situation than laymen suffering from the unexpected and alienating onset of psychosis or poisoning after accidentally eating hallucinogenic fungi with their wild mushroom stew (see Letcher 2006: 49–68). The former were, at least most of the time, well aware that they had ingested a mind-altering substance and could rely on the limited duration of its effects. To them, the occurrence of psychopathological symptoms was not unsettling and excruciating but the desirable outcome of a deliberate intervention to be followed with great curiosity. A symptom perceived as pathological in a patient appeared to the self-experimenters as a normal reaction to the given pharmaceutical stimulus. The test subjects encountered the medical personnel examining them as colleagues engaged in a common scientific enterprise, not as authorities in a mental institution. And instead of having to comply with the passive role of patient, their self-experimentation was part of a heroic professional ethos. No wonder many of them remembered their mescaline experiences fondly.

In his famous essay on the epistemological problem of how to understand alien forms of mental life, Thomas Nagel (1974: 439) asked himself what it was like to be a bat—and immediately warned that, to answer this question, it would not be sufficient to imagine oneself having webbing on the arms and flying around with a sonar system to catch insects in one's mouth: "In so far as I can imagine this (which is not very far), it tells me only what it would be like for *me* to behave as a bat behaves. But that is not the question. I want to know what it is like for a *bat* to be a bat. Yet if I try to imagine this, I am restricted to the resources of my own mind, and those resources are inadequate to the task." This argument would also apply to the ingestion of psychedelics for the purpose of understanding what it was like to be schizophrenic. Even if Masters and Houston (1966: 18, 51, 136) had been right in blaming psychosis-like episodes under the influence of psychedelic drugs on set and setting, it appeared questionable how similar these experiences really were to schizophrenia. Ironically, it seemed as if set and setting could liken hallucinogenic experiences to schizophrenic psychoses, but it was also set and setting that put a categorical limit on these approximations.

The current generation of researchers promoting the revival of hallucinogen research have acknowledged the difference in experience between "naturally" occurring psychoses and experimentally induced highs. As they are primarily interested in objectifiable neurobiological and neuropsychological aspects of the model psychoses, their approaches are significantly less challenged by this divergence than Beringer's experiential model. Moreover, Gouzoulis and her colleagues have even tried to turn the dissimilarity into an argument that helps rehabilitate the hallucinogen model of psychosis. If only set and setting of the drug experience and the onset of psychosis are identical, then, they suggest, the experiences would also be identical:

> If somebody is given psychedelics without his knowledge, he cannot recognize the artificial nature of his state. When such experiments were performed, the effects were sometimes indistinguishable from acute paranoid-hallucinatory psychoses. The situation of a patient with initial acute psychosis is comparable with that of somebody who has ingested psychedelic drugs unknowingly. Both experience pervasive alterations of perception, thinking and affectivity and know nothing about the origin of these alterations. Knowledge of the artificial nature of the state is therefore not a valid criterion for distinguishing between acute endogenous psychoses and psychedelically induced altered states of consciousness. (Gouzoulis-Mayfrank et al. 1998: 66; cf. Hermle et al. 1988: 55)

Gouzoulis also attributed educative value to the participation of psychiatric staff in hallucinogen trials. She told me that it improved their "ability to take the patient's perspective, which enables one to feel how best to approach him. If you have experienced yourself how important it is that the other has a reliable presence while keeping a certain distance, you will be able to handle psychotic patients more carefully. Many of our test subjects report back that the experiment made them more empathic and secure in dealing with their patients. But, of course, that's not the primary purpose of our studies."

MODELS OF PSYCHOSIS: EXPERIENTIAL, DESCRIPTIVE, EXPLANATORY

Before elaborating any further what the primary purpose of revived model psychosis research was, we need to explicate more of its epistemological history. For Beringer's model of psychosis was not merely an experiential model. Based on the firsthand experiences of his test subjects, he also established a descriptive model of psychosis. Following Karl Jaspers's (1923: 35) psychiatric phenomenology, Beringer attached great importance to the description of the soul "from inside," drawing from introspective self-reports rather than solely a psychiatrist's clinical gaze on a subject's behavior.[6] The participants of the mescaline trial were supposed to produce written accounts of their experiences. By collecting and analyzing these reports, Beringer produced a general phenomenological account of the psychosis-like effects of mescaline. Following Rachel Ankeny's article "Fashioning Descriptive Models in Biology" (2000), such a description can itself be regarded as a pre-explanatory or descriptive model of mescaline inebriation, which, in turn, served as a model of psychosis. Hence, the descriptive model served as a second-order model of psychosis. In order to fulfill this function, the description had to emphasize those properties that the intoxication had in common with psychotic, particularly schizophrenic, episodes.

Beringer's phenomenological account was developed through a process of abstraction. What was presented as the prototype of mescaline inebriation was an ideal-typical construct. It presented a certain pattern of recurring symptoms, which Beringer brought out by analyzing the reports of approximately sixty subjects. From these he tried to extrapolate what mescaline did as such—independent of the individual test persons and changing situations. The multitude of responses the drug provoked in different people at different points in time made it particularly difficult to identify the properties attributable to the drug itself. However, Beringer (1927: iii) claimed that by looking at a sufficiently great number of experiments he had been able to extract a recurrent set of symptoms, which he identified as effects of the drug (as opposed to those produced by the states and traits of the test subjects).[7] This is what pharmacologicalism looked like before the age of randomized placebo-controlled trials.

The resulting descriptive model was no objective representation of psychosis. The phenomenological approach to psychiatry for which the Heidelberg clinic was well-known was primarily informed by another epistemic virtue preceding objectivity, namely, truth-to-nature. Since the eighteenth century, this form of knowing had aspired to the extraction of the typical from the mass of natural particulars. Instead of having mechanical instruments record every insignificant detail to be conveyed, without further mediation, an experienced researcher was expected to select, compare, judge, and generalize on the basis of sustained observation. When objectivity emerged a century later, it did not replace but rather dislocated truth-to-nature (Daston and Galison 2007: 55–113). One of the practices in which truth-to-nature was rejuvenated was the formation of ideal types, which another, recently deceased member on the Heidelberg faculty, Max Weber (1949/1904), had proposed as a method for the cultural sciences. At about the same time as the German psychologist Heinrich Klüver (1926, 1928) (by then already at the University of Minnesota) described a number of typical geometric patterns, which subjects reported seeing under the influence of mescaline, he also published an article on the reception of Weber's notion of ideal types in psychology and psychopathology, especially in the work of Weber's friend Karl Jaspers. In the tradition of truth-to-nature and in opposition to objectivity, Klüver emphasized that the quality of any such type classification was largely dependent on the knowledge and experience of the individual author (a contingency that the proponents of objectivity had sought to eliminate). When Beringer (1927) derived the essential character of "the" mescaline inebriation from the multitude of collected experience reports, he did not average them (not least because they were qualitative, not quantitative accounts) but instead selected the features he knew to be typical of the phenomenon. Regarding the formation of such ideal types, Weber (1949/1904: 111) had cautioned his readers not to mistake them for objective knowledge: they only provided "concepts and judgments"—or descriptive models, we might add—"which are neither empirical reality nor reproductions of it but which facilitate its analytical ordering in a valid manner."

The empirical material from which Beringer developed his account of the mescaline inebriation consisted of introspective self-observations. But, like Moreau before him, Beringer was convinced that mental disorders were disorders of the brain. Thus, he anticipated that eventually his description of analogies between hallucinogen intoxication and acute stages of schizophrenia would serve as a basis for investigating the physical foundations of the psychopathological phenomena, which these conditions had in common. He hoped that one day biochemical research on the effects of mescaline might reveal "the disorders of intermediary metabolic processes (autointoxication process, endocrine metabolic toxins, etc.)" in the acute phase of schizophrenia (Beringer 1927: 114). But his own approach did not provide the means to directly examine the biological substratum of mescaline inebriation. The life processes underlying the drug's effects and the existence of endogenous psychosis-inducing molecules remained purely speculative. As a phenomenological psychiatrist, Beringer was neither eager to push this kind of theorizing much further nor did he make an effort to study the biochemistry of mescaline intoxication and schizophrenia himself. After all, phenomenological psychiatry was more committed to "understanding" than to explaining mental illness causally.

But other researchers used Beringer's account as a framework for the exploration of explanatory questions. The shift from Beringer's descriptive, pre-explanatory model to explanatory models of psychosis took place in the 1950s. At the time, several groundbreaking discoveries and innovations in the field of psychopharmacology initiated a process of reorientation in psychiatry toward the life sciences (Thuillier 1999). Of particular importance were the discoveries of lysergic acid diethylamide by the Swiss pharmaceutical company Sandoz in 1943 and of the antipsychotic chlorpromazine by the French company Rhône-Poulenc in 1951. LSD soon eclipsed mescaline as the leading hallucinogenic drug in psychiatry and became one of the discipline's most important research tools. Meanwhile, chlorpromazine not only helped to alleviate certain symptoms of schizophrenia but was also capable of inhibiting some of the effects of LSD and mescaline (Hoch 1955; Denber and Merlis 1956). At the time, the drug was categorized as an "ataractic," after the Greek term *ataraxia* for peace of mind—one of the main spiritual goals of ancient philosophy (Hadot 1995). Ataractics (soon to be denounced as chemical straitjackets) were celebrated for liberating psychotic patients by making them more indifferent toward their surroundings (Caldwell 1970). Such a stoic equanimity appeared to be the opposite of the mind-opening effects of psychedelics that were said to sensitize subjects to their environment by sabotaging the "cerebral reducing valve" (even though ancient philosophers had regarded cosmic consciousness not as inimical but as complementary to freedom from worry). The antagonism of hallucinogens and antipsychotics was taken to constitute an experimental system that would allow investigation of causes as well as potential pharmacotherapies of psychosis in healthy volunteers.

But stabilizing this experimental system turned out to be difficult. Some researchers found that, although low doses of chlorpromazine effectively blocked LSD, larger doses actually enhanced its behavioral effects (Aghajanian and Freedman 1968: 1186). Others reported that chlorpromazine only alleviated nausea, vomiting, dizziness, reduction in motor activity, and anxiety but not—as one could have expected from the treatment of an experimental psychosis—hallucinations and delusions (Passie et al. 2008: 306).

Although psychoanalytic and phenomenological approaches continued to be prevalent in psychiatry, the blossoming of psychopharmacology in the 1950s initiated a second wave of biological psychiatry, which—in contrast to its nineteenth-century antecedent—focused less on postmortem neuroanatomy than on in vivo brain chemistry (Shorter 1997; Rose 2003b). In the context of this molecularization of psychiatry, the Swiss researchers Roland Fischer and Felix Georgi (Fischer et al. 1951) took up, but differentiated, the analogy of hallucinogen intoxication and schizophrenia. Mescaline, they claimed, produced a state resembling the catatonic form of schizophrenia (manifested by stupor), while LSD provoked a hebephrenic variant (marked by disorganized behavior and flattened, often inappropriate affect). From this they inferred a toxic genesis of mental disease. An error in the metabolism of the liver, they postulated, produced an "endogenous autotoxin" triggering schizophrenic episodes. Beringer's descriptive model of psychosis led them to propose an explanatory model based on the hypothesis that different forms of schizophrenia were caused by different toxic metabolites. While Beringer had only speculated about this, Fischer and Georgi tested the assumption experimentally by examining metabolic disorders that were provoked by mescaline and LSD, especially the effects of these drugs on liver function.

In a similar vein, a number of researchers, especially in the United States and Canada, hypothesized various metabolites as potential agents in the pathogenesis of schizophrenia. The most elaborate and prominent postulate was the transmethylation hypothesis by Humphry Osmond, John Smythies, and Abram Hoffer. They suspected an erroneously methylated hallucinogenic derivate of adrenaline to be the cause (Hoffer et al. 1954; Hoffer and Osmond 1959; Healy 2002: 182–191; Baumeister and Hawkins 2004; Dyck 2008). The emergence and consolidation of such explanatory models of psychosis triggered a quest for an endogenous hallucinogen that induced the mental disorder.

Epistemologically, these explanatory models of psychosis resembled Beringer's experiential model and differed from his second-order descriptive model in that the model and the modeled were situated on the same ontological level. But in the explanatory model, hallucinogen intoxication and schizophrenia were equally regarded as molecular rather than experiential phenomena. Here, Max Weber's distinction between ideal-typical description and a world consisting of nothing but particulars did not apply. In the explanatory model of psychosis, there was no such disjunction between the conceptual and the material: the experimental intervention itself was the representation (see Fox Keller 2000). Its epistemology was flat.

At the same time, however, this materialized model continued to be imbued with a conceptualization of hallucinogen inebriation as psychosis, situated on the level of mental phenomena. Presupposing such a congruence of phenomenology and mechanism, the step from descriptive to explanatory model was daring because phenomenological similarity between a pharmacologically induced and a naturally occurring state does not necessarily imply similar underlying mechanisms (Canguilhem 1989: 148). The explanatory model of psychosis that was based on the assumption that schizophrenia was caused by an endogenous hallucinogen reached its limits when LSD and mescaline were shown to induce tolerance: their repeated administration led to diminishing effects. Thus, if an LSD-like substance was indeed responsible for schizophrenia, the disease should subside within a few days—which was clearly not the case (Vannini and Venturini 1999: 207).

A second explanatory model of psychosis was proposed shortly after the transmethylation hypothesis. The so-called serotonin hypothesis of schizophrenia grew out of the discovery that the neurotransmitter serotonin was, chemically speaking, an indoleamine like LSD. And LSD was found to antagonize some of the nonpsychotropic effects of serotonin on arteries and the rat uterus. Consequently, John Gaddum (1954) suggested that deficient serotonin activity in the brain might bring about mental disturbances. His own experience with LSD on Good Friday 1953 convinced him that "it is possible that 5-HT [serotonin] in our brains plays an essential part in keeping us sane and that this effect of LSD is due to its inhibitory action on the 5-HT in the brain" (quoted in Baumeister and Hawkins 2004: 282; see also Healy 2002: 204). At the same time, David Woolley and Edward Shaw (1954) speculated more specifically that a lack of serotonin might be the neurochemical substrate of schizophrenia. In contrast to the neurotoxin theories discussed above, the serotonin hypothesis did not require a new type of molecule but rather assumed that an imbalance of a naturally occurring brain chemical was responsible for schizophrenia and could be modeled with hallucinogens.

But it did not take long until Woolley and Shaw (1956) found that LSD antagonized only some of the effects of serotonin, while acting just like the neurotransmitter in other respects. Therefore, an excess and a deficiency of serotonin appeared to be equally good explanations of schizophrenia. The consequently destabilized serotonin hypothesis and the underlying hallucinogen model of psychosis were soon overshadowed by the dopamine hypothesis of schizophrenia, which was associated with an alternative pharmacological model of psychosis. This theory, developed in the 1960s and 1970s by Jacques van Rossum, Arvid Carlsson, Solomon Snyder, and others, also followed the logic of chemical imbalance but attributed schizophrenic psychosis to dopamine rather than serotonin. By stimulating dopamine D2 receptors, high doses of amphetamine had been found to provoke psychotic states, while the classical antipsychotics chlorpromazine and haloperidol could be shown to disrupt this effect by blocking this particular subtype of dopaminergic receptors (Baumeister and Francis 2002).

The dopamine hypothesis of schizophrenia, David Healy wrote, did not just displace the transmethylation hypothesis but wrote it out of history, breaking free from the latter's entanglement with the counterculture. In contrast to Humphry Osmond's model of psychosis, the dopamine hypothesis of schizophrenia was widely propagated by the pharmaceutical industry because, by providing a persuasive mechanism of action, it helped to market antipsychotic medicines (Healy 2002: 192, 207–219). It also outclassed the competing serotonin hypothesis because the relationship between amphetamine and dopamine was less ambiguous than the one between LSD and serotonin. And considering that the available antipsychotics had turned out to be dopamine receptor antagonists, both the serotonin hypothesis and the hallucinogen model of schizophrenia were called into question. Neither serotonin-receptor-binding psychedelics like mescaline, LSD, or psilocybin nor the newly discovered group of glutamate-receptor-binding substances comprising phencyclidine (PCP) and ketamine fit into this scheme. None of these drugs demonstrated a predominantly dopaminergic activity.

As the theoretical underpinning of the explanatory hallucinogen model was called into question, the American brain researcher Solomon Snyder (1989: 175) also challenged the descriptive model by questioning its clinical plausibility: "Psychotomimetic drugs such as LSD by definition elicit psychosis. However, the psychosis that follows LSD ingestion is clearly unlike schizophrenia. Few psychiatrists will mistakenly label an individual under the influence of LSD as a schizophrenic. By contrast, many amphetamine users admitted to hospitals have been diagnosed as paranoid schizophrenic until the history of drug use was uncovered days or weeks later. In this sense, amphetamine psychosis is one of the best drug models of schizophrenia."

Together with the explanatory model, the experiential model was also eliminated from the official epistemic culture of academic and corporate pharmaceutics in the course of the 1970s. This was partly because, alongside double-blind randomized placebo-controlled trials, objectivity and its fear of all things subjective had come to dominate drug research. In psychopharmacology, Beringer's commitment to truth-to-nature had largely gone out of fashion. But the ostracism of self-experimentation was also an effect of the institutionalization of medical ethics that had begun in the 1960s. The protection of human subjects not only guarded unwitting citizens from unscrupulous scientists and greedy corporations but also barred employees of universities or drug companies from risky research practices for which their institutions might be liable. Of course, the previous chapter has shown that contemporary pharmacological research, at least in the realm of hallucinogens, continues to be informed by personal drug experiences. But conflicts like the one between Rudolf Brenneisen and Paul Dietschy (described in chapter 3) also indicate how problematic the experiential dimension of psychopharmacological investigations has become. A few years after my fieldwork, this practice was abolished in Swiss psychedelic research. In cross-cultural comparison, the German case of publicly conceptualizing hallucinogen trials as medical self-experiments had become an anomaly and not the norm.

In sum, when the dopamine hypothesis of schizophrenia became paramount in the 1970s, the use of hallucinogen-induced states as models of schizophrenic psychoses stopped making sense. The model psychosis researchers affected by the recently introduced severe regulatory constraints on psychedelic research did not have enough confidence in their research agenda to resist the growing political pressure on their work. Thus, human experimentation with hallucinogens died down in scientific institutions. Those who had always doubted the analogy between hallucinogen inebriation and psychosis took this development as an affirmation of their critique. The use of hallucinogens as an experiential, descriptive, and explanatory model of psychoses appeared to be an impasse and was soon abandoned.

Yet less than two decades later, the model psychosis paradigm made a comeback. Why did academic psychiatry change its mind about the scientific value of psychedelic drugs?

EXPERIMENTAL PSYCHOSIS REDIVIVUS

At the time of my fieldwork, Euphrosyne Gouzoulis-Mayfrank, professor of experimental psychiatry at the University of Cologne, was the most prominent proponent of model psychosis research in Germany and had participated in the effort to bring this tradition back to life. At first, she had not been particularly interested in hallucinogens, and she continued to be known in the neuropsychedelic community for not being a "recreational pharmacologist," strictly separating work from play. In contrast to other people in the field, Gouzoulis presented herself as a psychosis, not as a hallucinogen, researcher. In the mid-1980s, having finished a dissertation on the dopaminergic control of respiration, she was trained as a psychiatrist at Freiburg Medical School. The director of the psychiatric clinic, Rudolf Degkwitz, had known Kurt Beringer personally and had kept what was left of Beringer's mescaline stocks. As a chemical analysis had shown the material to be in perfectly good condition, he suggested to two of his senior physicians, Leo Hermle and Manfred Spitzer, that it be used for experiments. As a resident on their ward, Gouzoulis joined their team and thus helped to revive Beringer's mescaline model of psychosis.

In the 1980s, this model appeared tenable again because, in the meantime, the dopamine hypothesis of schizophrenia had been relativized. Its validity was questioned by some of its very inventors, Solomon Snyder and Arvid Carlsson, who warned that just because the classical antipsychotics acted on D_2 receptors did not necessarily mean that an abnormality in these receptors was the cause of schizophrenia—and no such abnormality could eventually be found in postmortem brains of schizophrenic patients (Baumeister and Francis 2002; Healy 2002: 214–215). Although the fact that antidopaminergic drugs like chlorpromazine and haloperidol reduced some of the symptoms of schizophrenia continued to suggest that dopamine played some important role, the newly discovered atypical antipsychotics (e.g., clozapine) were equally potent but targeted serotonin rather than dopamine receptors. Other findings suggested that glutamate, too, was involved in the pathogenesis of schizophrenic disorders. Since the condition could obviously not be explained by hyperactivity of the dopaminergic system alone, the dopamine hypothesis was supplemented by a reanimated serotonin hypothesis and the newly introduced glutamate hypothesis of schizophrenia. Thereby, hallucinogen-based models of psychoses were relegitimated.

However, as the dopamine hypothesis had not been refuted altogether, the claims now had to be articulated in a more modest fashion. Since the confusion about the contradictory relations between the indole-amine hallucinogens and serotonin had been resolved by the discovery of different subtypes of serotonin (5-HT) receptors, 5-HT_{2A} agonists like psilocybin could be used to model certain aspects of schizophrenia that were related to the putative underlying disorder of the serotonergic system, especially so-called positive symptoms such as hallucinations and disorganized thought, speech, and behavior. The effects of antiglu-tamatergic hallucinogens like ketamine, on the other hand, served as a model of supposedly glutamate-related deficits in schizophrenia that comprised "negative symptoms" like emotional blunting, apathy, and attention abnormalities (Gouzoulis-Mayfrank et al. 2005, 2006).

Two decades since the prohibition of psychedelics had taken effect, the political climate had changed as well. When Hermle, Spitzer, and Gouzoulis reinvigorated model psychosis research in Germany in the mid-1980s, they did not encounter much resistance. In fact, they had been encouraged by the director of their clinic and received state funding from Germany's largest research funding organization, Deutsche Forsc-hungsgemeinschaft. Gouzoulis assured me that she had never experi-enced any political pressure—only intense, but eventually successful, negotiations with ethics committees.

When, shortly thereafter, Vollenweider followed suit, he was also pleasantly surprised by how open the Swiss authorities responded to his applications. Had his embrace of the model psychosis paradigm—in contrast to the psychotherapeutic approach advocated by the Swiss Medical Association for Psycholytic Therapy—helped him to get gov-ernment support? "Yes, I think this helped," he told me. "But I have to say that my main concern was to come up with good testable hypothesis to get grants. When I spoke to Dietschy [at the Swiss Federal Office of Public Health], I realized that they didn't take such a narrow view of the matter. At the time, the psycholytic therapists also submitted a new project and he told them that they needed a clear-cut design, a well-defined hypothesis, statistics, et cetera. On the side of the authorities, the attitude was not that you could only get permission to work with hallucinogens if you sold your work as psychosis research."

In the United States, however, the situation was different. Mark Geyer, from the University of California, San Diego, recounted that he had been given career advice by the head of a training program at the National Institute of Mental Health (NIMH) *not* to submit any grant on hallucinogens to them. "If I wanted to survive, I should either go to the National Institute on Drug Abuse and look at the problems with hallucinogens, but I should not go to NIMH with a project on model psychosis." American psychiatry, he said, had dismissed the hallucinogen model of psychosis in the 1960s, even before the dopamine hypothesis of schizophrenia caught on. The opposition was political. "The guy at NIMH told me that they see LSD and California and they think 'fun and games,'" said Geyer. "That was one of the places where I got a sense that there are taboos and that there is an institutionalized system—the East Coast establishment—that was really going to look down on anybody who might have any experiential biases or openness."

At the same time, the advocates of psychedelic research in the United States also disapproved of the model psychosis paradigm. When MAPS founder Rick Doblin (1992/93: 17) attended the First International Conference of the European College for the Study of Consciousness in 1992, he was enthusiastic about the research already happening in Germany and Switzerland but appalled by its conceptual framing: "The European researchers often spoke about psychedelic experiences as 'model psychosis,' a term that deserves abandonment along with the term 'hallucinogen,' since however politically expedient those terms may be they both imply that psychedelic experiences can be discounted as crazy and distorted." Rejected by both psychedelic activists and government funding agencies, American model psychosis research had fallen through the cracks.

MORE THAN ONE, LESS THAN MANY DRUG ACTIONS

When I set out to study contemporary neuropsychedelia, one of the key questions I was interested in was the assumed incommensurability of roughly three or four conceptions of—well, of what? Unfortunately, there is no neutral umbrella term for me to use. *Hallucinogens, psychotogens,* and *psychotomimetics*—the words most commonly employed in the medical literature imply that these substances make an individual lose contact with reality. When Aldous Huxley and Humphry Osmond replaced this terminology with the more positive label *psychedelics,* that is, mind-manifesting drugs, they wanted to convey that these substances provided access to a spiritual or metaphysical reality, which usually escaped human perception. The related term *entheogens* also attributed spiritual significance to the drug experience as revealing the

"God within," but it has been critiqued for ignoring the role of set and setting in the generation of these experiences (Doblin 1992/93: 17), making it as essentializing or pharmacologistic as calling the drugs *hallucinogens* or *psychotogens.* Finally, the designation *psycholytics,* mind-loosening drugs, had psychoanalytic connotations that suggested the pharmaceuticals in question could facilitate access to the unconscious (a conception more prevalent among secular European than spiritually oriented American psychotherapists). All these terms share the assumption that hallucinogens or psychedelics (to continue using the words most common among my own interlocutors and in the academic literature at large) transform the relationship between subject and truth, but in mutually exclusive ways: by radically distorting perceptual and cognitive access to the world or by making a new ontological dimension available, which can either be taken at face value or be reduced to biological or depth psychological substrates. In the field, however, I quickly came to realize that the researchers I worked with did not think of these categories as incompatible. The revival of model psychosis research brought this to the fore.

Since, in Europe, the problem was not political resistance to the use of hallucinogens in medical research, the experimental psychosis researchers' first goal was to dispel lingering scientific doubts concerning the validity of the hallucinogen model. Systematically preparing the ground for its resuscitation, the group around Leo Hermle published a series of historically oriented review papers (Hermle et al. 1992, 1993). Between 1988 and 1989, they also ran a pilot study in which they administered Kurt Beringer's old mescaline to twelve colleagues to explore the resulting psychopathology. In order to vindicate their project, it was particularly important to refute the criticism by Osmond, Solomon Snyder, and many others who had called into question whether the symptoms of hallucinogen intoxications and schizophrenia were sufficiently similar. Countering the challenge that schizophrenia was characterized by auditory hallucinations while visual phenomena prevailed in psychedelic trips, the Hermle group pointed out that visual hallucinations were not uncommon in schizophrenics while acoustic hallucinations could also be provoked by hallucinogens. They also had to respond to the objection that schizophrenics who had already taken hallucinogens reported that their drug experiences had been altogether different from their psychotic experiences. With an article on psychedelic experiences in the early stages of schizophrenia, Gouzoulis-Mayfrank and colleagues (1994) addressed the clash of interpretive frameworks head-on. They showed that ecstatic and transcendental experiences were reported not only by mystically inclined drug users but also by schizophrenic patients.

Even though Gouzoulis's scientific work was entirely committed to the psychotomimetic paradigm, she did not conceive of it as contradicting psychedelic and psycholytic conceptions: "Something psychotomimetic can be psychedelic as well because a psychosis also manifests contents," she told me. "As such these contents are not always pathological, but the form in which they are expressed does not conform to the normal. What a psychotic person thinks and sees has partly to do with himself—just like a dream, which can also tell me about myself. But a dream is a dream and not reality."[8] Gouzoulis's assistant Jörg Daumann also confirmed that, as a test subject in their experiments with DMT, he had equally experienced the drug's psychotomimetic, psycholytic, and psychedelic qualities. Even though their group's work was based on the model psychosis paradigm, Daumann recounted not only how his body once liquefied and dripped on the floor but also the resurfacing of biographical memories and the noetic quality, which William James (1958/1902: 293) had presented as one of the hallmarks of mystical experience: "I had the impression of seeing truths and interrelations, which, previously, I had not understood as clearly. This went along with an elevated mood. I thought, this is how a guru must feel when he stands in front of his disciples and says: 'I have something important to tell you. Listen carefully!'"

This convergence of religion and mental illness can be traced back to nineteenth-century anthropology and psychology. In *The Varieties of Religious Experience* (1958/1902), James drew from an already vast literature on the psycho- and neuropathic origins of spiritual experiences. In a similar vein, Freud's reflections in *The Future of an Illusion* (1961/1927) portrayed religion as "the universal obsessional neurosis of humanity." Like him, most anthropologists conceived of religion as a more or less functional delusion, which, some believed, would be overcome in the process of social evolution (Evans-Pritchard 1965; Strenski 2008). In anthropology, this discourse culminated in the 1950s in a debate over the claim that shamans suffered from schizophrenia, hysteria, neurosis, or epilepsy (Kroeber 1952; Devereux 1956; Linton 1956). In Europe and North America, they would have been confined in a mental asylum, the argument went, but other cultures valued them as intermediaries between the human and the spirit worlds. The same logic could be applied to hallucinogens: elsewhere they had traditionally served spiritual, including shamanic, purposes, while Euro-Americans used them to model psychoses.

On the basis of this conceptual matrix, Huxley and Osmond redefined psychotomimetics as psychedelics. Thereby, they transvalued the nineteenth-century topos of religious experience as mental disorder into the notion of mental disorder as religious experience. But, despite the different normative undertones, these two conceptions remained partially connected by Huxley's assumption that the neurobiological substrate of both schizophrenia and hallucinogen intoxication was the breakdown of a filtering mechanism protecting the human brain against a flood of sensory and extrasensory sensations. In response, Huxley's most ferocious critic, the British scholar of religion (and intelligence officer) Robert Zaehner (1957: 84), accused him of reducing "all meditative and contemplative religion to pure lunacy." Timothy Leary (1965: 133), on the other hand, inferred that hallucinogen-induced psychoses were symptoms of an "ontological confusion" and "spiritual crisis": "It may be pathology, but it might be divine madness."

Despite the pronounced ideological differences marking this discursive field, it seems as if one relatively stable complex had emerged in the twentieth century that tied together spiritual experience, mental illness, and inner truth. William James's work significantly contributed to its consolidation by providing a pragmatist frame of noncontradiction, in which the divisive question of the origins of altered states of consciousness (psychological, biological, or supernatural) receded into the background while their practical consequences moved center stage. James (1958/1902: 29) reminded his readers that there was not a single state of mind, healthy or morbid, religious or atheist, that had no organic process as its condition. Hence, all states of mind needed to be evaluated by their "fruits for life." This, however, was a question not just of different frames of reference but of practice.

More recently, the Dutch ethnographer and philosopher Annemarie Mol has given this pragmatist way of thinking an ontological twist. She moves beyond mononaturalism and multiculturalism not by imagining nature in the plural but by showing how one medical condition can be "enacted" differently in different practices. Following her theory, there is not a single passive object, say LSD or psilocybin, which can be seen from different points of view—as a hallucinogenic, psychedelic, or psycholytic drug. "Instead, objects come into being," Mol (2002: 5) argues, "with the practices in which they are manipulated.

And since the object of manipulation tends to differ from one practice to another, reality multiplies." But it does so locally. Psychotropics always act in specific bodies and situations. Depending on dose, set, and setting, drug action is contingent on practice. For example, the difference between psychedelic and psycholytic was not just an interpretive one but also a difference in therapeutic approach—depth psychological vs. "transpersonal"—and dosage: American psychedelic therapists tended to administer larger doses than their psycholytically oriented colleagues abroad, thereby making the occurrence of profound spiritual experiences more likely (Ulrich and Patten 1991; Walsh and Grob 2006). When Roland Griffiths followed in Pahnke's footsteps studying mystical-type experiences occasioned by psilocybin, he also gave his subjects—all "religiously musical"—more of the drug than what Vollenweider had administered in his model psychosis studies (Griffiths et al. 2006). Furthermore, these sessions were guided by an experienced psychologist, there was no neuropsychological testing, and the clinical setting was loosened up by music. The very notion of "psychoactive drug" implies that it is defined not just by its chemical structure but by its actions and interactions. Therefore, the different effects that psilocybin produces in different contexts can be taken to indicate that, to put it in Mol's telling phrase, psilocybin (or any other psychedelic drug) is more than one—and yet less than many.

There are not two or more psilocybins (as Emilie Gomart [2002] has claimed for methadone), because the molecules used in different contexts share a chemical structure and the practices codetermining their effects are coordinated. Conceptually, they are harmonized by the notion of the brain as filter. When model psychosis research was brought to life again, Huxley's hypothesis of a "cerebral reducing valve" equally compromised in schizophrenic, hallucinogenic, and mystical experiences was rearticulated in the current vocabulary of information theory as a neurobiochemical "impairment of information processing, selective filtering, and decoding of experiences from long-term memory" (Hermle et al. 1993: 53). This conceptual matrix informed a whole series of experimental paradigms that studied so-called gating mechanisms as the neurophysiological equivalents of Huxley's "doors of perception" (M. Geyer 1998: 34): startle habituation, inhibition of return, P50 suppression, and so on. The most important one, prepulse inhibition (PPI), will be discussed in detail in the next chapter. They were all regarded as "prephenomenal" measures: relatively basic neural functions located somewhere between simple biochemistry and the complexities of mental illness. In addition to neuroimaging (which, apart from EEG, was not yet available in the 1950s and 1960s), these were the new methodological approaches distinguishing the revival of hallucinogen research from its previous incarnation. Even though there were pronounced ideological differences and even conflicts over the assessment of hallucinogens—not just in the neuropsychedelic world at large but even within the microcosm of the Vollenweider lab, for example—the notion of a disturbed filtering mechanism provided a conceptual bridge, a common matrix allowing researchers of different worldviews to put their names on the same scientific papers published in the same neuropsychopharmacology journals without violating their dearest convictions.

Different conceptions of hallucinogenic drugs, human beings, and the ontological makeup of the world were also coordinated with the help of self-rating scales. As tools for the transformation of qualitative experience into quantitative data, they provided a mechanism for steering clear of ideological conflicts. One might sympathize or not with the use of psychedelics to model psychoses, with the comparison of drug intoxication and meditation, or with the use of a "mysticism scale" to rate the effects of a psychotomimetic, but whether or not study results were scientifically acceptable depended primarily on the statistical significance of the data. In a way, the standardized questionnaires respected the impenetrable subjectivity of experience. If a test subject marked on a questionnaire that she sensed an all-embracing love or felt connected to a higher power, there was no way of contesting these statements scientifically. What mattered was that they were collected significantly more often from test subjects under the influence of the drug than under the placebo condition. And, if that was the case, there was probably a neural correlate, as there had to be a corresponding brain state for every mental phenomenon, provided that "mind is what the brain does." And what the brain did could be captured through neuroimaging measurements to be correlated with the introspective data provided by the self-rating scales.

This association of the subjective and the objective enabled researchers to ignore everything beyond the confines of the so-called mind-brain. The anchoring of meaning attributed to drug experiences in sociocultural formations and the controversial content of these experiences were bracketed off. Investigating neural correlates of altered states of consciousness with the tools of psychopharmacology did not require a decision about whether the contents of these experiences were imaginary or real. Methodologically, brain research on spiritual experiences neither presupposed nor demonstrated or disproved the existence of any divine realms or entities. In a newsmagazine article on neurotheology, Felix Hasler (2005) cited neuroscientist Andrew Newberg's study on meditating Tibetan monks and Franciscan nuns to support his claim that brain experiments could neither prove nor falsify the existence of God:

> [Newberg's] cogent culinary comparison: Eating an apple pie produces certain mental phenomena—for example, the enjoyment of the little raisins sprinkled in—going along with certain brain processes, which the neurologist can observe ("This is your brain on apple pie"). But, of course, the fact that these brain processes exist does not mean that the apple pie is a delusion. (To be even more pedantic: we cannot demonstrate the existence of the apple pie with absolute certainty, either.)
>
> The biggest of all big questions, whether God exists or not, cannot be answered by way of biotheological studies. Whether God created our brain—and, thereby, our ability to recognize him—or whether our brain created God will remain a matter of faith. Once again, the ontological sixty-four-thousand-dollar question leads to a dead end—but at least keeping with the times, using the high-tech methods of brain research. And, after all, the atheist acting enlightened also only believes that God does not exist.

In a field strained by tensions between the proponents of disenchantment and those working toward a spiritualization of the brain, scientific practice embodied a salutary agnosticism that preserved the possibility of an ongoing exchange between adherents of conflicting worldviews. Such mechanisms of toleration and collaboration had become necessary since psychotomimetic, therapeutic, and spiritual applications of hallucinogens were no longer distributed across the West and the rest but rather coincided in the same academic field and sometimes even in the same laboratories. Scientific practice not only helped to maintain a tense coherence between different perspectives but also allowed coordination among the varieties of hallucinogen action. Practical coordination made psilocybin (or any other psychedelic) not many, but manifolded—one drug with multiple facets (Mol 2002: 53–85).[9] Hence, psychotomimetic and mystical-type experiences induced by hallucinogenic drugs are neither ontologically separate phenomena nor are they the same phenomenon differently interpreted; rather they are pharmacospiritual states that are partially connected through a shared historical matrix.

STAGING SCHIZOPHRENIA

Several months after the experiment with Daniel Wetzel, pharmaco-psychologist Boris Quednow and I went to see Rimini Protokoll's latest production: Friedrich Schiller's drama *Wallenstein*. So far the ensemble's trademark had been a novel kind of documentary theater. Whereas German documentary theater in the 1960s was based on carefully researched true incidents eventually put on stage with professional actors, its renaissance since the late 1990s had been characterized by a radical break with such relationships of representation. Instead of playing the roles of historical or contemporaneous real-life figures, Rimini Protokoll's "experts of everyday life" were real-life figures themselves. They were exhibited as theatrical ready-mades, but they also contributed actively to the production of the performance. In the case of *Wallenstein*, however, Rimini Protokoll experimented with an alternative to both representationalist 1960s documentary theater and the group's previous "presentationalist" works. For the purpose of staging Schiller's drama about the betrayal of the seventeenth-century politician and general Albrecht von Wallenstein, Rimini Protokoll cast the play with people who had experienced different forms of treachery in their own lives: at the time of the German Democratic Republic, today's head of the Weimar police department was degraded by his colleagues because of a love affair with one of his coworkers; a young conservative politician told the story of how he was chosen and then dropped as his party's candidate for mayor of Mannheim; and a Vietnam veteran now living in Heidelberg recounted how his unit blew up its own inhuman commander. In a way, these people all played the parts of Wallenstein or his betrayers. But, instead of reciting Schiller's text, they talked about their own lives, bringing fragments of reality onto the stage. The dramatic recontextualization of these records of everyday theatricality served less as a mise-en-scène of Schiller's historical material than to produce new insights into the contemporary world from which they had been extracted. As Rimini Protokoll refrained from giving its actors any kind of professional training, such as diction exercises, their bodies did not serve as transparent media of the dramatic plot. Moments of clumsiness or hesitation on the part of the actors continuously reminded the audience that, even though the presented material was documentary in nature, it was also staged.

Similarly, in model psychosis research, the hallucinogen inebriation—a quite wayward piece of biological and psychospiritual life—was brought into the laboratory to stand for an equally opaque phenomenon, namely, schizophrenia. In psychiatric discourse, both phenomena were classified as psychoses. Speaking as a psychiatrist, Vollenweider was therefore right to object to the argument of my paper "Ceci n'est pas une psychose." But his other statement, quoted at the beginning of this chapter, that psychedelic experiences were "not simply" psychotic processes, indicated that the relationship of representation between these two psychophysical states was broken. Beringer had already been cautious not to overextend his assertion that there was a phenomenological resemblance between mescaline intoxication and schizophrenia. He did not want to claim an identity between the "intoxication psychosis" induced by the drug and schizophrenia proper unless the biochemical substrates of the two states had been identified. From the 1950s onward, the experiential identity of schizophrenia and a hallucinogenic high was repeatedly called into question. After almost a century of model psychosis research, there seemed to be consensus among the revivalists of psychedelic science that, from a neurobiological point of view, hallucinogen intoxications and schizophrenia were distinct phenomena.

However, hallucinogen inebriation did not have to be identical with the mental disease to serve as its model. In fact, the very definition of a model requires that it *cannot* be identical with its object. From a purely epistemological point of view, the distinctness of drug effects and schizophrenia does not refute the conception of the hallucinogen model of psychosis. In his book *Models* (1979), the philosopher of science Marx Wartofsky wrote that questioning degrees of approximation was a shabby complaint if one kept in mind the definition of a model: "Nothing which is a model is to be taken as a model of itself, nor of something identical with it" (4). Wartofsky reminded his readers of the metaphorical nature of models and the distinction between the model and what it was a model of. This raises the question of whether models are ever true. Do they ever represent their objects adequately?

Wartofsky (1979: xx, 6) answered this question by elaborating his concept of representation. Anything can be taken as a representation of anything else. There are no intrinsic properties that predetermine one thing to serve as a representation of another thing. For something to be a representation, human beings have to construe and construct it as such. But it is not "anything goes." A good model shares a *particular* set of features with the object. The choice of these features—and, hence, of the model itself—is a normative act that presupposes a certain practical orientation or aim.

By shifting the discussion from the nature of representations to the human activity of representing, Wartofsky opened philosophy to the history and anthropology of science. His problematization of representation is deeply rooted in what Foucault (1973) described as the *episteme* of man, emerging at the turn from the eighteenth to the nineteenth century when God ceased to serve as guarantor of a preestablished correspondence between the world and its representations. In the realm of epistemology, the "death of God" amounted to the clouding of representation. As a result, man—or rather, finite and fallible human beings like Gouzoulis and Vollenweider—took over the place of God in creating and answering for dense and opaque representations of the world and their own species. And yet no epistemic nihilism ensued.

Considering that models of psychosis serve a certain purpose, the relationship between these models and their object must be regarded as contingent but not arbitrary. Sidney Cohen (1972: 92–93), an American psychiatrist involved in model psychosis research in the 1950s, wrote: "The debate about whether LSD brings forth a model psychosis is rather futile; undeniably, it can induce a model of psychosis, but for the reasons mentioned it cannot duplicate schizophrenia. A model need not reproduce every aspect of the thing modeled. For example, a model of a bridge, in addition to its difference in size, is also of different material and construction. Nevertheless, it is possible to learn much about the actual bridge from it. Just so, much can be learned about schizophrenic symptoms from a study of LSD phenomena." Or, as Mark Geyer (1998: 34) put it more recently: "It is not necessary to argue that hallucinogens mimic all the symptoms of a complex disorder such as schizophrenia to believe that they affect some of the brain systems that can be disturbed in psychiatric illnesses. Thus, an understanding of hallucinogen actions may be relevant to specific aspects of schizophrenia rather than the entire complex syndrome." Thus, model psychosis research is based on a genuinely pragmatist understanding of models, best summed up by Manfred Spitzer (1999: 296): "Models are . . . neither true nor false. Instead, they are useful or not."

Consequently, there was no objectivity in the construction of the hallucinogen model of psychosis. Like the theater directors of Rimini Protokoll casting their protagonists (or this ethnographer selecting his field sites and vignettes), experimental psychosis researchers had to pick and choose the relevant features connecting their model to its object. But the way in which they got implicated in this kind of modeling did not match the epistemic virtue of truth-to-nature either. The scientists' approach was not primarily about constructing an ideal-typical representation by looking back on the rich experience acquired during a lifetime of learning but about looking ahead to new discoveries and innovations.

In this spirit, Gouzoulis (her colleagues Hermle and Spitzer had by now changed course) was persistently pursuing a comparative project that contrasted the effects of different hallucinogens to evaluate and differentiate their usefulness for the purpose of modeling different kinds and aspects of psychoses. "The pharmacological models that we have," she explained to me, "are models of different quality for different syndromes. The two main models are the serotonergic and the antiglutamatergic model, which model different psychotic syndromes. This produces clues concerning the connections between neurobiological parameters and types of psychosis. Therefore, it is very reasonable to use different models. One can say, 'With this substance we model this syndrome and with that substance another one.'" But Gouzoulis did not assume that schizophrenia and its drug models were based on an identical neurobiological substrate. The commonalities between the two were not presupposed but investigated. Moreover, what was found in the hallucinogen models was not believed to prove anything about the nature of schizophrenia, but could only serve as a hint inspiring further research in schizophrenic patients. In Gouzoulis's eyes, as she told me, the purpose of these models was "to give interesting clues, which then need to be verified in patient populations. However, the models only serve as supplements. Based on model psychoses alone nothing can be demonstrated. There is no way of safely extrapolating from the results of model psychosis research to mechanisms of psychosis. Hence, I need to check whether a model fits and if it does, then I have only gained another argument."

What is peculiar about these models is that they do not function as transparent representations of their object. Although object and model are distinct, they are situated on the same ontological level. In the experiential model of psychosis, it is an experience that serves as the model of another experience, while its neurobiological rearticulation presents a brain on hallucinogens as the model of a schizophrenic brain. This distinguishes the model psychoses (apart from the associated descriptive models) from other kinds of models. Mathematical models of economic development, three-dimensional models of molecules, or Vollenweider's neurocybernetic wiring diagrams are qualitatively different from their objects in the "real world." They are formal, not material, models because they are independent of their physical embodiments. These representations are not made of the same stuff as what they represent. In the case of the model psychoses, on the other hand, this ontological difference had been eradicated. Possessing a distinct materiality and depth, model psychoses functioned as scientific objects in their own right. They had a certain opacity that called for research on the model itself (whereas it was not necessary to chemically investigate the materials from which Watson and Crick had built their tin and cardboard model of DNA).

Even though much science aims at creating representations of how the world really is (with the ensuing philosophical problems of realism and objectivity), model psychosis research did not. Of course, the hallucinogen model served as a representation of schizophrenia, but this representation was neither assumed to correspond to nature nor was it the endpoint of knowledge production. Quite the opposite. It was only a beginning that aimed at certain achievements in the future, some representational (more adequate accounts of the neurobiology of schizophrenia), some pragmatic (better antipsychotic drugs). Wartofsky (1979: 142) spoke of models as a "technology for creating the future." By the phrase "creating the future," he meant "*acting* in such a way as to make the future conform to some present vision of it" (142–143). However, the hallucinogen intoxications had turned out to be phenomena too convoluted and recalcitrant to always meet the researchers' expectations.

Following Daniel Wetzel's cue to look at the experiment he took part in as a dramatic Müller-style performance, model psychosis research appears to be an "ontological theater," to use Andrew Pickering's (2009, 2010) term, staging a vision of the mind-brain in its interactions with drugs, people, ideas, and different environments as an exceedingly complex system. Ever since Jacques-Joseph Moreau de Tours's simulation of mental illness with hashish, pharmacological models of psychiatric disorders had been attempts to compensate for the lack of knowledge regarding the organic nature of naturally occurring psychopathologies (Solhdju 2011: 129). But if the drugs' pharmacological activity is contingent on the different ways in which they are used, we could also follow Annemarie Mol's (2002: 32–33) set of theatrical metaphors in saying that the psychotomimetics were "enacted" as such, partly by following an experimental protocol and an unwritten cultural script, but also by improvising while incalculable nonpharmacological factors entered the stage. These kinds of nonrepresentational models used to approach a multiplex world in a forward-looking manner I propose to call enactive models.

As such an enactive model, the hallucinogen model of psychosis can be taken to demonstrate that acknowledgment of the fact that we are living in a world of exceedingly complex systems does not have to paralyze scientific research. However, the goal is not to celebrate an "ontology of unknowability," the way Andrew Pickering (2010) does in his historical account of the entwinement of British cybernetics and the counterculture, but to analyze an experimental system that has, among other things, produced neurocybernetic models (like Vollenweider's cortico-striato-thalamo-cortical loops) that remove the lid from the black box of the brain to conceptualize its inner workings (a vision of cybernetics diametrically opposed to Pickering's). Many ends of model psychosis research continued to be epistemic, but not by immediately establishing an epistemic end point: true knowledge about schizophrenia.

Historian of science Hans-Jörg Rheinberger (1997) has argued that an experimental system needs to be sufficiently stable to maintain and reproduce itself while being flexible or loose enough to promote unpredictable events. As a research system, it can only keep going as long as it generates not only knowledge but also "the unknown," which requires further research. Following the molecular biologist François Jacob, Rheinberger (1997: 28) has characterized such setups as "machines for making the future." Experimental systems do not simply generate answers to questions that science poses to nature (as Francis Bacon had it); first and foremost, they materialize these questions and generate further questions. Thus, Rheinberger's characterization of experimental systems is highly reminiscent of Wartofsky's branding of models as "technologies for creating the future." But, unlike Wartofksy, Rheinberger has an open future in mind, a future that cannot be foreseen and that, almost by definition, will not conform to any present vision of it. As Gouzoulis pointed out, hallucinogens cannot answer any questions about schizophrenia. Used in an enactive model of psychosis, they can only produce more questions to be settled in another experimental system involving schizophrenic patients.

Hence, it was a pragmatist view of models that informed the concept of model psychosis, no more about truth and falsity than Rimini Protokoll's theatrical performances distinguished reality from fiction. The hallucinogen model of psychosis shared this tacit philosophy of science with so many other models in contemporary molecular biology as a domain where no division between theory and experiment, between representing and intervening, had obtained (Fox Keller 2000). Like *Blaiberg und sweetheart19* or *Wallenstein*, the hallucinogen model of psychosis introduced a dense, hazy, and resistant reality of its own into a space of representation. But, as we will see in the next chapter, this opacity allowed for surprises and occasionally thwarted the scientists' goals. Would this enactive model produce what its builders had promised: insights into the neurobiology of schizophrenia and development of better antipsychotic drugs?

Between Animality and Divinity

"We need to anthropologize the West: show how exotic its constitution of reality has been," suggested Paul Rabinow (1986: 241) more than twenty-five years ago. Although today the deliberate construction of Euro-American exotica might appear dated, this chapter cannot help but live up to the demand for anthropological distancing effects: it is about Americans trying to understand schizophrenia by startling mice, rats, and guinea pigs. The experimental measure that researchers invented—prepulse inhibition, or PPI—became the most widespread gating paradigm that translated Aldous Huxley's drug mysticism and a fairy tale by Hermann Hesse into model psychosis research.

The concept of PPI describes the following phenomenon: Sudden and intense sensory stimuli trigger a startle reflex, which comprises blinking as well as a jerk of the whole body. If a weak, nonstartling stimulus (e.g., a low noise referred to as prepulse) precedes the stimulus (e.g., a loud noise referred to as pulse), it inhibits the startle response. This prepulse inhibition of the startle reflex served as an operational measure for sensorimotor gating, that is, the capacity of the nervous system to filter out irrelevant stimuli. This phylogenetically old mechanism, preserved from mollusks to primates, was found to be impaired in schizophrenics but also in rats treated with hallucinogens. Thus, an animal model of the mental disease was born—simple enough to serve as a screening mechanism for new antipsychotic drugs.[1]

In Franz Vollenweider's and Euphrosyne Gouzoulis-Mayfrank's laboratories, this paradigm was also explored in humans. During my fieldwork in Zurich, I frequently volunteered for such startle sessions. When no drugs were involved, these experiments were rather uneventful. I would sit in the EEG lab for twenty minutes listening to white noise on a set of headphones. Every time I was about to doze off, a sudden burst of sound made me blink, while an electromyograph recorded whether a usually unnoticed prepulse had reduced the reflexive contraction of my facial muscles.

I only became interested in this experimental paradigm when I learned about its problem. Whereas schizophrenics and drugged rats showed a decreased PPI, Gouzoulis-Mayfrank and colleagues (1998) had discovered an *increased* PPI in healthy human subjects treated with psilocybin. Under the influence of the hallucinogen, test subjects' ability to filter out certain stimuli seemed even better than usual. It was thus again called into doubt whether psychedelics really opened any "doors of perception." Similar findings by Vollenweider and his American colleague Mark Geyer (Vollenweider et al. 1999) confirmed that, in this puzzling case, the animal model of psychosis adequately represented its object (i.e. schizophrenia), whereas its human counterpart failed to do so. My interlocutors were not sure yet what to make of these perplexing results. Did the limits of this reductionist paradigm mark out what made us distinctly human? After all, hallucinogens were associated with mental illness and mystical experience—two domains still largely attributed to humankind and humankind alone (despite increasing prescriptions of psychiatric drugs in veterinary medicine and an emergent discourse on spiritual experiences in nonhuman primates [Braitman forthcoming; Goodall 2010]). What better site for an anthropological investigation of how the revival of psychedelic research inflected notions of *anthropos* today?

PSYCHIATRIC DRUG DISCOVERY: FROM SELF-EXPERIMENTATION TO ANIMAL RESEARCH

In spring 2006, I moved from Franz Vollenweider's human lab in Zurich to Mark Geyer's animal lab in San Diego, where Geyer and his coworker David Braff had introduced PPI into psychiatric research. I had met Geyer at the LSD Symposium in Basel, where he invited me to spend time with his research group. I had arrived in San Diego just in time for the public seminar "Chemistry of the Mind," which he had organized together with the small start-up company Acadia Pharmaceuticals—in part to draw attention to Acadia's then most promising compound: a potential atypical antipsychotic called ACP-103. They had invited Arvid Carlsson, by then a Nobel Prize laureate; Les Iversen, an Oxford professor of pharmacology and former director of the neuroscience drug discovery program at Merck; and Alexander "Sasha" Shulgin who, since quitting his job as a research chemist at Dole Chemical Company in 1966, had dedicated his life to developing new psychedelic drugs in a private lab on his farm in Lafayette, California. Each of the speakers gave a lecture. Carlsson and Shulgin reminisced about their achievements and indulged in anecdotes, but no dialogue emerged. Even though the symposium's announced goal was to discuss the future direction of research and discovery in psychopharmacology, its participants seemed more concerned with the past.

The following morning, during a question and answer session with Carlsson and Shulgin, arranged for University of California, San Diego, students from the neuroscience, pharmacology, and psychiatry departments, Shulgin explained his reliance on self-experimentation as the royal road to drug discovery. He claimed that animal testing was of no value in defining the subjective effects of a psychoactive drug in humans. As he put it elsewhere, "I believe totally that assays such as nest building among mice, disruption of conditioned response, grooming, maze running, or motor-activity have no value in determining the psychedelic potential of a compound" (Shulgin and Shulgin 1991: xxii). In Shulgin's eyes, this potential lay in the drugs' ability to open different doors to different inner landscapes and to provide "greater clarity as to our responsibilities towards our own species and all others" (Shulgin and Shulgin 1997: xxvi). Which door exactly a particular substance would unlock, and which spiritual lesson it would teach, was not determinable by way of animal experiments. Therefore, Shulgin had tested each of the more than one hundred molecules that he had developed on himself.

Sitting in the audience, Mark Brann, the founder and president of Acadia, wanted the students to understand this seemingly outlandish practice historically:

I think there is an interesting context to put Sasha and Arvid into. Being in the pharmaceutical industry, I've met and interacted with many of the pioneers of the field of their age group. What people don't realize is that what Sasha did was extraordinarily common in the 1960s and '70s. When people were testing compounds to investigate drug structure/activity relationships, particularly when they were testing compounds where the animal correlates weren't extremely obvious, they would taste the drugs themselves. For example, I know people doing eye-care research. All the drugs they developed until about 1975 were tested by the chemists making them on their own eyes to see if they worked and whether they had any side effects. The pharma industry, up until the mid-'70s, knew this was occurring and that it was very facilitating of the drug programs. But by the mid-'70s, this was stopped because of the liabilities. You have to look back at the time to realize that what Sasha is doing seems very outrageous when you look at it from the perspective we are all trained in now. But, at that time, it was the norm. The perception until the mid-1970s was that people knew they were taking a risk; they were curious about the results; they were dedicated scientists who wanted to see progress, and they did it.

When I asked Brann why self-experimentation had since lost its legitimacy, he answered: "I would say that it's an outcome of the liability culture and the fact that the research individuals are doing at a pharma company is a collective responsibility. If someone did that in my company, we would immediately terminate them because of the exposure they would create for our efforts. Now that we are in an environment where each step in drug development is hyperregulated, if such an activity occurred it would expose the company."

Thus, to learn about the psychoactive effects of the latest compound in its drug development pipeline, Acadia had given ACP-103 to Geyer's lab for preclinical testing in animals. In the model psychosis paradigm, ACP-103 turned out to be a powerful 5-HT_{2A} inverse agonist that reversed hallucinogen-induced PPI deficits in rats. At the time of the seminar, ACP-103 was being tested in humans.

OPERATIONALIZING THE DOORS OF PERCEPTION

Mark Geyer's laboratory was part of the medical school of the University of California, San Diego (UCSD). It was located thirteen miles away from the main campus at the UCSD Medical Center in Hillcrest, a lively residential area serving as the hub of San Diego's gay and lesbian community. In contrast to the Zurich lab—which, apart from the EEG room and a second room equipped with a computer for neuropsychological testing, mostly consisted of tidy office space—the Geyer lab (see figure 12) was crammed with glassware, chemicals, scales, a big microscope, computer equipment, discarded rat cages, motion-tracking boxes, startle chambers, and Plexiglas containers full of screeching mice, rats, or guinea pigs that had been brought up from the vivarium for experimentation. It was a space for bench work. This buzzing atmosphere reflected the fact that—at least in comparison with human test subjects—the easy availability of laboratory animals allowed experiments to take place much more frequently. Often several trials were run at a time. Usually, they were conducted by the five technicians, while the four scientists sat in front of their computers processing data, writing papers, and designing new experiments. This did not mean that the scientists were not doing any practical work at all or that the technicians were entirely excluded from the intellectual part of the research process. But the division of labor was structured hierarchically: the higher the rank, the less hands-on work and the less contact with animals (an organization that also had a practical justification: over the years, animal researchers had not only risen in the hierarchy but also tended to develop allergies complicating their handling of animals).

Lab head Mark Geyer had ceased to do technical work altogether. He spent his time writing articles and rushing from meeting to conference call to the airport and back again. A man in his early sixties, he had become a senior figure in the field of behavioral neuropsychopharmacology. He was president of the Serotonin Club (an umbrella organization of serotonin researchers), fulfilled editorial functions for various neuropsychopharmacology journals, served as consultant for pharmaceutical companies, and was actively engaged in science policy programs of the National Institute of Mental Health (the very state-run research agency that had tried to dissuade him from conducting model psychosis research). For Geyer, the Heffter Research Institute, which he had cofounded with Dave Nichols and others to promote psychedelic science, was one project among others. Like Gouzoulis and unlike Vollenweider, he did not conceive of himself as a hallucinogen researcher in the first place. The focus of his career was on prepulse inhibition and related measures closely associated with, but not at all restricted to, schizophrenia research. In this enterprise, hallucinogenic drugs had simply come to serve as an important tool to manipulate and investigate PPI.

In a conversation, Geyer traced his fascination with the startle response back to the 1960s when, as a college student, he read a fairy tale titled "Iris" by the German writer Hermann Hesse:

> This is a short story about somebody admiring the blossom of a flower. I can't remember its content, but I remember coming out of it thinking of habituation and how important it is in life to keep a childlike view of the world, to maintain a sensitivity perceiving things as they really are rather than through a curtain of habituated inattentive muted responses to things

that may be beautiful or ugly or whatever. I became enamored with this notion of wanting to remain childlike and open to experience. One of the most important things to capture my intellectual attention very early on was habituation. Habituation is what keeps us from seeing things anew all the time.

PPI emerged at the intersection of several historical trajectories. One of them was the late but enthusiastic reception of Hermann Hesse's works by the American youth culture of the 1960s. In the early twentieth century, his novels had already been popular among the German *Wandervogel* youth movement. Having grown out of the protocountercultural milieu, which before World War I coalesced in the Swiss village of Ascona, they were appealing to young people as odysseys of spiritual development. Their heroes reject established society and set out in search of a better life to be found in a mystical realm of rewarding inwardness. By the 1960s, however, many German dissident students were strongly influenced by Marxist historical materialism. And the goal of Marxism was not mystical withdrawal from, but a political transformation of, the world. Therefore, the German student movement vigorously rejected the kind of irrationalism, spiritualism, and metaphysical escapism for which Hesse stood.

In America, on the other hand, at least the hippie strand of the counterculture had emerged as part of a major transformation of the American religious landscape. This Fourth Great Awakening was characterized by a turn toward experience-centered and often unchurched forms of spirituality (McLoughlin 1978: 179–216; Luhrmann 2005). This development also affected young Mark Geyer, who told me: "At the end of high school, I began to get interested in religion and spend one summer with a good friend of mine going around various churches. Every weekend, we attended a different service and grilled the leaders. I entered college with a continuing adolescent confusion or curiosity about things religious or spiritual. None of that ever shook my fundamental atheism. But that doesn't deny spirituality in my mind—it never has!—which is about a here and now kind of experience. It didn't take me long to dismiss organized religion." Drug experiences, especially with psychedelics, played an important role in this historical development (Fuller 2000: 84–89). Timothy Leary (1963: 173) praised Hesse's novels as trip manuals showing the way toward "a holy sense of unity and revelation," and American youth celebrated the German writer as a guide into the newly discovered ecstasies of the soul (Ziolkowski 1969; Schwarz 1970).

Hesse's fairy tale "Iris" (1995/1918), which Geyer had cherished so much as a young man but had forgotten by the time he was a successful and busy university professor, is exactly about this: the falling into oblivion of youthful devotion to an experience of enchantment. As a child, Anselm, the hero of the story, is captivated by the sight of a blue flower, the iris. His experience of childlike immersion is both sensuous and spiritual in that the visual serves as an allegory through which Anselm communes with the spirit and the eternal life that lie hidden behind the world of the senses. But, as he grows up, Anselm gets distracted by more worldly business. He pursues an academic career and becomes a professor. Feeling a sense of dissatisfaction, he asks a woman named Iris to marry him. She realizes that he has lost something that was important and sacred to him, which he is reminded of every time he calls her name. If he wants to be with her, she demands, he first has to set out and rediscover what it is that he lost.

Even though it is not known if Hesse ever took hallucinogenic drugs, Leary identified the sensuous spirituality sought by Hesse's characters with the psychedelic experience. And, like Hesse, Leary (1963: 173) was concerned about how to escape "the soundless deserts of mapped out reality." For this purpose, psychedelic drugs appeared to be appropriate tools. As Geyer (1998: 35) would put it more prosaically many years later, "Hallucinogens have often been suggested to enhance one's ability to see familiar things as novel."

Back in the 1960s, Geyer was a hippie. Against the background of Leary's reading of Hesse and other psychedelic literature, he interpreted his own hallucinogenic experiences as "spiritually relevant." As agents of spiritual experience, hallucinogens were meant to transform those who ingested them. As a psychopharmacology graduate student right at the time when the psychedelic revolution hit, Geyer told me, he often served as a trip guide for groups of ten to fifteen people, which gave him ample opportunity to observe where psychedelic drugs took others: "The most common benefit that people get from these experiences is some loosening of constraint and respect for a variety of people and behaviors that those who have never had such experiences have a hell of a time relating to. That includes the freedom to interact openly with other people and to understand one's own potential and accept one's limitations. Whether such self-awareness translates as well as it could into action is not always so clear." Drugs served as mediators that helped people internalize countercultural values by teaching them how "to do their own thing," in common parlance, and how to respect that others did theirs, instead of demanding social conformity.

But Geyer also witnessed the detrimental effects of this collective research in the wild. "I've seen a few who suffered from these drugs," he told me. "Whether or not they would have gone off the deep end anyways, the drugs certainly helped push these people into places that weren't compatible with society." And he began to imagine "what it would be like if one had such experiences without the drug—that it must be like what some psychiatric patients experience."

Here, another piece of inspiration came in. In 1963, when Geyer was still an undergraduate, he heard Aldous Huxley speak about the mystical revelations he had experienced under the influence of mescaline. Reading *The Doors of Perception* (2009/1954), Geyer learned about Huxley's idea that both hallucinogens and schizophrenia disturbed a "cerebral reducing valve," filtering out all stimuli that did not help an organism's survival and that this was how these altered states produced a sense of oneness with the cosmic consciousness that pervaded and animated the whole universe.

The idea that schizophrenia was associated with an inability to filter out an overabundance of sensory stimulation can be traced back to the Burghölzli psychiatrist Eugen Bleuler (1950/1911) and his German colleague Emil Kraepelin (1919). However, the first systematic elaboration of what could be called defective filter theories was only presented in 1961 (Healy 2002: 266). The psychologists Andrew McGhie and James Chapman (1961: 104) reported that schizophrenic patients often said such things as "I just can't shut things out" or "I'm attending to everything at once and as a result I do not really attend to anything." One of their schizophrenic subjects described the new quality of his perceptual experience in terms strikingly reminiscent of little Anselm's absorption by the sight of the blue flower: "I notice so much more about things and find myself looking at them for a longer time. Not only the color of things fascinates me but also all sorts of little things, like markings in the surface, pick up my attention" (105). With reference to developmental psychology, McGhie and Chapman interpreted this experience of psychosis in analogy to the experience of childhood: "Studies of early ego development . . . indicate that the first stages of infancy are characterized by an undifferentiated protoplasmic consciousness in which there is no differentiation between the self and the outside world" (110). In the researchers' eyes, schizophrenics lapsed back into this primitive mode of perception—also described in the mystical literature. They explained the peculiar quality of psychotic experience by the breakdown of a central filter screening out stimuli irrelevant to the task at hand: "Consciousness would be flooded with an undifferentiated mass of incoming sensory data. . . . Perception would revert to the passive and involuntary assimilative process of early childhood and, if the incoming flood were to carry on unchecked, it would gradually sweep away the stable constructs of a former reality" (112). Geyer told me that he took this to be a more scientific exposition of what he called the "Huxley gating failure notion."

In the 1960s, Geyer was not only a hippie but also a psychopharmacologist in the making, trying to translate Huxley's perennial philosophy and Hesse's quest for the blue flower of Romanticism (mediated by Leary) into scientific research on how habituation to repeatedly presented sensory stimuli could be disrupted pharmacologically. Geyer's eureka experience leading up to an experimental operationalization of Huxley's doors of perception and Hesse's childlike view of the world was triggered in 1968. That year, Geyer read a rather inconspicuous article by brain researcher George Aghajanian, who had inhibited habituation to startling sounds by electrically stimulating serotonergic midbrain raphe neurons in rats. As LSD had also been reported to disrupt habituation, Aghajanian concluded "that LSD-25 mimics the action of serotonin in the brain" (Sheard and Aghajanian 1968: 24). For Geyer, this finding opened up an experimental approach to studying what made us perceive things as they really are rather than through a curtain of habituation. "Boy, I thought this was the neatest study I had ever seen," he remembered. "So I immediately ran to the lab and started setting up a startle system to study serotonin and habituation."

Geyer built a makeshift prototype of the startle chamber. In the developed form that I got to see in the lab, this pressboard box contained a Plexiglas tube big enough to fit a rat as well as a loudspeaker (see figure 13). When in use, it emitted white noise, and a computer occasionally interrupted this murmur by generating startling or nonstartling sonic bursts referred to as pulses and prepulses. Alternatively, light flashes and air puffs could also be triggered to affect sense modalities other than hearing. Usually, a pulse was strong enough to elicit a full-blown startle reflex, which comprised a jerk of the whole body. The amplitude of this reflex and of its inhibition by a prepulse was registered by a piezo crystal under the Plexiglas tube, measuring the intensity of the animal's twitches.

Before examining PPI, however, Geyer and colleagues (1978) used the apparatus to replicate the finding that pretreatment with LSD also impaired the animals' habituation to repeatedly administered startle stimuli (without any nonstartling prepulses). In collaboration with the psychiatrist David Braff, Geyer additionally studied this startle habituation in schizophrenic patients. To test humans they had to design a different system: it consisted of a computer that presented acoustic startle stimuli through earphones and a potentiometer that electromyographically recorded eye blinks as the most persistent component of the startle (this is the device I had come to know in Zurich). This setup enabled Braff and Geyer (1982) to demonstrate that schizophrenics resembled rats treated with LSD in failing to habituate normally to startling stimuli. Thus, Huxley's doors of perception had taken the form of an animal model of psychosis.

But all beginnings are difficult. Geyer recalled that, when they had first proposed to the National Institute of Mental Health to study psychosis through the habituation of startle, the funding agency replied that startle was too simple to have anything to do with a complex disorder such as schizophrenia. "It turned out," Geyer told me, "that startle is fairly complicated." At the time, it had just been discovered that the startle reflex could be inhibited if the startling stimulus was preceded by a nonstartling one (Graham 1975). Unlike habituation, this prepulse inhibition of the startle reflex was considered to be a very basic, preattentive, and largely involuntary filtering mechanism. Geyer and Braff wanted to test whether PPI could serve as a readout of the neural processes underlying the attention deficits found in schizophrenic patients. But measuring PPI was technically more demanding than habituation. Geyer remembered: "We struggled because we only had this homemade system that I had built and it wasn't sophisticated enough. We had a very difficult time designing a more flexible startle system. We built the computers ourselves, literally on plywood. But we finally managed to set up a system that could do a prepulse test."

With this system, Braff and Geyer managed to demonstrate that schizophrenic patients also showed a reduced prepulse inhibition (Braff et al. 1978). They thereby introduced PPI into psychiatry. And again, Geyer's laboratory was able to reproduce this finding in rats treated with a variety of drugs, including hallucinogens (Swerdlow et al. 1986; Mansbach and Geyer 1989, 1991; Sipes and Geyer 1995; Krebs-Thomson et al. 2006). Moreover, they could show in animals that many already known antipsychotic drugs could normalize PPI after it had been disrupted by hallucinogens (Mansbach et al. 1988; Swerdlow et al. 1991; Bakshi et al. 1994; Sipes and Geyer 1995). This gave rise to the hope that hallucinogen-induced PPI deficits in rodents could serve as a high-throughput drug-screening mechanism that would help to identify new antipsychotics. As PPI turned out to be more replicable, reliable, and robust than habituation, Geyer and his coworkers soon began to focus their attention on this more promising measure of sensorimotor gating.

Establishing a new scientific fact or method requires the formation and extension of a network (Latour and Woolgar 1986: 183). One major obstacle for PPI to catch on was the lack of reliable and standardized measuring instruments. Geyer recounted to me that, "in the 1970s, there was one company called Columbus Instruments that made a startle system that was trash. Like others, we had made our own systems and they worked pretty well. But unless you were adept at that, there was only this one company building a crappy system. The people who used it were getting really bad data, threw their hands up, and said that PPI was a bad paradigm." In response, Geyer founded his own company, San Diego Instruments, in the early 1980s and developed more reliable commercial startle systems for animals and humans. He was reproached by some of his collaborators for inviting competition, making their technology available to everybody who was willing to pay for it. "Of course, that was true," Geyer said. "But, in science, the worst thing is to protect your little private niche and be ignored. And all that competition did was to bring us more notice."

The global marketing of standardized and dependable startle systems paved the way for the scientific takeoff of PPI. In the 1990s, the San Diego Instruments device, the SR-LAB, became the most widely used system for testing PPI and habituation in both academic laboratories and industry departments that were developing new antipsychotics. Whereas in 1981 there were only four published reports on PPI, more than two thousand articles could be found by July 2011. PPI had become one of the most influential paradigms in schizophrenia psychophysiology (Swerdlow et al. 2008) and was about to spread into neighboring fields of psychiatric research. Geyer's profanation of Hesse's "Iris" and Huxley's *Doors of Perception* had significantly contributed to the resurgence of hallucinogen research. "The similarity of PPI deficits in animal studies and schizophrenic patients," Vollenweider (1998: 29) wrote, "has revitalized interest in hallucinogens in the 1990s and prompted a concerted search into the neurotransmitter systems involved in modulating PPI in rodents."

STEWARDSHIP IN THE IRON CAGE

However much Geyer had a hand in reviving hallucinogen research through PPI, and despite his commitment to the Heffter Research Institute, his project did not lend itself to attracting people first and foremost fascinated by psychedelic drugs and everything they stood for. Hence, drug experiences did not play a prominent role in shoptalk at the Geyer lab. At the beginning of my stay, one of the technicians asked me what exactly I was looking at in their work. When I told him that I was interested in their research with hallucinogenic drugs such as LSD, he shrugged: "It's just another drug." The dominant view in the lab was that psychedelics were research tools that allowed altering the brain chemistry of laboratory animals in specific ways. Not that Geyer's collaborators were generally ignorant of the effects their tools had on the human mind. Some had personally experienced how *Psilocybe* mushrooms or LSD could radically alter the way we think, feel, and perceive the world. But these experiences had not played a decisive role in the formation of their personal and professional identities. And, in the lab, drug experiences were usually not spoken about openly. There seemed to be some degree of uneasiness based on the concern that admitting firsthand knowledge of the substances one was working with might have a negative effect on one's reputation as a scientist. The norms governing the discipline of psychopharmacology had come a long way since Kurt Beringer had expected his residents to partake in his mescaline trial.

Although for some, drug experiences were a precarious detail of their past, they were not a major cause of concern or fascination. What the researchers in Geyer's lab did worry about was not so much their experimentation with drugs as with animals. During my first days in the lab, I watched how the youngest technician was taught how to implant cannulas into the brains of mice. After the animals had recovered from this minor surgery, the device enabled direct infusion of drugs into specific parts of the brain instead of globally administering pharmacological agents. Such an anatomically differentiated approach appeared to be one of the most promising venues of neuropharmacology. However, for ethical reasons, it could only be pursued in animals. I took photos of the surgery, of mice that had already been operated on and were now running around in their cages with little tubes sticking out of their heads, as well as of the subsequent killing—or "sacrificing," as the researchers called it—of these "practice animals." The fact that I had photographed scenes likely to stir up public sentiments gave rise to speculations that I might be a clandestine animal rights activist infiltrating the lab to bring it into disrepute: a strategy that had been employed successfully by the most prominent American animal rights organization, People for the Ethical Treatment of Animals (PETA).[2]

Public pressure was high. During my fieldwork, British antivivisectionists had managed to threaten not just small academic labs but even a transnational pharmaceutical giant such as GlaxoSmithKline. The company's chief executive felt it necessary to stress that Glaxo had no plans to leave the United Kingdom because of the protests and urged other businesses to resist pressure from animal rights activists too. "This is not the time to flee the battlefield," he said (Cowell 2006). Although, historically, the animal protection movement was not as well established in the United States as in Great Britain, PETA campaigners in the States had successfully obtained the suspension of research funds and the termination of experiments in academic institutions.

In the late 1980s, Mark Geyer's lab had become the target of PETA as well. Two of Geyer's grants were subpoenaed under the Freedom of Information Act and he was twice nominated as Vivisectionist of the Year. During Animal Liberation Week, the activists held a candlelight vigil on campus to make known Geyer's treatment of animals. Rumor even had it that the protestors burned him in effigy. They decided to amplify their allegations of cruelty to animals by focusing on a PPI study in which Geyer had administered the infamous hallucinogen PCP, also known by its street name angel dust, to ninety-two rats. "Out of those twenty-five pages of grant proposal, that was what they wanted to protest against," Geyer remembered. "There were neurotoxin studies and burning holes into brains, that is, making lesions, but that didn't bother them. What seemed to upset them was giving rats PCP and startling them. We can get humans to volunteer for that kind of study. Franz [Vollenweider] does it all the time, using ketamine instead of PCP. Whether this was a reflection of a projective anxiety that made the PETA people anxious or whether they were strategic, thinking that this is something that people can relate to as being horrible, I don't know."

Even though PETA's protests did not impede Geyer's research, his laboratory had already been affected by the consequences of previous campaigns, which had led to a revision and tightening of the Animal Welfare Act in 1985. Of course, this is not to say that the animal rights activists' demands were fully implemented by the American government. The regulations put in place at the time did not grant animals any "rights." Rights continued to be an exclusively human domain. Rather, the management of laboratory animals was based on the principle of "animal welfare," a form of responsible stewardship aimed at the humane use of animals but not an abolition of their scientific and agricultural utilization.[3] Alongside the increasing regulation of research on human subjects, the gradual institutionalization of animal welfare since the 1960s had been part of the emergence of "the ethical" as a significant public space carved out between the legal and the political (Rabinow 2008: 84).

The care of laboratory animals was haunted by the philosophical problem of subjectivity, as articulated by Thomas Nagel (1974): no human could tell what it was like to be a guinea pig. In the "Orientation to Animal Research" class, which every student and employee at UCSD beginning to experiment on animals had to take, a veterinarian advised the audience to assume that, "if something is painful or distressful to us, most likely it is painful or distressful to the animal we work with." However, such anthropomorphizing inference, from human experience to the experience of other species, was disputed. An ethics textbook assigned to animal science students cautioned that animals might suffer *more* or *less* than humans: possibly less because of different forms of pain reception and because they could not anticipate or remember pain; or maybe more because they had less understanding of the origin, nature, and meaning of the inflicted pain (Orlands et al. 1998: 40–41). In the case of rodents, that is, the vast majority of laboratory animals, it was particularly difficult to tell how they felt: as a prey species they masked their overt signs of pain as much as possible to avoid being singled out by predators.

However, the regulatory apparatus administering animal welfare and suffering sidestepped such slippery philosophical questions by defining formal criteria for animal husbandry and research protocols. Federal law specified what was considered adequate housing, food, cage size, transportation carriers, handling of animals, oversight responsibilities, and so on. Furthermore, every institution that received public funding also had to establish an Institutional Animal Care and Use Committee (IACUC), comparable to the ethics committees for human subjects research, to review every individual study. But in a large-scale institution such as a university, only a strictly formalist procedure enabled a bureaucratic body like the IACUC to watch over the ethicality of an enormous number of scientists and the well-being of an even larger number of lab animals.

Besides processing protocols, IACUC was mandated to police and audit laboratories and vivaria. Laboratory staff were expected to keep records on everything they did in relation to animals—from medical checkups to experiments, from purchase to euthanasia. This produced a significant amount of paperwork. Geyer was not entirely opposed to this: "Some regulation was certainly needed," he told me, "because there were people who didn't have sensitivities to the health of animals." He felt that these people were not primarily psychologists and behavioral psychopharmacologists but medical researchers interested in biochemistry and toxicology who were oblivious to their animals' behavior. But he also thought of himself as representative of the field in regarding the increasing regimentation as "overkill." Animal rights groups had discovered that red tape was a weapon: the more bookkeeping, the less animal experimentation. Geyer expressed his irritation about this: "Many of the controls that are required now don't add to the well-being of the animals." He accused PETA of trying to institutionalize as many procedural checks and balances as possible to increase the cost of doing research, saying, "This is based on the correct belief that, every time we spend a hundred dollars on processing forms, those hundred dollars can't go into buying a rat."

As Mark Brann's remarks about the decline of pharmacological self-experimentation and Geyer's complaints about the excessive regulation of animal welfare indicate, psychedelic science seemed to have been reborn into Max Weber's "iron cage" of modernity against which the hippies had rebelled: an increasingly bureaucratic order was suffocating vocational passion (as personified by Brann's avid pharmaceutical researchers curious enough to experiment on themselves) and outsourcing an ethos of stewardship to institutionalized ethics bodies such as IACUCs and institutional review boards for human research. Almost a century earlier, Weber (1992/1920: 124) had wondered who would live in this cage in the future: "specialists without spirit, sensualists without heart"?

The discontent and irritation felt vis-à-vis this regulatory framework indicated that researchers had not fully internalized the norms that the animal welfare apparatus imposed on them. However, this is not to say that the scientists were unscrupulous and free of ethical concerns. In fact, they had developed an attitude slightly at odds with, but also complementary to, the audit culture that monitored their work. In contrast to the procedural ethics practiced by bureaucracies that ideally operated in a strictly formalistic and impersonal manner, this kind of ethos was embodied by individual researchers. The regulatory institutions relied on the fact that those scientists and technicians actually working with animals handled them conscientiously. Bench workers were expected to develop a certain sensibility in accord with the practice and principles of animal welfare as well as animal experimentation. In the "Orientation to Animal Research" course, the IACUC representative urged the participants "to take time to think about and develop a personal code of ethics that emphasizes animal welfare." The veterinarian who had explained in much detail how different lab animal species were to be housed, handled, and killed proclaimed: "Doing research with live animals is a privilege, not a right. Therefore, these animals need to be treated with utmost compassion and respect because obviously they are sentient beings sacrificing their lives to advance science and knowledge."

Or at least the *researchers* sacrificed the animals' lives to advance science and knowledge—and, thus, their own careers. But, sociological cynicism aside, it is worth paying attention to the scientists' talk about their "sacrificing" of animals. On the whole, modern religions have abandoned the cruel rites of the past. "Today a deity who should require bleeding sacrifices to placate him would be too sanguinary to be taken seriously," remarked William James (1958/1902: 257). Yet the notion of the sacrifice lives on in biomedicine as the arena of modernity's most sacred values: life and health (Rabinow 2003: 133). Used as a technical term for the killing of animals in the laboratory, this manner of speaking not only justifies the destruction of these "sentient beings" for the "higher" causes of scientific knowledge and medical progress. As the sociologist of science Michael Lynch (1988) has argued, the expression "to sacrifice" also designates the rendering of a flesh-and-blood animal into an analytic entity such as tissue samples or data sets on a hard disk—analogous to the ritual transformation of a profane into a sacred object. Of course, in animal labs, the decapitation and gassing of mice and rats is no solemn sacral act but business as usual. Like the devout offering to God, however, it is associated with mediating acts that, if carried out correctly, give the animal a significance that transcends and outlives its quickly disposed of corpse: its preserved remainders and numeric traces connect the realm of lived experience with an invisible realm of abstract relations and scientific concepts. The scientific sacrifice also resembles its religious counterpart in that it is based on an identification with the sacrificial victims by those who slaughter them (as in the killing of scapegoats): in the end, no funding body would provide resources for research on rat brains if such studies did not indirectly shed light on human brains.

It should be noted that the relationship between Geyer's interest in unchurched forms of spirituality and this semantic analogy of scientific and religious sacrifice is not genealogical but contrastive. The former is about the here and now: pure immanence; the latter about transcendence. Empirically speaking, Bruno Latour's account of religion is certainly not representative of religion per se, not even of his own professed Catholicism (at least not in the Vatican's authoritative understanding). But Latour (2005) can be read as a trenchant analysis of the case at hand when he maintains that it was science that generated transcendence and grasped the far and the distant by building long and complicated referential chains from instrumental recordings, calculations, and models to reach the invisible worlds of what is too small, too big, too far, too powerful, or too counterintuitive to be apprehended without such mediations. Religion, on the other hand, did not even try to reach anything beyond, Latour claims. Religion is not about the belief in anything otherworldly but rather aims at salvation by redirecting attention away from indifference and habituation toward the present moment and one's neighbors—including, we might suppose in Latour's case, nonhuman others (Hache and Latour 2010).

The cultivation of compassion and respect for those sentient beings sacrificed to advance medical knowledge belongs to the spiritual rather than procedural dimension of the animal welfare apparatus. It has inspired the kind of substantive ethical deliberations that no ethics committee could achieve. When I asked people in the lab where they drew the line in what they were willing to do to an animal, a postdoctoral researcher told me that he would never do pain experiments—even though he did not think of them as transgressing any moral limits. In fact, he thought of their potential to alleviate human suffering as highly valuable. When I brought up his attitude in a conversation with two of his colleagues, they said that they would not rule out conducting pain experiments categorically. But they were only willing to engage in such work if they were convinced that it was a "good study." One of them had conducted pain experiments at a pharmaceutical company but quit the job when she realized that the experiment had been badly designed. Conducting uninterpretable "half-assed" research without proper controls was a "waste of animals," they said. Every judgment of this kind had to be based on an ethical, practical, and scientific orientation in a particular situation, which an ethics committee on the other side of campus would always lack.

Such a "personal code of ethics," which animal experimenters were expected to develop, revealed an ambiguity in the scientists' attitudes toward animal welfare. On the one hand, they opposed what they perceived as an excess of bureaucratic constraints. On the other hand, individual researchers laid down their own norms, which were often more restrictive than the official regulations. These decisions presupposed a practical wisdom that was the product of a process of ethical self-formation but also of technical competence, scientific knowledge, and intimate familiarity with animal behavior. However one might judge animal experimentation, it did not seem as if the spirit of stewardship (including its religious connotation of being accountable to God for the diligent care and use of His creation) had entirely escaped from the iron cage. Was it possible that the little-loved external strictures had even helped imbue researchers with this sense of responsibility? Or were other motives at play as well?

LULLABY FOR A MOUSE

Adam Brown[4] was a sturdy, bearded twenty-seven-year-old Scot who had recently finished his PhD in psychology at the University of Edinburgh on an animal model of attentional performance (5-choice serial reaction time task). As a matter of principle, he never took illegal drugs. But he loved to drink. No beer, but wine and shots. He joked: "If I should ever end up at an Alcoholics Anonymous meeting, I will get up and say: 'My name is Adam. I'm a Scotsman. Get over it!'" He was standing in a small PPI laboratory wearing a blue lab coat, purple gloves, and a breathing mask that covered most of his face. During his thesis work, he had developed an allergy to mice and rats and the mask protected him. Today, he wanted to test whether the PPI deficit induced by the antiglutamatergic hallucinogen PCP was related to the fact that PCP also interacted with the dopaminergic system. For this purpose, he would measure prepulse inhibition in genetically engineered dopamine D_2 receptor knockout mice that were under the influence of PCP and compare the results to those of normal mice who had also received the drug.

Brown picked up a mouse, held it by the scruff of its neck, and injected a PCP solution into the cavity of its abdomen (see figure 14). All the while, he spoke to the mouse in a soft voice. The mouse squeaked and peed on his gloved hands. Brown administered one of two different doses or merely the "vehicle" (roughly equivalent to a placebo in a human trial), to the other mice for the first measurement. He put the already dosed animals into different compartments of a Plexiglas box. They immediately started digging about in the litter. They looked lively. But Brown explained to me that this was escape behavior, indicating that they were stressed out. Those that had received a high dose of PCP appeared rather sedated.

During the fifth and last round of this procedure, something unexpected happened. The very last mouse that Brown injected with a high dose responded in a manner very different from everything we had seen before: it got onto its hind legs and started to rapidly bounce against the cover of the box, over and over again, until it reeled and fell to the side, only to get up again, continuing to bounce against the transparent ceiling until it fell another time, and so forth. Brown said, "This is as drunk as I've ever seen a mouse." He watched this bizarre spectacle for a while and then, with a quiet and gentle voice, he began to sing to the mouse:

> Show me the way to go home
> I'm tired and I wanna go to bed
> I had a little drink
> about an hour ago
> and it's gone right to my head.
> No matter where I roam
> Through land or sea or home
> You will always hear me singing this song:
> Show me the way to go home.

After the experiment, I asked Brown why he had spoken and sung to the mouse. He replied that he wanted to make it as comfortable as possible for the animals:

> You need to build up rapport with them. If you don't treat them well, your experimental results won't turn out well. This does not apply so much to PPI, but it's definitely true for 5-choice [serial reaction time task], where you need to train the animals every day. It's important that you are anal about this. I got my worst experimental results after I broke up with my ex. My life became rather disorganized for a while. I went out a lot and came to work at different hours. This might have interfered with the animals' circadian rhythm. I didn't treat the animals badly, but not with as much care as I usually do, and they react very sensitively to this. Another reason for

speaking to them is that patients in a clinical setting are treated gently as well and we do try to mimic all aspects.

Note the subtle shift from ethics to epistemology, from making lab animals comfortable to getting good experimental results. After Brown brought this up, I realized that other people in the lab made very similar connections between method and care. One afternoon, two of Brown's colleagues were discussing that working with animals at the lab bench on a daily basis under the usual time pressure could easily lead to a desensitization to the ethical problems involved. But one of them remarked that she had recently grown more conscientious again since she had started doing stress experiments. To study stress under controlled conditions she had to carefully identify and eliminate all unwanted stressors that caused variance, especially for baseline measurements. Hence, she had to look after the well-being of the tested animals. Likewise, Mark Geyer told me:

> I think my sensibilities of animal welfare were formed during a time when we didn't have a lot of external guidelines or stricture on our behavior. Because of my interest in spontaneous behavior of a fairly healthy organism, I adopted such principles not so much out of concern for the welfare of the animals as concerns about the quality of the science. That incidentally meant that we wanted the highest quality of animal welfare. I don't mean to suggest that I was insensitive to those concerns, but that just wasn't the explicit motivation.

Even though ethical incentives were secondary to the scientists, it was as if there had been a higher moral order governing the world of animal laboratories: to achieve good results, the researcher needed to treat his animals well. This perspective on animal experimentation seemed to defy what Foucault (2005: 18–25) called "the Cartesian moment" in the particular relationship between subjectivity and truth that characterizes modernity.[5] The principle of method as elaborated in the seventeenth century broke with the ancient idea that access to truth required a certain ethical work on the self and shifted the conditions of possibility of knowledge fully into the epistemological realm. No matter who you are, you can get to the truth, if you only follow the rules of method.

PHARMAHUASCA AND THE HANDLING OF RATS, SET, AND SETTING

But modern scientists would not be modern scientists if they had not responded to this anachronism by trying to turn the required care into another standardized procedure to achieve more consistent and repro-ducible results. The historian of science Otniel Dror (1999) describes how Anglo-American physiologists, especially those studying stress and other endocrinological phenomena related to feelings, worked hard to make the laboratory a place of controlled emotions (as opposed to nature as a site of perpetually changing states of affective excite-ment). This necessitated attention to a great many different parameters. The presence of an observer, an animal's familiarity with this person, and the stress of being handled by her were as important as the time of the day, the makeup of the experimental space, possible previous experiences in this environment, or pheromone-containing excretions and other communications between laboratory animals. Of course, different species and members of those species responded differently to particular circumstances, which had to be taken into account as well. This wide spectrum of factors can be broadly divided into two dimensions commonly discussed in, but apparently not restricted to, hallucinogen research: the impact of preformed expectations and imme-diate surroundings on an organism's response to a pharmacological intervention. The problem of set and setting did not plague human experimentation alone.

One of the technicians explained to me that setting was particularly difficult to handle in animal research, as it was hard for us to imagine how a different species experienced its environment. He liked to read popular-science books on the train while commuting and had just fin-ished *Animals in Translation: Using the Mysteries of Autism to Decode Animal Behavior* (2005), coauthored by Temple Grandin, an autistic animal behavior expert specializing in the design of more humane slaughter systems. Grandin, according to the technician's summary, argued that animals, like autistic humans, could not see the forest for the trees: "They have less of an overview, they are awash in all the details and don't get the big picture. Coincidentally, this also seems to be true for schizophrenics. Hence, when you're dealing with rats, you don't know what they are picking up on. Seemingly irrelevant parameters can change the outcome of the experiment." If results from a different laboratory could not be reproduced, it might well be due to something in the lab's *Umwelt* (see Roepstorff 2001; Uexküll 2010/1934). But it was very difficult to determine whether this was the new paint or the whirring of a computer's ventilation, especially if one had never been to the other place and there were no controlled experiments to find out the cause.

The problem of set was addressed by establishing handling procedures for laboratory animals. Successful management of their expectations and affective states required preparing them emotionally for the laboratory experience. To get them used to laboratory routine, manipulations, and human beings, they were exposed to daily handling. Such procedures were standard practice in animal laboratories. When entering the vivarium (usually after shipment from the manufacturer) and before being enrolled in any study, each new animal was handled for about five minutes. "It's almost like body massage," Geyer explained. "We swing them around and rub them. It does tend to make them less reactive to handling in the future." Additionally, animals were picked up once a day for a brief medical checkup, which also allowed them to get accustomed to humans. But this cultivation of an interspecies relationship aimed not at mutual attachment (as in the petting of pets) but at detachment. Habituation was meant to make the rats indifferent to the otherwise stressful encounter with humans. By reducing the impact of the scientists' presence on the animal's behavior, the handling procedures served the epistemic virtue of objectivity (Candea 2010).

As the psychopharmacological effects of hallucinogens were believed to be particularly sensitive to set and setting, Geyer had developed a special "hallucinogen handling procedure," which I first came to observe in the context of a study on "pharmahuasca." Pharmahuasca is the synthetic equivalent of the hallucinogenic tea ayahuasca, which can be brewed from different plants, one of which had to contain DMT while the other one added a monoamine oxidase (MAO) inhibitor to prevent the metabolic breakdown of DMT by the gut and liver enzyme MAO after oral ingestion. The concoction was used in Amazonian shamanism for the purpose of divination, healing, and religious ceremonies. Just like the Euro-American experiments described in this book, these Amerindian rituals required careful management of the conditions under which the drug was taken. Dietary proscriptions had to be adhered to before the session, which helped appease the jealous guardian spirit of the ayahuasca vine. Instead of isolating individuals in a quiet lab, the inebriating beverage was usually drunk in a group and the ceremony was accompanied by songs and whistling incantations (Dobkin de Rios 1984: 178). The drug was meant to enable humans to communicate with animals and spirits. But hallucinogens were also given to domestic animals, such as misbehaving dogs, to make them understand human speech. The Runa, for example, scolded their canines in this intoxicated state to reinforce compliance with a code of conduct, which the animals were supposed to share with everybody else in the village (Kohn 2007).

This form of animism turned naturalism, as the present Euro-American default ontology, upside down (anyone having watched a cartoon with talking animals should be aware, though, that modern occidentals occasionally adopt animistic thought as well). The naturalist ethics and epistemology of animal experiments were based on the assumption that animals had substantially different and categorically unknowable minds, whereas their bodies were closely related to human corporeality. In the animist ontology of Amerindian perspectivism, on the other hand, all sentient beings, be they humans, animals, or spirits, saw themselves as persons and members of a culture. They all shared the subjective aspect of being and a spiritual component, an anthropoid soul, qualifying them as people. What separated them were their bodily natures and, correspondingly, their different points of view (Viveiros de Castro 1998, 2004). Ayahuasca and other hallucinogens were meant to enable both humans and nonhumans to cross these ontological boundaries to adopt the perspectives of other natural and supernatural beings.

By contrast, pharmahuasca was not administered to rats for them to commune with human beings but to learn about their physiological responses to the drug. Unlike the naughty Runa dogs, they did not receive this pharmaceutically clean combination of DMT and MAO inhibitor to listen and obey. Instead their bodies were made to provide information about this drug cocktail—translated by a chain of inscriptions into humanly interpretable data. Geyer was interested in the ayahuasca ingredient DMT as a psychotomimetic agent because, unlike LSD or psilocybin, DMT was produced by the human organism (if only in minuscule amounts) and did not provoke tolerance. Hence, the resurgence of model psychosis research had also restarted the search for an endogenous psychotogen responsible for extended psychotic episodes as experienced by schizophrenic patients.

The pharmahuasca study conducted by Geyer's lab was motivated by evidence that, contrary to what had been assumed so far, DMT's mechanism of action differed significantly from those of other serotonergic hallucinogens. Since Vollenweider had established his claim that the psychedelic effects of psilocybin were primarily mediated by a 5-HT_{2A} agonism, Geyer had come to suspect that DMT might mainly stimulate 5-HT_{1A} receptors. Before being able to differentiate between its impact on these two subtypes of serotonin receptors, he first had to define the drug's unique behavioral profile.

For this purpose, Geyer decided to focus on locomotor and investigatory behavior, which was recorded by behavioral pattern monitors. The original impetus for using locomotor activity measures was derived from the amphetamine model of psychosis based on the dopamine hypothesis of schizophrenia. The apparent similarity between symptoms of schizophrenia and the effects of high doses of stimulants aroused interest in cross-species studies. Among the most marked behavioral effects of this class of drugs were locomotor hyperactivity and stereotyped behaviors. Even though schizophrenics are usually not hyperactive, they frequently show repetitive or ritualistic movements (Geyer and Moghaddam 2002). This partial correspondence led to looking at such stereotypies in intoxicated rodents as an animal model of psychosis. Exploratory locomotion, on the other hand, was usually not regarded as a model but as a dimension of behavior, which different drugs affected in fairly characteristic ways. A comparison of the temporal and spatial patterns of movement recorded by a behavioral pattern monitor contributed to an analysis of behavioral correlates of different neurochemical drug actions.

One day before the actual experiment, the white Sprague-Dawley rats were brought up from the vivarium to the laboratory to get used to the environment in which they would soon receive the drug. The room containing the behavior tracker boxes, in which they would be tested, was bathed in red light and the fans were running—"as if testing were imminent," as the protocol for the hallucinogen-handling procedure demanded. As nocturnal animals the rats were kept under reversed lighting conditions to adjust their circadian rhythm to that of the humans working with them. The technician running the experiment quietly took the rats out of their boxes and weighed them (the administered dosage would depend on the individual rat's body weight). He covered their head with a piece of cloth to calm them down while gently pinching their back skin to simulate a subcutaneous injection. Finally, he briefly put them into a large Plexiglas box resembling the actual behavior tracker boxes, which they would only get to know on the following day. After all rats had been handled in this manner, they were returned to the animal room in the basement of the building. In my discussions with Geyer, he explained that this strange ritual had grown out of a curious observation in 1976:

> In the National Science Foundation summer program to train undergraduates, we conducted a big study to examine the relationship between structure and activity of a number of hallucinogens, including some of Sasha Shulgin's

compounds, with primitive versions of our startle paradigms and a holeboard [a chamber with holes in the floor and walls that serve as specific stimuli for the rats to investigate]. Despite Sasha's claims to the contrary, one can predict the effects of these substances by doing animal experiments.

The normal procedure was to inject the animals in the carrying cages with drug or vehicle and, ten minutes later, you pick them up and put them in their test environment. We had the impression that, when you took the LSD animals, they were responding differently to being picked up than the control animals. When they went into the chamber, first they weren't very active. They went into a corner, looked around, and wouldn't venture out very much, which is characteristic of what a rat does on LSD.

We wondered whether the drug made them hyperresponsive to being picked up. So we did a study in which we did the same thing, except we exaggerated the handling. We picked them up and put them into the chamber, taking the same amount of time, but we also held the animals upside down for 15 to 20, maybe even 30 seconds, which is a long time to hold a rat upside down. They don't like that. That produced a significant effect, which again was significantly increased by LSD. Even the vehicle animals responded by being less exploratory if they had been handled this way, but in the LSD animals this effect was even more pronounced.

The day after the preparatory handling procedure, the rats were brought up to the laboratory again. This time, they underwent the real experiment and were injected with pharmahuasca. The effect of the drugs manifested itself immediately. The rats looked dazed. They lay around and only crawled short distances. At the same time they seemed tense. The moment the technician reached into an open cage to grab one of them, it jumped out in a high arc and fell on the floor. The rat tried to get underneath the boxes but was too stupefied to escape (see figure 15). Placed inside the behavior tracker box, it sat in the corner staring at the wall until the door was closed and the measurement began. The behavioral pattern monitor contained several infrared photo beams, building up a Cartesian coordinate system that tracked the rat's patterns of exploratory locomotion in this new environment over the next sixty minutes. In contrast to animals that had only been injected with the vehicle, they were more reluctant to explore their new environment right away. Their avoidance of open spaces was even more distinct. They stayed close to the walls and in corners, which they apparently perceived as the safest places they could find. As Geyer said jokingly at the LSD Symposium, alluding to the experiments that the Central Intelligence Agency had conducted on unwitting American citizens in the 1950s and 1960s (Lee and Shlain 1992: 19–35): "All you can do in animals is a CIA experiment. They don't volunteer for this. So we can study 'bad trips' a lot better than any other response to psychedelics." Thus, fear of the new (neophobia) and of open spaces (agoraphobia) had been identified as two of the most typical behavioral responses of rats to hallucinogens. Here, the decisive role of the setting became evident.

To gain a better understanding of the neophobia-inducing effect of hallucinogens, Geyer tested rats on LSD in a "free exploration paradigm." In contrast to the "forced exploration" setting described above, the rat's home cage was connected to an unfamiliar behavior tracker box, allowing it to go back and forth between the two spaces. In spite of the effects of LSD, the animals moved around normally in the familiar space of the home cage, whereas they displayed increased fearfulness in the unknown space. Hence, this dread of the new could be entirely attributed neither to the drug nor to the environment but instead resulted from a drug-induced change of the animals' attitudes toward these different environments. The result was striking. Unlike psychostimulants or sedatives, psychedelics did not determine a largely uniform behavioral reaction, such as moving around a lot more or less. "As in humans," Geyer observed, "hallucinogens do not lead to consistent effects on the level of arousal as reflected in motor activity; rather, hallucinogens alter the manner in which the organism's behavior is influenced by the environment" (Geyer and Krebs 1994: 126). In both animals and humans, this "ecopharmacology" of psychedelics was strictly localized: a phenomenon that could not be captured with randomized placebo-controlled trials, which would have produced very different results depending on whether they been conducted in the home cage or in a new environment. If the Amerindians were right and all sentient beings experienced their habits and characteristics in the form of culture, this experiment could count as a culture-controlled trial in animal research—slightly at odds with the naturalist ontology otherwise pervading the work of Geyer's group.

The custom of familiarizing the rats with the laboratory on the day before the experiment, which had been derived from these observations, was supposed to minimize the impact of the novelty of the lab space on the rodents' behavior. Of course, such habituation did not eliminate the ecological conditioning of the animal mind. No sacrifice, no aspiration to universal knowledge would abstract these animals from space: they would always be either in familiar or unfamiliar places, and that would modulate the investigated drug actions. And who could tell how many other distinctions mattered from the rats' point of view?

Therefore, the scientists and technicians in Geyer's lab made every effort to control for set and setting. But they had also come to realize the limits of this endeavor. Take the "tall blond left-handed effect," for instance. One of Geyer's former collaborators found that LSD initially induced a decrease of locomotor activity, which was then followed by an increase in the second part of the measurement. When her colleagues tried to reproduce this finding, they did not succeed—with the exception of another woman in the lab who, like the first researcher, turned out to be a tall left-handed blond. Besides the expectable erotic anthropomorphizations, it remained unclear what the rats had picked up on. The technician who related this anecdote to me concluded: "Behavioral work is an art. It is partly science, partly common sense, but it is also an art."

BEYOND ANTHROPOMORPHISM: ANGELOLOGY AND BEHAVIORAL NEUROPSYCHOPHARMACOLOGY

Many of the discussions of animal research reported above, from the question of animal suffering to the interpretation of the neophobia of hallucinogen-intoxicated rats, revolve around the problem of understanding the mental life of other species. The seventeenth-century philosopher René Descartes thought they had no mental life at all. When dissecting live animals, he never wondered what that was like for them. In fact, Descartes (1984/1641) did not even ask himself what the world was like for other human beings. He was rather worried that his dreaming brain or an evil genius might dupe him into a false picture of the world. But he had no doubt that everybody who was awake and not misled by a malignant demon saw the world exactly as he did. The problem of subjectivity, as it arose in the nineteenth century, however, was that of the correspondence among minds rather than between a mental representation and the world. The question of understanding other minds (in anthropology: "the native's point of view") was posed as, "What is it like to be an X or to experience X?" (Daston and Galison 2007: 273–283).

So what is it like to be a rat? What is it like to be a rat injected with LSD? And, if one looks at animals treated with hallucinogens as models of psychosis, the question arises whether being a rat on LSD is anything like being a patient suffering from schizophrenia. Can there be animal models of so-called mental diseases (Barondes 2003: 113–127)? When I asked Brown, he answered as a good naturalist: "You shouldn't anthropomorphize animals. All you can say is that a mouse displays an anxiogenic response in a test. But that doesn't mean it actually experiences anxiety. You can only observe its behavior. Therefore, I wouldn't say that there are mental diseases in animals, but that doesn't mean you can't model them in animals." After all, the model and its object are not the same.

When Thomas Nagel (1974) posed the question of what it was like to be a bat, he did not doubt that bats experienced the world somehow. But he argued that neither our imagination nor any neuroscientific data could provide access to the subjective quality of this experience. Philosophy, he conceded, was conceptually ill equipped to explain how the inner life could be related to physical processes in the brain. The proposition that a mental state is a state of the body, he claimed, remained incomprehensible to us as long as we did not know what *is* might mean when serving to identify such disparate realms as mental and physical states. Nagel was an analytic philosopher who did not believe that empirical neuropsychological research could help to find an answer to this question. In his eyes, the dilemma was entirely conceptual. What was needed was an "objective phenomenology" not dependent on empathy or the imagination.

Historian of science Lorraine Daston (2005) has responded to this challenge by tracing the other-minds problem to a point in time preceding the emergence of subjectivity and objectivity. Before anthropomorphism became a scientific vice, it was a theological sin to apply human categories to God, angels, or animals. In medieval theology, there was much concern about how angels thought. The question was worrisome because these immaterial beings lacked sense organs and knew the world through immediate intuitions of universal forms only, but on their missions they had to watch over or address specific individuals. How could they tell which woman was Mary if all they had available were the abstract concepts of virginity and immaculacy? And yet no scholastic theologian ever puzzled over what it was like to be an angel. Instead they approached the problem structurally: in contrast to humans, angelic minds were said to identify individuals not through analysis but through synthesis, that is, by associating all intelligible forms in which the individual participated.

Drawing from cognitive ethology, twentieth-century neuropsychopharmacologists also circumvented the problem of subjectivity by developing a structural yet empirical (rather than scholastic) response to the other-minds problem in animal research. In the early 1980s, for instance, Mark Geyer used his findings concerning the LSD-induced neophobia in rats to explore structure-activity relationships of drugs. When giving rats lisuride, a drug built very similarly to LSD, it did not increase their avoidance of open and novel spaces. When given to humans, lisuride did not produce the perceptual, cognitive, and affective changes characteristic of psychedelic experiences either. Hence, it seemed as if the neophobia observed in animals could serve as a behavioral marker capable of predicting hallucinogenic effects in humans. Geyer concluded that "the animal model of hallucinogenic activity was sensitive enough to discriminate between lisuride and LSD, two drugs that differ primarily with respect to their hallucinogenic effects" (Geyer and Krebs 1994: 134).

However, at about the same time, Jon Koerner and James Appel (1982) demonstrated that, in drug discrimination tasks, rats failed to recognize "hallucinogenicity" as a property shared by psilocybin, LSD, and mescaline. Their behavior seemed to indicate that they grouped LSD with psilocybin while putting mescaline into a different category. This led the authors to suggest that rats might detect something other than hallucinogenicity, a different property not shared by all so-called hallucinogens. They concluded that animals possibly perceived the effects of hallucinogens in a very different way than humans and that the term *hallucinogen* might therefore be a misnomer in the context of drug discrimination studies in nonhumans. After all, the term designates a group of chemically and neurophysiologically disparate substances, the effects of which only human beings seem to experience as sufficiently similar to pigeonhole these compounds as one class of drugs. The described third-person behavioral observations do not enable humans to tune into the rats' perspective and know what they felt like when they are administered these different substances. But, like medieval angelology, they do provide insights into the workings of other minds that do not rely on empathy or imagination: an objective (and empirical) phenomenology of sorts.[6]

IDENTIFICATION: THE LOGIC OF ANIMAL MODELS

How was mental disease modeled in animals, then, if all one could observe was behavior? Before ethology took a cognitive turn, reopening the black box of mental life in the 1970s (Perler and Wild 2005: 43–48), the taboo against anthropomorphism had given rise to behaviorism as an approach that shunned any kind of speculation about other minds in favor of experimental investigation of behavior. This approach was based on the assumption that there was no essential difference between humans and other animals. To study behavior under controlled laboratory conditions, behaviorists introduced the rat as their prime model organism. Due to the animals' fecundity, rapid rate of development, small size, and ease of handling, housing, and feeding, they soon populated psychology departments across the United States (Bühler and Rieger 2006: 200–208). In 1938, the psychologist Edward Tolman expressed his conviction that "everything important in psychology (except such matters as the building of a super-ego, that is, everything save such matters as involve society and words) can be investigated in essence through continued experimental and theoretical analysis of the determiners of rat behaviour at a choice point in the maze" (quoted in Burt 2006: 100–101).

The inference from rat to human behavioral psychology, and the corresponding neurobiology, was based on the premises of a "general biology." This is commonly true for the use of model organisms, as the historian of science Hans-Jörg Rheinberger (2010a: 6) points out:

> Organisms used as models began to play a central role in the life sciences at the beginning of the twentieth century—that is, relatively late in history, given that modeling and the construction of models compose an essential dimension of the experimental practices of the sciences. That model organisms and the concept of model organism could emerge at all in this period presupposed the idea of a *general biology*, the notion that certain attributes of life were common to all living things and could consequently be experimentally investigated using *particular* organisms that were representative of all others. In previous centuries, it was the *differences* between various living creatures that had commanded the interest of scientists, who in the natural history tradition had sought to account for life forms in all their diversity. With the goal that biological knowledge now set itself, these differences were invested with an altered, instrumental meaning: they could be used to arrive, by way of such particularities, at general characteristics of life.

The most recent and currently most powerful rearticulation of the program of a general biology emerged in the context of the genome projects of the 1990s. As part of the Human Genome Project, the genomes of other species, serving as model organisms, were sequenced as well. The mouse, which by now had replaced the rat as the most commonly used laboratory animal (in the Geyer lab as elsewhere because mice were cheaper to house and more suitable for genetic engineering), was reported to have a 99 percent genetic homology to humans (Boguski 2002). This once led an envious yeast geneticist to remark: "I don't consider the mouse a model organism. The mouse is just a cuter version of a human, a pocket-sized human" (quoted in Rader 2004: 267).

In the case of behaviorist research in psychology and biology, including behavioral neuropsychopharmacology, the blurring of the human and the animal led to a paradoxical situation: one painstakingly tried to avoid anthropomorphizing animals while using them as substitutes for and models of humans. This practice appears less confusing when examined through the lens of Philippe Descola's anthropology of ontologies. Drawing from developmental psychology and cross-cultural comparison, Descola (2006) assumes that human beings are natural-born dualists who approach every encountered entity through a process of tentative identification by selectively attributing or denying it an interiority and physicality analogous to their own. The ontological framework of naturalism inverts the animism that informed the ayahuasca rituals of Amazonian tribes (which Descola studied ethnographically) by taking plants and animals to be essentially different or even devoid of inner life while attributing to them a similar kind of material composition. Thus, it made perfect sense for Euro-Americans to reject any kind of mental identification with experimental animals while using them as biological model organisms to learn about human conditions.

But this ontological division had become unstable. Operating at the very border of interiority and physicality, biological psychiatry and psychopharmacology constantly undermined the kind of dualism that Descola believes to be innate and specific to the human species. For the time being, the molecularization of psychiatry allowed for the heuristic bracketing of the intricacies of human and animal minds alike. Instead of getting caught up in the overly complex convolutions of the brain and its higher faculties, researchers focused on basic neurophysiological mechanisms, which all mammals shared. This style of thought had grown out of Emil Kraepelin's (1892) pharmacopsychology that studied the effects of various pharmacological agents on easily measurable "simple psychic processes." Mark Geyer's focus on the startle reflex is an excellent example of this recourse to the most basic neural functions for the purpose of tackling problems as complex as schizophrenia and other mental diseases. Did Geyer think of his animal work as reductionist? "In some sense, yes," he told me:

> And in some sense I also see my attempts at human work as reductionist. For instance, my suggestion that we use prepulse inhibition as a possible biomarker, as a tool for prediction of pharmacotherapies, is a conscious attempt to reduce the complexity of symptom-based assessment of therapeutic effects

to something that is measurable acutely or in a shorter time frame, that might be predictive of but is not the same as the hoped for therapeutic clinical outcome. That would have increased efficiency by virtue of its increased precision even though it has decreased meaning by virtue of its being more distant from the ultimate goal of treating the problems that the patient has. And patients don't have problems with PPI. I have no illusions about that. They never come in complaining about a PPI deficit. So it is quite distal to the real-world problems that the patients have and that we are trying to treat. But those problems are very hard to quantify. And so is the alleviation of those problems. Hence, for me, consciously, it is a reductionistic approach to reduce that complexity at the cost of ultimate meaning. The success or failure of such an approach is in its predictive power. That's what we're here in science to do and really not much else. There is really only one proof of the pudding in science and that is, can you predict what's gonna happen next? The rest is all fluff and theory and opinion.

ANTHROPOLOGICAL DIFFERENCE: THE CRISIS OF ANIMAL MODELS

Geyer conceived of the PPI model of schizophrenia in pragmatist terms. The question was not whether this enactive model was true but whether it would help identify a future antipsychotic that would not only undo hallucinogen-induced PPI deficits in animals but also improve the clinical condition of patients (it was hoped that Acadia's ACP-103 would make this hurdle). Yet this emphasis on prediction entailed one significant problem: so far, the application of prepulse inhibition as a preclinical screening tool for novel antipsychotics had not led to the development of a single new drug. "The jury is still out on its usefulness as a predictive tool in clinical therapeutics," Geyer admitted. In fact, the only antipsychotic drug ever discovered with the help of the hallucinogen model of psychosis was risperidone in 1985 (Colpaert 2003). One possible reason for the lack of success of the PPI approach had only come to the fore since Euphrosyne Gouzoulis-Mayfrank and Franz Vollenweider had discovered that, in contrast to rats and schizophrenics, healthy human subjects treated with psilocybin and MDMA did not show a decreased prepulse inhibition but an increase. These discrepancies between humans and animals had given rise to an ongoing discussion between Geyer's lab and the labs of Vollenweider and Gouzoulis.

Further studies conducted in San Diego had complicated the picture even more. The discrepancies were not restricted to humans and animals but turned out to be widely disseminated across species, to the extent that even mice and rats did not always produce the same results. When Vollenweider came to visit Geyer's group, the issue was raised in a lab meeting. The explanatory attempts were multiple, highly complex, and inconclusive. One researcher brought up interspecies differences in metabolism and different dosages administered to the differently sized organisms. A closer look at Gouzoulis's study revealed that, under the influence of psilocybin, PPI was differently affected at short intervals between prepulse and pulse than at long intervals—which was not the case in schizophrenics, and a first still unpublished study in animals did not point to any such interval dependence either. Moreover, Geyer's team had dosed its animals with psilocybin many times but never managed to get repeatable results. Consistent PPI deficits had only been produced with other hallucinogens such as mescaline, DOI, or DOM. In contrast to these phenethylamine-derived psychedelics, the tryptamine psilocybin had a much stronger effect on the 5-HT_{1A} receptor. Geyer told me that his own hypothesis was that

> 5-HT_{1A} contributions are opposite to 5-HT_{2A} contributions. This is based on the surprising finding that in the mouse we have very clearly opposite effects in 1A and 2A contributions, which again is not the case in rats. In rats, both 1A and 2A disrupts PPI. In the mouse, on the other hand, 2A reduces PPI as in the rat, while 1A increases PPI opposite to the rat and opposite to the 2A effect. But we don't know yet about the contributions of 5-HT_3, 5-HT_4, 5-HT_5, 5-HT_6, and 5-HT_7. That leaves open the question, which rodent is more predictive of what happens in humans? My speculation is that, in the 5-HT_{1A} system, the mouse is a better predictor of the human situation. That would be consistent with the observations of Efi [Gouzoulis] and Franz [Vollenweider] that MDMA and psilocybin increase PPI in humans.

Such psychedelic research after the counterculture era confirmed the lessons of an anthropology of science beyond critique. Did it need any further demonstration of "how impossible it is for a reductionist scientist to be reductionist" (Latour 2004a: 226)? Certainly not for Geyer: "We chose such a simple behavior that a lot of people think it's not relevant to anything complex, but it's certainly complex enough for me to get frustrated about it."

The problems encountered in cross-species studies of hallucinogens point toward a more extensive problematization of generalizability in biology. The French historical epistemologist Georges Canguilhem (2008/1965: 11) pointed out that, in the life sciences, any logical generalization was limited unforeseeably by the specificity of the object of observation and the experiment. He even suggested adding the name of the species in which a biological phenomenon had been observed to the name of the phenomenon itself to prevent rash generalizations.

Although the use of model organisms presupposes the idea of a general biology, the application of findings from one species to another has often turned out be problematic. Accordingly, philosopher of science Rachel Ankeny (2007) argues that model organisms be used to generate knowledge through a form of case-based reasoning. Comparisons between different model organisms and attention to similarities and differences alike contributes to our understanding of the manifold manifestations of life. As Rheinberger (2010a: 8) contends, it is exactly the vagueness and imprecision of the match between model organisms and what they are a model of that keeps the experimental system productive: "From the standpoint of the research process, models maintain their function for only as long as this representational relation remains somewhat hazy, only as long as we cannot say exactly what a particular model ultimately represents. The emergence of certainty about a particular question abolishes the need for models altogether."

Nevertheless, the fact that the discrepancies between human and animal research promised to give rise to a fruitful exchange between the laboratories in San Diego, Cologne, and Zurich did not comfort Mark Geyer. Still hoping to be able to use PPI to go beyond basic research and to contribute significantly to the development of new antipsychotic drugs, he preferred to see a successful generalization of the results obtained in preclinical animal studies in the form of accurate predictions of antipsychotic effects in patient populations. But many of the younger researchers in the labs in Zurich and San Diego had grown skeptical about this prospect. In response to my nagging questions concerning the alleged crisis of PPI, Geyer finally gave in, expressing his consternation about the divergence of human and animal studies, which to him was indicative of a much more fundamental problem in behavioral neuropsychopharmacology:

> If there is anything like crisis, that's the crisis we have. But in a sense it is a bigger crisis than just for PPI. I tried not to emphasize this, but it's a crisis for animal models. And, secondarily, it's a crisis for the psychotomimetic drug-induced psychosis model. There are two mismatches. The first one is that some of the drug effects that we know are very robust in animals—in rodents, both mice and rats, and some in monkeys—don't seem to play out faithfully in humans. There are obviously ways to hand-wave and explain this away. The easiest is that we haven't pushed the dose in human research in the way we can readily do in animals. It is conceivable that most of these apparent disparities are dose-related. I take some solace in the notion that we have the power to address these cross-species disparities. But it's really hard to have confidence that you're actually measuring the same behavior across

species. This is a threat to animal modeling in general. In the case of the startle reflex, we have as close to a homologous behavior as one can really imagine from mice to humans. We have lots of reasons to believe that it's the same behavior and the same neural circuits across species. So if we can't do predictive psychopharmacology with that degree of homology, how do we expect that other, more indirect models of cognitive phenomena in a rodent predict anything in humans? That's one of the current challenges to the field.

The difference between humans and animals that neuropsychopharmacologists were struggling with was not a qualitative or essential one like the *differentia specifica* in the tradition of philosophical anthropology. The reasons for the disparity between human and animal research discussed by Geyer and his colleagues involved quantitative differences in dose and the speed of metabolism, differences in anatomical distribution of enzymes and neurotransmitter receptors, and, consequently, differences in effect of hallucinogenic agents on the measure of prepulse inhibition. Like other life sciences, psychopharmacology had come to see life as consisting of a limited number of basic elements: the carbon chemistry of proteins, carbohydrates, and fats; the four nucleotides of DNA; or a reflex arc, such as the startle response shared by all mammals. Kraepelin's simple psychic processes had been further broken down into interactions between neurotransmitters such as serotonin (fulfilling a diverse array of functions from blood pressure to mood regulation and perception) and different types and subtypes of neurotransmitter receptors. In this ontological form, which the philosopher Gilles Deleuze (1999: 131) called the "unlimited-finite," a finite number of relatively simple components were assembled and reassembled in unlimited permutations (see Rabinow 1996b: 91–93; Marks 2006). The "neuromolecular gaze" (Abi-Rached and Rose 2010) still saw man as different from other animals, but only as much as all species differed from each other (not to speak of within-species differences, which, in light of inconsistent PPI measurements in schizophrenics, contributed to the breakup of the disease category of schizophrenia into a multiplicity of so-called endophenotypes). The resulting molecularization and animalization of the human, commonly denounced as reductionism, had become a site of fierce contention. But the crisis of animal models was not a point scored for humanists: not only because there was little reason to rejoice in the fact that no better medications for schizophrenic patients had been forthcoming, but also because it did not prove *Homo sapiens* to be special—just a little more of a mouse than a rat.

MOLECULARIZED GOD-FORM AND ANTHROPOLOGICAL MACHINES

The epistemic figure of the unlimited-finite, which Deleuze described in "On the Death of Man and Superman," an appendix to his book *Foucault* (1999), is intellectually liberating in that it breaks open the finitude of anthropological thought. In the last two chapters, we saw that the inherent limitations of the empiricotranscendental double of man continue to haunt not only the discipline of anthropology but also the neurosciences. "Can a brain study the brain, can consciousness understand consciousness?" agonized Felix Hasler. Seeing all of life through reductionist glasses, the neuromolecular gaze averts its eyes from the representational opacity and essential depth that constitutes the epistemic formation of the human sciences. By reducing complex things to a limited number of simple, basic building blocks, this flat ontology also allows the creation of new complexities by infinitely rearranging these elements. Here, the goal is not to bring to light the fundamentally veiled nature of neuronal man but to reform human and other biologies, as is happening in biotechnology and neuropsychopharmacology.

The birth of the neuromolecular gaze in the 1960s coincided with the first psychedelic era and the dream of "pushing human consciousness beyond its present limitations and on towards capacities not yet realized and perhaps undreamed of" (Masters and Houston 1966: 316). When announcing a "molecular revolution," Leary (1965) was hoping that hallucinogenic drugs would help to free people's divine brains from their cultural selves, conditioned by a destructive and insane American society. LSD would turn the "symbolic human mind" into many "infra-human and superhuman evolutionary forms": "an amoeba, a madman, a medieval saint" (116, 148). "The psychedelic experience," Leary (1970: 27) declared, "is the Hindu-Buddha reincarnation theory experimentally confirmed in your own nervous system. You re-experience your human forebears, shuttle down the chain of DNA remembrance. It's all there in your cellular diaries. . . . Our fathers, who art protein in heaven-within; and our round-fleshed holy mothers, hallowed be thy names." Psychedelic discourse brought together the finitude of reductionism with the infinity of an open-ended evolutionary process, in which a "molecular consciousness" would expand beyond the confines of the human mind into the realm of divinity.

Through Huxley's adoption of Leibniz's perennial philosophy, the infinite had also entered into neuropsychedelia in a historical form, preceding the inward-boundedness of the epistemic figure of man. In his reading of Foucault's *Order of Things,* Deleuze (1999: 102–103) points out that, before the emergence of this "Man-form," seventeenth- and eighteenth-century thought was organized by the "God-form" that related the forces within man (conceived as a being among others rather than a subject among objects) with those forces that raise things to infinity. For example, human understanding was taken to participate, in a limited way, in the infinite understanding of the Almighty. Huxley (2009/1954: 26) brought this God-form to bear on psychedelic drugs when he proposed that they enabled the finite human mind to commune with the "Mind at Large" that animated the entire universe. The history of PPI as an attempt at operationalizing this opening of the "doors of perception" can be understood as a transition from the God-form, elevating the human to infinity, to the new form of the "unlimited-finite," which is neither God nor man but—at least in Leary's vision—simultaneously infrahuman and superhuman. Or maybe it was less the reiteration of an epochal transition and more the formation of a contemporary assemblage of the old God-form and the current molecularization and animalization of human life, for Geyer did not conceive of his reductionism and fundamental atheism as incongruous with an immanentist spirituality. Neuropsychedelia is one of the key sites where this molecularized God-form has been emerging since the 1960s. In this ontological framework, *anthropos* is configured as one of a multitude of finite transitory life-forms that participate in the infinity of an evolutionary process that is constantly reshuffling a limited number of biological building blocks. And this immanent transcendence has taken the place of the sacred.

At the turn from the twentieth to the twenty-first century, something significant seemed to be happening in the borderland of humanity, animality, and the divine. The philosopher Giorgio Agamben (2004) has tried to capture this dynamic in the image of two "anthropological machines" working in both symmetry and opposition to each other. One assimilates the notion of the human to animal life through advances in genomics and the neurosciences, for example. The other machine operates in reverse, acculturating animals to human life by turning them into pets and model organisms that serve as substitutes for human beings. Ethologists and philosophers of the life sciences have begun to argue that "anthropodenial"—the mistaken refusal to attribute human mental characteristics to nonhuman creatures—might be as serious an epistemological error as anthropomorphism (De Waal 1999; Mitchell

2005; Sober 2005). Animal rights activists are trying to rescue laboratory animals by simultaneously advocating returning them to the wild (restoring their original animality) and granting them rights (making them legally equal to humans). Although more marginal than naturalism and often at odds with established institutions, animism is alive and well in Euro-America. Despite the antagonism of naturalism and animism, of humanization and animalization, and of political and biological life, the anthropological machines are producing common ground: a "zone of indistinction" resulting from the collapse of these two countermovements upon each other. In *Homo Sacer* (1998), Agamben paints a bleak picture of this process, defining occidental biopolitics as a perpetual but escalating reduction of human existence to "bare life." In this vein, the mind has come to be identified with the brain (and, consequently, death with brain death—a development that Agamben believes is deeply disconcerting). Descola (2006: 140) has diagnosed the resulting materialism as a recent anthropological anomaly: this form of monism breaks with the supposedly universal dichotomy of interiority and physicality, as articulated by the dualist ontologies of both animism and naturalism.

While humanists and representatives of various religious denominations (think of the President's Council on Bioethics during Leon Kass's tenure) have been fighting to preserve a distinct notion of humanity that does not dissolve into mere biology, Agamben responded to this challenge by transvaluing bare life. His book *The Open* (2004) is a utopian gesture toward a dawning messianic time when the two anthropological machines and their historical dialectic of nature and culture will first idle and then come to a standstill. This profane soteriology promises a natural life, no longer human nor animal, that is unsavable and completely abandoned by every spiritual element—and yet perfectly serene and blessed. What Agamben's vision encapsulates, however obscure it might be, is the convertibility of contemporary materialism and mysticism as two forms of monism. The last chapter will explore different ways in which these forms have been conjoined in neuropsychedelia.

6

Mystic Materialism

CEREBRAL PREDESTINATION

March 2006. The small conference "The Challenge to Freedom in the Twentieth Century: Psychoanalysis—Structuralism—Neuroscience" took place in the parsonage of Zurich's Grossmünster. The church was one of the strongholds of the Swiss reformation in the sixteenth century. From here, Huldrych Zwingli challenged the freedom of the will four hundred years before a cerebral predestination of our actions was inferred from neuroscientist Benjamin Libet's experiments (Libet et al. 1982; C. Geyer 2004). Two philosophers, a psychoanalyst, and Franz Vollenweider as representative of the neurosciences were invited to discuss what was perceived as a pressing problem: is our conscious experience of freely deciding our actions adequate, or is human behavior actually determined by social structures, the unconscious, or the brain?

During the conference, a church choir could be heard rehearsing in a different part of the building—as if to remind the audience of the long-standing but, in the wake of the neurohype, almost forgotten theological genealogy of this debate. Against the neural determinism advocated by some prominent German brain researchers turned public intellectuals, one of the philosophers defended the freedom of the will. We are only unfree, he argued, if we are incapable of doing what we think is right. To give an example, he pointed to addiction: we are deprived of liberty if we smoke even though we know that it would be better for us to abstain from nicotine. In the following coffee break, I found Vollenweider and other conference participants joking about their supposed lack of free will while puffing on cigarettes in front of the parsonage. One woman said she would not lament the absence of free will. Without it, at least she would not have to feel guilty about every cigarette.

Vollenweider's subsequent presentation was disillusioning—not so much with respect to "our" image of humankind but regarding the alleged challenge to freedom posed by the neurosciences. "When preparing this talk," Vollenweider told the audience, "I was almost disappointed by how little I found—even though I went over forty-eight books on brain research to see what is known about free will. The relevant chapters in there were hardly longer than a page. What you find is still mostly in the realm of philosophy." Consequently, Vollenweider contented himself with a detailed explanation of the now historical Libet experiments from the early 1980s and the little work done in their wake.

NEUROCHEMICAL SELVES: A JOKE?

One of the reasons I decided to do fieldwork on brain research facilities studying hallucinogenic drugs was that I was hoping to see how people conducted their lives in light of neuroscientific knowledge. When the neurosciences began to boom in the 1980s and 1990s, a few empirically oriented philosophers of mind predicted and advocated nothing less than a cultural revolution. In her book *Neurophilosophy* (1986), Patricia Churchland foresaw that our prescientific folk psychology would be eliminated and replaced by a scientifically enlightened self-conception. Eventually, all talk about subjective experience (not to speak of religious beliefs) would be done away with as the neurosciences gradually discovered how the brain worked and provided us with an objectivist vocabulary to talk about our inner lives. In its rejection of conventional manners of speaking and the corresponding social institutions, this radicalism, despite the different political undertones, was not so far removed from Timothy Leary's "neurological revolution," which had been propagated in an early neuralese dialect. In a similar vein, the German philosopher of mind Thomas Metzinger (2000a: 6) argued that, since the 1990s, brain research had generated "a new image of man . . . , an image that will dramatically contradict almost all traditional images man has made of himself in the course of cultural history." This is reminiscent of Philippe Descola's (2006) diagnosis of materialism as a historical novelty and anthropological anomaly.

But in contrast to Churchland's Enlightenment optimism, Metzinger perceived scientific progress as a hard road. As an heir of Max Weber, he presented the disenchanting pursuit of knowledge as a tragic and heroic enterprise. There is both an emotional and a sociocultural price to be paid for the advances of brain research:

> The emotional price consists in a certain unease: We feel insecure because many of our unscrutinized beliefs about ourselves suddenly seem obsolete. . . . There will be a sociocultural price for the current development as well. . . . First of all, the image we have of ourselves in a subtle, yet very effective way influences how we live our everyday life and how we interact with our fellow human beings. A popularized form of vulgar materialism following on the heels of neuroscience might therefore lead us to another, reduced kind of social reality. If our image of ourselves is a radically demystified image, then we run the risk of losing a lot of the magic and subtlety in our social relationships. (Metzinger 2000a: 7)

To cope with this distressing but inexorable development, Metzinger proposed two things. First, in analogy to technology assessments that serve to calculate risks and predict social consequences of new technologies, Metzinger called for an "anthropology assessment" to anticipate and analyze the sociocultural ramifications of emergent images of humankind. Second, this self-identified analytic philosopher surprisingly advocated a return to an ancient conception of philosophy as *cultura animi*. In his eyes, the greatest challenge posed by what we were learning about our cerebral nature was the question of how intellectual honesty and spirituality could ever be reconciled. Philosophy should again take on the task of cultivating the soul in the light of recent neuroscientific discoveries, possibly with the help of consciousness technologies such as meditation or psychedelic drugs. Thereby, Metzinger hoped to move away from a purely defensive position, which he perceived as prevalent in the humanities, toward laying the foundations for a "consciousness culture" by asking "positive questions," for example, what a future culture might look like that used the results of consciousness research in a fruitful way (Metzinger 2000a: 6–10, 2009: 207–240).

As an anthropologist of science, I share Metzinger's interest in the emergence of forms of life that are shaped by neuroscientific knowledge and neurotechnologies. It should be noted, however, that historically there is nothing new about monistic articulations of materialism. They can easily be traced back to Enlightenment thinkers like Julien Offray de La Mettrie, the German *Materialismusstreit* in the 1850s, and the militant atheism of late nineteenth-century French anthropology

(Breidbach 1997; Hagner 2000, 2007; Hecht 2003). An assessment of the affective and social consequences of this view of the human requires no cultural predictions, just history and ethnography. Thus, instead of engaging in speculative bioethics and historical prognoses, I decided to examine how people intimately familiar with both brain research and pharmacological consciousness technologies live and conceive of themselves today. For this purpose, hallucinogen researchers seemed like a particularly promising group to study. Many of them had entered into neuropsychopharmacology because they had previously experienced their object of investigation firsthand, attributing enough existential significance to these experiences to dedicate themselves to their investigation. I assumed that the powerful mind-altering effects of psychedelic drugs enabled researchers to internalize the neuroscientific knowledge that their work produced. Who else would have a better sense of what it meant—not just scientifically but also existentially—for inner experience to be determined by brain chemistry?

At first glance, it seemed as if the neuroscientists I encountered provided a glimpse into the reductionist and eliminativist future dreamt up by Churchland and some of her colleagues. When talking about themselves, the hallucinogen researchers I worked with frequently referred to brain anatomy and chemistry. "You must have blown your hippocampus with all the drugs you've taken," one researcher said in response to his colleague's tendency of getting lost in the city. Things said in a fit of temper were attributed to malfunctioning frontal lobes. One scientist who had just fallen in love was joking about his oxytocin level. E-mails were signed "Serotonergically yours." And, after I had given him the sociologist Nikolas Rose's (2003a) article of the same title to read, pharmacologist Felix Hasler began to speak of himself as a "neurochemical self."

But most of the time these things were said in a humorous or teasing manner. The explanatory gap between mind and brain lends itself to the logic of jokes that call into question the border between being a person and being a thing, between humanity and animality. With regard to clumsy comics, scatological jests, and ribaldry, the philosopher Simon Critchley (2002: 43) points out: "Humour functions by exploiting the gap between being a body and having a body, between—let us say—the *physical* and the *metaphysical* aspects of being human. What makes us laugh, I would wager, is the return of the physical into the metaphysical, where the pretended tragical sublimity collapses into a comic ridiculousness which is perhaps even more tragic." Such humor often reveals us as persons we would rather not be. There should be more romantic reasons for being in love than neuroendocrinology. Hasler told me: "Even though there is something sad or irritating at the heart of all this, humor serves as an outlet. By making fun of it, you take away some of the poignancy." What is laughed at is a self-description that is perceived as troubling. But the laughter is also liberating in that the human condition is simultaneously acknowledged and ridiculed.

This sense of elation, Hasler explained to me, was a recurrent aspect of the psychedelic experience, which often made the whole universe appear like a "cosmic joke" and elicited uncontrolled giggling. Alexander and Ann Shulgin (1997: 178) wrote: "The Laughing Buddha is an archetype, an illustration of what it is to stand on the knife-edge between Dark and Light, Death and Life, and survey the universe from there. This is a cosmic laughter, half pain and half bliss. One doesn't have to be a Buddha to know that place; it's inside every one of us mortals, and all that's needed is the willingness to open the door and step through." And psychedelics are presented as one way of taking that step of recognizing the folly of the world.

In contrast to Churchland's prediction of the replacement of first-person by third-person vocabularies, the comic rationality underlying the scientists' jokes was not eliminativist. The jocular play with the incongruity of perspectives quickly came to an end when life got serious, making the existentially detached attitudes of humor and science appear inappropriate. Then the neuroscientists readily reverted to talking about themselves rather than their brains. Hasler confirmed: "Of course, at the end of the day, our ostentatious coquetry with the self-perception as neurochemical selves is just a comical posture—and not genuinely experienced reality. Subjectively, lovesickness probably feels too real to be dismissed as an expectation discrepancy–based neuronal error message."

Yet not all humor in the laboratory reflected the uneasy relationship between scientifically detached and existentially engaged perspectives on life. Some was pure mockery marking social distinctions. On the one hand, derisive remarks about rainbow-colored socks and batik shirts worn by old hippies at the LSD Symposium served to set oneself apart from the psychedelic counterculture. On the other hand, the hallucinogen researchers' identity as serious scientists was also asserted satirically against the philosophical overselling of neuroscientific findings by popularizing colleagues and in public discourse. Ranting about the worthlessness of many neuroimaging studies during lunch, Vollenweider singled out a recent publication on moral decision making. "They put test subjects into the scanner," he recounted, "and asked them to solve moral dilemmas. Eventually, they found—reverential murmur, gazes toward the sky—that the amygdala was activated. Good heavens, where else was it supposed to light up? In the buttocks?" Similarly, Hasler explained: "When I make fun of the free will debate, about people who infer from an activation of the premotor cortex shortly before the conscious decision to move a finger that offenders can no longer be convicted, I can laugh out loud without any sense of 'I can't live with that and therefore I need to deride it.'" It was in this spirit that Vollenweider joked before his presentation at the Grossmünster: "If there really was free will, I wouldn't be giving that talk."

On the face of it, Metzinger seemed mistaken in claiming that recent advances in brain research effectively influenced how people live their everyday lives (see Vidal 2009: 9). The dualist ontology of naturalism proved persistent. Ian Hacking (2005, 2007b) has recently even argued that, despite the customary Descartes bashing in neuroscience and almost all philosophical camps, a closer look at cultural practices reveals that the vision of Cartesian mind-body dualism is not at all foundering but is about to be fulfilled. While philosophical, social scientific, and historical observers of brain research have repeatedly diagnosed or prognosticated an "objective self-fashioning" (Dumit 2004) of human beings into *homines cerebrales* (Hagner 2000), cerebral subjects (Ehrenberg 2004; Vidal 2005), pharmaceutical persons (Martin 2006), or neurochemical selves (Rose 2003a), it seemed as if no members of these strange tribes would show themselves. Is there a limit to the neurobiologization of human kinds (Kusch 1997)?

DEBUNKING DRUG MYSTICISM

Not only self-images but also the modern separation of facts and values first seemed untainted by the emergent monist discourse. Ridiculing the inference of legal reforms from the contested interpretation of a neuroscience experiment has reaffirmed the rejection of transitions from the descriptive to the normative, from what *is* to what *ought* to be. This dismissal of the "naturalistic fallacy" arose in the eighteenth century and was promoted to a cultural commonplace at the beginning of the twentieth century (Shapin 2008b: 10–12). In his 1917 speech, "Science as a Vocation" (1958/1919), Max Weber famously cited Leo Tolstoy's dictum: "Science is meaningless because it gives no answer to our question, the only question important for us: 'What shall we do and how shall we live?'" (143). Science can tell us how to technically achieve a certain goal but not whether this goal is also worth pursuing.[1]

In the laboratory, however, closer ethnographic inspection revealed that the narrowly constricted results of single experiments did not affect how scientists in the observed laboratories conducted their lives, but the more deeply rooted worldviews that framed their interpretations did. At the center of the researchers' discussions about the relationship between their scientific work and the way they lived was the question of what to make of the contents of hallucinogen-induced experiences.

Since my very first day in the Vollenweider lab, I had been aware of Patrick Kossuth's (PK) hostility toward drug mysticism. In an interview toward the end of my time in Zurich, he told me about his own experiences with psilocybin and ketamine as a test subject in his colleagues' studies.

NL: *Have these experiences brought drug mysticism any closer to you? Have they helped you to understand why some of your colleagues hold the view that hallucinogenic drugs provide access to a transcendent reality?*

PK: No, in fact, I understand them even less. Let's assume that I'm having a beautiful trip. I'm lying there, feeling well, seeing nice colors, interesting shapes, and the music sounds very special to me. I'm also having some unusual ideas. But, at any moment of the experiment, I know that I'm in this state because I took psilocybin. I rationally ascribed my experience to 5-HT_{2A} receptors and not to some higher power. For this reason, I didn't feel connected to anything supernatural. And even if I had thought that there was a higher entity controlling our fate or something like that, I would have told myself afterward: "Funny, you've really been going around the bend." All of this can be explained by the fact that certain processes establish connections between certain cells. I wouldn't have mystified this.

NL: *You once said to me that mysticism and the natural sciences were at odds with each other. That is contrary to what Albert Hofmann said at the LSD Symposium. He claimed that every natural scientist should also be a mystic marveling at the wonders of creation.*

PK: Then we need to define more clearly what is meant by the term *mystic*. You don't need drugs to experience the wonder of nature. I can simply sit down and think about the perversity of the fact that we exist at all. Just watch one of these films about the universe. Everywhere it's cold and dreadful, but here there were a couple of single cell organisms and today we're driving around in cars. That's completely incredible and crazy! But for this insight I don't need drugs.

The mystification of drugs in the context of brain research makes such investigations appear dubious. What I find interesting about the field of hallucinogen research is that some figures are treated like icons. They are adored and worshipped. Take Albert Hofmann, for example. There are people getting down on their knees in front of him, kissing his feet, and the conference hall is filled by a cheering crowd and some are dancing on the stage, I've heard. There is a discipleship. There is no doubt that Hofmann has made a large number of highly significant contributions to drug research from a natural scientific point of view. But let's compare him to, for example, Martin Schwab [a renowned neuroscientist at the University of Zurich], in whose department I did an internship. I can take any neuroscience textbook covering the regeneration of spinal cord injury and I will find his name. When it will be possible to cure paraplegia, he will have contributed a lot to that. But are there people dancing for him at a congress or kissing his feet? No, that doesn't happen. Why? Because these groups with mystical leanings need a god whom they can adore. They need a leader. But if you work as a natural scientist, you don't need this kind of thing. Hofmann and Schwab—they're both doing research on neural systems, but their followers are completely different. Mystification makes drug research look fishy.

Another opponent of drug mysticism in the Vollenweider laboratory was the German pharmacopsychologist Boris Quednow. According to an anecdote circulating in the lab, he once exploded during a discussion over a neoshamanistic ayahuasca clinic in Peru, which one of his colleagues had visited, exclaiming: "Why don't you stop this esoteric blathering! We're nothing but senseless bioautomatons!" As a matter of fact, however, Quednow's image of humankind was more complex and syncretic. As a neuroscientist, he thought of the mind as a function of the brain and had little sympathy for the evocation of power animals and supernatural forces. But, having undergone psychoanalysis while studying psychology, his way of thinking about himself and others seemed to owe more to his socialization in the "psy disciplines" than to brain research. When I asked him about his skepticism with respect to hallucinogen consumption, he provided a very intimate, self-reflective account of his own distance toward these substances and a psychological explanation for why others seek meaning in psychedelic experiences:

> As you know, I resist drug mysticism. I think a lot of people attribute a kind of significance to their drug experiences that is completely inapt. Basically, I think that drug mysticism is based on an overestimation of an experience, which you can also have—maybe not as intensively and over a longer period of time—if you deal with yourself and your past, if you're able to allow for certain fears and to look at particular aspects of your identity without being afraid. I also think that, as always, people tend to attribute a deeper meaning to experiences that they don't understand. And most people neither understand themselves nor their environment. Why should that be any different under hallucinogens? Only because it feels much more intense and immediate? I can't believe that. I'm convinced that most people taking hallucinogens are simply consuming these drugs, just like alcohol. Often, this whole talk about self-experience is nothing but a cover-up for a completely oral satisfaction of a hunger for experience.

Thus, Quednow explained the "overestimation" of the psychedelic experience psychoanalytically as a form of regression, whereas Kossuth reduced its contents to neurochemistry and rejected all religious interpretations and their corresponding forms of sociality. Thereby, both Quednow and Kossuth disenchanted drug mysticism. The conflict between such modern iconoclasm and the countermodern quest for spiritual experience was already at the heart of Weber's "Science as a Vocation" a half century earlier. This lecture at the university of Munich addressed an academic youth increasingly disappointed by the "intellectual constructions of science" perceived as "an unreal realm of artificial abstractions, which with their bony hands seek to grasp the blood-and-the-sap of true life without ever catching up with it" (Weber 1958/1919: 141). Consequently, many of these young people were prone to the cult of lived experience, especially mysticisms of every shade and color, all too willing to follow prophetic personalities pretending to have "experienced life" and offering unequivocal orientation (137). Weber perceived these forms of discipleship and the craving for "not only religious experience but experience as such" (143) as an immature backlash against the complex of science and secularization that constituted the backbone of modernity. Kossuth's irritation about the adoration of Hofmann in the psychedelic community and Quednow's condemnation of drug mysticism as "a completely oral satisfaction of a hunger for experience" echoed Weber's diagnosis of science and its discontents in the early twentieth century.

Both Kossuth and Quednow displayed attitudes of scientific detachment, but their judgments of drug mysticism were hardly value neutral. Implicated were the appreciation of intellectual autonomy (as opposed to seeking spiritual guidance), pharmacological Calvinism (in which insights are to be gained by work on the self rather than drug taking), a normative account of psychosexual development (pathologization of behavior labeled "oral"), and a naturalist or materialist worldview (devaluing all references to the supernatural as superstitions). Even the disenchanting description of hallucinogen experiences as a phenomenon attributable to 5-HT_{2A} receptor activation had a powerful normative undertow. Although science still does not tell you what to do here, it does tell you what *not* to do: because hallucinogenic experiences are nothing but neurochemistry and do not reveal any deeper meaning or cosmic truth, one should not take them as incentives to abandon the scientific life for the sake of a religious life (following spiritual leaders, seeking salvation in transcendental experiences, etc.). In short, the internalization of neuroscientific knowledge did provide a particular, if negative, orientation concerning the conduct of life after all.

FROM THE BIOLOGY OF THE MYSTICAL TO THE MYSTICISM OF BIOLOGY

In Kossuth's account, mysticism and materialism are presented as mutually exclusive. Transcendental experiences are either attributed to supernatural forces or to brain chemistry. Natural science and mysticism also appear to be antagonistic, as the mystical experience revolves around the union of subject and object, whereas scientific objectivity presupposes their strict separation. But this methodological separation does not necessarily imply a dualistic ontology. In principle, monistic convictions such as the materialist identification of mind and brain are compatible with certain kinds of mysticism.

From the Renaissance to the present, natural philosophy and subsequently the natural sciences emerged and developed in parallel with the conception of nature as a space of religious significance. Both early modern students of nature and nature mystics contemplated nature as divine creation. This object of knowledge was meant to have moral effects on the knower who sought to become less selfish and more tranquil (Shapin 2008b: 23–27). In the twentieth century, physicists such as Albert Einstein and Werner Heisenberg still described their scientific insights into the nature of the universe by way of analogy to mystical experiences. Since the life sciences have outdone physics in the disciplinary race for public recognition, this tradition of nature mysticism has been rearticulated as biomysticism (Vondung 2007). The German physicist and literary scholar Christoph Holzhey (2007: 10) defines biomysticism as a mysticism of the biological as opposed to the biology of the mystical. Biomystics are not primarily interested in the neural correlates of mystical experience. They rather conceive of the life sciences as a whole in quasi-mystical terms: when biologists study biology, life studies itself and the separation of subject and object is overcome. The eminent German neuroscientist Wolf Singer (2002: 61–62), for example, pointed out that, in brain research, a cognitive system observed itself fusing explanans and explanandum. But he also cautioned that evolution might not have selected for such self-knowledge and that our neural nature might therefore remain inscrutable and mysterious to us. Growing out of the epistemic predicament of "anthropological thought" (Foucault 1973), this mystique of life itself deviates from the Weberian narrative of disenchantment, not in assuming any supernatural forces, but in losing trust in the principal calculability and intelligibility of the world and human nature (Weber 1958/1919: 139).

In the life sciences, these mystical topoi have primarily been identified on the level of biological theory and speculation (Vondung 2007: 37). However, during my fieldwork in the Zurich laboratory, I met a researcher who had overcome the separation of subject and object at the level of experimental practice. By way of extensive psychopharmacological self-experimentation, he had moved from the neuroscientific naturalization of mystical experience to a decidedly modern brand of nature mysticism. Honza Samotar was a Swiss physician of Czech descent in his midthirties, about to finish his MD/PhD training and working on two theses simultaneously: one on insect navigation with respect to potential applications in robotics, the other on the effects of hallucinogenic drugs on the human brain.

Samotar (2006: 93) retrospectively presented his coming of age as a drug researcher in almost Cartesian terms: "When I started experimenting with altered states of consciousness my primary motivation was the search for reality. . . . Between 12 and 14 years of age, I doubted whether I could be sure about the existence of anything since everything was just mediated by my awareness. So the only thing that I could be certain existed were my own perceptions." Samotar hoped to be able to anchor his knowledge about the world in an unshakeable ego: "The search for reality implied the search for the real self" (94). Descartes (1984/1641) had meditated over the deceptive nature of his dreams and hyperbolized the resulting skepticism concerning sensory perceptions in order to eventually ground certainty about his own existence in the world in thought. Samotar also explored altered states of consciousness to move from radical doubt to sure knowledge. For him, however, not dreams, but drugs appeared to provide the royal road to an "Archimedean point of introspection": "It may seem strange to use psychoactive drugs for close inspection of reality. They are often considered to serve the opposite aim, namely to escape from reality. But turning anything off never was an end in itself for me. I rather saw it as a possible way to find firm ground" (Samotar 2006: 94, 96).

Samotar began to self-experiment with drugs when he was sixteen years old. Unlike most adolescents, he told me, he pursued his interest in mind-altering substances with methodical rigor and self-discipline:

> Mine was not the classical way of getting into drugs with one's friends. I deliberately looked for particular substances and then I planned specific experiments, which I conducted on my own—at the beginning still equipped with pen and ink, later on with a Dictaphone. The experiments began with rather harmless substances. This was mostly about practicing different forms of application. For example, I intravenously injected things from the kitchen, such as glucose. But, occasionally, that led to rather dramatic states—up to an almost anaphylactic reaction. Hashish was the first really inebriating substance I took. Interestingly, in my case, alcohol came later. First I was stoned, and then drunk. The first time I got drunk was in a self-experiment, completely on my own. I drank 2 dl of schnapps and, of course, I took notes on everything. That is, briefly summarized, how I got interested in the brain and consciousness.

From 1992 to 1995, as a medical student in his early twenties, Samotar had access to an isolation tank that a friend of his operated in the back room of his bookstore. Samotar used the tank after closing time to test the effects of about a dozen psychoactive drugs on himself. The isolation tank (also known as the samadhi tank, named after the Sanskrit term for unitive spiritual experiences) was developed in the mid-1950s by the American physician, consciousness researcher, and countercultural psychonaut John Lilly at the National Institute of Mental Health. To test whether the brain would fall asleep or continue to be mentally active without external stimulation, Lilly devised a tank in which human subjects float in saline solution at body temperature and in complete darkness and dead silence (Lilly 1978: 98–102; Langlitz 2006b). Given that experimental subjects were hardly indifferent to laboratory settings—however sterile and white, or rather because of their very sterility and whiteness—the goal was to create a truly neutral environment.

But Samotar did not only make use of Lilly's technology. Since he had read Lilly's *Center of the Cyclone: An Autobiography of Inner Space* (1972) at age seventeen, he also looked at Lilly's whole research strategy as a model: "Lilly's approach consisted of examining the mind scientifically as a system by isolating it," Samotar explained to me. "This was his original idea, which led to the construction of the samadhi tank. As little input, as little output as possible—allowing one to observe the mind in maximal purity as a scientific object." Samotar shared Lilly's assumption that, in order to study consciousness and consciousness alone, it had to be detached from its environment by depriving it of sensory stimulation (according to another informant, however, this goal was occasionally thwarted in the isolation tank when the saline solution burned a subject's anus—a painful reminder that human beings were not simply their brains). Samotar also followed Lilly in exposing this "purified" mind to a broad range of pharmacological interventions—from alcohol and cannabis to fly agaric, *Psilocybe* mushrooms, LSD, ketamine, MDMA, dextromethorphan, trihexiphenidyl, and laughing gas. In a systematic manner, Samotar explored the effects of these drugs and their combinations, compiling multidimensional tables to keep track of the permutations. By probing the neurochemical malleability of the human mind, he was hoping to find some constancy in the mental multiverse opened up by the psychedelic pharmacopoeia. In the tank, Samotar dictated real-time protocols of his experiences to a digital audiotape recorder so that he could compare these reports with each other. His goal was to discover or construct the "real self" as the lowest common denominator of the different mental states described, as a solid foundation of experience resisting all pharmacological challenges—but to no avail. He recounted:

> Basically, I asked myself a question, which, before me, John Lilly had already posed: to what extent can you change the experience of being and of the world and what remains invariant under all circumstances? That is to say, what are the experiential invariants of existence? Lilly reached the conclusion that there aren't any. I verified this empirically in my self-experiments and I came to the same conclusion: there are none. Everything is variable.

The only thing that remains the same is the point of departure to which I always return when the drug effects wear off.

Among the many different altered states that Samotar experienced, there were the kind of states reported in the mystical literature as conveying a sense of unity with the cosmos. What set Samotar apart from most aficionados of psychedelic mysticism was his attitude of scientific detachment. From his perspective, such uplifting experiences were just as valuable as the ones that were deeply horrifying and alienating:

> I have to say that bad trips are no problem for me. I had several bad trips in my life. Some of them were really bad—worst trips, so to speak. The fact that this hasn't put me off has to do with my motivation. If someone mostly takes drugs for hedonistic reasons, then he will keep his hands from a substance after it triggered a bad trip. For me, however, a dreadful experience is no reason to distance myself from the drug. In my eyes, a bad trip is as interesting as a good one, sometimes even a lot more interesting. My goal is to carry as much as possible from such altered states into everyday life. It doesn't matter whether I experience bliss or anxiety in these states. What's important is that the state differs from everyday consciousness and that it's describable. That's it.

The aim of Samotar's drug experimentation was self-knowledge, not self-care. What was striking about this unsparing self-relation was that, here, the will to knowledge even trumped the most fundamental survival instincts. Samotar disregarded his well-being and even put his life at risk without pressing cause. The logic of self-preservation underlying evolutionary accounts of humankind fails to explain such practices.

Samotar's attitude is modern and scientific in its disengagement from the concerns of the individual researcher. One of the hallmarks of modern science is the principle of method. This principle aims at the integration of investigations conducted by a potentially infinite sequence of inquiring subjects over time. The implication of the researchers' personal lives in their scientific activities is merely accidental, and their individual needs and desires in regard to truth cannot serve as a measure to evaluate the totality of the knowledge to be produced (Blumenberg 1983: 317–318). In the collective historical enterprise of scientific progress, it does not matter if single experiments fail. Even though such failures might be regrettable for the individual experimenter, the scientific community will still be able to learn from them. Giving the asceticism of method an existential twist, Samotar's paragon John Lilly (1972:

35) even welcomed what he described as a "near-lethal 'accident' "—a suicide attempt that he committed after his second LSD self-experiment. "No experiment is a failure," he concluded. "I had learned that death is not as terrifying as I had imagined it to be" (35).

Samotar's embrace of good and bad trips alike and the risks he took by ingesting new combinations of highly potent drugs were in line with this acceptance of severe hardship up to the point of self-destruction in the pursuit of knowledge. In this ethos, however, scientific detachment borders on mystical self-annihilation. The German philosopher Peter Sloterdijk (1996: 14) points to the religious genealogy of modern self-experimentation: "In his self-experiments, the modern individual takes the freedom to put himself to the test up to the limits of self-destruction. That is a pretty surprising trait. To find something comparable you need to go back to the idea of mystical self-annihilation that spread during the European Middle Ages, maybe also in Eastern schools of meditation. It seems to me that, today, elements that have already been tried out in Christian mysticism are being reiterated in a nontheological code—mostly in the language of intensified experience, of inebriation, of the sensation civilization."

According to Sloterdijk's historical anthropology, modern humankind has supplemented the rationality of self-preservation with the quest for self-intensification—or rather, intensification of experience, which can involve the transgression of the self and its inherent egocentrism. In modernity, mysticism is not on the wane but has acquired a new significance by entering into configurations that also include scientific elements. Samotar's self-experimental practice was marked as both scientific and mystical, not primarily due to occasional pharmacologically induced unitive experiences, but mostly because of the indifference and equanimity with which he faced both positive and negative experiences.

What distinguishes Samotar's mysticism of biology from the biology of the mystical (as investigated in neurotheological studies) is that its spiritual focal point is not the extraordinary mental states engendered by hallucinogenic drugs but rather the ordinary existence to which the self-experimenter eventually returns. Instead of trying to assimilate everyday life to the experiential mode of psychedelic trips, Samotar contemplated the difference between these two orders of experience to reinvigorate a sense of wonder, which has often been identified as the origin of philosophy. Honza Samotar's (HS) is a philosophical mysticism in tune with radical materialism and anticlericalism.

HS: In my eyes, the mystical cannot be found in such ego-
dissolution experiences, which make you feel at one with
everything. The truly mystical is that, when the drug effects
wear off, you always return to your point of departure in
everyday consciousness, to the baseline, so to speak. It's about
the fact that I can lose myself in a state in which I'm not human
anymore, in which I lack both individuality and sociality, in
which I have no lifetime because I'm eternal, being everything
and nothing, neither dead nor alive, not divided into subject and
object, not located in a universe with a beginning and an end—
and that this state eventually comes to an end. That I can even
remember it. In retrospect, I then tell myself: yes, there are states
in which I'm eternal, but then I'm not myself—then *it* simply is,
that state is. And, strangely enough, I always come back here, to
the same body at the same place. That's what I conceive of as
the mystical.

Others think of this as pure materialism. I can live with that
allegation very well. Partly through my drug experiments, I have
become an avowed materialist. I simply think: I am my brain
state. Full stop. And at the same time, I conceive of exactly this
as deeply mystical.

I'm speaking of the mystical in a Wittgensteinian sense.
Wittgenstein [1961: 149] wrote this brilliant sentence in his
Tractatus Logico-Philosophicus, to which I fully subscribe:
"It is not how things are in the world that is mystical, but
that it exists." In my eyes, the truly mystical is not what seems
amazing at first glance, but that which is the most amazing.
The more it amazes me, the more mystical it is. And it
amazes me a lot more that this life, as it is, so odd, so
absurd, so simple, and yet so complicated, that this is
what life is.

NL: *So you don't assign any particular value to your mystical
experiences?*

HS: No, particularly because of my experiences of altered states
of consciousness it seems extremely reprehensible to me how
certain religions and sects draw political, economic, and religious
capital from real or ostensible altered states. People are duped
when they are made to believe that certain states are more valuable than others. After all my experiences, I regard this as total

nonsense. Why should one state of mind be more valuable than another?

NL: *Does this have any consequences for your everyday life?*
HS: No, in my everyday life the assumption of an equivalence of all states of consciousness doesn't make a difference. There, I behave like any other organism. I don't touch the hot plate every day just because I think of pain as an interesting state.

BIOMYSTICAL PHOTOGRAPHY: NATURE OBSERVING ITSELF

The mystique surrounding mind-brain identity was also reflected artistically in the work of Marco Antonio Benz, an MD/PhD involved in model psychosis research in Vollenweider's lab. Next to his neuroimaging research on the effects of ketamine, Benz dedicated much time and energy to fine-arts photography. His pictures were on display and for sale at occasional exhibitions and on his website (www.mindscapes .ch). "Mindscapes" was the overarching concept tying together three series of photographs: *Urban Contemplations, Nature Introspections,* and *Highway Memories*. Apart from the latter series, which comprised abstract "light paintings" drawn with the headlamps and rear lights of cars passing by on American highways, Benz's work mostly consisted of landscape photography. The series titles *Urban Contemplations* and *Nature Introspections* pointed to the goal of an aesthetic integration of a concrete "outer reality" captured on film and an abstract mental sphere of concepts, cognitive processes, and states of mind. On his website, Benz described his project as follows: "I explore the potential of photographs to act as interfaces between outer physical and inner mental realities of contemplativeness. My photographic vision and intention has increasingly become influenced by my interest in the philosophy and science of consciousness, specifically the relationship between mind and matter, and my activity as an MD in brain research on altered states of consciousness."

Psychedelic drugs have been said to have had a significant impact on the history of art. A few anthropologists even wonder whether hallucinogen experiences did not give rise to indigenous art in the first place (Reichel-Dolmatoff 1978; Letcher 2006: 39–42). Some of the geometric-ornamental patterns typical of hallucinogen-induced visions are supposedly represented in Paleolithic rock art (Lewis-Williams and

Dowson 1988). In the nineteenth century, Romantic artists associated these forms with the rejection of scientific rationalism in favor of a primacy of the imagination (Betancourt 2007). As hallucinogenic drugs became popular in Euro-American culture in the mid-twentieth century, they became key elements of what came to be known as psychedelic art. Art critic Ken Johnson (2011) has even argued that, since the mass consumption of LSD in the sixties, practically all contemporary art has come to conform with a "psychedelic paradigm" (for a critique of this overstatement, see Langlitz 2012c). However, work labeled psychedelic was not only inspired by the artists' drug experiences but also drew from a whole range of artistic traditions, from art nouveau, surrealism, and pop art to Islamic ornaments and Buddhist mandalas (Grunenberg 2005; Grunenberg and Harris 2005; Rubin 2010).

The references to different kinds of religious art were not merely formal. In their book *Psychedelic Art,* which was instrumental in constituting the field, the hallucinogen researchers Robert Masters and Jean Houston (1968: 81) presented the mission of the new drug-inspired artwork as spiritual: "The art is religious, mystical: pantheistic religion, God manifest in All, but especially in the primordial energy that makes the world go, powers the existential flux. Nature or body mysticism: the One as an omnisensate Now."

Benz posited his photographic work in this spiritual, but not in the visual, tradition of psychedelic art. During one of our leisurely conversations on the terrace of the Burghölzli cafeteria, he explained to me on which level his work reflected his own drug experiences. Under the influence of hallucinogens, he also saw colorful geometric patterns and moving fractals and experienced visual defragmentation. It made sense to him that these phenomena reflected the organization of the visual cortex, as the psychologist Heinrich Klüver (1928) and, more recently, the computational neurobiologist Paul Bressloff claimed (Bressloff et al. 2001). But Benz emphasized that there was more to the hallucinogen experience than visions and perceptual distortions. Beyond this sensory hyperarousal there was a deeper experiential level associated with deep calm, relaxation, and clarity of consciousness. He had had the deepest experience of this sort as a test subject in one of his colleague's experiments, when he was lying stock-still in a PET scanner for two and a half hours while voyaging to the "antipodes of the mind." It was this level that he wanted to address in his pictures.

To demonstrate this point, Benz showed me a series of prints titled *Slot Canyon.* They displayed curved and grooved surfaces in different tones of red: dynamic, but soothing. The photos were taken in Antelope Canyon, a popular sightseeing spot in Arizona photographed again and again by millions of tourists and amateur photographers. Benz's pictures were so abstract that the viewer could not tell what they depicted. He emphasized that he refrained from digital manipulation. He did not want to alter reality or deny the specific and concrete nature of his motifs. Instead he made use of the documentary quality of the medium of photography to reveal material reality as amorphous matter devoid of meaning. In Benz's eyes, it was our conceptual categorizations and habitual observations that introduced distinctions and thereby assigned significance to things in the world—making the canyon a canyon, for instance. Hallucinogenic experiences, Benz explained, were consciousness-expanding in that they allowed us to gain a new perspective on the world. This is what he was also trying to accomplish through his photographic work. By enabling us *not* to recognize the canyon as a canyon, he enabled the viewer to take a fresh look. Benz wanted to turn the spectator's gaze from the way things appeared in everyday life to their unchanging mystical and metaphysical nature. On his website, he wrote: "For the purpose of transcending the particularity of the moment of light capture, my photographs attempt to provide the observer with an intuition of timelessness. Contemplative experience may lead to higher-order abstract mental concepts that are less bound to specific, transient, finite, and concrete embodiment. Such mental concepts may rather be about the essence of reality itself."

A glance at the history of twentieth-century fine-arts photography (or even just a Google Image search for "Antelope Canyon") reveals that the association of the high-modernist aesthetics of Benz's work with the psychedelic experience is contingent (but maybe no more contingent than the association in psychedelic culture of Mexican mushrooms with Buddhist mandalas or art nouveau graphics). While the PET images that Benz produced as a researcher served to visualize the brain activities recorded in the scanner, the artistic pictures taken in the canyon were actually not meant to represent the depicted rocks but to evoke a certain state of mind. He emphasized their performative over their symbolic qualities. Benz's use of photography as the emblem of mechanical objectivity conveying a subjective experience rearticulated the introspective tradition of modernist art, representing perception rather than the perceived (Ziff 1995), along with the naturalization of introspection in neurobiological consciousness research. In our conversations, Benz emphasized the importance of "the subjective loop of the physical that is perceived and the physical that perceives":

> I'm a monist. When we look at nature, we look at ourselves. This is a kind of introspection on different levels. Through the emergence of consciousness, nature has come to observe itself. Nature observes itself on a level beyond the individual. But, on the level of the individual, the observation of nature is also a kind of introspection. For example, looking at a horizon evokes certain feelings that cannot be expressed by words. These are memories taking us back to a point in natural history preceding language. There is something archetypical about a horizon that moves us. When I talk about introspection, about nature observing itself, this is based on the assumption that we are part of nature, that we are made from the same stuff, that, romantically speaking, we are stardust. On the level of the individual, the observation of nature allows us to experience deeply emotional, deeply touching inner spaces. I would like to foster this by producing images that do not constrain the eye by conceptual thought. I'm trying to show that outer spaces can also be inner spaces.

Benz's overarching interest was "the connection between consciousness and biology, between the subjective and the objective." "Within the possibilities of subjectivity," he added, "I'm particularly interested in the spiritual dimension." Here, the neurobiologization of consciousness met the Romantic association of spirituality and nature. The Romantic impulse Benz was trying to convey through his photographs was meant to counteract what he conceived of as the destructive potential of reductionist neuroscience. In Benz's eyes, human beings must feel embedded in a cosmic whole. But commitments to bigger causes, such as the preservation of the environment in the face of ecological catastrophe, are undermined by the individualizing image of humankind promoted by brain research.[2] Against this kind of naturalization of the mind, Benz brought up a variety of nature mysticism. But it neither aspired to glimpse a universe beyond material reality nor to withdraw from the world into a subjectivist realm of fantasy. Instead it aimed at an epiphanic vision found in this world, in the here and now, captured by photography. He made use of this medium to express and cultivate a this-worldly biomysticism.

PACKAGE TRIP TO THE URBIOLOGICAL

Monism comes in many shades and colors. As a doctoral student in Vollenweider's laboratory, Erich Studerus was equally wary of the discourses of materialist neuroscience and spirituality. "In spiritually oriented people," he told me, "I often see a neglect of the corporeal. They think the soul would be something higher than the body and all problems could be solved mentally. That's a reverse kind of reductionism." But Studerus also rejected the reduction of mind to brain. His discontent with the reigning paradigms of psychiatric drug research was so pronounced that he even refused to be called a psychopharmacologist:

> Psychopharmacological research is very much focused on the brain. But you can't reduce mental illness to a disequilibrium of neurotransmitter levels. We need to look at the body more holistically. What influence does the endocrine system have on the brain? Which roles do vitamins and minerals play? These aspects are often overlooked because of the increasing specialization in medicine, but also because too much research is paid for by pharmaceutical companies interested in bringing drugs to the market. I'm growing increasingly convinced that many mental problems are consequences of bodily imbalances. I see the biggest shortcoming, not in a disregard for psychology or spirituality, but in a neglect of the urbiological conditions of our existence. For example, our nourishment has totally changed since the Stone Age, we're exposed to environmental toxins, and we don't get enough sunlight and exercise.

This view was reinforced through a series of drug experiences Studerus had had in a shamanic setting in Amazonia. A test subject from an MDMA study, which he had conducted in the Vollenweider lab, had told him about a place called Takiwasi. This addiction treatment center located in the Peruvian rain forest was run by Jacques Mabit, a Catholic physician from France, in collaboration with indigenous shamans. In a ritual context, the hallucinogenic vine of ayahuasca was meant to help addicts come to terms with the existential emptiness they had previously tried to fill with crack cocaine and other habit-forming substances. But Takiwasi also catered to spiritual seekers from abroad, whom anthropologist Marlene Dobkin de Rios has unfavorably referred to as "drug tourists" (Dobkin de Rios 1994; Dobkin de Rios and Rumrrill 2008: 69–86): Europeans and Americans out for visionary experiences in authentic shamanic settings. Having grown interested in transpersonal psychology and aboriginal healing practices, Studerus eventually booked a so-called personal evolution seminar at Takiwasi. After preparing in an isolated jungle hut with four days of intermittent purging and fasting, Studerus underwent four ayahuasca sessions that took him from what he described as cold and cerebral visions of other planets to an experience of his physical foundations. Studerus recounted that, in contrast to Mabit, who had interpreted his visions both in depth-psychological and shamanistic terms, the indigenous shamans attributed less significance to Erich's visions than to his vomiting (purgation is a common side effect of ayahuasca). This seminar, he said in retrospect, sowed the seeds of his growing attention to materialist philosophies (including Nietzsche's) as well as the most basic conditions of life and, almost paradoxically, his waning interest in treatments based on altered states of consciousness.

Studerus conceived of his experience at Takiwasi as highly enriching, but he did not see how such shamanic practices could be integrated into life back home in Switzerland:

> Introducing an equally powerful and convincing drug ritual in the West seems very difficult to me. The question is whether one can simply create such a practice. I remember a discussion with Jacques Mabit, in which I argued that a techno party was as much of a ritual as an ayahuasca session. He said that a ritual was nothing arbitrary one could simply create, but was based on a long tradition. He was enormously afraid of changing even the smallest detail, as the procedure was exactly determined by shamans and plant spirits. For him, the ritual was sacrosanct. Of course, one can dismiss this as superstition, but the ritual probably only becomes so powerful and convincing because the shamans regard its rules as sacred. Without the power of suggestion, a shamanic session would not work. Those running such a drug ritual need to exude absolute security, authority, and expertise. In the case of experimental subjects easily impressed by scientific authorities, a researcher might be able to fulfill this function as well. In my eyes, however, a scientist is not in the least capable of keeping up with a Peruvian shaman because the latter has techniques at his disposal that have stood the test of millennia.

Whether *traditional* is the right word to describe the rituals conducted at Takiwasi may be called into question. It was not so long ago (maybe as recent as 1992, when the center was founded) that Amazonian *curanderos* began to work in multidisciplinary teams with medical doctors, psychologists, and educators to treat crack addicts from the city and Westerners striving for "personal evolution." Anthropological scholarship has also suggested that rituals can be reconfigured or invented anew while maintaining their transformative power (Jungaberle et al. 2006). In fact, a research team funded by the Heffter Research Institute demonstrated that the use of ayahuasca by the Brazilian União do Vegetal Church facilitated the remission of psychopathology (Grob et al. 1996)—in spite of a highly syncretic ritual context that mingled Catholicism and Christian spiritism with African and Amerindian traditions that had only emerged since 1962. Thus, in principle, the introduction of new drug rituals into a given cultural context appears to be possible.

But Studerus's skepticism concerning the creation of a place for ayahuasca in his home country also reflected a lack of spiritual momentum in contemporary Swiss culture. Despite the growing recognition that even Europe has never been entirely secular, and contrary to the diagnosis of a global resurgence of religion, there is no spiritual reawakening on the European horizon. Neither is an Alpine equivalent of the União do Vegetal about to emerge, nor do neoshamanic rituals gain much traction. The resulting vacancies have not been filled through the process of secularization (Blumenberg 1983). Although brain researchers have been endowed with and have claimed the (frequently contested) authority to address all things human and even divine, they have not come to serve as modern priests or shamans. The discourse and ethos of science do not lend themselves to warm hearts, nor do they feed souls, work wonders, or provide answers to big questions of meaning. As we saw in chapter 3, the neuroscientists in Vollenweider's laboratory availed themselves of the power of suggestion for ethical and epistemological purposes, that is, to collect data while maintaining the test persons' well-being in the laboratory, but they did not work toward a lasting ethical and spiritual transformation of their subjects. The goal of scientific research is factual knowledge, not betterment and salvation. Even though the neuroscientific investigation of psychedelic drugs has significantly advanced our understanding of their psychopharmacological effects, it has done precious little to generate new ritual contexts that consolidate and secure applications of these substances in Western lifeworlds (the clinical use of psychedelics is a different story; see Langlitz and Hermann 2012).

PERENNIAL NEUROPHILOSOPHY

A youthful philosophical question—"What is real? What is not real?"—marked the outset of Franz Vollenweider's (FXV) intellectual trajectory at age eighteen. When, in his midtwenties, he discovered hallucinogenic drugs, he hoped they could help him find an answer. He turned to brain research expecting it to shed light on the puzzling experiences he had had with these substances. But it gradually dawned on him that the scope of present-day neuroscientific experimentation might be too narrow to answer the big questions raised by philosophy and psychedelic experiences.

FXV: During a hallucinogen intoxication, I can experience time as passing very slowly, almost standing still, or as accelerated. Either there is a rush of associations or this great calm allowing you to let go. Then you feel that you've reached eternity. Is it eternity or does your inner meter work differently? That's the kind of question I'm interested in. It's tempting to say that it's not the meter. Some people claim that, in such moments, you've been spread out in the universe, in the atman. Where does madness begin?

NL: *An experience of eternity paradoxically implies that it is possible to observe timelessness in time. The problem with any kind of mystical experience of oneness is that, if all is one, it can't be observed. At least not based on bivalent logics distinguishing the object of observation from something else.*

FXV: Yes, there are many questions like this, but you need to ask yourself: Does this have to be studied? Should the state pay for this?

NL: *Together with Mark Wittmann [see Wittmann et al. 2007], you examined the alteration of time perception under psilocybin influence. Could your work on the temporal organization of experience be described as an attempt to examine Kantian forms of intuition, such as time and space, neurophysiologically?*

FXV: Yes, absolutely.

NL: *Would you describe this research as an operationalization of philosophical thought?*

FXV: I would like to say so, but maybe we haven't got the necessary tools yet. I've had several conversations with the philosopher Thomas Metzinger. He said that his book *Being No One* [2003] contains some suggestions for new experiments and asked us whether we could operationalize them. He is very interested in these issues, for example, in the question of to what extent we construct and simulate the world. Is the trip only a hallucination? But I often wonder whether we aren't doing classical psychophysiology of a peculiar state of mind and to what extent this allows us to address philosophical questions.

In contrast to eliminativist neurophilosophers, Vollenweider was too critical of the narrowly confined methods of neuroscience to simply brush off first-person accounts. But he was equally cautious not to be duped by the seeming self-evidence of subjective experience. "It would be nice," he told me, "if this so-called mysticism, these ecstatic states, would not just be simulations, if they would tap something, if hallucinogens allowed us to penetrate this Platonic world. But I can't get rid of the doubt that I simply simulate all this."

Vollenweider has looked for answers to this question in books such as Huston Smith's *Cleansing the Doors of Perception* (2000) or *Beyond the Postmodern Mind* (2003). While Timothy Leary was at Harvard, Smith was a young professor of philosophy, teaching a few blocks away at the Massachusetts Institute of Technology. Ever since his first hallucinogenic experience in Leary's house on New Year's Day 1961, Smith (1964) was concerned with the question of whether drug experiences had religious import. Following Aldous Huxley, he became an avid advocate of the perennial philosophy, that is, the belief that all religions were built around the same cross-cultural and transhistorical core, namely, the mystical experience. In the light of Walter Pahnke's Good Friday experiment in 1963, he argued that, given the right set and setting, psychedelics could induce this prototypical spiritual experience indistinguishable from religious experiences occurring spontaneously.

Like Smith and many members of the psychedelic community, Vollenweider was a perennialist—or, in the words of his colleague Felix Hasler, a "neuroperennialist." In a public talk I attended at Hebbel Theater in Berlin, Hasler described a shift from *philosophia perennis* to *neurobiologia perennis*: "What students of religion since Leibniz have discussed as *philosophia perennis,* namely, that all religions share the same core of absolute truth, is currently undergoing a modern neurobiological reinterpretation. Maybe the spiritual experiences of human beings do not resemble each other across cultures because they point to the same God or universal truth but simply because human brains all work alike."

In Vollenweider's eyes, this eternal philosophy was not a matter of faith but of experience: "I do not doubt the existence of such transcultural phenomena," he told me. "The basic question is whether these states open something up." At this point, Vollenweider parted from Smith's account. Huston Smith (2000) was a believer, convinced of the existence of an "Ultimate Reality" revealed by religious experiences, including those induced by drugs. When rereading Smith's work, Vollenweider was looking for evidence to support the existence of such a higher realm. Eventually, he laid the books aside, as disappointed in them as he was with the free will debate. "How can Smith corroborate this claim ontologically?" Vollenweider asked. "This is purely subjective. It can't be established in natural scientific terms. And even if you could translate it into natural scientific language, you still wouldn't know if the brain didn't simulate all this."

Despite his underlying skeptical attitude, Vollenweider's desire to verify and possibly study the beyond with scientific objectivity and empirical rigor is reminiscent of the goals of late nineteenth-century spiritists' attempts to establish a "science of God" by employing the means of experimental psychology (Monroe 2008). In both cases, religion is modeled on science, the assumption being that spiritual truths are to be established or disproved through chains of inscriptions and translations—just like scientific facts. This ostensible compatibility of modern science and religion is based on the assumption that they both teach us that things are not as they seem, that there is an unseen world behind the observed one. Following Bruno Latour's (2005) account, science generates technical mediations and brings this unseen world into the purview of human beings. But does not religion have to be conceptualized differently?

Although Huston Smith believed in the metaphysical contents of transcendent experiences, his thinking was in the pragmatist tradition of William James and he was not primarily concerned with whether such experiences referred to anything in the world or beyond. Nor did he assume that a neurological origin of mystical experiences contradicted their religious significance. More important to him was whether these experiences were spiritually transformative. Even though Smith was convinced that psychedelic experiences were genuine religious experiences, he did not assume that they would be able to give faith. Instead, he argued, they would only have transformative effects if the subject was already faithful and engaged in spiritual exercises:

> Drugs appear to be able to induce religious experiences; it is less evident that they induce religious lives. It follows that religion is more than a string of experiences. This is hardly news, but it may be a useful reminder, especially to those who incline toward "the religion of religious experience." . . . The conclusion to which the evidence seems currently to point is that it is indeed possible for chemicals to enhance religious life, but only when they are set within the context of faith (conviction that what they disclose is true) and

discipline (exercise of the will toward fulfilling what the disclosures ask of us). (H. Smith 1964: 528–530)

The idea, however, that the *philosophia perennis* was about seeing things not only as they truly are but also as "a path to be walked," that it might be about not only insight and knowledge but also virtue and care (H. Smith 2003: 55), seemed alien to Vollenweider: "Why would it be a way of life? There is no code of practice. It's not like a Zen order where people practice. This just happens to you: either something opens up or it doesn't." Even though Vollenweider was convinced that, if people had more of this kind of consciousness, it would reduce fear and aggression while promoting altruism and serenity, he also told me that he did not draw any rules of conduct from it. His perennial neurophilosophy was concerned with the theological question of whether the world was imbued with divinity, but solely on the levels of epistemology and ontology, which were disconnected from ethics—at least from an ethics understood in the strongly normative sense of a moral order prescribing what one should do.

COSMIC PLAY

The failure of brain research to solve the big philosophical questions neither led Vollenweider to abandon science in favor of psychedelic piety nor drove him into a positivistic rejection of all questions exceeding the epistemic capacities of science. Instead he developed an outlook of partial detachment, in which he let go of the earnest quest for epistemological, ontological, and theological foundations. Even though neuroscientific experiments did not answer these questions, Vollenweider stopped perceiving them as pressing. "There was a time," he remembered, "when questions concerning the reality of mystical experiences were extremely important to me. About ten years ago, I really wanted to know. I thought: I experienced it myself—and yet the doubts lingered on. Today, I think that it's a bit stupid that I was bothered by these questions. Maybe I'm just getting older. Now what's important for me is that I'm enjoying myself."

In comparison with philosophy and religion, Vollenweider perceived science as the "more delightful game." Strolling through the alleys of Zurich during the lunch break of the "Challenge to Freedom" conference, he explained to me that he loved to read philosophical texts but that ultimately he was glad to work as a natural scientist. In comparison to the austerity of philosophy, with all its dry definitions, natural science was playful: "There, I can manipulate something. I take much pleasure in tinkering with a data set using new software, or trying out new instruments to make something novel become visible. In research, it's very small things. When I have an idea about how to do something, that's a kick for me. Then I'm happy. That other thing, contemplating and immersing myself in transcendence, I can still do when I'm dead."

Starting from Max Weber's insight into the limits of science, its inability to answer the final questions of life, Vollenweider developed a very different attitude toward scientific inquiry. Whereas Weber described and advocated modern science as a vocation, adopting an ethos deeply rooted in Protestantism, Vollenweider conceived of science as a game. If it had any religious underpinnings at all, they appeared to be more inspired by the Hindu conception of *līlā*—the cosmic playfulness of the divine absolute to be joyfully embraced—than by grave Christian asceticism. Maybe it was no historical coincidence that this notion of the gods' free and irresponsible frolics, which first blossomed in the fourth century when caste restrictions came to be systematically enforced by Brahmanical dynasties, were imported by the 1960s countercultures that rebelled against the capitalist drivenness, technocratic overregulation, and stale moralism of Western societies (Hein 1995; Hospital 1995). According to Vollenweider's own account, psychedelic drugs played an important role in cultivating his ludic approach to science as a way of life.

NL: *What do you gain from hallucinogen experiences?*

FXV: Hallucinogens cause a perspectival change. Apart from experiencing a normal state of mind, you then also experience a very different perspective. Between these two states a space of reflection opens up. Take the koans in Zen Buddhism, for example. You can't solve them rationally. But in such states you sometimes experience that things that you usually perceive as separate are connected in one gestalt. What these perspectival transformations show you is how extremely restricted our conception of reality is. All these potentialities. We play with them. A trip is about reality and the play of thoughts.

NL: *This implies that, under the influence of hallucinogens, you can experience things usually beyond our imagination.*

FXV: Yes, you find answers to questions such as, what does the clapping of one hand sound like? But the image that then comes up is not essential. It's not about the content of consciousness but about experiencing the playfulness of the world, how things fold and unfold, how they manifest and disappear. That's what you can learn. But all this content—forget about it! It only leads to pseudoreligiosity! Abstracting from experience, that's the realization, that's what you're being shown. And not this kind of "Oh, I'm one with everything, everybody likes me, and there is a man with a beard." You hear such stories constantly. It's all anthropomorphisms and projections. What is liberating about the hallucinogen state resembles the story of the Hindu yogi Maharishi: He is suffering for twenty years until he realizes that suffering is no solution. Then he steers a middle course. He eats, has sex, and enjoys life. It's simply as it is. He enters into the flux of reality. If you tense up in abstraction you become Jesus. [*Laughs.*] That's not what I'm desperate to do. What I learned from hallucinogens is this playfulness. Every time I come down, I'm astonished: all of a sudden, you're neurotic again, you're busy, running after science, writing grants, et cetera. That's all important! That's all unimportant! When you break through to this inner calm, this play of nature and the cosmos, then you're one step ahead.

Eventually, the Hindu motif of divine playfulness also appears to dissolve tensions between the ultimately real and the realm of ordinary experience in a joyous masquerade of changing perspectives (Fost 1998). Yes, the world might be an illusion: the playground of the gods or a neuronal game. From this perspective, liberation is not achieved by maintaining the freedom of the will against its deterministic challenges from posthumanist philosophy, structuralist sociology, and the neurosciences but by seeing through the unreality of the phenomenal world. "When you jettison these attachments to perceive something deeper," Vollenweider told me, "then you relativize a lot of things that you usually do. The term *enlightenment* is used in the sense of a spontaneous mystical experience that shakes you. But I don't think that such a singular experience can last. The saints have been tempted by the devil again and again."

DISILLUSIONMENTS

Three years after leaving the Vollenweider lab, I returned to Zurich for one of my occasional follow-up visits. On my last night, I met with

Felix Hasler in a trendy bar, where he announced that, after thirteen years, he was quitting hallucinogen research. Hasler had entered the field in the early 1990s. His doctoral work at Rudolf Brenneisen's lab on drug safety, pharmacodynamics, and pharmacokinetics of psilocybin had helped to prepare the ground for the psychedelic resurgence by convincing regulators in Switzerland, Germany, the United States, and elsewhere that psilocybin could be securely administered to human subjects in experimental settings. But two decades into the revival, Hasler had lost the spirit of optimism that had fired its early days. He was disappointed by both psychedelic science and drugs:

> One of the reasons I'm leaving is that, in my salad days, I had hoped for a much bigger outcome. I really had the somewhat idealistic expectation that it would be possible to learn about human nature, the nature of consciousness, and the pharmacological basis of schizophrenia. We were also hoping to demonstrate some kind of mental enhancement. With amphetamines this wouldn't be difficult. But in all of our psilocybin studies we have never ever been able to show any robust improvements. Probably our methods of measurement fail to capture the essence of such states. Thus, the longer I've worked in this area, the more disillusioned I've become with the results.

The revival of hallucinogen research in the 1990s coincided with the emergence of a public discourse on neuropsychopharmacology dominated by the problematization of enhancement. "Smart drugs" such as Ritalin were reported to be used increasingly for the purpose of "cognitive enhancement," or "brain doping." Both critics and advocates believed that such substances would give their users an advantage in the neoliberal rat race. At the same time, antidepressants were refashioned as "mood enhancers," no longer prescribed to treat a medical condition, but liberally taken to feel "better than well." Some bioethicists, neurophilosophers, and transhumanists even imagined the invention of "moral enhancers." Of course, none of this was entirely new. Timothy Leary and the hippies had already hoped that psychedelics would turn us into a more virtuous, more creative, and happier species. In the 1960s and 1970s, many researchers were convinced that their work would contribute to propelling human consciousness toward unheard of capacities. In the 1990s, however, these utopian dreams gave way to a less fanciful conception of enhancement as optimization of already known human capacities. In contrast to the psychedelic explorations of human potential, this one-dimensional notion of enhancement lent itself to an experimental operationalization. In the reigning paradigms of psychopharmacology, all relevant aspects of human life were captured as rating-scale scores or performance measures.

Vollenweider and his group repeatedly expressed their frustration over the fact that the effects of psychedelics escaped such measurements or that their subjects' performance even deteriorated under the influence. One possible explanation for the researchers' failure to scientifically demonstrate any of the benefits, which so many users claim to have experienced, might be that what the drugs are doing is too subtle to be picked up, given the limited financial resources available for testing. The effects of psychotropics are hardly ever as pronounced as those of antibiotics, for example. When penicillin was discovered decades before randomized placebo-controlled trials became the gold standard of pharmacological research, it did not take any such elaborate study design and powerful statistical tools to pick up the drug's impressive therapeutic efficacy: patients who would otherwise have died suddenly survived. In psychopharmacology, however, it is usually small differences between verum and placebo that need to be carved out. The smaller the difference, the more subjects are needed—and the more money has to be paid to compensate and insure them. As hallucinogen research does not promise to be lucrative, it is hardly funded by industry. In consequence, hallucinogen trials are usually based on a small number of cases (10–20 subjects per trial, sometimes even fewer), which might not be sufficient to pick up all of the drugs' effects.

However, anyone who has experienced psychedelics firsthand will know that their impact is everything but subtle. The problem of measuring enhancement effects might also be due to the fact that, despite the striking potency of hallucinogens, their effects have turned out to be relatively indeterminate. Too many nonpharmacological factors, prominently summed up under the rubric of set and setting, affect the outcome. As modern psychopharmacology discards case studies as merely anecdotal, focusing on large (or not so large) numbers of test subjects instead, pronounced effects in individuals tend to be averaged out in the final analysis. The question of how to approach the complexity of psychobiological phenomena that depend on an organism's interactions with its environment continues to be unresolved. It was early on in my fieldwork that Felix Hasler pointed out to me that the main obstacle to hallucinogen research came from within. It was not political repression that was the problem but the lack of more suitable epistemic practices.

Whether the failure to prove enhancement effects and therapeutic benefits was because of a small effect size or high inter- and intraindividual variability, it led to a disenchantment with psychedelics. In opposition to the vocal enthusiasts populating the scene, Vollenweider emphasized to me that hallucinogens were no wonder drugs:

> I've always asked myself why there are so many people in the field of hallucinogen research who do funny things such as taking drugs all the time and overrating these experiences. They present them as if they were something ultimate, as if you just had to take these drugs and you got cured and there would be peace in the world. We've already had that in 1968. If it would work, these goals would have been achieved long ago. I don't like this kind of glorification. This morning, I wrote a paper listening to Bach. When I write, I like Bach. But when I don't have to concentrate, I prefer jazz-rock. I have different means of being happy. That's also how it is with hallucinogens. They're no panacea, that's nonsense. And probably they're only for people who are more or less healthy.

By stressing their nonmedical use (in the public debate, often denounced as "cosmetic psychopharmacology"), Vollenweider fashioned hallucinogens as psychopharmacological equipment to aid the good life. Comparing their effects with the enjoyment of music, however, he shifted them from the register of enhancement to that of eudaemonia. "For me, the hallucinogenic experience is first and foremost something sensual," he said. "It's also intellectually stimulating, but more than that it's about opening up the senses." In the fabric of Vollenweider's life, the aesthetic nature of this experience was thereby entwined with his passion for playing percussion and for the "painting orgies" in which he regularly indulged. It was particularly this aesthetic quality of the drug experience that had drawn him from patch-clamp research on single cells ("dry as dust") to psychedelic science as a way of life.

Despite this mutual pervasion of life and science, Vollenweider and his collaborators emphatically renounced the proselytizing of many 1960s psychedelic researchers and advocates. In Hasler's eyes, their generation was no longer on a revolutionary mission. In contrast to some of their American colleagues, especially those rallying behind MAPS, most members of the Heffter Research Institute had abandoned the messianic hope that drug-induced consciousness expansion would ring in a new age. The Dionysian ecstasy of hallucinogen inebriation was carefully dispensed and measured in the laboratory and integrated in rather Apollonian practices of methodical self-experimentation and a composed self-care that took place in private.

Heffter had been founded in 1993 in an atmosphere of departure. Shortly after the raising of the Iron Curtain, a critical historical moment seemed to have arrived. In an early call for funding, the founders of Heffter had written of the coincidence of rapidly changing social orders, the restructuring of economic powers, and an unprecedented interest in the relationship of brain and mind, which the neuroscientific investigation of psychedelic substances would help to elucidate in an unparalleled manner (Heffter Research Institute n.d.: 1). In the summer of 2010, half a year after Felix Hasler told me about his plan to quit, I saw him again, this time in Berlin. He had found a place at the Max Planck Institute for the History of Science (where I had spent more than two years as a postdoctoral fellow), and he was writing a popular-science book deflating what he called "neuromythology" (Hasler 2012).[3] In the book, Hasler critiqued the "brain overclaim syndrome" (Morse 2006), that is, the inflationary use of neuroscience to explain the lifeworld and to promote political agendas with reference to neuroimaging data. Twenty years after US president George H.W. Bush had proclaimed the Decade of the Brain, and after the founders of Heffter had climbed on this bandwagon to promote the revival of hallucinogen research, Hasler felt disillusioned by both neuroscience and psychedelic drugs.

The often promised neurological revolution had never happened. Neither had Timothy Leary's utopian hopes for a liberation of the divine brain from the constraints of culture come true, nor was the overcoming of folk psychology predicted by eliminativist neurophilosophers about to materialize—not even among the neuroscientists themselves. Hasler (2009: 26) wrote in one of his popular articles: "The consequent implementation [of neuroreductionism] in everyday life is lacking. Eventually it is unlikely that one day we will say, 'Hey, today my *gyrus fusiformis* is yet again so poorly perfused that I almost didn't recognize my neighbor.'" What would it mean for neuropsychedelia if both the Romantic dreams of the sixties and the subsequent hopes for a neuroscientific Enlightenment waned as the twentieth century slipped into history?

THE STONY ROAD OF NORMAL SCIENCE

The ground floor of the warehouse located in an industrial area around Berne was filled with antiques. Passing by some dusty armchairs and a padded cobra in a basket, I climbed up the staircase to the exhibition space: an unheated hall with a concrete floor, filled with large-format black-and-white digital prints of photographs taken by Felix Hasler and his friend Nenad Brcic. Among the recurrent motifs were spiritual experiences: from devout Catholic women prostrating on the floor of a Croatian church, to a Pentecostal exorcism in Brazil, to German Jesus freaks (an evangelical youth culture), to the guests of a wellness hotel worshiping the sun in their morning meditation.[4] In a video installation, Honza Samotar's face, strangely twisted by the effects of ketamine, floated in a samadhi tank where Hasler and Brcic had filmed him in night mode. Samotar's voice groaned from one of the DAT tapes recorded during his early self-experiments: "Oh my God, 100 mg was too much"—before continuing to report visions of divine beings bowing in front of him. In the background, Arvo Pärt, one of the pioneers of mystic minimalism, was playing. In the restroom, a loudspeaker voice spoke about pharmacologically and electromagnetically induced religious experiences. The exhibition was titled *Vague Ideas about Life— and the Trouble Arising for Those Who Seek Meaning.* Hasler's opening address revealed his conception of neuroperennialism as organizing the exhibition by bridging the different cultural and denominational practices on view. As Hasler and Brcic put it in an online announcement of their show: "We allow ourselves the provocation of confronting religious experiences with other forms of transcendence that are surrounded by less nimbus in order to raise the question of whether all of these are not merely neuronal disorders."

In contrast to the pathos displayed by the New Atheists (e.g., Dawkins 2006; Dennett 2006) or their militant nineteenth-century forebears (Hecht 2003), Hasler communicated his reductionist message in a visual language and tone of writing marked by irony rather than zeal. In a conversation with a visitor of the exhibition, he tellingly referred to his own atheism as a "hobby." His faith in science was too shaken to serve as a substitute for hope of religious salvation. Even though humorous, the exhibition title, *Vague Ideas about Life,* revealed a deeper feeling of existential disorientation that also affected his sense of science as a vocation.

In the *Protestant Ethic* (1992/1920), Max Weber described the formation of the idea of the calling during the Reformation as a key element of the emergence of capitalism. As the epitome of the religious life shifted from monasticism to everyday activity, the fulfillment of duty in worldly callings took the place of otherworldly forms of asceticism. What Weber (1958/1919) described as science as a vocation was one outcome of this spiritual development. Vocational activity is characterized by the fact that it is pursued as an end in itself. The decision to become a scientist, Weber cautioned, required not only cutting back one's economic expectations, but also accepting the intellectual and spiritual limits of science: the willingness to dedicate a significant part of one's life to finding answers to narrowly constructed questions that provided neither meaning nor salvation. Usually, an individual scientist's extensive work on a single piece of the jigsaw does not even solve any of the bigger problems of her discipline, let alone human existence.

This was what Mark Geyer meant when he told me: "If I wanted to understand the relationship between brain and behavior, which is the general thing I'm after scientifically, I would stop doing research. That's a very inefficient way given how much information is out there that I'm not aware of. I could increase my understanding a lot more by just reading than by doing. If my personal edification was the goal, then this would be a really stupid way of going about it." Over the years, he recounted, it had become harder and harder for him to feel enthusiastic about his research findings: "I fully appreciate and understand the gradual accrual of validated information. That is the process of science. But you start getting a little jaded and skeptical because you so often had the experience that, five years later, either you or somebody else finds some flaw in your results." Geyer's own response to this problem was to shift his professional libido away from scientific bench work: "It is not uncommon for people as they get older and more senior to see their continued contribution, their value, in legacy building rather than fact finding. If, at this point of my career, I would be trying to do something that outlasts me, it would be trying to train students, academics having a positive, multiplicative influence, and changing policies, changing systems that endure." And a reform of science policy was exactly what Geyer was working toward through his engagement in the MATRICS initiative that aimed at a different regulation of the development of antipsychotic drugs (Bromley 2008).

Geyer and Vollenweider, despite their discontents, are highly dedicated scientists. But I hesitate to describe the ethos of Vollenweider and many of the younger researchers in his lab as vocational in the stern Weberian sense (with the notable exception of Boris Quednow). Vollenweider pursued science for its own sake, but he did so as a game to be enjoyed without the solemnity marking the Protestant genealogy of a calling. The secularized theology informing the ethos of modern science was at odds with the mystical leanings pervading psychedelic research.[5] Considering that neuroscience laboratories are highly competitive workplaces, which usually leave their inhabitants little room for leisure activities, it was striking that, after-hours, many people in Vollenweider's lab spent much time and energy on parascientific practices related to, but not identical with, their scientific interest in hallucinogen experiences: Honza Samotar's systematic self-experimentation; the photographic work of Marco Benz and Felix Hasler; Hasler's forays and eventual migration into science writing; or Vollenweider's involvement in philosophical conversations. When I related this observation to Hasler, he agreed: "The fact that almost all Swiss hallucinogen researchers pursue activities outside of but closely related to their day-to-day business is indeed remarkable. This is probably due to the fact that the original, perhaps exaggerated expectations concerning meaningfulness and true insight in research can hardly be fulfilled. You at least wanted to explain consciousness and, *en passant,* cure schizophrenia—and find yourself attaching PPI electrodes."

In comparison with MAPS' highly ambitious goal of reforming mainstream culture by opening it up to psychedelics, the Heffter Research Institute's attempt to consolidate hallucinogen research as a scientific field appeared modest. At the time of my fieldwork, however, even this aim was far from being realized. During a discussion with Geyer and Vollenweider about the future of psychedelic science, Geyer stated: "The intention has been and still is to build more systematically the next generation of researchers. That that has not been adequately successful is quite clear to us. But I don't think it's for lack of willingness and interest. It's for lack of resources." On the basis of this diagnosis, Heffter recruited donors who endowed an Aldous Huxley Training Grant and an Albert Hofmann Fellowship to support doctoral students, and the institute sought further funding for career development at the assistant professor level. But Vollenweider also pointed to the fact that too many young researchers interested in hallucinogens lacked the stamina necessary to stay in the field. Felix Hasler had been regarded as a promising candidate to be built up, but he eventually decided against a life in science. As I write this book, many of the doctoral students I met during my fieldwork have also left the laboratory and some even the field of neuropsychopharmacology. "They do their thesis and then it's over," Vollenweider said. "That's the tragedy. In Switzerland, we can use these substances much more easily than in the US, but nobody does it. Sometimes I ask myself, will everything break down when I leave?"

By now, the revival of hallucinogen research is more than twenty years old. The Decade of the Brain has long passed. Even though packaging psychedelics in the fashionable vocabulary of the neurosciences has returned legitimacy to hallucinogen research, it has not made up for Leary's failed neurological revolution. Undoubtedly, the renewed investigation of psychedelics has significantly advanced neuroscientific knowledge. For example, it has contributed to an understanding of the cortical metabolism and neurochemical substrates of psychotic processes, elucidated the role of serotonin and glutamate receptors in cognitive and perceptual processing, and opened up new experimental venues for the treatment of post-traumatic stress disorder, cluster headaches, and end-of-life anxiety in patients suffering from terminal illness (Nichols 2004; Geyer and Vollenweider 2008). But this scientific progress has taken place just the way Weber described: it has been hard-earned, piecemeal, and in itself has not provided much moral, spiritual, or intellectual edification. Even though psychedelic scientists attended, at least tacitly, to set and setting, the reintroduction of these drugs into neuropsychopharmacology neither marked a paradigm shift nor the emergence of a novel *episteme*. Within the boundaries of what Thomas Kuhn (1962) had called "normal science," they developed innovative experimental designs. But, after what happened in the 1960s, hallucinogen researchers would have been the last to vociferously challenge the hegemony of randomized placebo-controlled trials. Throughout, the revival has been based on mainstreaming, not on overtly disputing the status quo. It has proceeded through slow and diligent scientific work that, although not solely committed to the epistemic virtue of objectivity, did not predetermine its outcomes.

Considering that the literature of consciousness research is brimming with calls for a paradigm shift, this pursuit of normal science might be found wanting. It might also disappoint historians of science who, since the twentieth century, have paid much attention to scientific revolutions and epistemic breaks, as well as anthropologists following the current trend of focusing on "the emergent" (replacing the encounter with a cultural other instead with first contact with an unknown future). But without normal science no scientific knowledge would ever be consolidated, and no more broadly accepted psychedelic culture could be rebuilt—and this is exactly what academic hallucinogen researchers have quietly been striving for. Although the problem of set and setting imposes itself most forcefully on psychedelic science, it might not yet be the time to loudly call for culture controls and field studies. Or at least hallucinogen research might not be the right corner of neuropsycho-pharmacology to start their implementation, if one wishes its ongoing resurgence to further build momentum.

But, as we have seen in this as well as previous chapters, the revival of academic studies of psychedelic drugs not only generated scientific knowledge but also stimulated experimentation with different forms of life. The resulting ethical orientations were not so much characterized by aggressive reductionism and a self-assured sense of being on the side of scientific progress as by exploratory movements from which no stable formation has yet emerged. The hallucinogen researchers I worked with were no modern Don Juans teaching the anthropologist their way of knowledge. The cerebral savages of the strange land of psychedelic science turned out to be travelers themselves, looking for ways of integrating hallucinogenic experiences into their twenty-first-century Western lives.

Now that both ethnographer and reader have had a chance to meet at least a few self-proclaimed monists, it appears conceivable that the neuropsychedelic assemblage of the classical God-form and the recent molecularization and animalization of human life might engender a new form: a mystic materialism less committed to a neurotheology of mystical experiences than to a biomysticism in awe of life itself. But this form is still fragile and its contours fuzzy. It is far from having stamped out all dualist sentiments. Naturalism (in Descola's sense) is alive and well—just like the Euro-American varieties of animism. These are no logical contradictions, just a reminder that epochal breaks and cultural wholes have always been in the eye of the beholder. Neuropsychedelia is no exception. The ethnographic portraits presented in this chapter might give a sense of the fact that every person is "a people unto him- or herself," the expression of a possible world (Viveiros de Castro, quoted in Candea 2011: 148). Each of these miniature "anthropology assessments" provides a different answer to my colleague Emily Martin, who once wondered why the "monadic sociality" of mind-brain identity might appeal to certain contemporaries.[6] If you like Leibnizian neologisms and are not yet tired of the *neuro-* prefix, call this account an ethnographic "neurodicy"—even though the metaphysical optimism of living in the best of all possible worlds has long since been shaken.

Conclusion

Fieldwork in Perennial Philosophy

ANTHROPOLOGY OF THE PERENNIAL

Ethnographic narratives often end with the anthropologist coming back home. Having gone through the motions of a dialectic between self and other, he arrives at a deeper understanding of his own cultural identity. For my part, I did not return to where I come from, the predominantly Catholic Rhineland in Germany. Instead I found myself an anthropology professor in New York. After a hectic semester, teaching students who lift their spirits with Prozac and write their term papers while on Ritalin and Adderall, I have spent an oppressive Manhattan summer at my desk, intoxicated by the old and new drugs of the Protestant work ethic (Schivelbusch 1992: 15–84): high doses of caffeine and occasional bouts of Provigil. They neither expanded my consciousness nor enhanced my thinking, but they did enable me to work on this book for longer hours. As I am about to bring it to a close, I try to remind myself what the whole journey has been about.

The point of departure of this inquiry was no traditional anthropological or philosophical problem, but an experience: the wonder, shame, and buzzing confusion I felt when I first took LSD, initially losing myself in a psychotic delusion, later on being filled with a deep sense of inner peace and ontological security. Although, contrary to Timothy Leary's (1965: 113–114) predictions, psychedelic trips never became part of the academic canon, the incident raised different philosophical questions— "live questions," as William James would have called them—regarding the truth-value of subjective experience and the reconcilability of spirituality and materialism in a disenchanted world. At the time of that first trip, I kept my preoccupation with these problems confined to the introspective mirror maze of my diary. Since regurgitating my own experience did not provide a way out of these conundrums, I eventually abandoned both the questions and the drugs—only revisiting them about a decade later while discovering how intellectually liberating anthropological fieldwork can be.

The Oxford philosopher John Austin (1970b) coined the phrase *fieldwork in philosophy* to designate his practice of approaching philosophical problems by attending to the ways in which they were reflected in ordinary language use. When studying the social conditions enabling and delimiting philosophical thought in the French academe, the sociologist Pierre Bourdieu (1990) availed himself of the expression as a label for his own project. Eventually, it was taken up once again by Paul Rabinow (1989, 2003), who used it for lack of a better term for his attempt to anthropologically describe emergent responses to problematizations that he deemed of philosophic import but that were not necessarily the subject matter of philosophy seminars. After writing a book on Lacan's psychoanalytic practice of variable-length sessions in relation to his predominantly philosophical discussions of temporality, the idea of fieldwork in philosophy appealed to me (Langlitz 2005)—especially as the outward orientation of ethnographic observations promised to mobilize the blockage of my previously fruitless psychedelic meditations. However animating inner experience might be for any kind of philosophical inquiry, it is also restraining in that one remains confined to one's own mind. And, in contrast to purely archival and textual work that I had conducted as a historian of medicine, fieldwork located the philosophical questions raised by my drug experience in a much richer experiential context, bringing into view flesh-and-blood people, institutions, affects, objects, and practices omitted from written accounts. It promised to reconnect philosophy as concept work to the ancient conception of philosophy as a way of life (Hadot 1995).

If, in antiquity, philosophy was about spiritual exercises that prepared the subject for the reception of a truth that would transfigure his very being, modern science and academic philosophy have largely divorced access to truth from such ethical work on the self, making this access solely dependent on knowledge. Even though the preceding chapters have revealed exceptions to this rule on the level of scientific practice, they have also shown that the ethical dimension of the modern quest for truth is almost always subordinated, if not external to epistemic goals. And methodically acquired knowledge does not save anyone's soul but is accumulated in an infinite process of serving "humankind" rather than the particular human being acquiring it. The inevitably resulting discontents have given rise to a long-standing problematization of the unedifying relationship between the modern subject and truth (Foucault 2005).

In *The Perennial Philosophy* (2004/1944), Aldous Huxley lamented the alienation of professional philosophers from direct spiritual knowledge (ix). Not that he would have had any personal acquaintance with the "Divine Ground" himself. His own conversion from agnostic British intellectual, who never wrote about eternal verities without a sense of irony, to an advocate of mysticism concerned about the spiritual malaise of modern life had been a rather cerebral affair. As a resident of Hollywood, he became involved with the Vedanta Society of Southern California, but his attempts at yogic meditation did not take him far. As *The Perennial Philosophy* had been written before the psychiatrist and model psychosis researcher Humphry Osmond introduced Huxley to mescaline and LSD, the book is devised as an annotated anthology of mystical experiences, which people other than the author, coming from many different religions and historical periods, had reported. Although Huxley had adopted the term *philosophia perennis* from Leibniz, he emphasized that "the thing—the metaphysic that recognizes a divine Reality substantial to the world of things and lives and minds; the psychology that finds in the soul something that places man's final end in the knowledge of the immanent and transcendent Ground of all being—the thing is immemorial and universal" (vii).

When Leibniz spoke of a perennial philosophy in a frequently quoted letter from 1714, which Huxley must have had in mind, he did not invent the expression but borrowed it from the Vatican librarian Agostino Steuco, who had published a book titled *De perenni philosophia* in 1540. Although modernity was about to dawn, this Renaissance theologian did not proclaim a break with the past as the Protestant reformers did when seceding from the Roman Church. Here, contemporaneously with the great modern divide, a nonmodernity came into being that sought to produce harmony from discord. At a time when Europeans began to encounter more and more ethnic groups unlike themselves, Steuco explained the corruption of the divine wisdom, in which men in paradise had still participated, by the human race's scattering into all parts of the world. Living far apart from each other, people only recognized what mattered to their own lives. But, in principle, all peoples, including pagans and Protestants, had continued to have access to the same original wisdom since the beginning of the human species, a wisdom that Steuco wanted to reconstruct (Ch. Schmitt 1966; Schmidt-Biggemann 2004: 428–434).

This line of thought can be traced up to universalist positions in twentieth-century anthropology. Huxley (2004/1944: 20) approvingly (if imprecisely) quoted from Paul Radin's *Primitive Man as Philosopher*: "No progress in ethnology will be achieved until scholars rid themselves once and for all of the curious notion that everything possesses a history; until they realize that certain ideas and certain concepts are as ultimate as man, as a social being, as specific physiological reactions are ultimate for him, as a biological being."[1] Among these supposedly timeless concepts, Huxley emphasized, was monotheism. It should be noted, however, that Radin did not claim that all human beings had always been monotheists. Reminiscent of Geoffrey Lloyd's (2007) recent survey of the latest state of the nature vs. nurture debate, Radin (1957/1927: 364–374) rather stressed differences between individuals within a particular culture and epoch instead of between these totalities. In Radin's eyes, there had always been explicit monotheists in every tribe—just like there were proponents of materialism, animism, and other religious temperaments. What varied historically and cross-culturally was only the distribution of these types within different populations.

In the 1980s, this perennialist heritage of anthropology came under attack. Talal Asad argued that the anthropological category of religion did not correspond to an aspect of life shared by all human beings but was itself a historical construction. The earliest systematic attempts at producing a universal definition of religion in the sixteenth and seventeenth centuries were not just contemporaneous with the rise of the perennial philosophy: they were its very essence. Because of the category's specifically Christian genealogy, Asad (1993: 54) claimed, the anthropologist could not simply conduct cross-cultural comparisons of what were taken to be different religions; rather he or she would have to unpack "the comprehensive concept which he or she translates as 'religion' into heterogeneous elements according to its historical character." If, in the preceding chapters and on the following pages, the term *religion* has been and will occasionally be employed without such qualification, the reason is simple: in my fieldwork there was no problem of cultural translation.[2] From my American interlocutors, I simply incorporated their English references to "religion," and I translated the Swiss

(German) *Religion* as "religion" without worrying much about what might have gone missing along the way. All cultures involved have a predominantly Christian past. With the import of Asian philosophies, however, a turn away from this patrimony has set in within Western societies. As a result, not anthropologists, but spiritual seekers in Europe and America, many inspired by psychedelics and psychedelia, came to decompose the category of religion on their own, discarding organized forms of worship and a belief in the supernatural while maintaining and cultivating an experience-centered spirituality. The West had begun to anthropologize itself.

For the universalist conception of religion to be called into question, the scholarly world did not have to wait until anthropology's Foucauldian return to history, either. Half a millennium before, Steuco's contemporaries had already been well aware of how difficult, nay impossible, it was to extrapolate not just the lowest common denominator but, as Huxley put it, the "highest factor" shared by all religions and wisdom traditions. Early modern critics of the Neoplatonic *philosophia perennis* remembered all too well how medieval theologians had already struggled to bring the pagan philosophy of Aristotle into accord with Christianity. This difficult undertaking required making philosophy the "servant of theology": a purely theoretical activity that did not interfere with a way of life to be guided by the church, not by the philosophical practices of ancient Greece (Ch. Schmitt 1966: 523; Hadot 1995: 270). And Steuco's project of getting the whole world and all of history to agree was a lot more ambitious than that. Of course, the twentieth-century university professors whom Huxley (2004/1944: viii) had accused of having no access to direct spiritual knowledge, as they did not even try "to make themselves loving, pure in heart, and poor in spirit," reciprocated by not giving his rearticulation of the perennial philosophy a particularly warm welcome. For Huxley's all-embracing wisdom was not based on systematic historical and cross-cultural analysis but amounted to an anthological potpourri, including mystical thinkers from many different traditions that ranged from Christianity and Sufism to Hinduism and Taoism while ignoring others such as Confucianism or Judaism (Bronkhorst 2001).

But Huxley's approach was in line with an epistemological tradition that is both ancient and contemporary, namely, eclecticism. In antiquity, eclectics were philosophers who did not belong to any recognized school. Defying the conventions of discipleship, they selected doctrines as they pleased from many different sources. The most famous work promoting this attitude is Diogenes Laertius's *Lives and Opinions of Eminent Philosophers,* a book written in the second century before Christ to enable students to learn from different masters, from both their theories and their conduct of life.[3] At first glance, such a largely anecdotal doxography (reminiscent of an unreflective ethnography of ancient philosophers) seems ill-suited to modern knowledge practices that rely, at least according to the grand narrative of the seventeenth-century Scientific Revolution, on rational thought, direct experience, and empirical data, not on the views of others (but see Shapin 1994).

It is this epistemological modernism that fills neuroscientifically oriented philosophers of mind, such as Patricia Churchland and Thomas Metzinger, with contempt for so-called continental philosophy, which continues to cherish old texts and revered authors. However secular most contemporary practitioners of this hermeneutic mode of inquiry might be, they have adopted (and refunctioned) a practice of revealed religions, which are always dependent on tradition since revelations are events in time that can only be preserved through cultural transmission (Schmidt-Biggemann 2004: 34). However, just as the secession of modern Christianity was accompanied by the emergence of a non-modern (but not pre- or antimodern) *philosophia perennis,* the birth of modern science was accompanied by a resurgence of eclecticism. At a time when submission to epistemic authority was challenged as never before, the freedom to pick and choose from different schools of thought offered an alternative to the notorious *querelle des anciens et des modernes.* As one eighteenth-century eclectic put it: "one should not seek truth by oneself, nor accept or reject everything written by ancients and moderns" (quoted in Kelley 2001: 585). Instead, eclectics joined the old, largely descriptive doxographical tradition with the search for universal truths. They exercised their "liberty of philosophizing," guided by the novel practice of critical history, which did not promote relativism but aimed at wisdom and utility. Examining old and new doctrines (including the external conditions under which these doctrines had come into being), they assembled those that appeared to be veracious and consequently everlasting in useful ways that accommodated the spirit of particular times and places (Kelley 2001).

From the start, eclecticism was the perennialists' mode of philosophical inquiry. In his attempt to uncover the *philosophia perennis* and thereby facilitate religious unity in an era rife with interconfessional violence, Leibniz self-consciously selected and synthesized what seemed valuable to him from different systems and periods of history—not only drawing from philosophy but trying to assimilate competing knowledge-making practices from all areas of scholarship. The perennial philosophy is based on the unity of science: a science that is both historical and universal, grounded not in the autonomy of human reason but in the participation of finite human beings in an infinite wisdom beyond the rational capacities of man (Ch. Schmitt 1966: 530–531; Loemker 1989; Schmidt-Biggemann 2004: 412, 445; Whitmer 2009). When Aldous Huxley discussed the latest schizophrenia and drug research alongside the Upanishads and the mystical writings of Meister Eckhart, he reinvigorated both the eclectic and the perennialist tradition in a century deeply divided between the "two cultures" of the sciences and the humanities (Snow 1964). After the latest remake of this academic sectarianism—the science wars of the 1990s—an anthropology of the perennial appears to be one possible response to the deadlock between modern scientists (and their philosophical allies), who are often wistfully cut off from the meaningful cosmos of the past, and critical humanities scholars and social scientists, who conceive of themselves as an epistemic counterculture.

In retrospect, the inquiry documented in this book appears to be a kind of fieldwork in perennial philosophy. It has sketched a critical history but has primarily focused on an ethnographic examination of what became of the Huxleyan variety of perennialism in late twentieth- and early twenty-first-century neuropsychedelia: model psychosis research, biomysticism, and *neurobiologia perennis*. Entering into these new configurations, the perennial took a contemporary form. The God-form was molecularized: in the neuropsychopharmacology of psychedelic drugs, the previously transcendent infinity of the divine merged with the unlimited-finite shaping molecular biology on a purely immanent plane. The derivative anthropology of the infrahuman and the superhuman did not replace, but had come to coexist with, the nineteenth-century figure of man, despite the inherent instability of this empiricotranscendental doublet.

All three forms—the God-form, the Man-form, and the form of the infrahuman/superhuman—come with their own chronotopes. The God-form relates human finitude to eternity. In the Man-form, this finitude is cut off from the infinity of time. It is constituted by history, which determines and is determined by human beings. Historicization reveals everything pointing beyond this finitude to be a human projection, appearing and disappearing at certain moments in this human—all too human—time-form. As historical thought has begun to historicize itself, it has come to be supplemented and transformed by yet another chronotope that corresponds to the unlimited-finite of molecularization. Although Reinhart Koselleck (2004: 99) traced this contemporaneity of the noncontemporaneous all the way back to antiquity, it has only taken up a more prominent place in historical consciousness in recent decades, as globalization has come to mix up the remnants of social evolutionism and as a sprawling memory culture is trying to preserve as much of the past as possible (Rohbeck 2004: 12). Instead of conceiving of time as a linear series of events, this form of temporality is marked by simultaneities of elements from all times: the old and the new are assembled and reassembled in what Hans Ulrich Gumbrecht (2010) called a "broad present." Since the resulting polytemporal clusters are no longer characterized by breaks with past epochs, Bruno Latour (1993) referred to them as "nonmodern." I will follow Giorgio Agamben's (2009) and in particular Paul Rabinow's (1999, 2008) terminology, calling this time-form "the contemporary." In accord with its inherent logic, the contemporary is not posthistorical, for it has not eliminated the preceding chronotopes the way history has superseded the eternity of the divine. The contemporary has rather juxtaposed and connected prior chronotopes in an ephemeral moment, constantly recalibrating the recent past and the near future.

The contemporary rearticulation of the perennial in the molecular matrix of the unlimited-finite, here described in the context of neuropsychedelia, renews the olden present of the eternal in the current moment. It gives fresh vigor to what Mark Geyer called spirituality: an unhabituated attention to the here and now. "Here and now, boys," is also what the mynah birds from Huxley's (spatial, not temporal) utopia *Island* (1962) never tire of reminding the inhabitants of Pala. "Why 'Here and now'?" asks the modern European protagonist of a native girl. "'Well . . .' She searched for the right words in which to explain the self-evident to this strange imbecile. 'That's what you always forget, isn't it? I mean, you forget to pay attention to what's happening" (10).[4] And thereby people lose sight of the "great primordial facts" of life. As psychedelic chemist Alexander Shulgin noted after a self-experiment with one of the numerous novel compounds that he had derived from phenethylamine and tryptamine hallucinogens: "Funny, I'd forgotten that what comes to you when you take a psychedelic is not always a revelation of something new and startling; you're more liable to find yourself reminded of simple things you know and forgot you knew— seeing them freshly—old, basic truths that long ago became clichés, so you stopped paying attention to them" (Shulgin and Shulgin 1991: 262). What fills these eternal verities with life again is their eclectic reconfiguration with discourses, practices, and chemical compounds from other times and places. Perennialism produces recombinant truths and spiritual exercises that fit the here and now.

Despite the maybe surprising formal proximity of the perennial (in its "contemporary" rearticulation) and the contemporary (in Rabinow's sense), these two chronotopes do not match entirely. The contemporary captures singularities but is not oriented toward universals. The perennial, by contrast, attends to singular rearticulations of the universal. In response to a world experienced as contingent, malleable, and open, Rabinow's (1999: 181) anthropology of the contemporary advocates the cultivation of a nominalist sensibility of constant change. Before him, Clifford Geertz (2000: 134–135) had momentously dismissed anthropological universals as either being large banalities or poorly founded. It seems to me, though, that the extraordinary universality of the genetic code—or, to a lesser but still significant degree, of neurochemicals such as serotonin, or arguably of religious beliefs—is neither trivial nor so ill-founded as to be automatically shrugged off. What has come to escape not only many anthropologists devoted to contingencies and differences but also post-Enlightenment thought more broadly is a sense of wonder (Daston and Park 1998: 329–363), which Honza Samotar expressed so eloquently: the wonder about the fact "that this life as it is, so odd, so absurd, so simple, and yet so complicated, that this is what life is." Life in all its iridescent universality.

The interesting anthropological question is how archaic and more or less universal elements enter into new polytemporal ensembles. Of course, such work does require a sensibility of constant change, but also a perennialist sensibility of the eternal return of the same. For the perennial is not the everlasting, but the recurrent: it shows up again and again under widely differing circumstances (Bronkhorst 2001: 187). Thus, an anthropology of the perennial is no perennial anthropology. It is not about what is constant in human life, but about the incessant need for rearticulations and revivals. If the spiritual values a universal dimension of humankind (and other sentient beings), its universality cannot be presupposed in the way of Leon Kass (2002) and Francis Fukuyama (2002) but has to be freshly achieved time after time—through perennial philosophies, religious speech-acts, sacred rituals, psychedelic drugs, or other practices of mediation (see Latour 2002: 205–207). As the previous chapters have shown, in the age of molecular neurobiology, the mystical tradition derived from Huxley's perennialism no longer appeals to a transcendent God but has taken the immanent form of mystic materialism.

ONTOLOGIES AND OBSERVATIONS

Materialism, mystic materialism, the belief in a cosmic consciousness existing independently of the brain, not to speak of animism and totemism: since its inception, anthropology has dealt with this problem of multiple ontologies. Ontology is a branch of philosophy, especially metaphysics, dealing with the nature of being, including the question of whether nature is all that is or whether there are other, not just subordinate, but genuinely distinct realms of existence such as culture, the mind, or the supernatural. Ontology became an anthropological problem when non-Western people began to tell Western ethnographers about entities and powers that had no place in Euro-American cosmologies, for example, a multitude of deities in a world reigned over by the one and only God of monotheism, or hallucinogen-induced spirit journeys through a disenchanted universe. The inquiry presented in this book, however, started out not just as an "anthropology at home" but from a personal experience of the anthropologist as a young man puzzled by the coincidence of psychotic and religious elements in his first LSD experience. Here, the clash of materialist and supernaturalist ontologies did not take place between cultures or groups of people within one culture, but inside a single person. Framing the problem in this way was not just ethnocentric, but unabashedly self-centered. Why then approach it through anthropological fieldwork?

The place of us humans in a larger ontological framework is a question of philosophical anthropology. Philosophy proper would have offered different ways of addressing it, such as a phenomenological ontology of the psychedelic experience, a linguistic analysis of the concepts of nature and the supernatural, or a deconstruction of their dichotomy. However, the problem as discussed in this book is neither purely conceptual nor is it confined by the structure of consciousness; it is located in a complex and initially ill-defined historical and cultural situation, which has been created by real people, powerful institutions, and potent drugs that supposedly expand consciousness and dissolve the ego. Thus, it seemed appropriate to get out of the armchair and into the field to work through an experience that was not primarily psychological but biological, cultural, and historical. The problem at the heart of this inquiry was the result of forces and discourses affecting many of my contemporaries as well—and maybe not just my contemporaries. It is such an aggregate situation that anthropological fieldwork in philosophy responds to.

The assemblage of model psychosis research and the neurotheology of mystical experiences here described as neuropsychedelia both frame and mirror the problem that arose from my own experience with hallucinogenic drugs. Loosely following Ian Hacking (2002: 37), I assume that many of our philosophical perplexities result from the fact that concepts and practices have memories, which escape us. We have come to put this equipment to new uses while having forgotten about its past. Eclecticism without critical history still generates a perennial philosophy of sorts—not one that reinvigorates ancient questions and basic truths that long ago became clichés, but one that gnaws on seemingly eternal problems without understanding where they have come from. Just think of the conflicts between natural scientists propagating objectivity and humanities scholars defending the subjective, who both fail to notice that the two concepts emerged side by side and continue to be structurally interlocked: whatever images of the mind at work that electroencephalographers or PET scanners might produce, the subjective will never be eliminated or reduced to anything objective, for the concepts of subjectivity and objectivity are mutually constitutive. The link between mysticism and psychosis is more contingent but equally historical, rooted in nineteenth-century strife between supporters of the Christian churches and antiecclesiastic scientists and intellectuals, not least agnostic and atheist anthropologists. Their common battleground provided the conceptual matrix for present-day skirmishes over psychedelic drug mysticism, but it also enabled the transvaluation of experimental and other psychoses into spiritual experiences. The pragmatist philosophy of religion articulated by William James (1958/1902) reconciled the tension between these two conceptions by redirecting attention from the origins (natural or supernatural) to the effects of experiences.

From their critiques of religion as "a hallucination or an infantile disease," many nineteenth- and early to mid-twentieth-century anthropologists and psychologists inferred "that the time for religion is past" (Evans-Pritchard 1965: 100). In light of the spectacular empirical failure of this secularization thesis, some contemporary proponents of a so-called New Naturalism in the study of religion have come to concede that, "for better or worse, religious belief in the supernatural seems here to stay" (Atran 2002: 280).[5] Just like their pathologizing forebears, these cognitive anthropologists seek to explain those higher powers that have always captured the human imagination. But, given that this "infantile disease" could neither be cured nor outgrown in the past century, they have stopped conceptualizing religion as a pathology and instead present it as the (by-)product of evolutionarily adaptive processes. A hardwired animistic ontology based on a naturally selected agency-detection system has been postulated to account for the attribution of intentions and other mental faculties to inanimate natural and imagined supernatural entities. This tendency to overreact to figures in the dark and voices in the wind has helped human beings to survive, because mistaking a nonagent for an agent is usually less harmful than failing to detect an agent such as a lethal predator (Barrett 2000; Boyer 2001: 144–148; Atran 2002: 78–79). It follows that a predisposition to religious thought can no longer be dismissed as a remnant of primitive culture, but must be acknowledged as part of human nature.

The American literary critic Barbara Herrnstein Smith (2009) has accused the proponents of these views of slipping from methodological to metaphysical naturalism—a charge that could also be leveled against many of the nineteenth-century critics of religion. Advocated by cognitive anthropologists and psychologists, the New Naturalism is a naturalism in Philippe Descola's dualist sense. Although cognitive anthropology has naturalized representations as functions of brain processes, they continue to serve as explanations for why people see the world in different, often illusory ways (Holbraad, in Carrithers et al. 2010: 182). Just like cultural anthropology, cognitive anthropology is committed to an ontology that presupposes one nature and many different (cognitive and/or cultural) representations of it, one world and many minds endowed with distinct worldviews. In this context, ontology is at work on two levels: first, in the anthropological sense of multiple ontologies providing alternative conceptual frameworks to understand the question of what kind of entities exist, for example, through the lenses of a supposedly innate animism and a contingently derivative supernaturalism; second, in the philosophical or metaphysical sense of one arguably correct theory of the nature of being and its basic categories, which, in this case, is naturalism. The naturalist ontology of science is taken to trump the folk ontologies of animism and supernaturalism by explaining them away in naturalistic terms, allowing no reference to "mysterious incalculable forces," as Weber (1958/1919: 139) put it in his definition of the disenchantment of the world.

Such a commitment to naturalism is one trajectory in the project of anthropology that can be traced from the late nineteenth century to the present. It came to be rivaled by a professedly antiontological approach when, in the mid-twentieth century, social and cultural anthropology began to focus on meaning and the rationalities of different systems of thought and action. In this tradition, anthropology is defined as a discipline of second-order observation. Its task is to observe *how* others observe the world and to refrain from trying to simultaneously observe *what* they observe. One of the protagonists of this turn, the Catholic convert Edward Evans-Pritchard (1965: 17) proclaimed that, as an anthropologist, he was not concerned with the truth or falsity of religious belief: "As I understand the matter, there is no possibility of *knowing* whether the spiritual beings of primitive religions or any others have any existence or not. . . . The beliefs [for the anthropologist] are social facts, not theological facts, and his sole concern is with their relation to each other and to other social facts. His problems are scientific, not metaphysical or ontological." In Evans-Pritchard's eyes, questions of ontology were purely speculative and better left to philosophers—and one's personal faith.

In spite of the fact that, in sociocultural anthropology, ontology was subsequently verboten, the discipline has recently come to attend to metaphysical problems again. In fact, ontology has become one of its key sites of contention ever since the seemingly neutral ontological facade of multiculturalism has been identified as a cover-up of mononaturalism, which is believed to serve as an inexhaustible source of ethnocentric bias (Strathern 1980; Viveiros de Castro 1998; Holbraad 2008; Carrithers et al. 2010). One of the driving forces reintroducing ontology into anthropological discourse was the advent of science studies. Another Catholic, Bruno Latour (1993: 54), has provided an account of how the sociology of science tried to provide a social explanation of science the way Émile Durkheim had explained religion by reducing it to a function of "society." But science turned out too hard a nut to crack unless one also took into account the nonhuman actors populating laboratories and codetermining scientific research. Latour claimed that the failure of social explanations of science in retrospect also revealed the failure of social explanations of religion. In opposition to social explanations of anything, he proposed to redescribe the world in terms of actor networks that connected human and nonhuman entities through an incessant work of translation and mediation, in turn conducted by machines and researchers, scientific instruments and angels (129). The underlying actor-network theory postulates that nature, culture, society, and God have no agency of their own and therefore cannot serve as explanations of what is happening in the world—instead they are being constructed by mediators whose agency is not predetermined but emerges from their interactions with each other in a network.

Against this theoretical background, Latour not only provided a sketchy ethnographic description of the ontology of the moderns as discursively dividing human and nonhuman actors (mind and body, subject and object, culture and nature, etc.), but also proposed a non-modern ontology of his own that acknowledged the continuity and connectedness between human and nonhuman entities. He countered modern ontology with his own observation that, against their professions, the moderns were actually generating more and more hybrids, combining rather than separating human and nonhuman entities—and thus had never been truly modern. This shift from second- to first-order observation marks Latour's anthropology as an empirical philosophy that also deals with the kind of metaphysical and ontological questions excluded from Evans-Pritchard's conception of anthropology as a science of social facts.

At the beginning of my fieldwork, I often had to explain to scientists what I was doing in their laboratories. Taking my cues from Niklas Luhmann (1998) and Paul Rabinow (2008), but actually following a much broader anthropological tradition, I usually told them that I was practicing second-order observation: while they were looking at drugs, I was looking at them. Second-order observers pretend to be neutral with respect to the makeup of the world, but they implicitly presuppose a dualist ontology of one objective world and many subjective worldviews—and this is compatible with the prevailing ontology of neuropsychopharmacology. At some point, however, I found myself challenging the mononaturalism built into the drug researchers' experimental designs—and consequently the multiculturalism of my own anthropological framework. I realized that by arguing for the historical and cultural contingency of hallucinogen experiences, I was already calling into question the essentialist or pharmacologicalist conception of drugs that underlies randomized placebo-controlled trials. But the drug-induced experiences to which I had been privy myself when serving as a test subject were not just mental but also biological states that collapsed the dichotomies of mind/body, subject/object, and nature/culture.

In the history of science studies, one of the key objections to taking material agency seriously had been sociological concerns that this would require giving up analytic authority to the scientists themselves (Collins and Yearley 1992; Pickering 1993). I did not share this worry because I had experienced the material agency of psychedelic drugs firsthand and, having been trained as a physician before entering anthropology, I also felt well equipped to discuss pharmacological questions with my interlocutors. Considering that these drug researchers were significantly more knowledgeable about the details of their work than I was, it seemed perfectly appropriate to largely respect their analytic authority, not because they also had a degree in medicine, biology, or psychology, but because they managed to establish their authority through sound argument and earned trust in their exchanges with me and their colleagues. Yet I saw no need to refrain from practical judgments, squaring personal experience, scientific facts, social knowledge, and other epistemic resources in a form of contemporary *phronesis*. When I rightly or wrongly disagreed with my informants about the ontological framework of their work and the ensuing study designs, I used an invitation from the journal *Zeitschrift für Kulturwissenschaften* to engage in an interdisciplinary debate about my position with pharmacopsychologist Boris Quednow and a biological psychiatrist from Berlin (Bajbouj 2010; Langlitz 2010b; Quednow 2010b). Unlike sociology, anthropology is a field that, at least in its holist past, integrated social scientific and biological knowledge, and the ontological thrust reintroduced through science studies provides a venue for reanimating this intellectual breadth without necessarily lapsing back into the discipline's metaphysical naturalism, old or new. The end point of this development will hopefully be a multifaceted but monist epistemology and ontology for anthropology and other fields.

But neuropsychedelia is not only a zone of indistinction between nature and culture, the human and the animal; it also defines itself in relation to an even more contested third pole: the divine. The last chapters have shown how the transcendent dimension of the God-form has been brought inside the immanence of mystic materialism. The exclusion of supernatural entities—be they the Mind at Large, angels, or the loving DMT elves encountered by Rick Strassman's (2001: 173) test subjects—is significant because it shows that, contrary to the surface of Latour's argument, we have been modern indeed and continue to retain modern practices and attitudes, even though the latter no longer constitute a coherent modern chronotope (see Shapin 1992: 358–359).

Andrew Pickering (2009, 2010) is right: "ontology makes a difference," not just discursively, because the way people imagine the world affects how they act in it, and their actions recursively shape their ontological visions. Different ontological frameworks and their corresponding ethics and epistemologies do not produce a gap between what people say they are doing and what everybody has in fact always been doing, but they have significant effects. For example, by dividing up the world into competing shares of nature and culture, mononaturalism and multiculturalism prevent neuropsychopharmacology from inventing study designs that do justice to the fact that hallucinogen effects cannot be broken up into an essential pharmacology and supplemental placebo effects. The history of experimental psychosis research demonstrates that the epistemic virtue of truth-to-nature gave rise to research practices very different from those striving for objectivity, such as Kurt Beringer's phenomenological approach to mescaline inebriation or, in a modified form, the enactive model of psychosis. Consequently, methodical detachment is not just a self-misunderstanding of would-be moderns, who are actually becoming even more enmeshed in the network of hybrids whose existence they still steadfastly deny, but has led to the demise of a rich culture of pharmacological self-experimentation, which had catalyzed many important advances in the field.

I followed Latour's initiative to reconnect anthropology to ontology, which, as a branch of metaphysics, had been discarded by most late twentieth-century anthropologists and a great many philosophers. But I have not adopted his division between his own theory and what people in the field are saying and doing. I did my best to keep the epistemology of this book as flat as the ontology of model psychosis research or of the unlimited-finite: no boring into the depths of the human, no God's-eye view from nowhere and from everywhere. Not only did I place my cultural and biological self in the world that I have described, but I also tried to bring many of my scholarly points of reference onto that same plane. Weber's work on the Protestant ethic and the role of science in modern life was taken up by the psychedelic counterculture and continued to be so pertinent to my own analysis because his work had grown out of a common cultural matrix (remember his visits to Ascona). Historically, science studies emerged as a critical response to the same technocracy that the hippies rebelled against, not least by propagating the use of hallucinogenic drugs. The current dissociation of hallucinogen researchers from their field's countercultural past mirrors the ongoing reevaluation of critique in the anthropology of science, which has come to break with a subject position that deems itself external (if not antagonistic) to science and society. In this vein, I have shown how neuropsychopharmacological knowledge was constructed, while drawing from it in a realist manner to build my own account, interweaving historically much older forms of knowledge with the latest neuroscience. This chronotope of the contemporary, which has come to concern many of my peers, shares the epistemology of early modern eclecticism with the perennial philosophy that pervades neuropsychedelia to this day. Throughout this book, fieldwork and concept work, first-order and second-order observations, have taken place on the same rugged ontological, epistemological, and ethical ground.

BACK TO US: FROM FIELDWORK TO PHILOSOPHICAL ANTHROPOLOGY

This landscape is a physical, historical, and logical space that I shared with the people I met in the field and whose publications I read at my desk. In good anthropological tradition, this book has been about them. But it has also been about us—and here I deviate from the anthropological language game of "us" and "them." By "us" I do not mean us moderns, occidentals, or anthropologists as opposed to the people "we" study. Instead I mean to include myself as another inhabitant of the world I have been writing about. I do so, not to objectify the knowing subject in an act of staged self-reflection, but to draw the reader's attention to the difficult relationship between ethnography and anthropology, between fieldwork and philosophy.

Traditionally, cultural anthropology wrote about its subjects from a third-person perspective while trying to capture the "native's point of view"—an endeavor that is epistemologically as inherently flawed as the neuroscientists' attempt to objectively record the neural correlates of subjective experience. Since the late 1970s, the genre of ethnographic writing has come to comprise self-reflexive first-person narratives (e.g., my experience as a test subject) and dialogic second-person components (e.g., the public debate between myself and Boris Quednow), but overall it continues to aim at the description of others. Such empirical accounts save their readers from parochialism and enable them to ground their judgments in circumstantial knowledge of the world. In his book *Anthropological Futures* (2009: 217), Michael Fischer reminds us that Kant dedicated a large part of his pedagogic career to teaching a course that was eventually published as *Anthropology from a Pragmatic Point of View* (2006/1798). Kant's course addressed university students who did not yet have the experience required to make the knowledge of his philosophical seminars speak to their own lives. In a world too large and too complex for us to acquire firsthand familiarity with all its far-flung recesses, such an anthropological *Bildung* with cosmopolitan intent is a lifelong process and would appear to be even more pertinent today than in the eighteenth century. Fischer seems to suggest that at least one possible future of anthropology lies in reanimating its function of providing such an experiential foundation to philosophical thought—a vision I sympathize with. But he does not explain how to move from these empirical prolegomena to an anthropology in the philosophical sense.

This transition is problematic because it requires switching between third-person and first-person perspective. Philosophy might take a detour through the other, but ultimately it has to return to its point of departure, to the care of the self (Foucault 1985, 1986; Hadot 1995) or questions such as Kant's (1992/1800: 538) "What can I know?," "What ought I to do?," and "What may I hope?," which all refer to a fourth question: "What is man?" As an ethnography, this book primarily gives an account of what *they* could know, how *they* conducted their lives, and what *they* were hoping for. None of this provides a direct answer to my own concern about how to reconcile my materialist convictions with the drug-induced spiritual experience that I reported at the outset of this book. Above, I did not change from talking about "them" to talking about "us" to signal that I identify with "their" way of life. The key contention of the last chapter was that, even though the described varieties of mystic materialism point to a new form of perennialism that reconciles biology and spirituality, no stable cultural formation has yet emerged: for me, "going native" is not even an option. Moreover, even if there was a flourishing neuropsychedelic culture, its bare existence would not be a good reason to adopt such a lifestyle. The fact that Kant's fourth question "What is man?" reverts to a third-person perspective indicates that the preceding questions did not ask what "I," as psychological subject or member of a particular cultural community, but what I—or maybe better, what "we," as human beings—can know, should do, and may hope for (Tugendhat 2007: 36–39). In the eighteenth century, anthropology grew out of Enlightenment philosophy that reflected on humanity to break the bonds of tradition: it thereby privileged *anthropos* over *ethnos*. Thus, Kant's grammatical switch can serve to remind us of an ancient philosophical virtue, which the *Aufklärung* made its motto: *Sapere aude!* "Have courage to use your own understanding!" (Kant 1983/1784: 41). But, if the noble savages' ways of life are not presented as models to imitate (the way countercultural anthropologists like Carlos Castaneda [1968] or Michael Harner [1980] did regarding shamanic hallucinogen use), then how are we ever to return from ethnography to anthropology or from fieldwork in philosophy to philosophy proper?

One possible response to this question lies hidden in perennialism, even though it needs to be given a contemporary form. The perennial philosophy nourishes an awareness of the fact that many building blocks of a good life are already out there, to be found in different times and places, but need to be reassembled with new elements to meet the demands of the here and now. The eclectic epistemology underlying this approach requires continuously assessing and reassessing all components—an activity inconsistent with cultural relativism—while maintaining an orientation toward the universal. Not the universality of transhistorical truths and anthropological constants, but one akin to the universality of DNA or certain neurochemicals: molecules that we share not only with all humans but also with distant and ancient life-forms. In these species, they might fulfill very different functions—depending not just on the nature of the organism but also on its current situation (see Churchland 2011: 32, 50). And yet they are the same compounds. Translated into an anthropological perspective, such a view casts aside the notion of essential incommensurabilities, be they between historical epochs, national cultures, scientific paradigms, academic disciplines, or religious traditions. This cosmopolitan perennialism does not assume that there are no differences, but that we should think about them more in the way that neuropsychopharmacologists conceive of the differences between mice, rats, and humans than the way in which the philosophical anthropology of old thought about anthropological difference, in the singular and without a shared molecular matrix.

DILIGENCE AND SURRENDER

As an anthropologist of psychopharmacology, I have, in recent years, frequently been contacted by journalists. They hardly ever wanted to know about my work on the revival of hallucinogen research, but called to talk about cognitive enhancement. The question they worried about was whether we were on a slippery slope to a *Brave New World*. As the psychedelic counterculture of the 1960s waned, Huxley's utopia *Island* was eclipsed from the public debate over nonmedical drug use. A recent

German newspaper article on "brain doping" noted nostalgically, "In the past, drugs were meant to liberate from societal constraints, today neuroenhancers promote work frenzy" (Auf dem Hövel 2010). One of the key contentions of this debate is that pharmaceuticals like Ritalin, Adderall, and Provigil (although most widely used, caffeine is usually omitted) improve the cognitive performance of their consumers. This poses an ethical problem, the critics argue, because it gives the users of these drugs an undue advantage in a highly competitive knowledge society, imagined as a perpetual sporting contest. Of course, this question was also discussed among the drug researchers I worked with. Together, we looked at the scientific literature, sampled the substances, thought about the experiences of people we knew, and came to the conclusion that it was what Boris Quednow called a "phantom debate" (Quednow 2010a; see also Hasler 2010; Langlitz 2010a). Pointing to the meager and inconsistent results of pharmacological attempts to push cognitive performance into the supernormal range, he contended, "Given that usually our brains already perform to the best of their ability and that the homeostasis of this organ is very sensitive, general enhancement for everyone seems strictly limited" (Quednow 2010a: 154).

Since about 2010, such voices critical not of the ethicality but of the efficacy of so-called smart drugs have come to be heard more often in the media. At the beginning of the twentieth century, the German psychiatrist Max Seige described how the cultural histories of psychotropic drugs were moving in circles: first they were celebrated as wonder drugs, then demonized, and eventually they were put to limited use (Snelders et al. 2006). At this point, they usually drop out of public controversy as the next substance is made into a projection screen for societal hopes and fears. It seems as if cognitive enhancers are about to enter the pragmatic postdystopian phase of the Seige cycle. Just like psychedelics: in the 1950s, hallucinogens were the cutting edge of psychopharmacology; in the 1960s, a social problem; and, since the revival of academic research in the 1990s, a more sober attitude has achieved the upper hand. For both cognitive enhancers and hallucinogens, the expectation to maximize our existing cognitive or perceptual capacities has largely been disappointed.

But this is not to deny the significant biocultural potential of both classes of drugs. For better or worse, cognitive enhancers, which Quednow (2010a: 154) suggested be called "vigilance or motivation enhancers" instead, increase self-discipline and diligence in an academic world that has indeed come to resemble Weber's iron cage but that also leaves room for Vollenweider's gay science or the joy of writing a book like this one. One should not forget that the use of psychostimulants to facilitate intellectual work has had a hedonistic component ever since caffeine stimulated discussions among Enlightenment scholars in seventeenth-century coffeehouses and Ritalin helped hippie students earn their university degrees. Some of those who managed to reconcile their quest for mystical elation with the Protestant work ethic required by the scientific rat race have featured prominently in this book.

Psychedelics, by contrast, might not lend themselves to any kind of enhancement (*pace* McKenna 1993 and Doyle 2011). I mentioned that what I learned from the debate with Quednow and from Erich Studerus's research (Studerus et al. 2012) was that, even though hallucinogenic drug action was shaped by the circumstances of administration, neither the pharmacologistic focus on the substance nor the culturalist focus on the context could account for much: 80 percent of the variance in the anxiety scores reported by test subjects still remained unexplained. Similarly, Mark Geyer had to admit that his laboratory had been unable to stabilize the effects of psilocybin in a measure as simple as PPI in rats. These observations indicated a massive blind spot on both sides of the modern nature/culture divide, with one party striving for control of experience through neurochemical intervention and the other by carefully preparing set and setting. Not that the laboratory experiments in Zurich or San Diego had ever been out of control: we have seen how the researchers effectively managed their human and animal subjects' emotions. But, at least in the human case, this could not preclude a broad spectrum of different experiences ranging from the bliss of *unio mystica* to the paranoid mood of a "bad trip." Significantly, one of the most effective ways for test persons to recover their poise was to overcome the urge to control an uncontrollable biopsychological situation. As researcher Patrick Kossuth had learned the hard way: "You need to let go." Surrender: virtue of the mystics—pharmacologically wrung from a staunch opponent of drug mysticism. But maybe it is an attitude worth cultivating in response to the ontology of exceedingly complex systems that escape all calculation (Pickering 2010).

Psychopharmacologically, I take both Studerus's empirical data and this ethnographic anecdote to put a question mark over enhancement and therapeutic applications of psychedelics, since regular consumers, patients, pharmaceutical companies, and regulatory agencies would expect predictable effects. On the anthropological level, the tight limits of successfully controlling for set and setting appear to reflect the limits of the emancipatory potential of culturalism and historicism: what is contingent is not necessarily amenable to future improvement, especially if a phenomenon is complex (a feature that the objects of neuroscience and anthropology have in common). Not always, but sometimes, one needs to accept the finitude of human understanding and intervention and take things as they are: serenely, often sadly affirming this world when it cannot be changed instead of cultivating an otherworldly orientation. Activism is well and good, but occasionally the mystical ethos of quietism provides a more viable alternative (Magee 2010).

Historically, mysticism grew out of various religious traditions that were based on beliefs that appear untenable in light of how we conceive of the world today. Occasionally, my interlocutors raised the question of a higher, possibly supernatural reality, but usually without much conviction. The God-form had been deprived of its transcendent dimension. As a *cultura animi* in the age of cognitive neuroscience, neuropsychedelia is less driven by faith than by experience—by feelings not of oneness with something otherworldly but of connectedness with a material world infinitely larger than one's own finite existence. The New Naturalists notwithstanding, no religious belief in the supernatural persisted in this form of mystic materialism. Yet a mystical relationship to the world of things, lives, and minds was maintained. According to Huxley's perennial philosophy, this attitude was at the heart of each of the world's religious traditions. However, the remaking of perennialism into a perfectly this-worldly spiritual orientation did not show mystic materialism to be yet another religion but rather demonstrated that the historical link between religion and mysticism had always been contingent and had, in this case, been disarticulated.

This ethnographic observation concurs with Ernst Tugendhat's (2003) philosophical anthropology of mysticism. *Anthropos,* Tugendhat contends, is a restless animal searching for peace of mind. What prevents human beings from attaining it is their specific self-relation: they fundamentally care about themselves, worrying about how to conduct their lives in the face of untoward events always looming on the horizon. This is why there is philosophy in the first place. Mysticism aims at overcoming this inherently disquieting egocentrism. Paradoxically, it is a care of the self that seeks freedom from all care of the self. In Tugendhat's analysis, religion, ideal-typically understood as the belief in one or more supernatural powers, presents a different response to the same problem of contingency: how to deal with the fact that the world does not always conform to human will? In theist religion, human beings pray to the gods and bring sacrifices, hoping that these transcendent beings will intervene from outside into the course of the world on behalf of their worshippers. Ultimately, it is a magical and instrumental relationship to the world, aiming at the fulfillment of human wishes. In mysticism, on the other hand, it is these very wishes, their significance, that is being relativized: the goal is to achieve tranquility, not by getting what one was hoping for (even for others), but by taking oneself and one's hopes and fears less seriously (121–124).

It was such detachment from the self, not an expectant orientation toward the supernatural, which was expressed when Alexander Shulgin spoke about the cosmic laughter inside each of us, when Honza Samotar declared that "bad trips" were not a problem for him, when Marco Benz tried to inspire the viewers of his photographs to give precedence to the protection of the environment over their own wants and desires, or when Franz Vollenweider described how tapping the play of the cosmos enabled him to put into perspective what Weber (1958/1919: 156) had called "the demands of the day." It is characteristic of this discourse that it is less about expanding one's consciousness to grasp an Ultimate Reality than about experiencing the dissolution of the ego—and that these experiences are considered less important than the philosophical orientations that they engender. Of course, historically and ethnographically there have been and continue to be many entanglements between religion and mysticism. But Tugendhat's ideal-typical distinction enables us to understand how these elements could be disassembled and how one of them, mysticism, could be reassembled with other elements, some derived from the Protestant ethic, in the secular form of contemporary neuropsychedelia. It allows putting an end to the double-entry bookkeeping of materialist persuasions and experiences deemed religious.

Thus fieldwork in perennial philosophy moves beyond ethnography and begins to provide philosophical tools to remediate some of the spiritual ills of late modern life. In what ways these discourses will be supplemented by pharmacological equipment depends on whether the scientists and activists fueling the psychedelic revival will be able to maintain its momentum. So far no drugs have been registered for medical purposes. In the United States, the Religious Freedom Restoration Act allows members of the Native American Church and the syncretist churches of União do Vegetal and Santo Daime the ceremonial use of peyote and ayahuasca, but neither America nor Switzerland or other European countries provide legal frameworks for applications that are neither medical nor religious but spiritual in a secular sense. The provision of LSD in state-controlled meditation centers, as envisioned by Albert Hofmann, is not on the horizon. And another backlash is always possible. But we are not living in a *Brave New World* and hope cannot be found on a remote *Island,* either. Neuropsychedelia has moved beyond these Huxleyan frameworks, in both their countercultural and humanistic renderings. And its story is far from over.

Notes

1. A diagnosis seconded from the left by Ian Hacking (2009).

2. All terms used to designate "hallucinogenic drugs," or however else one prefers to refer to this class of substances, are charged with conflicting worldviews. I follow anthropological tradition, usually employing the terms most frequently used by the people I worked with, *hallucinogens* and *psychedelics,* without necessarily subscribing to the beliefs and attitudes accompanying the use of these terms. Although the categorization of these compounds as hallucinogens has become vastly unpopular within the contemporary psychedelic drug scene, the terms *hallucinogens* and *psychedelics* continue to be the ones used in the academic literature. In December 2011, both terms scored above 20,000 hits in the PubMed database, whereas alternative designations such as *entheogens* or *ecodelics* were found less than 10 times.

3. For a genealogy of one such technocratic society, namely, in France, see Rabinow (1989).

4. The distinction between technical optimization (as a maximization of existing capacities for the purpose of personal or instrumental gains) and flourishing (as a pursuit of the good life that does not presuppose that human capacities are already known in advance) has been borrowed from Paul Rabinow (2009).

5. Another example of early anthropological self-experimentation with hallucinogens was an experimental reenactment of a Native American religious ceremony with drums, rattles, and peyote songs. A group of anthropologists, sociologists, and psychologists at the University of Pennsylvania (including the young Howard Becker) ingested peyote buttons under these conditions to better understand, among other things, how peyotists came to claim that it was not them but God who was shaking the rattle (Fernberger 1932).

6. For a discussion of the problem of drug safety regarding not well-understood illicit, especially psychedelic, substances marketed on the Internet, see Langlitz (2009).

7. As Hamilton Morris has pointed out to me, the situation might actually be more complicated than these quotes from the DEA and the EU suggest. While the use of classical hallucinogens has indeed gone down (especially after the American authorities busted William Leonard Pickard's LSD laboratory in 2000—see chapter 2), there are some indications that, subsequently, the sales of so-called research chemicals went up. Many of these synthetic psychedelics are not yet controlled and can be purchased through the Internet (see Langlitz 2009). As these compounds are usually distributed by weight of pure powder rather than in prepackaged doses, they initially posed new challenges to counternarcotics bookkeeping, even when they did not slip under the regulatory radar. "When substances were seized," Morris explained in an e-mail, "officials were faced with new questions like, 'How many doses are there in a gram of 2C-T-21?'" So far, however, the surge of research chemicals in a small and relatively scientifically literate experimental drug scene has not provoked much public concern.

8. This understanding of naturalism is more restrictive than and possibly diverges from its more common definition as a metaphysics that assumes that the fundamental makeup of reality is exhausted by nature and contains nothing supernatural. I decided to adopt Descola's peculiar usage of the term because the worldviews of many (often self-identified) naturalists featured in this book—from Weber's cosmology of disenchantment to contemporary cultural and cognitive anthropology of religion and the animal researchers' rejection of anthropomorphism—presuppose a discontinuously structured interior realm (marked by unbridgeable differences between moral values, mental and cultural representations, or species-relative cognition) that is not made of supernatural stuff but organized dissimilarly from the exterior dimension of reality where differences are thought to be gradual. By contrast, I will reserve the term *materialism* for monist ontologies that also assume that there can be no entities violating the laws of nature but that do not share this twofold structure.

9. I highlight accounts that make psychedelics and antidepressants appear antagonistic, as I take them to reflect the most common conceptions of these substances. However, this should not obliterate the fact that they have also been likened. In her *Prozac Diary,* Lauren Slater (1999: 93) describes the spiritual transformation she underwent under the influence of the antidepressant: "What does it mean . . . that my burgeoning contemplative bent does not come directly from God but from Prozac? Might this mean that Prozac is equal to God? This is an awful, awful thought. So turn it around. Primitive cultures often use drugs as a means of accessing their gods. That's better. Maybe Prozac is to the modern world what peyote is to the Indians."

CHAPTER 1 PSYCHEDELIC REVIVAL

1. On the importance of the "principle of measured sloppiness" for experimental systems, see Rheinberger (1997: 78). Following Rheinberger's histori-

cal epistemology, Jeannie Moser (2007) analyzed the figuration of LSD as an "epistemic thing" in Hofmann's research.

2. A Google Scholar search for this period, conducted on 13 March 2011, found 768 publications with *LSD* in the title. As this search engine does not index all mid-twentieth-century journals that published studies on hallucinogenic drugs, the actual number is presumably higher. Dyck (2008: 15) reports more than 1,000 articles. See also Passie (1997).

3. Smaller religious associations using psychedelic drugs (for example, the Temple of the True Inner Light or the Peyote Way Church of God) have managed to subsist without legal sanction or prosecution since the 1970s, even though they never received permission. I thank Hamilton Morris for this piece of information.

4. I have excluded discussion of the research chemicals scene and its use of the website www.erowid.org presented in my article "Pharmacovigilance and Post–Black Market Surveillance" (2009) from this book, as *Neuropsychedelia* focuses on the revival of *academic* hallucinogen research. Another step toward a scholarly treatment of psychedelic amateur science can be found in Doyle (2011). But a detailed historical and ethnographic account has yet to be written.

5. Of course, not everybody in the psychedelic community agreed with the mainstreaming strategy adopted by MAPS and the Heffter Research Institute. At the LSD Symposium in 2006, for example, there were many echoes of the 1960s counterculture. In one of the conference halls, Bruce Eisner gave a seminar on Aldous Huxley's *Island*. With a few friends, Eisner had worked to keep the psychedelic movement alive during three decades of cultural repression. In 1990, they established the nonprofit educational organization Island Foundation. Inspired by Huxley's utopian novel, they were hoping to find some remote place in the world to build a sanctuary where an experimental community could use hallucinogens in a way similar to the fictional use of the psychedelic moksha on the equally fictional island of Pala (Eisner 2006). But neither this nor any other neocountercultural endeavor had any significant impact on the revival of academic hallucinogen research.

6. Hagner (2009) coined the term *neuroscientific Biedermeier* to describe the transformation of the concept of the unconscious in brain research. Whereas, in the nineteenth century, the unconscious emerged as a motor of artistic production always working on the brink of madness, contemporary neuroscience has turned unconscious neural processes into mechanisms that ease the burden of consciousness. The unconscious used to be seen as conflictive and potentially subversive to the social order but is now regarded as harmless and even psychophysiologically functional.

7. Fetzer Institute, www.fetzer.org (retrieved 15 June 2012).

CHAPTER 2 SWISS PSILOCYBIN AND US DOLLARS

1. See McCann and Ricaurte (2000) and Vollenweider et al. (2001).

2. For a third case, a grassroots security apparatus monitoring the designer drug market, see Langlitz (2009).

3. Similarly, Steven Shapin (1994: 409–417) points to the officially marginalized but practically still highly significant role of trust in individual actors and institutions in the other major area of rationalization: science.

4. Clinically, however, there was a growing interest in "dirty drugs," since highly selective antidepressants like the selective serotonin reuptake inhibitors (SSRIs) had been found less effective than drugs affecting several neurotransmitter systems at a time (Healy 2002: 220).

5. Grim (2005) has called the numbers presented by the authorities into question, arguing that the amount of LSD seized in this raid was significantly less than what the Drug Enforcement Administration claimed. For an insider's account of life in the missile silo, Pickard's arrest, and the disconcerting events in its wake, see Hamilton Morris's documentary, *Getting High on Krystle,* available from www.vice.com/hamiltons-pharmacopeia/getting-high-on-krystle (retrieved 26 February 2012).

6. It was the first clinical trial, if one does not count the hardly controlled and largely undocumented LSD experiments of the SAPT in the late 1980s and early 1990s.

CHAPTER 3 THE VARIETIES OF PSYCHEDELIC LAB EXPERIENCE

1. Whether it is possible to extract such singular events from the very significant noise of electroencephalographic recordings is questionable. Usually, it takes a large quantity of neural responses to a repeated stimulus for a particular pattern to become visible. By contrast, Cahn's reasoning was that striking neuropsychological events (such as a *unio mystica*) must have been building up for a while and that this extended process would leave traces in the readout.

2. Later on, revised versions of the APZ questionnaire were introduced as OAV (Bodmer et al. 1994) and 5D-ASC (Dittrich et al. 2010). For a critical discussion of these self-rating scales, especially of the three-dimensional structure of the APZ and OAV scales, see Studerus et al. (2010).

3. For the analog of Heisenberg's uncertainty principle in brain research, see also Steven Rose (1973: 23–24).

4. To protect the privacy of these two subjects, their names have been changed.

5. To protect the privacy of this test subject, his name has been changed.

6. High scores on the APZ subscale dread of ego dissolution showed a positive correlation with metabolic hyperactivation of the anterior cingulate cortex, while oceanic boundlessness was negatively correlated with increases of the frontomedial-temporolateral ratio or the frontolateral-temporolateral ratio in the left hemisphere (Vollenweider et al. 1997b: 365–366).

7. For a more positive assessment of Leary's naturalistic studies at Harvard, see Das and Metzner (2010: 35–36)

8. James's account also referred back to earlier work by Bergson (Myers 1986: 354).

9. Many critical observers have interpreted functional neuroimaging as a new form of phrenology—a contemporary remake of Franz Joseph Gall's much derided nineteenth-century attempt of mapping mental properties, talents, and

character traits onto the skull and into the brain (Uttal 2001; Dumit 2004; Hagner 2006). Vollenweider's approach did not fit into this scheme in that he investigated mental states, not traits. But, more importantly, the mathematical correlation between metabolic changes in different anatomical locations and quantified introspective accounts served less to equate one brain region with one psychological function than to open up a perspective on the brain at a systems level. This allowed Vollenweider to confirm his hypothesis that psilocybin and ketamine, even though affecting distinct neurochemical pathways, would both activate the frontal cortex and a number of overlapping regions. "These findings demonstrated," Vollenweider (1998: 25) concluded, "that not a single brain region, but distributed neuronal networks, are involved in psychedelic and psychotic symptom formation." Unlike classical neuropsychology, which inferred the cerebral location of a mental function from correlating circumscribed brain lesions to resulting functional deficits, the systemic approach enabled by neurocybernetics and functional imaging (which allows looking at the brain as a whole) has led to the development of theories that explain the interplay of different parts of the brain that execute a certain function (Beaulieu 2002: 73).

10. Roland Fischer reported that, when subjects looked at optically distorted images, hallucinogens increased visual acuity by disturbing a "corrective" mechanism that enabled human beings to perceive their surroundings undistorted even if they really were distorted (Fischer et al. 1970; Hill and Fischer 1971). Assuming that such acuity must have been of greater adaptive value than the optimization of visual information that *Homo sapiens* had apparently been selected for, Terrence McKenna (1993) inferred that early hunter-gatherers were able to find more food once they began using *Psilocybe* mushrooms as "chemical binoculars." More recently, this "stoned ape theory" has informed Richard Doyle's *Darwin's Pharmacy* (2011). Both Richard Hill's and Fischer's much more modest scientific claim and McKenna's wildly speculative just-so natural history present subjective experience and the inebriated organism's performance as in accordance with each other—a conception that research conducted at the Vollenweider lab could not corroborate.

CHAPTER 4 ENACTING EXPERIMENTAL PSYCHOSES

1. To protect the privacy of this informant, his name has been changed.

2. For another account of how a theater director turned to neuroscience for its theatrical potential, see Tobias Rees's (2006) work on the artistic collaboration between the French brain researcher Alain Prochiantz and the playwright Jean François Peyret.

3. Suspension points in original.

4. Delirium was regarded as the exemplary mental disorder in the first half of the nineteenth century (Jay 1999: 19; Healy 2002: 180). The concept of psychosis was introduced by Karl Friedrich Canstatt and Ernst von Feuchtersleben in the 1840s (Janzarik 2003)—at about the time of Moreau's experiments, but he did not yet make use of it.

5. Osmond was referring to Osmond and Smythies (1952). A systematic argument disputing the comparability of hallucinogen-induced and endogenous psychotic states was subsequently articulated by Leo Hollister (1962).

6. Jaspers, however, believed that nothing valuable could be learned from administering "poisons" to healthy test subjects (Healy 2002: 213).

7. Andreas-Holger Maehle (1995: 294) describes a very similar approach for self-experiments with opium in the eighteenth century, in which a form of scientific objectivity was achieved by way of collectivization of subjective experiences: "Overall, the example of opium research shows how different, at first contradictory, observations in self-experiments contribute to the development of a kind of collective subjective experience eventually condensed to a profile of action of the drug. Thereby, subjectivity is elevated to a new form of scientific objectivity." However, considering that usage of the terms *objective* and *subjective* changed significantly in the course of the eighteenth century, Maehle's choice of words might well be anachronistic (see Daston and Galison 2007: 27–35).

8. In this quote, Gouzoulis's use of the term *psychedelic* appears to be closer to the standard usage of *psycholytic,* emphasizing the revelation of otherwise hidden aspects of an individual's psychic life rather than the experience of unity with a cosmic mind.

9. A related account of the "multidimensionality of phenomena" can be found in Lloyd (2007).

CHAPTER 5 BETWEEN ANIMALITY AND DIVINITY

1. Earlier attempts at constructing a hallucinogen-based animal model of schizophrenia in the 1950s have been described by Thuillier (1999) and Balz (2010: 108).

2. As several informants who contributed to this chapter expressed their concern about acts of revenge by animal rights activists, many figures in this chapter will remain nameless.

3. For another case of stewardship in science, the management of a high-throughput lab by a laboratory technician, see Rabinow and Dan-Cohen (2005: 62–96).

4. To protect the privacy of this informant, his name has been changed.

5. For a critique of Foucault's notion of the "Cartesian moment," see Hadot (2002: 263–264).

6. A closely related if not identical approach to the problem of other minds, sidestepping both introspectionism and behaviorism, has also been articulated by the neuroscientist Joseph LeDoux (2002: 200–234).

CHAPTER 6 MYSTIC MATERIALISM

1. For a powerful neurophilosophical challenge to rejections of the "naturalistic fallacy," see Churchland (2011) and my own review of this book (Langlitz 2012a).

2. Benz's discourse combines a materialist variety of psychedelic mysticism with the ecologically oriented mysticism that Bron Taylor (2010) describes in *Dark Green Religion.* These are two contemporary forms of spirituality that share an adoration of life itself.

3. Usually, it is the anthropologist who "goes native." Hasler's is the rare case where the native ventures into the anthropologist's world.

4. Many images on display at the exhibition are available online at http://neuroculturelab.photoshelter.com/gallery/Vague-Ideas-about-Life/G00007mN QzhkfiWY (retrieved 2 June 2010).

5. Not surprisingly, one of the most outspoken opponents of drug mysticism in the Zurich lab, Boris Quednow, conformed most significantly with the conception of science as a vocation. The other vehement antimystic, Patrick Kossuth, diverged from this Weberian ideal type in aspiring to and eventually taking up a job in the pharmaceutical industry because he was unwilling to put up with the financial vagaries and low income marking academic careers. For a historical account of the ethos of industrial science as an occupation rather than a vocation, see Shapin (2008b).

6. I refer to Emily Martin's presentation "Identity, Identification, and the Brain," given at the "Neurocultures" workshop at the Max Planck Institute for the History of Science, Berlin, in 2009. A video recording of her presentation is available from http://mediathek.mpiwg-berlin.mpg.de/mediathekPublic/versionEins/Conferences/Neurocultures/Emily-Martin.html (retrieved 28 July 2011). Martin (2010) covers much of the same ground without using the apt expression "monadic sociality."

CONCLUSION: FIELDWORK IN PERENNIAL PHILOSOPHY

1. Huxley slightly but significantly misquoted Radin (1957/1927: 373), who did not at all question the historicity of concepts and physiological reactions. What Radin challenged throughout his book was the assumption that everything had an *evolutionary* history. The original quote reads: "No progress will ever be achieved, however, until scholars rid themselves, once and for all, of the curious notion that everything possesses an evolutionary history; until they realize that certain ideas and certain concepts are as ultimate for man as a social being as specific physiological reactions are for him as a biological entity. Both doubtless have a history; but in the one case its roots lie in presocial man and in the other in the lower organisms."

2. Of course, Asad (1986: 155–156) is well aware of the fact that cultural translation is not always required. In response to Ernest Gellner's (1970) critique of this anthropological practice as an excessively charitable interpretive approach, which makes even the most incoherent and absurd native assertions appear reasonable, Asad does not aim at a cultural translation of Gellner's claims by showing how they make sense in a particular social context, but rather contests them outright as incoherent. The precondition for this aggressive stance is that Gellner and Asad speak the same language and are part of the same epistemic culture

3. For a contemporary book in this tradition, see Critchley (2008).

4. Suspension points in original.

5. This point had already been made in the 1970s by sociobiologist Edward O. Wilson (1978).

Bibliography

Aarburg, Hans-Peter von, and Michael Stauffacher. 2004. From law enforcement to care: Changed benefits and harm of heroin use in Switzerland through a shift in drug policy. In *European Studies on Drugs and Drug Policy: Selected Readings from the 14th International Conference of the European Society for Social Drug Research (ESSD)*, edited by Tom Decorte and Dirk Korf, 21–47. Brussels: VUB University Press.

Abi-Rached, Joëlle, and Nikolas Rose. 2010. The Birth of the Neuromolecular Gaze. *History of the Human Sciences* 23 (1):11–36.

Adam, Armin. 2006. *Politische Theologie: Eine kleine Geschichte*. Zürich: Pano Verlag.

Agamben, Giorgio. 1998. *Homo sacer: Sovereign Power and Bare Life*. Stanford (CA): Stanford University Press.

———. 2004. *The Open: Man and Animal* Stanford (CA): Stanford University Press.

———. 2009. *What Is an Apparatus?* Stanford (CA): Stanford University Press.

Agar, Jon. 2008. What happened in the sixties? *British Journal for the History of Science* 41 (4):567–600.

Aghajanian, George K., and Daniel X. Freedman. 1968. Biochemical and morphological aspects of LSD pharmacology. In *Psychopharmacology: A Review of Progress, 1957–1967*, edited by Daniel Efron, 1185–1193. Washington (DC): US Government Printing Office.

Altman, Lawrence. 1987. *Who Goes First? The Story of Self-Experimentation in Medicine*. New York: Random House.

Amendt, Günter. 2008. *Die Legende vom LSD*. Frankfurt/M.: Zweitausendeins.

Angst, Jules. 1967. Gefahren des LSD. *Schweizer medizinische Wochenschrift* 97 (42):1404.

————. 1970. Halluzinogen-Abusus. *Schweizer medizinische Wochenschrift* 100 (16):710–715.

Ankeny, Rachel. 2000. Fashioning descriptive models in biology: Of worms and wiring diagrams. *Philosophy of Science* 67:260–272.

————. 2007. Wormy logic: Model organisms as case-based reasoning. In *Science without Laws. Model Systems, Cases, Exemplary Narratives*, edited by Angela N.H. Creager, Elizabeth Lunbeck, and M. Norton Wise, 46–58. Durham (NC): Duke University Press.

Asad, Talal. 1986. The concept of cultural translation in British social anthropology. In *Writing Culture: The Poetics and Politics of Ethnography*, edited by James Clifford and George E. Marcus, 141–164. Berkeley: University of California Press.

————. 1993. *Genealogies of Religion: Discipline and Reasons of Power in Christianity and Islam*. Baltimore: Johns Hopkins University Press.

Atran, Scott. 2002. *In Gods We Trust: The Evolutionary Landscape of Religion*. New York: Oxford University Press.

Auf dem Hövel, Jörg. 2010. Ich, nur besser. *Der Freitag*, 8 July, 6.

Austin, John. 1970. A plea for excuses. In *Philosophical Papers*, edited by J.O. Urmson and G.J. Warnock, 175–204. Oxford: Oxford University Press.

Baars, Bernard. 2003. The double life of B.F. Skinner: Inner conflict, dissociation and the scientific taboo against consciousness. *Journal of Consciousness Studies* 10 (1):5–25.

Bajbouj, Malek. 2010. Kulturlose affektive Neurowissenschaften oder kulturadjustierte Neuropsychopharmakologie? *Zeitschrift für Kulturwissenschaften* (2):71–73.

Bakshi, Vaishali, Neal Swerdlow, and Mark Geyer. 1994. Clozapine antagonizes phencyclidine-induced deficits in sensorimotor gating of the startle response. *Journal of Pharmacology and Experimental Therapeutics* 271 (2):787–794.

Balz, Viola. 2010. *Zwischen Wirkung und Erfahrung—eine Geschichte der Psychopharmaka: Neuroleptika in der Bundesrepublik Deutschland, 1950–1980*. Bielefeld (Germany): Transcript.

Barber, Bernard. 1941. A socio-cultural interpretation of the peyote cult. *American Anthropologist* 43 (4):673–675.

Barondes, Samuel. 2003. Better than Prozac: Creating the next generation of psychiatric drugs. New York: Oxford University Press.

Barrett, Justin L. 2000. Exploring the natural foundations of religion. *Trends in Cognitive Science* 4 (1):29–34.

Baumeister, Alan A., and Jennifer L. Francis. 2002. Historical development of the dopamine hypothesis of schizophrenia. *Journal of the History of the Neurosciences* 11 (3):265–277.

Baumeister, Alan A., and Mike F. Hawkins. 2004. The serotonin hypothesis of schizophrenia: A historical case study of the heuristic value of theory in clinical neuroscience. *Journal of the History of the Neurosciences* 13 (3):277–291.

Beaulieu, Anne. 2002. Images are not the (only) truth: Brain mapping, visual knowledge, and iconoclasm. *Science, Technology, and Human Values* 27 (1):53–86.

Beauregard, Mario, and Vincent Paquette. 2006. Neural correlates of a mystical experience in Carmelite nuns. *Neuroscience Letters* 405:186–190.

Becker, Howard. 1963. *Outsiders: Studies in the Sociology of Deviance*. London: Free Press of Glencoe.

Bellah, Robert. 1999. Max Weber and world-denying love: A look at the historical sociology of religion. *Journal of the American Academy of Religion* 67 (2):277–304.

Ben-Ari, Eyal. 1987. On acknowledgments in ethnographies. *Journal of Anthropological Research* 43 (1):63–84.

Berge, Jos Ten. 1999. Breakdown or breakthrough? A history of European research into drugs and creativity. *Journal of Creative Behavior* 33 (4):257–276.

Bergson, Henri. 1932. *The Two Sources of Morality and Religion*. London: Macmillan.

Beringer, Kurt. 1927. *Der Meskalinrausch: Seine Geschichte und Erscheinungsweise*. Berlin: Julius Springer.

Betancourt, Michael. 2007. A taxonomy of abstract form using studies of synesthesia and hallucination. *Leonardo* 40 (1):59–65.

Birkenhauer, Theresia. 2004. Der Text ist der Coyote . . . Und man weiß nicht, wie er sich verhält. In *Der Text ist der Coyote: Heiner Müller; Bestandsaufnahme,* edited by Christian Schulte and Brigitte Maria Mayer, 11–34. Frankfurt/M.: Suhrkamp.

Bittner, Stefan. 2009. Die romantische Wende nach 1968: Das Beispiel der Schweizer Aussteiger-Gruppierung Bärglütli. In *1968–1978: Ein bewegtes Jahrzehnt in der Schweiz,* edited by Janick Marina Schaufelbuehl, 237–247. Zürich: Chronos.

Bleuler, Eugen. 1950/1911. *Dementia Praecox; or, The Group of Schizophrenias*. New York: International Universities Press.

Blum, Richard. 1964. Conclusions and commentary. In *Utopiates: The Use and Users of LSD-25,* edited by Richard Blum, 265–293. New York: Atherton.

———. 1969. A cross-cultural study. In *Society and Drugs. Drugs I: Social and Cultural Observations,* edited by Richard Blum, 135186. San Francisco: Jossey-Bass.

Blumenberg, Hans. 1983. *The Legitimacy of the Modern Age*. Translated by Robert Wallace. Cambridge (MA): MIT Press.

Boas, Franz, Alfred L. Kroeber, Aleš Hrdlička, J.P. Harrington, M.R. Harrington, Weston LaBarre, Vicenzo Petrullo, Richard Evans Schultes, Elna Smith, and Chief Fred Lookout (Osage). 1937. *Documents on Peyote: Statements by F. Boas, A.L. Kroeber, A. Hrdlicka, J.P. and M.R. Harrington, W. La Barre, V. Petrullo, R.E. Schultes, Elna Smith, and Chief Fred Lookout (Osage) against U.S. Senate Bill 1399 (Feb. 8), Seventy-Fifth Congress, First Session*. Mimeographed, 137817. Washington (DC): Government Printing Office.

Bodmer, Ines, Adolf Dittrich, and Daniel Lamparter. 1994. Außergewöhnliche Bewusstseinszustände—ihre gemeinsame Struktur und Messung. In *Welten des Bewusstseins*. Vol. 3, *Experimentelle Psychologie, Neurobiologie und Chemie,* edited by Albert Hofmann and Hanscarl Leuner, 45–58. Berlin: VWB—Verlag für Wissenschaft und Bildung.

Boguski, Mark. 2002. Comparative genomics: The mouse that roared. *Nature* 420:515–516.

Boller, Boris. 2005. *Drogen und Öffentlichkeit in der Schweiz: Eine sozialanthropologische Analyse der drogenpolitischen Kommunikation der 1990er Jahre.* Zürich: LIT Verlag.

Bourdieu, Pierre. 1990. Fieldwork in philosophy. In *In Other Words: Essays Towards a Reflexive Sociology,* 3–33. Stanford (CA): Stanford University Press.

Bourguignon, Erika. 1973. *Religion, Altered States of Consciousness, and Social Change.* Columbus: Ohio University Press.

Boyer, Pascal. 2001. *Religion Explained: The Evolutionary Origins of Religious Thought.* New York: Basic Books.

Braff, David, and Mark Geyer. 1982. Habituation of the blink reflex in normals and schizophrenic patients. *Psychophysiology* 19 (1):1–6.

Braff, David, Claudia Stone, Enoch Callaway, Mark Geyer, Ira Glick, and Likh Bali. 1978. Prestimulus effects of human startle reflex in normals and schizophrenics. *Psychophysiology* 15 (4):339–343.

Braitman, Laurel. Forthcoming. *Animal Madness.* New York: Simon and Schuster.

Breidbach, Olaf. 1997. *Die Materialisierung des Ichs: Zur Geschichte der Hirnforschung im 19. und 20. Jahrhundert.* Frankfurt/M.: Suhrkamp.

Bressloff, Paul, Jack Cowan, Martin Golubitsky, Peter Thomas, and Matthew Wiener. 2001. Geometric visual hallucinations, Euclidean symmetry and the functional architecture of the striate cortex. *Philosophical Transactions of the Royal Society* 356 (1407):299–339.

Brickman, Ronald, Sheila Jasanoff, and Thomas Ilgen. 1985. *Controlling Chemicals: The Politics of Regulation in Europe and the United States.* Ithaca (NY): Cornell University Press.

Briggle, Adam. 2009. The Kass Council and the politicization of ethics advice. *Social Studies of Science* 39 (2):309–326.

Broad, Charlie Dunbar. 1949. The relevance of psychical research to philosophy. *Philosophy* 24 (91):291–309.

Bromley, Elizabeth. 2008. Pharmaceutical dreams: The search for cognition-enhancing medications for schizophrenia. PhD dissertation, Anthropology, University of California, Los Angeles.

Bronkhorst, Johannes. 2001. The perennial philosophy and the law of karma. In *Aldous Huxley between East and West,* edited by C.C. Barfoot, 175–189. Amsterdam: Rodopi.

Bühler, Benjamin, and Stefan Rieger. 2006. *Vom Übertier: Ein Bestiarium des Wissens.* Frankfurt/M.: Suhrkamp.

Burt, Jonathan. 2006. *Rat.* London: Reaktion Books.

Bush, George H.W. 1990. Presidential proclamation 6158.

Büttner, Jean-Martin. 2006. Halluzinogene als Medikament und Sakrament. *Tages-Anzeiger,* 18 January.

Cahn, Rael. 2005. Neurophysiological correlates to the experience of self and binocular rivalry stimulus processing as modulated by meditation and psilocybin administration. Unpublished study proposal.

———. 2006. Neurophysiological correlates to sensory and cognitive processing in altered states of consciousness. PhD dissertation, Neuroscience, University of California, San Diego.

Caldwell, Anne. 1970. *Origins of Psychopharmacology: From CPZ to LSD.* Springfield (IL): Charles C. Thomas Publisher.

Candea, Matei. 2010. "I fell in love with Carlos the meerkat": Engagement and detachment in human–animal relations. *American Ethnologist* 37 (2):241–258.

———. 2011. Endo/exo. *Common Knowledge* 17 (1):146–150.

Canguilhem, Georges. 1989. *The Normal and the Pathological.* New York: Zone Books.

———. 2008/1965. *Knowledge of Life.* New York: Fordham University Press.

Carrithers, Michael, Matei Candea, Karen Sykes, Martin Holbraad, and Soumhya Venkatesan. 2010. Ontology is just another word for culture: Motion tabled at the 2008 meeting of the Group for Debates in Anthropological Theory, University of Manchester. *Critique of Anthropology* 30:152–200.

Carter, Olivia, D. Burr, John Pettigrew, Guy Wallis, Felix Hasler, and Franz Vollenweider. 2005. Using psilocybin to investigate the relationship between attention, working memory, and the serotonin 1A and 2A receptors. *Journal of Cognitive Neuroscience* 17:1497–1508.

Castaneda, Carlos. 1968. *The Teachings of Don Juan: A Yaqui Way of Knowledge.* Berkeley: University of California Press.

Churchland, Patricia S. 1986. *Neurophilosophy: Toward a Unified Science of the Mind-Brain.* Cambridge (MA): MIT Press.

———. 2011. *Braintrust: What Neuroscience Tells Us about Morality.* Princeton (NJ): Princeton University Press.

CIA Historical Review Program. 1977. "Truth" drugs in interrogation. In *Project MKULTRA, the CIA's Program of Research in Behavioral Modification: Joint Hearing before the Select Committee on Intelligence and the Subcommittee on Health and Scientific Research of the Committee on Human Resources United States Senate,* 25–33. Washington (DC): US Government Printing Office.

Clark, Andy, and David Chalmers. 1998. The extended mind. *Analysis* 58 (1):7–19.

Clarke, Adele. 2012. Turning points and trajectories in a surprising and late blooming career. *Studies in Symbolic Interaction* 38:75–102.

Clifford, James. 2005. Rearticulating anthropology. In *Unwrapping the Sacred Bundle: Reflections on the Disciplining of Anthropology,* edited by Daniel Segal and Sylvia Yanagisako, 25–48. Durham (NC): Duke University Press.

Clifford, James, and George E. Marcus, eds. 1986. *Writing Culture: The Poetics and Politics of Ethnography.* Berkeley: University of California Press.

Cohen, Sidney. 1972. *The Beyond Within: The LSD Story.* New York: Atheneum.

Cohen, Sidney, and Keith S. Ditman. 1962. Complications associated with lysergic acid diethylamide (LSD25). *Journal of the American Medical Association* 181:161–162.

Cohn, Simon. 2008. Making objective facts from intimate relations: The case of neuroscience and its entanglements with volunteers. *History of the Human Sciences* 21 (4):86–103.

Collins, Harry M., and Steven Yearley. 1992. Epistemological chicken. In *Science as Practice and Culture*, edited by Andrew Pickering, 301–326. Chicago: University of Chicago Press.

Colpaert, Francis C. 2003. Discovering risperidone: The LSD model of psychopathology. *Nature Reviews* 2:315–320.

Cowell, Alan. 2006. Oxford seeks more curbs on protests to aid animals. *New York Times,* 19 May. Available from www.nytimes.com/2006/05/19/world/europe/19animal.html (retrieved 15 June 2012).

Crick, Francis. 1990. *What Mad Pursuit: A Personal View of Scientific Discovery.* New York: Basic Books.

Crick, Francis, and Christof Koch. 1990. Towards a neurobiological theory of consciousness. *Seminars in the Neurosciences* 2:263–275.

Critchley, Simon. 2002. *On Humour.* New York: Routledge.

———. 2008. *The Book of Dead Philosophers.* New York: Vintage Books.

d'Aquili, Eugene G., and Andrew B. Newberg. 2002. The neuropsychology of aesthetic, spiritual, and mystical states. In *NeuroTheology: Brain, Science, Spirituality, Religious Experience,* edited by Rhawn Joseph, 243–250. San Jose: University Press.

Daemmrich, Arthur. 2004. *Pharmacopolitics: Drug Regulation in the United States and Germany.* Chapel Hill: University of North Carolina Press.

Das, Ram, and Ralph Metzner. 2010. *Birth of a Psychedelic Culture: Conversations about Leary, the Harvard Experiments, Milbrook and the Sixties.* Santa Fe: Synergetic Press.

Daston, Lorraine. 1992. Objectivity and the escape from perspective. *Social Studies of Science* 22:592–618.

———. 1994. Historical epistemology. In *Questions of Evidence: Proof, Practice, and Persuasion across the Disciplines,* edited by James Chandler and Arnold I. Davidson, 282–289. Chicago: University of Chicago Press.

———. 2005. Intelligences: Angelic, animal, human. In *Thinking with Animals: New Perspectives on Anthropomorphism,* edited by Lorraine Daston and Gregg Mitman, 37–58. New York: Columbia University Press.

———. 2009. Science studies and the history of science. *Critical Inquiry* 35 (4):798–813.

Daston, Lorraine, and Peter Galison. 2007. *Objectivity.* New York: Zone Books.

Daston, Lorraine, and Katharine Park. 1998. *Wonders and the Order of Nature, 1150–1750.* New York: Zone Books.

Davenport-Hines, Richard. 2002. *The Pursuit of Oblivion: A Social History of Drugs.* London: Phoenix.

Davis, Fred, and Laura Munoz. 1968. Heads and freaks: Patterns and meanings of drug use among hippies. *Journal of Health and Social Behavior* 9 (2):156–164.

Davis, Thomas J. 1996. Images of intolerance: John Calvin in nineteenth-century history textbooks. *Church History* 65 (2):234–248

Dawkins, Richard. 2006. *The God Delusion*. New York: Houghton Mifflin Company.

De Waal, Frans. 1999. Anthropomorphism and Anthropodenial: Consistency in our Thinking About Humans and Animals. *Philosophical Topics* 27:255–280.

DeGrandpre, Richard. 2006. *The Cult of Pharmacology: How America Became the World's Most Troubled Drug Culture*. Durham (NC): Duke University Press.

Deleuze, Gilles. 1999. *Foucault*. London: Continuum.

Denber, Herman C.B., and Sidney Merlis. 1956. Studies on mescaline IV: Antagonism between mescaline and chlorpromazine. In *Psychopharmacology: A Symposium Organized by the Section on Medical Sciences of the A.A.A.S. and the American Psychiatric Association and Presented at the Berkeley Meeting, December 30, 1954*, edited by Nathan S. Kline, 141–144. Washington (DC): American Association for the Advancement of Science.

Dennett, Daniel. 2006. *Breaking the Spell: Religion as a Natural Phenomenon*. New York: Penguin.

Descartes, René. 1984/1641. Meditations on first philosophy. In *The Philosophical Writings of Descartes*, vol. 2, 3–62. Cambridge (UK): Cambridge University Press.

Descola, Philippe. 2005. *Par-delà nature et culture*. Paris: Éditions Gallimard.

———. 2006. Beyond nature and culture. *Proceedings of the British Academy* 139:137–155.

Devereux, Georges. 1956. Normal and abnormal: The key problem of psychiatric anthropology. In *Some Uses of Anthropology: Theoretical and Applied*, edited by J.B. Casagrande and T. Gladwin, 23–48. Washington (DC): Anthropological Society of Washington.

Devonis, David C. 2012. Timothy Leary's mid-career shift: Clean break or inflecton point? *Journal of the History of the Behavioral Sciences* 48 (1):16–39.

Dillon, Michael, and Luis Lobo-Guerrero. 2008. Biopolitics of security in the 21st century: An introduction. *Review of International Studies* 34:265–292.

Dittrich, Adolf. 1985. *Ätiologie-unabhängige Strukturen veränderter Wachbewußtseinszustände: Ergebnisse empirischer Untersuchungen über Halluzinogene I. und II. Ordnung, sensorische Deprivation, hypnagoge Zustände, hypnotische Verfahren sowie Reizüberflutung*. Stuttgart: Ferdinand Enke Verlag.

———. 1994. Psychological aspects of altered states of consciousness of the LSD type: Measurement of their basic dimensions and prediction of individual differences. In *50 Years of LSD: Current Status and Perspectives of Hallucinogens*, edited by A. Pletscher and Dieter Ladewig, 101–120. New York: Parthenon Publishing Group.

Dittrich, Adolf, Daniel Lamparter, and Maja Maurer. 2010. *5D-ASC: Questionnaire for the Assessment of Altered States of Consciousness; A Short Introduction*. Zurich: PSIN PLUS.

Dobkin de Rios, Marlene. 1975. Man, culture, and hallucinogens: An overview. In *Cannabis and Culture*, edited by Vera Rubin, 401–416. The Hague: Mouton Publishers.

————. 1984. *Hallucinogens: Cross-Cultural Perspectives*. Prospect Heights (IL): Waveland Press.

————. 1994. Drug tourism in the Amazon. *Anthropology of Consciousness* 5 (1):16–19.

Dobkin de Rios, Marlene, and Roger Rumrrill. 2008. *A Hallucinogenic Tea, Laced with Controversy: Ayahuasca in the Amazon and the United States*. Westport (CT): Praeger Publishers.

Dobkin de Rios, Marlene, and David Smith. 1977. The function of drug rituals in human society: Continuities and change. *Journal of Psychedelic Drugs* 9 (3):269–275.

Doblin, Rick. 1989a. International interest in MDMA research. *MAPS Newsletter* 2 (1):3.

————. 1989b. Switzerland leads the way. *MAPS Newsletter* 1 (2):1.

————. 1991. Pahnke's "Good Friday Experiment": A long-term follow-up and methodological critique. *Journal of Transpersonal Psychology* 23:1–28.

————. 1992. Overview. *MAPS Newsletter* 3 (2):1.

————. 1992/93. Worlds of consciousness researchers. *MAPS Newsletter* 3 (4):16–17.

————. 1998. Dr. Leary's Concord Prison Experiment: A 34-year follow-up study. *Journal of Psychoactive Drugs* 30 (4):419–426.

————. 2000. Regulation of the medical use of psychedelics and marijuana. PhD dissertation, Kennedy School of Government, Harvard University, Cambridge (MA).

————. 2002a. A clinical plan for MDMA (ecstasy) in the treatment of post-traumatic stress disorder (PTSD): Partnering with the FDA. *MAPS Bulletin* 7 (3):5–18.

————. 2002b. Letter from Rick Doblin, PhD, MAPS president. MAPS Bulletin 7 (3):3–4.

————. 2003. Letter from Rick Doblin, PhD, MAPS president. *MAPS Bulletin* 8 (1):3.

————. 2007. Interview with Rick Doblin. NeuroSoup.com, 7 June 2007 (retrieved 14 December 2009).

————. 2008. Keeping the psychedelic dream alive: An interview by Arran Frood, New Scientist. Posted 2 September. *New Scientist* (2671). Available from www.maps.org/media/view/interview_keeping_the_psychedelic_dream_alive (retrieved 15 June 2012).

Downing, Joseph. 1986. The psychological and physiological effects of MDMA on normal volunteers. *Journal of Psychoactive Drugs* 18 (4):335–340.

Doyle, Richard M. 2011. *Darwin's Pharmacy: Sex, Plants, and the Evolution of the Noösphere*. Seattle: University of Washington Press.

Dreyfus, Hubert. 1991. *Being-in-the-World: A Commentary on Heidegger's Being in the World, Division I*. Cambridge (MA): MIT Press.

Dreyfus, Hubert, and Paul Rabinow. 1982. *Michel Foucault: Beyond Structuralism and Hermeneutics*. Chicago: University of Chicago Press.

Dreysse, Miriam, and Florian Malzacher, eds. 2007. *Experten des Alltags: Das Theater von Rimini Protokoll*. Berlin: Alexander Verlag.

Dror, Otniel. 1999. The affect of experiment: The turn to emotions in Anglo-American physiology, 1900–1940. *Isis* 90 (2):205–237.

Dumit, Joseph. 2002. Drugs for life. *Molecular Interventions* 2 (3):124–127.

———. 2004. *Picturing Personhood: Brain Scans and Biomedical Identity.* Princeton (NJ): Princeton University Press.

Dyck, Erika. 2008. *Psychedelic Psychiatry: LSD from Clinic to Campus.* Baltimore: Johns Hopkins University Press.

Ehrenberg, Alain. 2004. Le sujet cérébral. *Esprit* (November):130–155.

Eisner, Bruce. 2006. LSD and Aldous Huxley's *Island*: Setting sail for a better country. *Gaia Media News* 5:18–20.

Elliott, Carl. 2004. Pursued by happiness and beaten senseless: Prozac and the American Dream. In *Prozac as a Way of Life,* edited by Carl Elliott and Tod Chambers, 127–140. Chapel Hill: University of North Carolina Press.

Epstein, Steven. 1996. *Impure Science: AIDS, Activism, and the Politics of Knowledge.* Berkeley: University of California Press.

———. 2007. Patient groups and health movements. In *The Handbook of Science and Technology Studies,* 3rd ed., edited by Edward J. Hackett, Olga Amsterdamska, Michael Lynch, and Judy Wajcman, 499–540. Cambridge (MA): MIT Press.

Evans-Pritchard, Edward Evan. 1965. *Theories of Primitive Religion.* Oxford: Oxford University Press.

Fahrenkurg, Hermann. 1995. Drogenpolitik. In *Illegale Drogen in der Schweiz, 1990–1993: Die Situation in den Kantonen und der Schweiz,* edited by Hermann Fahrenkrug, Jürgen Rehm, Richard Müller, Harald Klingemann, and Regine Linder, 161–188. Zürich: Seismo.

Farber, David. 2002. The Intoxicated state/illegal nation: Drugs in the sixties counterculture. In *Imagine Nation: The American Counterculture of the 1960s and '70s,* edited by Peter Braunstein and Michael William Doyle, 17–40. New York: Routledge.

Färber, Thomas, and Bernhard C. Schär. 2008. Zwischen bürgerlicher Reform und jugendlicher Revolte: die Nonkonformisten. In *Bern 68: Lokalgeschichte eines globalen Aufbruchs—Ereignisse und Erinnerungen,* edited by Bernhard C. Schär, Ruth Ammann, Stefan Bittner, Marc Griesshammer, and Yves Niederhäuser, 15–27. Baden: hier+jetzt.

Fernberger, Samuel W. 1932. Further observations on peyote intoxication. *Journal of Abnormal and Social Psychology* 26 (4):367–378.

Fischer, Michael M.J. 2009. *Anthropological Futures.* Durham (NC): Duke University Press.

Fischer, Roland, Felix Georgi, and P. Weber. 1951. Psychophysische Korrelationen. VIII. Modellversuche zum Schizophrenieproblem: Lysergsäurediäthylamid und Mescalin. *Schweizer medizinische Wochenschrift* 81:817–818.

Fischer, Roland, Richard M. Hill, Karen Thatcher, and James Scheib. 1970. Psilocybin-induced contraction of nearby visual space. *Agents and Actions* 1 (4):190–197.

Fisher, Philip. 2002. *The Vehement Passions.* Princeton (NJ): Princeton University Press.

Fost, Frederic F. 1998. Playful illusion: The making of worlds in Advaita Vedānta. *Philosophy East and West* 48 (3):387–405.

Foucault, Michel. 1973. *The Order of Things: An Archaeology of the Human Sciences.* New York: Random House.

———. 1985. *The Use of Pleasure: The History of Sexuality*. Vol. 2. New York: Vintage Books.

———. 1986. *The Care of the Self: The History of Sexuality*. Vol. 3. New York: Vintage Books.

———. 1997. Preface to *The History of Sexuality*, vol. 2. In *Essential Works of Michel Foucault*, vol. 1, *Ethics: Subjectivity and Truth*, edited by Paul Rabinow, 199–205. New York: The New Press.

———. 2003. *Society Must Be Defended: Lectures at the Collège de France, 1975–76*. New York: Picador.

———. 2005. *The Hermeneutics of the Subject: Lectures at the Collège de France, 1981–1982*. New York: Palgrave Macmillan.

———. 2006. *Psychiatric Power: Lectures at the Collège de France, 1973–74*. Houndmills (UK): Palgrave Macmillan.

———. 2007. *Security, Territory and Population: Lectures at the Collège de France, 1977–78*. Houndmills (UK): Palgrave Macmillan.

Fox Keller, Evelyn. 2000. Models of and models for: Theory and practice in contemporary biology. In *Proceedings of the 1998 Biennial Meetings of the Philosophy of Science Association*, part 2, *Symposia Papers, Philosophy of Science* 67 (Suppl.):S72–S86.

Francom, P., D. Andrenyak, H.K. Lim, R.R. Bridges, R.L. Foltz, and R.T. Jones. 1988. Determination of LSD in urine by capillary column gas chromatography and electron impact mass spectrometry. *Journal of Analytical Toxicolology* 12 (1):1–8.

Franklin, Sarah. 2005. Stem cells R us: Emergent life forms and the global biological. In *Global Assemblages: Technology, Politics, and Ethics as Anthropological Problems*, edited by Aihwa Ong and Stephen Collier, 59–78. Malden (MA): Blackwell Publishing.

Freud, Sigmund. 1961/1927. *The Future of an Illusion*. In *The Standard Edition of the Complete Psychological Works of Sigmund Freud*, vol. 21 (1927–1931), *"The Future of an Illusion," "Civilization and Its Discontents," and Other Works*, edited by James Strachey, 1–56. London: Vintage.

———. 1961. *Civilization and Its Discontents*. Translated by James Strachey. New York: W.W. Norton & Company.

Frith, Charles H., Louis W. Chang, Danny L. Lattin, Robert C. Walls, Jack Hamm, and Rick Doblin. 1987. Toxicity of methylenedioxymethamphetamine (MDMA) in the dog and the rat. *Fundamental and Applied Toxicology* 9 (1):110–119.

Fukuyama, Francis. 2002. *Our Posthuman Future: Consequences of the Biotechnology Revolution*. London: Profile Books.

Fuller, Robert. 2000. *Stairways to Heaven: Drugs in American Religious History*. Boulder (CO): Westview Press.

Furst, Peter. 1972. *Flesh of the Gods: The Ritual Use of Hallucinogens*. New York: Praeger.

———. 1976. *Hallucinogens and Culture*. San Francisco: Chandler & Sharp.

Gaddum, John H. 1954. Drugs antagonistic to 5-hydroxytryptamine. In *Ciba Foundation Symposium on Hypertension: Humoral and Neurogenic Factors*, edited by G.E.W. Wolstenholme and M.P. Cameron, 75–77. Boston: Little, Brown and Company.

Geertz, Clifford. 1973. *The Interpretation of Cultures: Selected Essays*. New York: Basic Books.

———. 2000. *Available Light: Anthropological Reflections on Philosophical Topics*. Princeton (NJ): Princeton University Press.

Gellner, Ernest. 1970. Concepts and society. In *Rationality: Key Concepts in the Social Sciences*, edited by Bryan R. Wilson, 18–49. London: Basil Blackwell.

Geyer, Christian, ed. 2004. *Hirnforschung und Willensfreiheit. Zur Deutung der neuesten Experimente*. Frankfurt/M.: Suhrkamp.

Geyer, Mark. 1998. Why study hallucinogenic drugs in animals? *Heffter Review of Psychedelic Research* 1:33–38.

Geyer, Mark, and Kirsten Krebs. 1994. Serotonin receptor involvement in an animal model of the acute effects of hallucinogens. In *Hallucinogens: An Update*, NIDA Research Monograph 146, edited by G.C. Lin and R.A. Glennon, 124–156. Rockville (MD): National Institute on Drug Abuse.

Geyer, Mark, and Bita Moghaddam. 2002. Animal models relevant to schizophrenia disorders. In *Neuropsychopharmacology: The Fifth Generation of Progress*, edited by Kenneth Davis, Dennis Charney, Joseph Coyle, and Charles Nemeroff, 689–701. Philadelphia: Lippincott, Williams, and Wilkins.

Geyer, Mark, Lyle Peterson, Gary Rose, David Horwitt, Roger Light, Lynne Adams, John Zook, Richard Hawkins, and Arnold Mandell. 1978. The effects of lysergic acid diethylamide and mescaline-derived hallucinogens on sensory-integrative function: Tactile startle. *Journal of Pharmacology and Experimental Therapeutics* 207 (3):837–847.

Geyer, Mark A., and Franz X. Vollenweider. 2008. Serotonin research: contributions to understanding psychoses. *Trends in Pharmacological Sciences* 29 (9):445–453.

Gibbon, Sahra, and Carlos Novas, eds. 2008. *Biosocialities, Genetics and the Social Sciences: Making Biologies and Identities*. London: Routledge.

Gomart, Emilie. 2002. Methadone: Six effects in search of a substance. *Social Studies of Science* 32 (1):93–135.

Goodall, Jane. 2010. Why it is time for a theological zoology. In *Wenn sich Tiere in der Theologie tummeln: Ansätze einer theologischen Zoologie*, edited by Rainer Hagencord, 10–20. Regensburg (Germany): Pustet.

Gouzoulis-Mayfrank, Euphrosyne, Karsten Heekeren, Anna Neukirch, Martin Stoll, Carsten Stock, Maja Obradovic, and Karl-Artur Kovar. 2005. Psychological effects of (S)-ketamine and N,N-dimethyltryptamine (DMT): A double-blind, cross-over study in healthy volunteers. *Pharmacopsychiatry* 38:301–311.

———. 2006. Inhibition of return in the human 5HT(2A) agonist and NMDA antagonist model of psychosis. *Neuropsychopharmacology* 31 (2):431–441.

Gouzoulis-Mayfrank, Euphrosyne, Karsten Heekeren, Bernhard Thelen, H. Lindenblatt, Karl-Artur Kovar, Henning Sass, and Mark Geyer. 1998. Effects of the hallucinogen psilocybin on habituation and prepulse inhibition of the startle reflex in humans. *Behavioural Pharmacology* 9 (7):561–566.

Gouzoulis-Mayfrank, Euphrosyne, Leo Hermle, and Henning Sass. 1994. Psychedelische Erlebnisse zu Beginn produktiver Episoden endogener Psychosen. *Der Nervenarzt* 65:198–201.

Grandin, Temple, and Catherine Johnson. 2005. *Animals in Translation: Using the Mysteries of Autism to Decode Animal Behavior.* New York: Scribner.

Green, A. Richard. 2008. Gaddum and LSD: The birth and growth of experimental and clinical neuropharmacology research on 5–HT in the UK. *British Journal of Pharmacology* 154 (8): 1583–1599.

Green, Martin. 1986. *Mountain of Truth: The Counterculture Begins; Ascona, 1900–1920.* Hanover (NH): University Press of New England.

Greenfield, Robert. 2006. *Timothy Leary: A Biography.* Orlando (FL): Harcourt.

Griffiths, Roland, William Richards, Una McCann, and Robert Jesse. 2006. Psilocybin can occasion mystical-type experiences having substantial and sustained personal meaning and spiritual significance. *Psychopharmacology* 187 (3):268–283.

Grim, Ryan. 2005. The numbers touted by the government in its big LSD bust just don't add up. *Slate Magazine,* 14 March. Available from www.slate .com/articles/news_and_politics/hey_wait_a_minute/2005/03/the_91pound_ acid_trip.single.html (retrieved 15 June 2012).

Grinspoon, Lester, and James Bakalar. 1979. *Psychedelic Drugs Reconsidered.* New York: Basic Books.

Grob, Charles. 2002. Psychiatric research with hallucinogens: what have we learned? In *Hallucinogens: A Reader,* edited by Charles Grob, 263–291. New York: Jeremy P. Tarcher / Putnam.

Grob, Charles, Dennis McKenna, James Callaway, Glacus Brito, Edison Neves, Guilherme Oberlaender, Oswaldo Saide, Elizieu Labigalini, Cristiane Tacla, Claudio Miranda, Rick Strassman, and Kyle Boone. 1996. Human psychopharmacology of hoasca, A plant hallucinogen used in ritual context in Brazil. *Journal of Nervous and Mental Disease* 184 (2):86–94.

Grunenberg, Christoph, ed. 2005. *Summer of Love. Psychedelische Kunst der 60er Jahre.* Frankfurt/M.: Hatje Cantz Verlag.

Grunenberg, Christoph, and Jonathan Harris, eds. 2005. *Summer of Love: Psychedelic Art, Social Crisis, and Counterculture in the 1960s.* Liverpool: Liverpool University Press.

Gumbrecht, Hans Ulrich. 2010. *Unsere breite Gegenwart.* Frankfurt/M.: Suhrkamp.

Gursky, Andreas, and Heinz-Norbert Jocks. 1999. "Das Eigene steckt in den visuellen Erfahrungen" (Interview). *Kunstforum international* (145):249–265.

Hache, Émilie, and Bruno Latour. 2010. Morality or moralism? An exercise in sensitization. *Common Knowledge* 16 (2):311–330.

Hacking, Ian. 1995. The looping effects of human kinds. In *Causal Cognition: A Multidisciplinary Debate,* edited by Dan Sperber, David Premack, and Ann Premack, 351–383;. Oxford: Oxford University Press.

———. 2002. *Historical Ontology.* Cambridge (MA): Harvard University Press.

———. 2005. The Cartesian vision fulfilled: Analogue bodies and digital minds. *Interdisciplinary Science Reviews* 30 (2):153–166.

———. 2007a. Kinds of people: Moving targets. *Proceedings of the British Academy* 151:285–318.

———. 2007b. Our neo-Cartesian bodies in parts. *Critical Inquiry* 34:78–105.

———. 2009. The abolition of man. *Behemoth: A Journal on Civilisation* 2 (3):5–23.

Hadot, Pierre. 1995. *Philosophy as a Way of Life: Spiritual Exercises from Socrates to Foucault.* Oxford: Blackwell.

———. 2002. *What Is Ancient Philosophy?* Cambridge (MA): Harvard University Press.

Hagner, Michael. 1996. Der Geist bei der Arbeit: Überlegungen zur visuellen Präsentation cerebraler Prozesse. In *Anatomien medizinischen Wissens: Medizin, Macht, Moleküle,* edited by Cornelius Borck, 259–286. Frankfurt/M.: Fischer.

———. 2000. *Homo cerebralis: Der Wandel vom Seelenorgan zum Gehirn.* Frankfurt/M.: Insel.

———. 2006. *Der Geist bei der Arbeit: Historische Untersuchungen zur Hirnforschung.* Göttingen (Germany): Wallstein.

———. 2007. Hirnforschung und Materialismus. In *Weltanschauung, Philosophie und Naturwissenschaft im 19. Jahrhundert,* vol. 1, *Der Materialismus-Streit,* edited by Kurt Bayertz, Myriam Gerhard, and Walter Jaeschke, 204–222. Hamburg: Meiner.

———. 2009. Das Unbewusste zwischen Subversion und neurowissenschaftlichem Biedermeier. In *Das Unbewusste: Krisis und Kapital der Wissenschaften; Studien zum Verhältnis von Wissen und Geschlecht,* edited by Christina von Braun, Dorothea Dornhof, and Eva Johach, 27–43. Bielefeld (Germany): Transcript.

Halter, Martin. 2006. Alles ist erleuchtet. *Frankfurter Allgemeine Zeitung,* 20 January, 34.

Haraway, Donna. 1991. A cyborg manifesto: Science, technology, and socialist-feminism in the late twentieth century. In *Simians, Cyborgs, and Women: The Reinvention of Nature,* 149–181. New York: Routledge.

Harner, Michael J. 1973. Preface. In *Hallucinogens and Shamanism,* edited by Michael Harner, vii–viii. Oxford: Oxford University Press.

———. 1980. *The Way of the Shaman.* New York: Harper & Row.

Harrington, Anne. 2008. *The Cure Within: A History of Mind-Body Medicine.* New York: W.W. Norton & Company.

Harrison, Ann. 2006. LSD: The geek's wonder drug? *Wired,* 16 January. Available from www.wired.com/science/discoveries/news/2006/01/70015?currentPage=all (retrieved 16 June 2012).

Hartman, Alan, and Leo Hollister. 1963. Effect of mescaline, lysergic acid diethylamide and psilocybin on color perception. *Psychopharmacologia* 4:441–451.

Hasler, Felix. 2005. Ein Gefühl, schöner als Glück. *Weltwoche* (50). Available from www.weltwoche.ch/ausgaben/2005-50/artikel-2005-50-ein-gefuehl-scho.html (retrieved 15 June 2012).

———. 2006. Alle lieben Albert. *Die Weltwoche,* 19 January, 12–14.

———. 2007. LSD macht keinen zum Genie [interview by Thomas Gull and Roger Nickl]. *Unimagazin* (2):39–42.

———. 2009. Stoppt den Neurowahn! Neuroökonomie? Neuromarketing? Alle machen Hirnforschung. *Das Magazin*, 23 October. http://dasmagazin .ch/index.php/stoppt-den-neurowahn (retrieved 25 October 2010; no longer available).

———. 2010. Kann auch mal gründlich daneben gehen. *Der Freitag*, 8 July, 7.

———. 2012. *Neuromythologie: Eine Streitschrift gegen die Deutungsmacht der Hirnforschung*. Bielefeld (Germany): Transcript.

Hasler, Felix, D. Bourquin, Rudolf Brenneisen, T. Bär, and Franz X. Vollenweider. 1997. Determination of psilocin and 4-hydroxyindole-3-acetic acid in plasma by HPLC-ECD and pharmacokinetic profiles of oral and intravenous psilocybin in man. *Pharmaceutica Acta Helvetiae* 72 (3):175–184.

Healy, David. 1997. *The Antidepressant Era*. Cambridge (MA): Harvard University Press.

———. 1998. *The Psychopharmacologists*. Vol. 2. London: Chapman & Hall.

———. 2002. *The Creation of Psychopharmacology*. Cambridge (MA): Harvard University Press.

Hecht, Jennifer Michael. 2003. *The End of the Soul: Scientific Modernity, Atheism, and Anthropology in France*. New York: Columbia University Press.

Heffter Research Institute. N.d. *Research at the Frontiers of the Mind: Case for Support*. Brochure.

Heffter Research Institute. 2001. What is the Heffter Research Institute? *Heffter Review of Psychedelic Research* 2:iii–iv.

Hein, Norvin. 1995. Lílā. In *The Gods at Play: Līlā in South Asia*, edited by William S. Sax, 13–20. New York: Oxford University Press.

Hermle, Leo, Euphrosyne Gouzoulis, Godehard Oepen, Manfred Spitzer, Karl-Artur Kovar, Dieter Borchardt, Matthias Fünfgeld, and M. Berger. 1993. Zur Bedeutung der historischen und aktuellen Halluzinogenforschung in der Psychiatrie. *Der Nervenarzt* 64:562–571.

Hermle, Leo, Godehard Oepen, and Manfred Spitzer. 1988. Zur Bedeutung der Modellpsychosen. *Fortschritte der Neurologie, Psychiatrie* 56:48–58.

Hermle, Leo, Manfred Spitzer, D. Borchardt, and Euphrosyne Gouzoulis. 1992. Beziehungen der Modell- bzw. Drogenpsychosen zu schizophrenen Erkrankungen. *Fortschritte der Neurologie, Psychiatrie* 60:383–392.

Herzberg, David. 2009. *Happy Pills in America: From Miltown to Prozac*. Baltimore: Johns Hopkins University Press.

Hess, David, Steve Breyman, Nancy Campbell, and Brian Martin. 2007. Science, technology, and social movements. In *The Handbook of Science and Technology Studies*, 3rd ed., edited by Edward J. Hackett, Olga Amsterdamska, Michael Lynch, and Judy Wajcman, 473–498. Cambridge (MA): MIT Press.

Hesse, Hermann. 1995/1918. Iris. In *The Fairy Tales of Hermann Hesse*, 242–263. New York: Bantam Book.

Hettling, Manfred. 1998. Bürgerlichkeit: Eine ungesellige Gesellfigkeit. In *Eine kleine Geschichte der Schweiz: Der Bundesstaat und seine Traditionen*, edited by Manfred Hettling, Mario König, Martin Schaffner, Andreas Suter, and Jakob Tanner, 227–264. Frankfurt/M.: Suhrkamp.

Hill, Richard M., and Roland Fischer. 1971. Interpretation of visual space under drug-induced ergotropic and trophotropic arousal. *Agents and Actions* 2:122–130.

Hillebrand, Jennifer, Deborah Olszewski, and Roumen Sedefov. 2006. *EMCDDA Thematic Papers—Hallucinogenic Mushrooms: An Emerging Trend Case Study.* Lisbon: European Monitoring Centre for Drugs and Drug Addiction.

Hobson, J. Allan. 2001. *The Dream Drug Store: Chemically Altered States of Consciousness.* Boston: MIT Press.

Hoch, Paul H. 1955. Comments: Experimental psychiatry. *American Journal of Psychiatry* 111:787–790.

Hoffer, Abram, and Humphry Osmond. 1959. The adrenochrome model and schizophrenia. *Journal of Nervous and Mental Disease* 128 (1):18–35.

Hoffer, Abram, Humphry Osmond, and John Smythies. 1954. Schizophrenia: A new approach. II: Result of a year's research. *Journal of Mental Science* 100 (418):29–45.

Hofmann, Albert. 1983. *LSD: My Problem Child; Reflections on Sacred Drugs, Mysticism, and Science.* Boston: J.P. Tarcher.

Holbraad, Martin. 2008. Definitive evidence, from Cuban gods. *Journal of the Royal Anthropological Institute* 14 (Suppl. s1):S93–S109.

Hollister, Leo. 1962. Drug-induced psychoses and schizophrenic reactions, a critical comparison. *Annals of the New York Academy of Sciences* 96:80–88.

Holmes, Douglas, and George Marcus. 2004. Cultures of expertise and the management of globalization: Toward the re-functioning of ethnography. In *Global Assemblages: Technology, Politics, and Ethics as Anthropological Problems,* edited by Stephen Collier and Aihwa Ong, 235–252. London: Blackwell.

Holzhey, Christoph. 2007. Einleitung. In *Biomystik. Natur—Gehirn—Geist,* edited by Christoph Holzhey, 7–22. München: Wilhelm Fink Verlag.

Horgan, John. 2003. *Rational Mysticism: Dispatches from the Border between Science and Spirituality.* Boston: Houghton Mifflin Company.

Hospital, Clifford. 1995. Līlā in early Vaisnava thought. In *The Gods at Play: Līlā in South Asia,* edited by William S. Sax, 21–34. New York: Oxford University Press.

Huxley, Aldous. 1932. *Brave New World.* London: Chatto & Windus.

———. 1959. *Brave New World Revisited.* London: Chatto & Windus.

———. 1962. *Island.* New York: Harper & Row.

———. 1980. *Moksha: Writings on Psychedelics and the Visionary Experience, 1931–1963.* London: Chatto & Windus.

———. 2004/1944. *The Perennial Philosophy.* New York: HarpersCollins.

———. 2009/1954. *The Doors of Perception and Heaven and Hell.* New York: HarperCollins.

Jack, Anthony, and Andreas Roepstorff. 2003. Why trust the subject? *Journal of Consciousness Studies* 10 (9–10):v–xx.

James, William. 1958/1902. *The Varieties of Religious Experience.* New York: New American Library.

———. 1999/1898. Human immortality: Two supposed objections to the doctrine. Preface to second edition. In *William James: Writings, 1878–1999,* edited by Gerald Myers, 1098–1127. New York: Library of America.

Janke, Wilhelm, ed. 1983. *Response Variability to Psychotropic Drugs*. New York: Pergamon.

Janzarik, Werner. 2003. Der Psychose-Begriff und die Qualität des Psychotischen. *Nervenarzt* 74 (1):3–11.

Jaspers, Karl. 1923. *Allgemeine Psychopathologie*. Berlin: Springer.

———. 1963. *General Psychopathology*. Translated by J. Hoenig and Marian Hamilton. Manchester: Manchester University Press.

Jay, Martin. 2005. *Songs of Experience: Modern American and European Variations on a Universal Theme*. Berkeley: University of California Press.

Jay, Mike, ed. 1999. *Artificial Paradises: A Drugs Reader*. London: Penguin.

Johnson, Ken. 2011. *Are You Experienced? How Psychedelic Consciousness Transformed Modern Art*. Munich: Prestel.

Jones, John Alan. 1953. The Sun Dance of the Northern Ute. Anthropological Papers no. 47. *Bulletin of the Bureau of American Ethnology* 157:203–263.

Jonnes, Jill. 1996. *Hep-Cats, Narcs, and Pipe-Dreams: A History of America's Romance with Illegal Drugs*. Baltimore: Johns Hopkins University Press.

Jordan, George Jefferjs. 1927. *The Reunion of the Churches: A Study of G. W. Leibnitz and His Great Attempt*. London: Constable.

Joseph, Rhawn, ed. 2002. *Neurotheology: Brain, Science, Spirituality, Religious Experience*. San Jose: University Press.

Joyce, Kelly. 2008. *Magnetic Appeal: MRI and the Myth of Transparency*. Ithaca (NY): Cornell University Press.

Jungaberle, Henrik, Rolf Verres, and Fletcher DuBois, eds. 2006. *Rituale erneuern: Ritualdynamik und Grenzerfahrung aus interdisziplinärer Perspektive*. Gießen (Germany): Psychosozial-Verlag.

Kant, Immanuel. 1983/1784. What is enlightenment? In *Perpetual Peace, and Other Essays on Politics, History, and Moral Practice*. Indianapolis: Hackett.

———. 1992/1800. *Lectures on Logic*. Translated by Michael Young. Cambridge (UK): Cambridge University Press.

———. 2006/1798. *Anthropology from a Pragmatic Point of View*. Translated by Robert Louden. New York: Cambridge University Press.

Kass, Leon. 2002. *Life, Liberty and the Defense of Dignity: The Challenge of Bioethics*. San Francisco: Encounter Books.

———. 2003. Beyond therapy: Biotechnology and the pursuit of human improvement. President's Council on Bioethics. Available from http://bioethics.georgetown.edu/pcbe/background/kasspaper.html (retrieved 15 June 2012).

———. 2008a. A chat with George W. Bush's conscience (Interview by Francis Wilkinson). *Discover Magazine*, 20 February. Available from http://discovermagazine.com/2008/feb/20-a-chat-with-george-w-bush.s-conscience (retrieved 15 June 2012).

———. 2008b. How brave a new world? *Society* 45:5–8.

Kelley, Donald R. 2001. Eclecticism and the history of ideas. *Journal of the History of Ideas* 62 (4):577–592.

Kerlikowske, R. Gil. 2009. Statement of R. Gil Kerlikowske at the International Association of Chiefs of Police Annual Conference, 6 October, Denver (CO).

Klerman, Gerald. 1972. Psychotropic hedonism vs. pharmacological calvinism. *Hastings Center Report* 2 (3):1–3.

Kluckhon, Clyde, and Dorothea Leighton. 1946. *The Navaho*. Cambridge (MA): Harvard University Press.

Klüver, Heinrich. 1926. M. Weber's "ideal type" in psychology. *Journal of Philosophy* 23 (2):29–35.

———. 1928. *Mescal: The "Divine" Plant and Its Psychological Effects.* London: Kegan Paul, Trench, Trubner, and Company.

———. 1966. *Mescal and Mechanisms of Hallucination.* Chicago: University of Chicago Press.

Koerner, Jon, and James Appel. 1982. Psilocybin as a discriminative stimulus: Lack of specificity in an animal behavior model for "hallucinogens." *Psychopharmacology* 76 (2):130–135.

Kohn, Eduardo. 2007. How dogs dream: Amazonian natures and the politics of transspecies engagement. *American Ethnologist* 34 (1):3–24.

Kometer, Michael. 2006. Elektrophysiologische Korrelate visueller und kognitiver Prozesse und deren Modulation durch Psilocybin. Lizentiatsarbeit, Psychology, University of Zurich.

Kometer, Michael, B. Rael Cahn, David Andel, Olivia L. Carter, and Franz X. Vollenweider. 2010. The 5-HT2A/1A agonist psilocybin disrupts modal object completion associated with visual hallucinations. *Biological Psychiatry* 69 (5):399–406.

Koselleck, Reinhart. 2002. The temporalization of utopia. In *The Practice of Conceptual History: Timing History, Spacing Concepts.* Stanford (CA): Stanford University Press, 84–99.

———. 2004. *Futures Past: On the Semantics of Historical Time.* Translated by Keith Tribe. New York: Columbia University Press.

Kraepelin, Emil. 1882. Über psychische Zeitmessungen. *Schmidts Jahrbücher der in- und ausländischen gesammten Medicin* 196:205–213.

———. 1892. *Ueber die Beeinflussung einfacher psychischer Vorgänge durch einige Arzneimittel: Experimentelle Untersuchungen.* Jena (Germany): Gustav Fischer.

———. 1919. *Dementia Praecox and Paraphrenia.* Edinburgh: Livingstone.

Kramer, Peter. 1993. *Listening to Prozac: A Psychiatrist Explores Antidepressant Drugs and the Remaking of the Self.* New York: Penguin Books.

Krebs-Thomson, Kirsten, Erbert Ruiz, Virginia Masten, Mahalah Buell, and Mark Geyer. 2006. The roles of 5-HT1A and 5-HT2 receptors in the effects of 5-MeO-DMT on locomotor activity and prepulse inhibition in rats. *Psychopharmacology* 189 (3):319–329.

Kroeber, Alfred L. 1952. *The Nature of Culture.* Chicago: University of Chicago.

Kucinich, Dennis. 2002. Spirit and stardust. *MAPS Bulletin* 7 (3):19–24.

Kuhn, Thomas S. 1962. *The Structure of Scientific Revolutions.* Chicago: University of Chicago Press.

Kusch, Martin. 1997. The sociophilosophy of folk psychology. *Studies in History and Philosophy of Science* 28 (1):1–25.

LaBarre, Weston. 1960. Twenty years of peyote studies. *Current Anthropology* 1 (1):45–60.

LaBarre, Weston, David McAllester, James S. Slotkin, Omer C. Stewart, and Sol
Tax. 1951. Statement on peyote. *Science* 114:582–583.

Langlitz, Nicolas. 2005. *Die Zeit der Psychoanalyse: Lacan und das Problem
der Sitzungsdauer.* Frankfurt/M.: Suhrkamp.

———. 2006a. Ceci n'est pas une psychose: Toward a historical epistemology
of model psychosis. *BioSocieties* 1 (2):158–180.

———. 2006b. Tripping in solitude: Introducing Honza Samotar by way of
John Lilly. In *Introspective Self-Rapports: Shaping Ethical and Aesthetic
Concepts, 1850–2006,* Preprint 322, edited by Katrin Solhdju, 81–92. Berlin:
Max-Planck-Institut für Wissenschaftsgeschichte.

———. 2007. The Office of Experiments' truth serum threat: Notes on the
psychopharmacology of truthfulness. In *sk-interfaces: Exploding Borders
in Art, Technology and Society,* edited by Jens Hauser, 118–124. Liverpool:
FACT/Liverpool University Press.

———. 2009. Pharmacovigilance and post–black market surveillance. *Social
Studies of Science* 39 (3):395–420.

———. 2010a. Das Gehirn ist kein Muskel. *Frankfurter Allgemeine
Sonntagszeitung,* 3 January, 52.

———. 2010b. Kultivierte Neurochemie und unkontrollierte Kultur [Debate
with Malek Bajbouj, Boris Quednow, and Ludwig Jäger]. *Zeitschrift für
Kulturwissenschaften* (2):61–88.

———. 2012a. Aristotelian Neurophilosophy for Big Children. *BioSocieties* 7
(1):98–101.

———. 2012b. Delirious brain chemistry and controlled culture: Exploring the
contextual mediation of drug effects. In *Critical Neuroscience: A Handbook
of the Social and Cultural Contexts of Neuroscience,* edited by Suparna
Choudhury and Jan Slaby, 253–262. London: Wiley.

———. 2012c. Review of Ken Johnson's *Are You Experienced? How Psychedelic
Consciousness Transformed Modern Art. Leonardo Reviews Quarterly,* May.
Available from http://leonardo.info/reviews/may2012/langlitz_johnson.php
(retrieved 15 June 2012).

Langlitz, Nicolas, and Anne Kirstine Hermann. 2012. Der Tod, in anderem
Licht betrachtet. *Frankfurter Allgemeine Sonntagszeitung,* 22 July 2012, 54.

Latour, Bruno. 1993. *We Have Never Been Modern.* Cambridge (MA): Harvard
University Press.

———. 1999. *Pandora's Hope: Essays on the Reality of Science Studies.*
Cambridge (MA): Harvard University Press.

———. 2002. *Jubiler ou les tourments de la parole religieuse.* Paris: Les
Empêcheurs de Penser en Rond.

———. 2004a. How to talk about the body? The normative dimension of
science studies. *Body and Society* 10 (2–3):205–229.

———. 2004b. *Politics of Nature: How to Bring the Sciences into Democracy.*
Cambridge (MA): Harvard University Press.

———. 2004c. Why has critique run out of steam? From matters of fact to
matters of concern. *Critical Inquiry* 30 (2):225–248.

———. 2005. "Thou shall not freeze-frame," or, how not to misunderstand
the science and religion debate. In *Science, Religion, and the Human*

Experience, edited by James D. Proctor, 27–48. Oxford: Oxford University Press.

Latour, Bruno, and Steve Woolgar. 1986. *Laboratory Life: The Construction of Scientific Facts.* Princeton (NJ): Princeton University Press.

Lattin, Don. 2010. *The Harvard Psychedelic Club: How Timothy Leary, Ram Dass, Huston Smith, and Andrew Weil Killed the Fifties and Ushered in a New Age for America.* New York: HarperOne.

Leary, Timothy. 1965. *Turn On, Tune In, Drop Out.* Berkeley: Ronin.

————. 1968. *High Priest.* New York: New American Library.

————. 1970. *The Politics of Ecstasy.* London: MacGibbon & Kee.

————. 1983. *Flashbacks: A Personal and Cultural History of an Era; An Autobiography.* New York: G.P. Putnam's Sons.

————. 2001. *Your Brain Is God.* Berkeley: Ronin.

Leary, Timothy, George Litwin, and Ralph Metzner. 1963. Reactions to psilocybin adminstered in a supportive environment. *Journal of Nervous and Mental Disease* 137 (6):561–573.

Leary, Timothy, and Ralph Metzner. 1963. Hermann Hesse: Poet of the interior journey. *Psychedelic Review* 1 (2):167–182.

Leary, Timothy, Ralph Metzner, and Richard Alpert. 1964. *The Psychedelic Experience: A Manual Based on the Tibetan Book of the Dead.* New Hyde Park (NY): University Books.

LeDoux, Joseph. 2002. *Synaptic Self: How Our Brains Become Who We Are.* New York: Penguin.

Lee, Martin, and Bruce Shlain. 1992. *Acid Dreams: The Complete Social History of LSD; The CIA, the Sixties, and Beyond.* New York: Grove Press.

Leonard, Irving. 1942. Peyote and the Mexican Inquisition, 1620. *American Anthropologist* 44 (2):324–326.

Letcher, Andy. 2006. *Shroom: A Cultural History of the Magic Mushroom.* London: Faber and Faber.

Levine, Joseph. 1983. Materialism and Qualia: The explanatory gap. *Pacific Philosophical Quaterly* 64:354–361.

Lewis-Williams, J.D., and Thomas A. Dowson. 1988. Signs of all times: Entoptic phenomena in Upper Palaeolithic art. *Current Anthropology* 29:201–245.

Libet, Benjamin, E.W. Wright, and C.A. Gleason. 1982. Readiness-potentials preceding unrestricted "spontaneous" vs. pre-planned voluntary acts. *Electroencephalography and Clinical Neurophysiology* 54 (3):322–335.

Lilly, John. 1972. *The Center of the Cyclone: An Autobiography of Inner Space.* New York: Julian Press.

————. 1978. *The Scientist: A Novel Autobiography.* Philadelphia: J.B. Lippincott Company.

Lim, H.K., D. Andrenyak, P. Francom, R.L. Foltz, and R.T. Jones. 1988. Quantification of LSD and N-dimethyl-LSD in urine by gas chromatography/resonance electron capture ionization mass spectrometry. *Analytical Chemistry* 60 (14):1420–1425.

Lindemann, Gesa. 2005. Beobachtung der Hirnforschung. *Deutsche Zeitschrift für Philosophie* 53 (5):761–781.

Lindesmith, Alfred. 1938. A sociological theory of drug addiction. *American Journal of Sociology* 43:593–609.

Linke, Angelika, and Joachim Scharloth, eds. 2008. *Der Zürcher Sommer 1968: Zwischen Krawall, Utopie und Bürgersinn.* Zürich: Verlag Neue Zürcher Zeitung.

Linton, Ralph. 1956. *Culture and Mental Disorder.* Springfield (IL): C.C. Thomas.

Lloyd, Geoffrey E.R. 2007. *Cognitive Variations: Reflections on the Unity and Diversity of the Human Mind.* Oxford: Clarendon Press.

Lock, Margaret. 1995. *Encounters with Aging: Mythologies of Menopause in Japan and North America.* Berkeley: University of California Press.

———. 2002. *Twice Dead: Organ Transplants and the Reinvention of Death.* Berkeley: University of California Press.

Lock, Margaret, and Vinh-Kim Nguyen. 2010. *An Anthropology of Biomedicine.* Malden (MA): Wiley-Blackwell.

Loemker, Leroy E. 1989. Introduction: Leibniz as philosopher. In *Gottfried Wilhelm Leibniz: Philosophical Papers and Letters,* 2nd ed., edited by Leroy E. Loemker, 1–69. Dordrecht: Kluwer.

Luhmann, Niklas. 1998. *Observations on Modernity.* Stanford (CA): Stanford University Press.

Luhrmann, Tanya. 2003. Metakinesis: How God becomes intimate in contemporary U.S. Christianity. *American Anthropologist* 106 (3):518–528.

———. 2005. The art of hearing God: Absorption, dissociation, and contemporary American spirituality. *Spiritus* 5:133–157.

Lumholtz, Carl. 1902. *Unknown Mexico.* Vol. 1. New York: Charles Scribner.

Lynch, Michael. 1988. Sacrifice and the transformation of the animal body into a scientific object: Laboratory culture and ritual practice in the neurosciences. *Social Studies of Science* 18 (2):265–289.

MacAndrew, Craig, and Robert Edgerton. 1969. *Drunken Comportment: A Social Explanation.* Chicago: Aldine.

Maehle, Andreas-Holger. 1995. Selbstversuche und subjektive Erfahrung in der Opiumforschung des 18. Jahrhunderts. *Würzburger Medizinhistorische Mitteilungen* 13:287–297.

Magee, Glenn Alexander. 2010. Quietism in German mysticism and philosophy. *Common Knowledge* 16 (3):457–473.

Malabou, Catherine. 2008. *What Should We Do with Our Brain?* New York: Fordham University Press.

Mansbach, Robert, and Mark Geyer. 1989. Effects of phencyclidine and phencyclidine biologs on sensorimotor gating in the rat. *Neuropsychopharmacology* 2:299–308.

———. 1991. Parametric determinants in prestimulus modification of acoustic startle: Interaction with ketamine. *Psychopharmacology* 105:162–168.

Mansbach, Robert, Mark Geyer, and David Braff. 1988. Dopaminergic stimulation disrupts sensorimotor gating in the rat. *Psychopharmacology* 94 (4):507–514.

Markoff, John. 2005. *What the Dormouse Said: How the 60s Counterculture Shaped the Personal Computer Industry.* London: Viking.

Marks, Harry. 1997. *The Progress of Experiment: Science and Therapeutic Reform in the United States, 1900–1990.* Cambridge (UK): Cambridge University Press.

Marks, John. 2006. Molecular biology in the work of Deleuze and Guattari. *Paragraph* 29 (2):81–97.

Martin, Emily. 2006. The pharmaceutical person. *BioSocieties* 1 (3):273–287.

———. 2010. Self-making and the brain. *Subjectivity* 3 (4):366–381.

Masters, Robert E.L., and Jean Houston. 1966. *The Varieties of Psychedelic Experience: The Classic Guide to the Effects of LSD on the Human Psyche.* New York: Holt, Rinehart & Winston.

———. 1968. *Psychedelic Art.* New York: Grove Press.

McAllister, William. 2000. *Drug Diplomacy in the Twentieth Century: An International History.* New York: Routledge.

McCann, Una D., and George A. Ricaurte. 2000. Caveat emptor: Editors beware. *Neuropsychopharmacology* 24:333–334.

McGhie, Andrew, and James Chapman. 1961. Disorders of attention and perception in early schizophrenia. *British Journal of Medical Psychology* 34:103–116.

McKenna, Terrence. 1993. *Food of the Gods: The Search for the Original Tree of Knowledge.* New York: Bantam.

McLoughlin, William. 1978. *Revivals, Awakenings, and Reform: An Essay on Religion and Social Change in America.* Chicago: University of Chicago Press.

Mead, Margaret. 1928. *Coming of Age in Samoa: A Psychological Study of Primitive Youth for Western Civilisation.* New York: Morrow.

Meckier, Jerome. 1978. Coming of age in Pala: The primitivism of *Brave New World* reconsidered in *Island. Alternative Futures* 1:68–90.

Metzinger, Thomas. 2000a. Introduction: Consciousness research at the end of the twentieth century. In *Neural Correlates of Consciousness: Empirical and Conceptual Questions,* edited by Thomas Metzinger, 1–16. Cambridge (MA): MIT Press.

———. 2000b. The subjectivity of subjective experience: A representationalist analysis of the first-person perspective. In *Neural Correlates of Consciousness: Empirical and Conceptual Questions,* edited by Thomas Metzinger, 285–306. Cambridge (MA): MIT Press.

———. 2003. *Being No One: The Self-Model Theory of Subjectivity.* Cambridge (MA): MIT Press.

———. 2009. *The Ego Tunnel: The Science of the Mind and the Myth of the Self.* New York: Basic Books.

Miller, Timothy. 1991. *The Hippies and American Values.* Knoxville: University of Tennessee Press.

Mitchell, Sandra. 2005. Anthropomorphism and cross-species modeling. In *Thinking with Animals: New Perspectives on Anthropomorphism,* edited by Lorraine Daston and Gregg Mitman, 100–117. New York: Columbia University Press.

———. 2009. *Unsimple Truths: Science, Complexity, and Policy.* Chicago: University of Chicago Press.

Mol, Annemarie. 2002. *The Body Multiple: Ontology in Medical Practice.* Durham (NC): Duke University Press.

Monastersky, Richard. 2006. Religion on the brain. *Chronicle of Higher Education* 52 (38):A14.

Monroe, John Warne. 2008. *Laboratories of Faith: Mesmerism, Spiritism, and Occultism in Modern France.* Ithaca (NY): Cornell University Press.

Mooney, James. 1896. The mescal plant and ceremony. *Therapeutic Gazette* 12:7–11.

Moreau de Tours, Jacques-Joseph. 1845. *Du haschisch et d'aliénation mentale: Études psychologiques.* Paris: Masson et Cie.

Morgan, Philip, Suzanne Shanahan, and Whitney Welsh. 2005. Brave new worlds: Philosophy, politics, and science in human biotechnology. *Population and Development Review* 31 (1):127–144.

Morse, Stephen J. 2006. Brain overclaim syndrome and criminal responsibility: A diagnostic note. *Ohio State Journal of Criminal Law* 3:397–412.

Moser, Jeannie. 2007. Die Metamorphosen des Dämons: Figurationen eines epistemischen Dings bei Albert Hofmann. In *ZfK—Zeitschrift für Kulturwissenschaften,* vol. 1, *Fremde Dinge,* edited by Michael Frank, Bettina Gockel, Thomas Hauschild, Dorothee Kimmich, and Kirsten Mahlke, 99–108. Bielefeld (Germany): Transcript.

Müller, Ulrich, Paul Fletcher, and Holger Steinberg. 2006. The origin of pharmacopsychology: Emil Kraepelin's experiments in Leipzig, Dorpat and Heidelberg (1882–1892). *Psychopharmacology* 184:131–138.

Myerhoff, Barbara. 1974. *Peyote Hunt: The Sacred Journey of the Huichol Indians.* Ithaca (NY): Cornell University Press.

———. 1975. Peyote and Huichol worldview: The structure of a mystic vision. In *Cannabis and Culture,* edited by Vera Rubin, 417–438. The Hague: Mouton Publishers.

———. 1976. Organization and ecstasy: Deliberate and accidental communitas among Huichol Indians and American youth. In *Symbol and Politics in Communal Ideology: Cases and Questions,* edited by Sally Falk Moore and Barbara Myerhoff. Ithaca (NY): Cornell University Press.

Myers, Gerald. 1986. *William James: His Life and Thought.* New Haven (CT): Yale University Press.

Nagel, Thomas. 1974. What is it like to be a bat? *Philosophical Review* 83 (4):435–450.

Newberg, Andrew, Abass Alavi, Michael Baime, Michael Pourdehnad, Jil Santanna, and Eugene d'Aquili. 2001. The measurement of regional cerebral blood flow during the complex cognitive task of meditation: A preliminary SPECT study. *Psychiatry Research: Neuroimaging Section* 106 (2):113–122.

Nichols, David. 2004. Hallucinogens. *Pharmacology and Therapeutics* 101 (2):131–181.

———. 2006. The molecule that changed the world. *Gaia Media News* 5:1–5.

Noë, Alva. 2004. *Action in Perception.* Cambridge (MA): MIT Press.

Novak, Steven. 1997. LSD before Leary: Sidney Cohen's critique of 1950s psychedelic drug research. *Isis* 88 (1):87–110.

O'Donnell, Mike, and Bryn Jones, eds. 2010. *Sixties Radicalism and Social Movement Activism: Retreat or Resurgence?* London: Anthem Press

Olff, Sabine. 2006. Leises Comeback von LSD und Co. Halluzinogene werden wieder zur Behandlung von Ängsten und Traumata eingesetzt. *SonntagsZeitung*, 8 January, 68.

Ong, Aihwa, and Stephen Collier. 2005. Global assemblages, anthropological problems. In *Global Assemblages: Technology, Politics, and Ethics as Anthropological Problems*, edited by Aihwa Ong and Stephen Collier, 3–21. Malden (MA): Blackwell Publishing.

Oppenheimer, Mark. 2003. *Knocking on Heaven's Door: American Religion in the Age of Counterculture.* New Haven (NH): Yale University Press.

Oreskes, Naomi. 1996. Objectivity or heroism? On the invisibility of women in science. *Osiris* 11:87–113.

Orlands, Barbara, Tom Beauchamp, Rebecca Dresser, David Morton, and John Gluck. 1998. *The Human Use of Animals: Case Studies in Ethical Choice.* New York: Oxford University Press.

Osmond, Humphry. 1957. A review of the clinical effects of psychotomimetic agents. *Annals of the New York Academy of Sciences* 66 (3):418–434.

Osmond, Humphry, and John Smythies. 1952. Schizophrenia: A new approach. *Journal of Mental Science* 98:309–315.

Otto, Rudolf. 1958. *The Idea of the Holy.* Oxford: Oxford University Press.

Pahnke, Walter. 1963. *Drugs and Mysticism: An Analysis of the Relationship between Psychedelic Drugs and the Mystical Consciousness.* Cambridge (MA): Harvard University.

Pahnke, Walter, and William Richards. 1966. Implications of LSD and experimental mysticism. *Journal of Religion and Health* 5 (3):175–208.

Passie, Torsten. 1996/97. Hanscarl Leuner: Pioneer of hallucinogen research and psycholytic therapy. *MAPS Newsletter* 7 (1):46–49.

———. 1997. *Psycholytic and Psychedelic Therapy Research 1931–1995: A Complete International Bibliography.* Hannover: Laurentius Publishers.

Passie, Torsten, John H. Halpern, Dirk O. Stichtenoth, Hinderk M. Emrich, and Annelie Hintzen. 2008. The pharmacology of lysergic acid diethylamide: A review. *CNS Neuroscience and Therapeutics* 14:295–314.

Peirano, Mariza G.S. 1998. When anthropology is at home: The different contexts of a single discipline. *Annual Review of Anthropology* 27:105–128.

Perler, Dominik, and Markus Wild. 2005. Der Geist der Tiere—eine Einführung. In *Der Geist der Tiere: Philosophische Texte zu einer aktuellen Diskussion,* edited by Dominik Perler and Markus Wild, 10–74. Frankfurt/M.: Suhrkamp.

Perrine, Daniel. 2001. Visions of the night: Western medicine meets peyote, 1887–1899. *Heffter Review of Psychedelic Research* 2:6–52.

Petrullo, Vicenzo. 1934. *The Diabolic Root: A Study of Peyotism, the New Indian Religion, Among the Delawares.* Philadelphia: University of Pennsylvania Press.

Petryna, Adriana. 2009. *When Experiments Travel: Clinical Trials and the Global Search for Human Subjects.* Princeton (NJ): Princeton University Press.

Pickering, Andrew. 1993. The mangle of practice: Agency and emergence in the sociology of science. *American Journal of Sociology* 99 (3):559–589.

———. 2009. The politics of theory: Producing another world, with some thoughts on Latour. *Journal of Cultural Economy* 2 (1–2): 197–212.

———. 2010. *The Cybernetic Brain: Sketches of Another Future*. Chicago: University of Chicago Press.

Pieters, Toine, and Stephen Snelders. 2007. From King Kong pills to mother's little helpers: Career cycles of two families of psychotropic drugs; The barbiturates and benzodiazepines. *Canadian Bulletin of Medical History* 24 (1):93–112.

Polanyi, Michael. 1958. *Personal Knowledge: Towards a Post-Critical Philosophy*. Chicago: University of Chicago Press.

Porter, Theodore. 1986. *The Rise of Statistical Thinking, 1820–1900*. Princeton (NJ): Princeton University Press.

———. 1992. Quantification and the accounting ideal in science. *Social Studies of Science* 22 (4):633–651.

Prentiss, D. W., and Francis P. Morgan. 1895. *Anhalonium lewinii* (mescal buttons): A study of the drug, with special reference to its physiological action upon man, with report of experiments. *Therapeutic Gazette* 11 (9):577–585.

Quednow, Boris. 2005. *Folgen des Ecstasy-Konsums: Neurobiologische Grundlagen kognitiver Defizite bei MDMA-Konsumenten*. Frankfurt/M.: Peter Lang.

———. 2010a. Ethics of neuroenhancement: A phantom debate. *BioSocieties* 5 (1):153–156.

———. 2010b. Tyrannische Neurobiologie und unterdrückte Kultur des psychotropen Erlebens. *Zeitschrift für Kulturwissenschaften* (2):79–84.

Rabinow, Paul. 1986. Representations are social facts: Modernity and postmodernity in anthropology. In *Writing Culture: The Poetics and Politics of Ethnography*, edited by James Clifford and George E. Marcus, 234–261. Berkeley: University of California Press.

———. 1989. *French Modern: Norms and Forms of the Social Environment*. Chicago: University of Chicago Press.

———. 1996a. Artificiality and enlightenment: From sociobiology to biosociality. In *Essays on the Anthropology of Reason*, 91–111. Princeton: Princeton University Press.

———. 1996b. *Essays on the Anthropology of Reason*. Princeton (NJ): Princeton University Press.

———. 1999. *French DNA: Trouble in Purgatory*. Chicago: University of Chicago Press.

———. 2003. *Anthropos Today: Reflections on Modern Equipment*. Princeton (NJ): Princeton University Press.

———. 2008. *Marking Time: On the Anthropology of the Contemporary*. Princeton (NJ): Princeton University Press.

———. 2009. Prosperity, amelioration, flourishing: From a logic of practical judgment to reconstruction. *Law and Literature* 21 (3):301–320.

Rabinow, Paul, and Talia Dan-Cohen. 2005. *A Machine to Make a Future: Biotech Chronicles*. Princeton (NJ): Princeton University Press.

Rader, Karen. 2004. *Making Mice: Standardizing Animals for American Biomedical Research, 1900–1955.* Princeton (NJ): Princeton University Press.

Radin, Paul. 1957/1927. *Primitive Man as Philosopher.* New York: Dover Publications.

Rasmussen, Nicolas. 2008. *On Speed: The Many Lives of Amphetamine.* New York: New York University Press.

Rees, Tobias. 2006. Plastic reason: An anthropological analysis of the emergence of adult cerebral plasticity in France. PhD dissertation, Anthropology, University of California, Berkeley.

Reichel-Dolmatoff, Gerardo. 1978. Drug-induced optical sensations and their relationship to applied art among some Colombian Indians. In *Art in Society: Studies in Style, Culture and Aesthetics,* edited by Michael Greenhalgh and Vincent Megaw, 289–304. London: Duckworth.

Reynolds, Simon. 1999. Generation ecstasy: Into the world of techno and rave culture. New York: Routledge.

Rheinberger, Hans-Jörg. 1997. *Toward a History of Epistemic Things: Synthesizing Proteins in the Test Tube.* Stanford (CA): Stanford University Press.

———. 2010a. *An Epistemology of the Concrete: Twentieth-Century Histories of Life.* Durham (NC): Duke University Press.

———. 2010b. *On Historicizing Epistemology. An Essay.* Translated by David Fernbach. Stanford (CA): Stanford University Press.

Ricaurte, George, Jie Yuan, George Hatzidimitriou, Branden Cord, and Una McCann. 2002. Severe dopaminergic neurotoxicity in primates after a common recreational dose regimen of MDMA ("ecstasy"). *Science* 297:2260–2263.

———. 2003. Retraction. *Science* 297:1479.

Roberts, Andy. 2008. *Albion Dreaming: A Popular History of LSD in Britain.* London: Marshall Cavendish Editions.

Roepstorff, Andreas. 2001. Brains in scanners: An Umwelt of cognitive neuroscience. *Semiotica* 134 (1/4):747–765.

Rohbeck, Johannes. 2004. *Geschichtsphilosophie zur Einführung.* Hamburg: Junius.

Rose, Nikolas. 1999. *Powers of Freedom: Reframing Political Thought.* Cambridge (UK): Cambridge University Press.

———. 2003a. Neurochemical selves. *Society* 41 (1):46–59.

———. 2003b. The Neurochemical self and its anomalies. In *Risk and Morality,* edited by R. Ericson, 407–437. Toronto: Toronto University Press.

———. 2007. *The Politics of Life Itself: Biomedicine, Power, and Subjectivity in the Twenty-First Century.* Princeton (NJ): Princeton University Press.

Rose, Steven. 1973. *The Conscious Brain.* New York: Weidenfeld and Nicolson.

Rosenfeld, Seth. 2001. William Pickard's long, strange trip: Suspected LSD trail leads from the Bay Area's psychedelics era to a missile silo in Kansas. *San Francisco Chronicle,* 10 June, A1.

Roszak, Theodore. 1968. *The Making of a Counter Culture: Reflections on the Technocratic Society and Its Youthful Opposition.* Garden City (NY): Anchor Books.

————. 1986. *From Satori to Silicon Valley: San Francisco and the American Counterculture*. San Francisco: Don't Call It Frisco Press.

Roth, Gerhard. 1997. *Das Gehirn und seine Wirklichkeit: Kognitive Neurobiologie und ihre philosophischen Konsequenzen*. Frankfurt/M.: Suhrkamp.

Rothman, David. 1991. *Strangers at the Bedside: A History of How Law and Bioethics Transformed Medical Decision Making*. New York: Aldine de Gruyter.

Rubin, David S., ed. 2010. *Psychedelic: Optical and Visionary Art since the 1960s*. Cambridge (MA): MIT Press.

Rühle, Alex. 2006. LSD-Kongress in Basel: Kinners, mir wird so blümerant. *Süddeutsche Zeitung*, 17 January. Available from www.sueddeutsche.de/kultur/lsd-kongress-in-basel-kinners-mir-wird-so-bluemerant-1.433626 (retrieved 15 June 2012).

Samotar, Honza. 2006. Tripping in solitude. In *Introspective Self-Rapports: Shaping Ethical and Aesthetic Concepts, 1850–2006*, Preprint 322, edited by Katrin Solhdju, 93–103. Berlin: Max-Planck-Institut für Wissenschaftsgeschichte.

Sandel, Michael. 2002. What's wrong with enhancement. President's Council on Bioethics. Available from http://bioethics.georgetown.edu/pcbe/background/sandelpaper.html (retrieved 15 June 2012).

Sandison, Ronald. 1997. LSD therapy: A retrospective. In *Psychedelia Britannica. Hallucinogenic Drugs in Britain*, edited by Antonio Melechi, 53–86. London: Turnaround.

Saner, Luc, ed. 1998. *Auf dem Weg zu einer neuen Drogenpolitik*. Basel: Helbing & Lichtenhahn.

Saunders, Nicholas. 1993. *E for Ecstasy*. London: Nicholas Saunders.

Schär, Bernhard C. 2008. "1968" als wiederbelebte bürgerliche Revolution—Einleitung. In *Bern 68: Lokalgeschichte eines globalen Aufbruchs—Ereignisse und Erinnerungen*, edited by Bernhard C. Schär, Ruth Ammann, Stefan Bittner, Marc Griesshammer, and Yves Niederhäuser, 6–13. Baden: hier+jetzt.

Schivelbusch, Wolfgang. 1992. Tastes of Paradise: A Social History of Spices, Stimulants, and Intoxicants. New York: Pantheon Books.

Schmidt-Biggemann, Wilhelm. 2004. *Philosophia perennis. Historical Outlines of Western Spirituality in Ancient, Medieval and Early Modern Thought*. Dordrecht: Springer.

Schmitt, Carl. 2005. *Political Theology: Four Chapters on the Concept of Sovereignty*. Chicago: University of Chicago Press.

Schmitt, Charles. 1966. Perennial philosophy: From Agostino Steuco to Leibniz. *Journal of the History of Ideas* 27 (4):505–532.

Schüle, Christian. 2006. Geld lehrt beten: Wie die amerikanische Templeton Foundation ihren Reichtum einsetzt, um die Wissenschaft auf den Weg des Glaubens zu bringen. *Die Zeit*, 4 May. Available from www.zeit.de/2006/19/templeton1_xml (retrieved 15 June 2012).

Schwarz, Egon. 1970. Hermann Hesse, the American youth movement, and problems of literary evaluation. *PMLA* 85 (5):977–987.

Segal, Daniel, and Sylvia Yanagisako. 2005. Introduction. In *Unwrapping the Sacred Bundle: Reflections on the Disciplining of Anthropology*, edited by

Daniel Segal and Sylvia Yanagisako, 1–23. Durham (NC): Duke University Press.

Sessa, Ben. 2008. Is it time to revisit the role of psychedelic drugs in enhancing human creativity? *Journal of Psychopharmacology* 22 (8):821–827.

Shapin, Steven. 1992. Discipline and bounding: The history and sociology of science as seen through the externalism-internalism debate. *History of Science* 30:333–369.

———. 1994. *A Social History of Truth: Civility and Science in Seventeenth Century England*. Chicago: University of Chicago Press.

———. 2008a. Science and the modern world. In *The Handbook of Science and Technology Studies*, 3rd ed., edited by Edward J. Hackett, Olga Amsterdamska, Michael Lynch, and Judy Wajcman, 433–448. Cambridge (MA): MIT Press.

———. 2008b. *The Scientific Life: A Moral History of a Late Modern Vocation*. Chicago: University of Chicago Press.

———. 2010. *Never Pure: Historical Studies of Science as If It Was Produced by People with Bodies, Situated in Time, Space, Culture, and Society, and Struggling for Credibility and Authority*. Baltimore: Johns Hopkins University Press.

Shapin, Steven, and Simon Schaffer. 1985. *Leviathan and the Air-Pump. Hobbes, Boyle, and the Experimental Life*. Princeton (NJ): Princeton University Press.

Sheard, Michael H., and George Aghajanian. 1968. Stimulation of midbrain raphé neurons: Behavioral effects of serotonin release. *Life Sciences* 7:19–25.

Shonle, Ruth. 1925. Peyote, the giver of visions. *American Anthropologist* 27 (1): 53–75.

Shorter, Edward. 1997. *A History of Psychiatry: From the Era of the Asylum to the Age of Prozac*. New York: John Wiley.

Shulgin, Alexander, and Ann Shulgin. 1991. *PIHKAL: A Chemical Love Story*. Berkeley: Transform Press.

———. 1997. *TIHKAL: The Continuation*. Berkeley: Transform Press.

Singer, Wolf. 2002. *Der Beobachter im Gehirn: Essays zur Hirnforschung*. Frankfurt/M.: Suhrkamp.

Sipes, Thomas, and Mark Geyer. 1995. DOI disruption of prepulse inhibition of startle in the rat is mediated by 5-HT2A and not by 5-HT2C receptors. *Behavioural Pharmacology* 6:839–842.

Slater, Lauren. 1999. *Prozac Diary*. New York: Penguin.

Sloterdijk, Peter. 1996. *Selbstversuch: Ein Gespräch mit Carlos Oliveira*. München: Carl Hanser Verlag.

Slotkin, J.S. 1955. Peyotism, 1521–1891. *American Anthropologist* 57 (2):202–230.

Smith, Barbara Herrnstein. 2009. *Natural Reflections: Human Cognition at the Nexus of Science and Religion*. New Haven (CT): Yale University Press.

Smith, Huston. 1964. Do drugs have religious import? *Journal of Philosophy* 61 (18):517–530.

———. 2000. *Cleansing the Doors of Perception: The Religious Significance of Entheogenic Plants and Chemicals*. New York: Jeremy P. Tarcher/Putnam.

————. 2003. *Beyond the Postmodern Mind: The Place of Meaning in a Global Civilization*. Wheaton (IL): Quest Books.

Smith, Roger. 2005. Does reflexivity separate the human sciences from the natural sciences? *History of the Human Sciences* 18 (4):1–25.

Snelders, Stephen, and Charles Kaplan. 2002. LSD therapy in Dutch psychiatry: Changing socio-political settings and medical sets. *Medical History* 46:221–240.

Snelders, Stephen, Charles Kaplan, and Toine Pieters. 2006. On cannabis, chloral hydrate, and career cycles of psychotropic drugs in medicine. *Bulletin of the History of Medicine* 80:95–114.

Snow, C.P. 1964. *The Two Cultures*. Cambridge (UK): Cambridge University Press.

Snyder, Solomon H. 1986. *Drugs and the Brain*. New York: Scientific American Books.

————. 1989. *Brainstorming: The Science and Politics of Opiate Research*. Cambridge (MA): Harvard University Press.

Sober, Elliott. 2005. Comparative psychology meets evolutionary biology: Morgan's Canon and cladistic parsimony. In *Thinking with Animals: New Perspectives on Anthropomorphism*, edited by Lorraine Daston and Gregg Mitman, 85–99. New York: Columbia University Press.

Solhdju, Katrin. 2011. *Selbstexperimente: Die Suche nach der Innenperspektive und ihre epistemologischen Folgen*. München: Fink.

Spitzer, Manfred. 1999. *The Mind within the Net: Models of Learning, Thinking, and Acting*. Cambridge (MA): MIT Press.

Star, Susan Leigh. 1989. Regions of the Mind. Brain Research and the Quest for Scientific Certainty. Stanford (CA): Stanford University Press.

Star, Susan Leigh, and James Griesemer. 1999. Institutional ecology, "translations," and boundary objects: Amateurs and professionals in Berkeley's Museum of Vertebrate Zoology, 1907–1939. In *The Science Studies Reader*, edited by Mario Biagioli, 505–524. New York: Routledge.

Stevens, Jay. 1987. *Storming Heaven: LSD and the American Dream*. New York: Atlantic Monthly Press.

Stewart, Omer C. 1987. *Peyote Religion: A History*. Norman: University of Oklahoma Press.

Stocking, George W. 1992. *The Ethnographer's Magic and Other Essays in the History of Anthropology*. Madison: University of Wisconsin Press.

Strassman, Rick. 2001. *DMT: The Spirit Molecule; A Doctor's Revolutionary Research into the Biology of Near-Death and Mystical Experiences*. Rochester (NY): Park Street Press.

Strathern, Marilyn. 1980. No nature, no culture: The Hagen case. In *Nature, Culture and Gender*, edited by Carol MacCormack and Marilyn Strathern, 174–222. Cambridge (UK): Cambridge University Press.

————. 2000. Introduction: new accountabilities. In *Audit Cultures: Anthropological Studies in Accountability, Ethics and the Academy*, edited by Marilyn Strathern, 1–18. London: Routledge.

Strenski, Ivan. 2008. The spiritual dimension. In *A New History of Anthropology*, edited by Henrika Kuklick, 113–127. Malden (MA): Blackwell.

Strickland, Stuart Walker. 1998. The ideology of self-knowledge and the practice of self-experimentation. *Eighteenth-Century Studies* 31 (4):453–471.

Studer, Brigitte, and Janick Marina Schaufelbuehl. 2009. Die 68er Bewegung und ihre Auswirkungen in der Schweiz—Einleitung. In *1968–1978: Ein bewegtes Jahrzehnt in der Schweiz,* edited by Janick Marina Schaufelbuehl, 9–33. Zürich: Chronos.

Studerus, Erich, Alex Gamma, Michael Kometer, and Franz X. Vollenweider. 2012. Prediction of psilocybin response in healthy volunteers. *PLoS ONE* 7 (2):1–12.

Studerus, Erich, Alex Gamma, and Franz Vollenweider. 2010. Psychometric evaluation of the altered states of consciousness rating scale (OAV). *PLoS ONE* 5 (8):1–19.

Styk, Juraj. 1992/93. The Political and Psychological Dynamics of Psychedelic Psychotherapy in Switzerland. *MAPS Newsletter* 3 (4):21–23.

Suter, Andreas. 1998. Neutralität: Prinzip, Praxis und Geschichtsbewußtsein. In *Eine kleine Geschichte der Schweiz: Der Bundesstaat und seine Traditionen,* edited by Manfred Hettling, Mario König, Martin Schaffner, Andreas Suter, and Jakob Tanner, 133–188. Frankfurt/M.: Suhrkamp.

Swerdlow, Neal, David Braff, Mark Geyer, and George Koob. 1986. Central dopamine hyperactivity in rats mimics abnormal sensory gating of the acoustic startle response in schizophrenics. *Biological Psychiatry* 21:23–33.

Swerdlow, Neal, V.A. Keith, David Braff, and Mark Geyer. 1991. Effects of spiperone, raclopride, SCH 23390 and clozapine on apomorphine inhibition of sensorimotor gating of the startle response in the rat. *Journal of Pharmacology and Experimental Therapeutics* 256 (2):530–536.

Swerdlow, Neal, Martin Weber, Ying Qu, Gregory. Light, and David Braff. 2008. Realistic expectations of prepulse inhibition in translational models for schizophrenia research. *Psychopharmacology* 199 (3):331–388.

Tanner, Jakob. 1990. Rauschgiftgefahr und Revolutionstrauma: Drogenkonsum und Betäubungsmittelgesetzgebung in der Schweiz der 1920er Jahre In *Schweiz im Wandel: Studien zur neueren Gesellschaftsgeschichte,* edited by Sebastian Brändli, 397–416. Basel: Helbing & Lichtenhahn.

———. 2009. "Doors of perception" versus "mind control": Experimente mit Drogen zwischen kaltem Krieg und 1968. In *Kulturgeschichte des Menschenversuchs im 20. Jahrhundert,* edited by Birgit Griesecke, Marcus Krause, Nicolas Pethes, and Katja Sabisch, 340–372. Frankfurt/M.: Suhrkamp.

Taylor, Bron. 2010. *Dark Green Religion: Nature Spirituality and the Planetary Future.* Berkeley: University of California Press.

Taylor, Charles. 1992. *Sources of the Self: The Making of the Modern Identity.* Cambridge (MA): Harvard University Press.

Thompson, Laura. 1948. Attitudes and acculturation. *American Anthropologist* 50 (2):200–215.

Thuillier, Jean. 1999. *Ten Years That Changed the Face of Mental Illness.* Translated by Gordon Hickish. London: Martin Dunitz.

Tone, Andrea. 2008. *The Age of Anxiety: A History of America's Turbulent Affair with Tranquilizers.* New York: Basic Books.

Tresch, John. 2011. Experimental ethics and the science of the meditating brain. In *Neurocultures: Glimpses into an Expanding Universe,* edited by Francisco Ortega and Fernando Vidal, 49–68. Frankfurt/M.: Peter Lang.

Tugendhat, Ernst. 2003. *Egozentrizität und Mystik: Eine anthropologische Studie.* München: Beck.

———. 2007. *Anthropologie statt Metaphysik.* München: Beck.

Turner, Fred. 2006. *From Counerculture to Cyberculture: Stewart Brand, the Whole Earth Network, and the Rise of Digital Utopianism.* Chicago: University of Chicago Press.

Uexküll, Jakob von. 2010/1934. *A Foray into the Worlds of Animals and Humans.* Minneapolis: University of Minnesota Press.

Ulrich, Robert, and Bernard Patten. 1991. The rise, decline, and fall of LSD. *Perspectives in Biology and Medicine* 34 (4):561–578.

US Drug Enforcement Agency (2003). Pickard and Apperson sentenced on LSD charges: Largest LSD lab seizure in DEA history. DEA news release, 31 March. Available from www.justice.gov/dea/pubs/states/newsrel/2003/sanfran033103.html (retrieved 15 June 2012).

———. 2006. LSD 2006. DEA fact sheet, 13 December. Available from www.dea.gov/concern/lsd.html (retrieved 15 June 2012).

Uttal, William. 2001. *The New Phrenology: The Limits of Localizing Cognitive Processes in the Brain.* Cambridge (MA): MIT Press.

Vannini, Claudio, and Maurizio Venturini. 1999. *Halluzinogene: Entwicklung der Forschung, 1938 bis in die Gegenwart; Schwerpunkt Schweiz.* Berlin: VWB—Verlag für Wissenschaft und Bildung.

Vidal, Fernando. 2005. Le sujet cérébral: Une esquisse historique et conceptuelle. *Psychiatrie, Sciences Humaines, Neurosciences* 11 (3):37–48.

———. 2009. Brainhood, anthropological figure of modernity. *History of the Human Sciences* 22 (1):5–36.

Viveiros de Castro, Eduardo. 1998. Cosmological deixis and Amerindian perspectivism. *Journal of the Royal Anthropological Institute* 4 (3):469–488.

———. 2004. Exchanging perspectives: The transformation of objects into subjects in Amerindian ontologies. *Common Knowledge* 10 (3):463–484.

Vollenweider, Franz X. 1992/93. New avenues in the search for biological correlates of altered states of consciousness: From model to practice. *MAPS Newsletter* 3 (4):18–20.

———. 1998. Recent advances and concepts in the search for biological correlates of hallucinogen-induced altered states of consciousness. *Heffter Review of Psychedelic Research* 1:21–32.

Vollenweider, Franz, Reese Jones, and Matthew Baggott. 2001. Caveat emptor: Editors beware. *Neuropsychopharmacology* 24:461–463.

Vollenweider, Franz X., K. Leenders, Christian Scharfetter, A. Antonini, P. Maguire, J. Missimer, and Jules Angst. 1997a. Metabolic hyperfrontality and psychopathology in the ketamine model of psychosis using positron emission tomography (PET) and [18F]fluorodeoxyglucose (FDG). *European Neuropsychopharmacology* 7 (1):9–24.

Vollenweider, Franz X., K. Leenders, Christian Scharfetter, P. Maguire, O. Stadelmann, and Jules Angst. 1997b. Positron emission tomography and fluorodeoxyglucose studies of metabolic hyperfrontality and psychopathology in the psilocybin model of psychosis. *Neuropsychopharmacology* 16 (5):357–372.

Vollenweider, Franz X., S. Remensberger, Daniel Hell, and Mark A. Geyer. 1999. Opposite effects of 3,4-methylenedioxymethamphetamine (MDMA) on sensorimotor gating in rats versus healthy humans. *Psychopharmacology* 143 (3):365–372.

Vollenweider, Franz X., Margreet Vollenweider-Scherpenhuyzen, Andreas Bäbler, Helen Vogel, and Daniel Hell. 1998. Psilocybin induces schizophrenia-like psychosis in humans via a serotonin-2 agonist action. *NeuroReport* 9 (17):3897–3902.

Vondung, Klaus. 2007. Von der Naturmystik zur Biomystik. In *Biomystik. Natur—Gehirn—Geist,* edited by Christoph Holzhey, 23–39. München: Fink.

Wake, Archbishop W., D. E. Jablonski, and Otakar Odložilík. 1934. Protestant reunion in the 18th century. *Slavonic and East European Review* 13 (37):119–126.

Wallace, Anthony F. C. 1959. Cultural determinants of response to hallucinatory experience. *Archives of General Psychiatry* 1 (1):58–69.

Walsh, B. Timoth, Stuart N. Seidman, Robyn Sysko, and Madelyn Gould. 2002. Placebo response in studies of major depreession: Variable, substantial, and growing. *Journal of the American Medical Association* 287:1840–1857.

Walsh, Roger, and Charles Grob, eds. 2005. *Higher Wisdom: Eminent Elders Explore the Continuing Impact of Psychedelics.* Albany: State University of New York Press.

Walsh, Roger, and Charles S. Grob. 2006. Early psychedelic investigators reflect on the psychological and social implications of their research. *Journal of Humanistic Psychology* 46 (4):432–448.

Wartofsky, Marx. 1979. *Models. Representation and the Scientific Understanding.* Dordrecht: D. Reidel Publishing Company.

Wasson, Gordon, Albert Hofmann, and Carl Ruck. 1978. *The Road to Eleusis: Unveiling the Secret of the Mysteries.* New York: Harcourt Brace Jovanovich.

Weber, Max. 1946. Bureaucracy. In *From Max Weber: Essays in Sociology,* edited by H. H. Gerth and C. Wright Mills, 196–244. New York: Oxford University Press.

———. 1949/1904. "Objectivity" in social science and social policy. In *The Methodology of the Social Sciences,* 50–112. Glencoe (IL): Free Press.

———. 1958/1919. Science as a vocation. In *From Max Weber: Essays in Sociology,* edited by H. H. Gerth and C. Wright Mills, 129–146. New York: Oxford University Press.

———. 1992/1920. *The Protestant Ethic and the Spirit of Capitalism.* London: Routledge.

Weil, Andrew. 1972. *The Natural Mind. An Investigation of Drugs and the Higher Consciousness.* Boston: Houghton Mifflin Company.

Whimster, Sam. 2001. Im Gespräch mit Anarchisten: Max Weber in Ancona. In *Sinnsuche und Sonnenbad: Experimente in Kunst und Leben auf dem*

Monte Verità, edited by Andreas Schwab and Claudia Lafranchi, 43–59. Zürich: Limmat Verlag.

Whitmer, Kelly J. 2009. Eclecticism and the technologies of discernment in Pietist pedagogy. *Journal of the History of Ideas* 70 (4):545–567.

———. 2010. The model that never moved: The case of a virtual memory theater and its Christian philosophical argument, 1700–1732. *Science in Context* 23 (3):289–327.

Wilson, Edward O. 1978. *On Human Nature.* Cambridge (MA): Harvard University Press.

Wittgenstein, Ludwig. 1961. *Tractatus Logio-Philosophicus.* London: Routledge & Kegan Paul.

Wittmann, Marc, Olivia Carter, Felix Hasler, B. Rael Cahn, Ulrike Grimberg, Philipp Spring, Daniel Hell, Hans Flohr, and Franz X. Vollenweider. 2007. Effects of psilocybin on time perception and temporal control of behaviour in humans. *Journal of Psychopharmacology* 21(1):50–64.

Wolfe, Tom. 1968. *The Electric Kool-Aid Acid Test.* New York: Farar, Straus and Giroux.

Woolley, David W., and Edward Shaw. 1954. A biochemical and pharmacological suggestion about certain mental disorders. *Science* 119:587–588.

———. 1956. Some serotoninlike activities of lysergic acid diethylamide. *Science* 124:121–123.

Zaehner, Robert Charles. 1957. *Mysticism: Sacred and Profane; An Inquiry into Some Varieties of Praeternatural Experience.* London: Oxford University Press.

Ziche, Paul. 1999. Das Selbstbild des Denkens: Introspektion als psychologische Methode. In *Video Ergo Sum. Repräsentation nach innen und außen zwischen Kunst und Neurowissenschaft,* edited by Olaf Breidbach and Karl Clausberg, 82–98. Hamburg: Verlag Hans-Bredow-Institut.

Zieger, Susan. 2008. Victorian hallucinogens. In *Romanticism and Victorianism on the Net.* Available from www.erudit.org/revue/ravon/2008/v/n49/017857ar .html (retrieved 15 June 2012).

Ziff, Stewart. 1995. Beyond the context: Landscapes, pictures, and the epistemology of image-making. *Leonardo* 28 (5):437–439.

Zinberg, Norman. 1984. *Drugs, Set, and Setting: The Basis for Controlled Intoxicant Use.* New Haven (CT): Yale University Press.

Ziolkowski, Theodore. 1969. Saint Hesse among the hippies. *American German Review* (2):19–23.

Zweifel, Urs. 1998. Polizeilicher Ordnungsdienst im "Aufbruch '68." In *Dynamisierung und Umbau: Die Schweiz in den 60er und 70er Jahren,* edited by Mario König, Georg Kreis, Franziska Meister, and Gaetano Romano, 183–199. Zürich: Chronos Verlag.

Index

Abi-Rached, Joëlle, 28
Abnormal Mental States questionnaire
(APZ), 90, 100–101, 103, 105, 129,
135, 270nn1,2,5
Acadia Pharmaceuticals, 168–69, 197
ACP-103, 168–69, 197
Actor-Network Theory, 93, 256
Adderall, 243, 262
Adrenaline, 146
Agamben, Giorgio, 202–203, 250
Agar, Jon, 92
Aghajanian, George, 174
Alcohol and alcoholism, 9, 28, 50, 67, 101,
122, 183, 212, 215, 216
Alpert, Richard (Ram Dass), 78
Altered states of consciousness. *See*
consciousness
Altruism, 230
Amerindian perspectivism, 188
Amphetamine, 6, 13, 148–49, 189, 233. *See
also* methamphetamine
Angel dust. *See* phencyclidine
Angels and angelology, 138, 193–94,
256–57
Angst, Jules, 99–100, 102
Animal models, 23, 54, 166–203, 272n1.
See also model organisms
Animal rights movement, 92, 178, 180,
203, 272n2. *See also* People for the
Ethical Treatment of Animals

Animism 18–19, 188, 196, 203, 241, 246,
252, 254
Ankeny, Rachel, 143, 199
Anthropodenial, 202
Anthropological difference (or *differentia
specifica*), 23, 200, 261
Anthropological fieldwork 2, 16, 124,
132, 244, 252–53, 259–261. *See also*
ethnography
Anthropological machines, 202–203
Anthropological thought. *See* Man, epistemic figure of
Anthropology, 16–17, 123, 201, 206, 243,
246, 257; of the contemporary, 251;
cultural, 6, 18–19, 117–21, 120–21,
254–55, 259; as cultural critique,
12–13; cognitive, 47, 253–54, 268n8;
historical, 218; holistic, 22, 120, 257;
interpretive, 119; of modernity, 17; of
the perennial, 249, 251; philosophical,
19, 23, 200, 252, 259–261, 264; physical, 119, 257; of science, 19, 160, 198,
206, 258; symbolic 119.
Anthropology assessment, 206, 241
Anthropology at home, 19, 252
Anthropomorphism, 193–94, 202, 232,
268n8
Antidepressants, 3, 27, 123, 233, 268n9.
See also selective serotonin reuptake
inhibitors

Printed in Great Britain
by Amazon